W9-ALN-552

A SPIRAL APPROACH TO FINANCIAL MATHEMATICS

A Spiral Approach to Financial Mathematics

NATHAN TINTLE

*Department of Mathematics, Dordt College,
Sioux Center, IA, United States*

NATHAN SCHELHAAS

Principal Financial Group, Des Moines, IA, United States

TODD SWANSON

*Department of Mathematics, Hope College, Holland,
MI, United States*

ACADEMIC PRESS

An imprint of Elsevier

Academic Press is an imprint of Elsevier
125 London Wall, London EC2Y 5AS, United Kingdom
525 B Street, Suite 1650, San Diego, CA 92101-4495, United States
50 Hampshire Street, 5th Floor, Cambridge, MA 02139, United States
The Boulevard, Langford Lane, Kidlington, Oxford OX5 1GB, United Kingdom

Copyright © 2018 Elsevier Inc. All rights reserved.

No part of this publication may be reproduced or transmitted in any form or by any means, electronic or mechanical, including photocopying, recording, or any information storage and retrieval system, without permission in writing from the publisher. Details on how to seek permission, further information about the Publisher's permissions policies and our arrangements with organizations such as the Copyright Clearance Center and the Copyright Licensing Agency, can be found at our website: www.elsevier.com/permissions.

This book and the individual contributions contained in it are protected under copyright by the Publisher (other than as may be noted herein).

Notices
Knowledge and best practice in this field are constantly changing. As new research and experience broaden our understanding, changes in research methods, professional practices, or medical treatment may become necessary.

Practitioners and researchers must always rely on their own experience and knowledge in evaluating and using any information, methods, compounds, or experiments described herein. In using such information or methods they should be mindful of their own safety and the safety of others, including parties for whom they have a professional responsibility.

To the fullest extent of the law, neither the Publisher nor the authors, contributors, or editors, assume any liability for any injury and/or damage to persons or property as a matter of products liability, negligence or otherwise, or from any use or operation of any methods, products, instructions, or ideas contained in the material herein.

British Library Cataloguing-in-Publication Data
A catalogue record for this book is available from the British Library

Library of Congress Cataloging-in-Publication Data
A catalog record for this book is available from the Library of Congress

ISBN: 978-0-12-801580-3

For Information on all Academic Press publications
visit our website at https://www.elsevier.com/books-and-journals

Working together
to grow libraries in
developing countries

www.elsevier.com • www.bookaid.org

Publisher: Candice Janco
Acquisition Editor: Scott Bentley
Editorial Project Manager: Susan Ikeda
Production Project Manager: Mohana Natarajan
Cover Designer: Mark Rogers

Typeset by MPS Limited, Chennai, India

CONTENTS

PREFACE

A traditional approach to mathematics and statistics education involves direct instruction of techniques and tasks for problem solving, presenting topics in a sequence, which scaffolds students from simpler problems to more complex problems, with a focus on algorithms, equations, and computation (http://en.wikipedia.org/wiki/Traditional_mathematics). Alternative approaches (e.g., reform mathematics) tend to emphasize conceptual understanding, critical thinking, and problem solving. While debate between the two approaches continues, comparative studies show that students using these alternative (reform) approaches tend to perform similarly on basic skills tests but have enhanced conceptual understanding and problem solving skills (http://www.nctm.org/news/content.aspx?id = 12320). This conceptual approach can also be seen in the recently adopted Guidelines for Assessment and Instruction in Statistics Education [GAISE (http://www.amstat.org/education/gaise/)], which emphasize six recommendations for statistics education: (1) emphasize statistical literacy and develop statistical thinking, (2) use real data, (3) stress conceptual understanding, rather than mere knowledge of procedures, (4) foster active learning in the classroom, (5) use technology for developing conceptual understanding and analyzing data, and (6) use assessments to improve and evaluate student learning.

While some curricula for Calculus, Introductory statistics and K-12 mathematics and statistics have been reenvisioned from the ground up to embrace this conceptual approach, few other college level mathematics and statistics courses have been reenvisioned from the ground up, including most financial mathematics (FM) courses or other courses taken as part of an Actuarial Science program. At best, curricula have been "updated" by sprinkling in some new language and problems on an existing course framework. In order to attain the benefit of students who have a deeper conceptual understanding of topics in FM, while simultaneously preparing students for actuarial certification exams, we will develop a full course-length textbook, which embraces GAISE-like guidelines (adopted for FM topics). We state these guidelines here:

(1) Emphasize FM literacy and develop financial math thinking,

(2) Use real financial data and real situations,

(3) Stress conceptual understanding, rather than mere knowledge of procedures,

(4) Foster active learning in the classroom,

(5) Use technology for developing conceptual understanding and analyzing data and financial situations, and

(6) Use assessments to improve and evaluate student learning.

To do this we have (1) reordered the typical content covered in a FM course to embrace a spiral approach to educating students about financial concepts and financial problem solving, (2) integrated exposition, examples and explorations, (3) integrated use of technology, and (4) used real data and real situations throughout. The following sections briefly summarize our approach across the four main distinctives:

1. Spiral approach. Typical FM books have the following characteristics:

   a. Chapters are organized by major financial concept (e.g., Time value of money, annuities, loans, etc.), and within each chapter, both the large and small concepts are given equal treatment [e.g., compound interest, simple interest, continuous (force) and discount are each given a section] even though some concepts (compound interest) will be used more than the others in later chapters.

   b. Students are presented with a laundry list of equations in every chapter, with little sense of priority. Many of the equations are similar/related, but students do not always make the connections.

To combat these deficiencies, we propose a syllabus, which gently introduces the major financial concepts in the most realistic manner possible. For example, topics like loans and refinancing come early, as does compound interest, while topics like discount and arithmetically increasing annuities come later. This allows us to spiral over important financial concepts throughout the text, instead of relegating them to a single section of a single chapter in the middle or end of the course. This approach has the benefit of (1) ensuring students see the most important financial concepts early in the course, (2) that these basic concepts are reinforced throughout the semester as the concepts are revisited while learning some of the minor (related) concepts, and (3) students having a balanced preparation for Exam FM if that is their goal (read more on student audience at the end of the preface).

Notably, this approach also allows us to judiciously present equations to students; the most important, fundamental equations and learning objectives are presented early in the course when they have pedagogical value (i.e., they reinforce fundamental understanding of the financial concepts). Early presentation (Unit 1) of these key formulas also maximizes student exposure, leading to increased retention of key concepts. More subtle/nuanced and/or less important equations are relegated until later in the course (Unit 2), when they can be introduced on top of a solid foundational understanding of the key concepts and only for those students for whom such material would be beneficial.

2. **Integration of exposition, examples, and explorations.** Every section includes exposition about the topic of that section, at least one example to illustrate how to apply the ideas and methods presented, and at least one exploration that students work through to learn more about the topic and gain experience with applying the topic. We offer maximal flexibility for instructors to decide on the order in which they will present sections and components within sections, and what they will ask students to do in class vs outside of class. For example, one instructor could ask students to read exposition and examples outside of class and spend class time leading students through explorations. Another instructor might present exposition and examples in class and ask students to work through explorations outside of class. *To facilitate this flexibility, examples and explorations within a section are written so that neither depends on the other,* allowing the instructor to present either one first and, furthermore, it is not necessary for students to do both if the student feels confident in their understanding after either just the example or just the exploration.

3. **Easy-to-use technology integrated throughout.** Implementing a conceptual approach to FM requires effective use of technology. Rather than asking students to learn to use only a financial calculator, we have designed easy-to-use Excel spreadsheets that allow students to explore financial concepts and their behavior to provide a complementary view to merely seeing an equation, while simultaneously learning an important skill for business practice and personal finance. BA-II PLUS calculator instructions are not included because they are easily and freely available online. Actuarial students should make it a point to practice with/learn the calculator at a time that they think is best for their own learning style—this could be "along the way" or it could be "at the end." On the other hand, Excel is the "coin of the realm" when it comes to practical, hands-on problem solving. Excel spreadsheets are provided for most chapters and students are regularly

asked to go to the Excel spreadsheets in order to explore concepts and solve problems. Like the calculator, we've limited explicit and detailed Excel instructions since this depends greatly upon the student's version of Excel and operating system. Instead, students and instructors should find plenty of Excel help online. This "find your own technology help" should help students greatly as they transition to the "real world" where such independent research and problem solving is necessary.

4. **Real data from real financial situations.** We utilize real data from real financial situations throughout the book. These situations are taken from a variety of fields of application, to maximize student interest and to see the vast application of key financial concepts. We try to balance examples both from personal finance (e.g., student loans) and corporate decision-making (e.g., protecting a company's assets and liabilities from interest rate changes). We've also tried to point out to students places where we are illustrating a topic that we think is no longer of great practical value given recent advances in computation for FM. These cases are primarily in Unit 2 where we have included some topics primarily because they are on the FM Actuarial certification exam.

WHY THE CHANGES IN CONTENT SEQUENCING?

The traditional approach to teaching FM starts with simple, unrealistic financial situations, with an emphasis on formulas and computation. Alternatively, we start with practical, conceptual problems for which students have a good intuition. For example, while an amortized loan has a challenging formula, the key concepts (e.g., payback must include interest + principal; the larger the payment the quicker the loan is paid off) are relatively straightforward and intuitive. By starting students in a place where their intuition is correct, students are then asked to explore FM concepts using a mix of role playing activities and graphical and numerical examples. The goal is to build on students natural intuition—building toward complex, but intuitive, formulas, while downplaying the role of minor corollary level formulas and formulas used only for the sake of computation—most of which we have tried to relegate to the second unit of the course. This approach yields students a deeper, more solid understanding of FM concepts without sacrificing understanding of formulas and ability to solve problems.

▶ WHAT ABOUT CHANGES IN PEDAGOGY?

In addition to changes to the content of the course, we have also substantially changed our pedagogical approach from passive (e.g., listening to lectures) to active learning which engages the full range of students' senses. Each chapter contains a number of explorations for the students to complete, in addition to example-driven exposition of concepts. These materials allow for a variety of instructor-determined approaches to content delivery including approaches where examples/concepts are presented first by the instructor, then explored by the student or vice versa.

Student explorations involve a variety of tactile learning experiences: role-playing examples (you be the bank, I will be the borrower) and using Excel spreadsheets for explorations. The explorations are flexibly designed to be completed by students working individually, in small or large groups, and/or inside or outside of class.

Concepts are introduced using compelling examples explained in an easy-to-understand format that limits technical jargon and focuses on conceptual understanding. We have also included key idea boxes and "Think about it" questions to help students understand what they read, identify core concepts, and be engaged readers. Overall, we advocate utilizing a small amount of instructor-led interactive lectures and discussions, but mainly focusing on engaging and strengthening different student learning processes by way of a variety of active, self-discovery learning experiences for students.

In addition to the explorations and examples, each chapter contains an extensive set of exercises: (1) rote exercises, (2) conceptual problems, (3) application problems based on real financial situations and real data, and (4) sample problems from the Financial Mathematics Actuarial Certification exam.

STUDENT AUDIENCE AND HOW TO UTILIZE THE MATERIALS

Finally, we note that there are two primary target audiences of this textbook (1) students who are pursuing a potential career as an actuary and preparing to take the FM exam and (2) students wishing to gain a solid understanding of FM for personal and, possibly, professional purposes (e.g., small business owners; Chartered Financial Analysts, CFA; accounts).

Students Hoping to Gain a Solid Understanding of Financial Mathematics Concepts

For students who do not intend to sit for the FM certification exam, the entirety of Unit 1 (Chapters 1–5) should provide a solid mathematical foundation on which to operate for future personal and professional financial decision making. The Unit can be covered in a half to full-semester long course, depending on the amount of time, depth of coverage and amount of time devoted to homework exercises in each chapter. Importantly, we believe that this material is appropriate regardless of whether or not a student has taken Calculus, and by relying heavily on technology (Excel, calculators) in Unit 1, it provides a practical foundation without making the course get bogged down on algebra techniques. That said, for instructors or courses where a secondary objective is algebra practice, all equations are provided and instructors can opt to restrict technology usage on exams and certain assignments to allow for students practice their algebra skills.

Students Hoping to Pass Actuarial Certification Exam FM

For students considering the actuarial profession and planning to sit for the FM certification exam, we believe this course provides a deeper, conceptual understanding of the concepts than most other curricula available. By spending time in Unit 1 which, may at times, seem simple for some of these students, students will be ensured to have a very strong, conceptual foundation on which to layer the more nuanced, technical and detailed concepts which come up in Unit 2. Along the way, students will gain practice with Excel which is an important "resume builder" for their future profession—no practicing actuary is actually going to use the BA-II Plus to do financial calculations in their everyday work! Some additional practical advice for these students (and their instructors) to pass the exam is provided in the section titled "To the student" which follows.

TO ALL STUDENTS

This book is about finance, not mathematics. Mathematics books tend to focus on what can be done mathematically and let the formulations of mathematical proofs act as the roadmap through the curriculum. Because this book is about finance, we will let financial concepts be the roadmap through the curriculum, and not focus on concepts just because we can do them, but because they are done and are used in financial practice by actuaries, financial experts and everyday citizens in daily life. With this in mind, we will

1. Use notation only when necessary, not everywhere it is possible
2. Focus on formulas that are useful in daily practice and help to reinforce intuitive understanding, not focusing on niche formulas
3. Start exploration of concepts using a mix of intuition, simple mathematics and spreadsheets (Excel)

By the time you finish Unit 1, which is a good stopping place unless you plan to go on and take the actuarial certification exam, you should have a solid mathematical foundation on which to operate for future personal and professional financial decision making, along with a solid set of Excel experiences you can use when making decisions about loans, savings and investments. Many people in the world today have little to no financial acumen. When you finish Unit 1, you will. Use it wisely!

TO THE ACTUARY STUDENT

We'd love to be able to say that exam FM follows this same set of goals as those described above. We believe that, for the most part, they do. However, to make sure you are as prepared as possible to succeed on exam FM, the latter half of the book "fills in the gaps" and "spirals over" some topics to make sure we explicitly dealt with some of the nuanced topics of the actuarial exam. Most curricula throw these topics at students early and often. Our experience is that these nuanced topics get in the way of deep understanding for most students. This can lead to shallow understanding and lots of memorization to pass the exam. It can also contribute to a lack of "retention" of key financial concepts for later exams as well as when you become a "real" actuary in your internship or job after you graduate. Therefore, our advice is not to rush through Unit 1 to get to the "hard stuff." You will likely find some of the topics in Unit 1 straightforward. Great! Use the opportunity to make sure you really understand these ideas. Practice solving these problems with Excel and your calculator. Excel, while not allowed on the FM exam, will be an invaluable tool for you when you start your professional life. It is what you will actually use in day-to-day life—not a financial calculator. Learning how to use Excel now will help build your resume as you compete for internships and jobs. Finally, even in Unit 1, we've include sample exam problems at the end of every chapter. If you are truly, deeply understanding the concepts in Unit 1, you should be able to solve these problems as you go. Our experience, however, is that these problems are challenging for students and so be ready to roll up your sleeves, dig into them and be thankful that you haven't dived right into all of the Unit 2 nuance yet!

So what about the topics in Unit 2? If we had taken time to talk about them earlier in the course, they would have gotten in the way of your big picture, global, conceptual understanding of FM. When you get to Unit 2, be ready to go back and review key ideas from Unit 1 if they are shaky. This will help immensely with your long-term retention of the concepts. And, of course, be ready to roll up your sleeves and get to work! By now, you should be comfortable enough with Excel that you can quickly go to Excel and solve problems to check your answer or build more intuition before trying to figure out how to solve the same problem using your financial calculator and a pencil and paper.

Finally, even once you've worked through those later chapters, you shouldn't expect to take and pass the exam. What remains for you to do? Practice, practice and more practice. Our goal is to provide you with a solid foundation—actually, our goal is to provide you with the most solid foundation you could possibly get in any first course in FM using any book. We believe you'll get it. When you are done, you will be conceptually familiar with every topic on the exam. But, when you're done with our book you'll be ready for practicing. The experts say that you should anticipate 300—400 hours of study for exam FM. Our experience is that this is pretty accurate. After working through this curriculum from start to finish, you should be about halfway there. So, what next? There are many test prep programs out there and sets of additional practice exam questions. Do them. When you find those areas you need more work on, we suggest you brush up on the fundamentals using this book, and then go practice some more to get faster and faster and move on from strong conceptual understanding, to be able to quickly and readily solve any problem.

Why do we think this is the best approach? If you jump into the nuance, without understand the concept, you will probably spend a lot more time feeling lost and frustrated—getting questions wrong because of a conceptual misunderstanding vs an algebraic mistake. Our approach ensures you have a strong foundation on which you can build your mastery level of understanding. If you jump right into the online prep guides, manuals and systems you'll probably be lost more than you need to be given that won't really understand the "Why" behind the problems you are trying to solve. If you've got the right foundation, your "test prep" time can be all about speed and problem recognition instead of struggling to keep your head above water. Best wishes on your studying!

Introduction to Financial Mathematics

CHAPTER ONE

Savings: Fundamentals of Interest

Abstract

Saving money for the future is something that many people know they should do, and yet, too few people actually do. Saving requires planning for the future and delaying gratification—being willing to wait to buy until you have the money in hand, instead of using a credit card or taking a bank loan. In this chapter, we will explore the mathematics behind compound interest—a powerful concept that lies at the heart of most arguments as to why saving (whether for a car, college or retirement) is something most financial experts believe you should do. We will explore compound interest in simple situations with a single deposit, and more complex situations with multiple transactions. We will see how spreadsheet tools like Microsoft Excel can simplify complex financial calculations and allow you to quickly evaluate the impact of changes in savings habits, interest rates, and time frames on account balances.

Keywords: Compound interest; nominal interest; cash flow; simple interest; effective interest

SECTION 1.1. SIMPLE AND COMPOUND INTEREST

At some point in your life, you probably had someone tell you to put your money in the bank. Perhaps, it was a grandparent who gave you money for your birthday and then told you to "Have fun, but put some of it in the bank." Maybe it was a parent telling you when you came home with your first paycheck to "Put some of it in the bank to save for college." You might have asked them, or asked yourself, why? There are a number of answers to that question, and you probably have some answers in mind already. One reason for putting your money in the bank is safety—money in a basic savings account at many banks is insured, meaning that even if the bank goes out of business, gets robbed, or burns down, you won't lose your money. That's probably safer than keeping your money in your wallet or under your mattress. Another reason to put money in the bank is to help you save for a big purchase, like college or a car, at some point in the future.

A Spiral Approach to Financial Mathematics.
DOI: https://doi.org/10.1016/B978-0-12-801580-3.00001-0
© 2018 Elsevier Inc.
All rights reserved.
3

Big purchases are hard to make without the advance preparation of putting some money aside now so the financial "pain" of the large purchase isn't as big later. Of course, you can save for a big purchase (even if you don't have that big purchase in mind right now) knowing that at some point, whether you want to or not, you will likely have to make a big purchase. Furthermore, some people say that saving money is one of the three things we should do with money we earn (the others being spending and donating) as part of a healthy and balanced lifestyle. Finally, another reason to save is *interest*. When you put your money in the bank instead of under your mattress, the bank gives you additional money in return—a sort of "thanks" for letting them use your money for a while. So, putting $100 in a savings account at the bank today might mean you have $102 at the end of the year, whereas if you put $100 under your mattress now, you won't have more than $100 under your mattress at the end of the year. Now a $2 difference isn't much, but neither is $100 or 1 year. If the time period is longer and/or the dollar amount is larger, the extra money you earn (the interest) grows. This can end up making for a big difference between bank savings and mattress stuffing! In this section, we'll talk about the basic financial principles of simple and compound interest, which act as a foundation for most of the advanced concepts in this text.

Learning objectives

By the end of this section, you should be able to

- Understand the basic concept of compound interest and its advantages as compared to simple interest.
- Use Excel to quickly compute savings account balances for a single deposit to an account with a fixed rate of interest with compounding.
- Understand the impact of more time, higher interest rates and larger starting balances on resulting balances in accounts with compound interest.

EXAMPLE 1.1. SAVING MONEY TO STUDY ABROAD

At the end of your freshman year of college, you decide that you want to study abroad in your senior year to experience another culture.

Fortunately, through hard work, studying, and saving during high school, you have earned enough scholarships and saved enough money to cover the costs of your basic 4-year education, but the study abroad program will cost $18,000 more for the semester you are gone (including some spending money, travel, and the higher tuition). You need to have this money ready to go by the start of your senior year. There are three summers between now and then.

Think about it

Will you be able to afford to go on the study abroad experience without taking a loan? How hard will you have to work the next three summers to pull it off? What kind of a savings account should you put your money in at summer's end?

Let's assume that you think you can find a job this summer working for 12 weeks earning $10.50 an hour after taxes, and that you will be able to work full time each week (40 hours/week). This means that if you live at home and don't have any real expenses, you should be able to earn 40 (hours/week) $\times$ $10.50/hour = $420/week. For 12 weeks, this amounts to 12 (weeks) $\times$ $420/week = $5,040 saved by the end of the summer.

But, what should you do with your money at the end of the summer? Is a **certificate of deposit** (CD) better than a basic savings account?

Definition

A CD is a type of savings account that prespecifies the length of time that the deposit will be held by the bank with a prespecified, usually unchanging, interest rate. Penalties are often incurred if money is withdrawn (taken out) sooner.

CDs typically pay more **interest** than a basic savings account, so you think maybe you'll put your money in a CD since you don't need your money for over a year. So, what is interest?

Definition

Interest is the amount of money the bank or other depositing institution pays you for the privilege of storing (and using!) your money. Usually interest is paid as a percentage of the amount deposited and is paid at regular, predetermined intervals.

Interest is what the bank pays you for the privilege of using your money. We usually think of banks as keeping our money safe, and they do, but the reality is that banks are using your money for their own investments and to loan to other people. Another way to think of it is that you are loaning the bank your money and, as is typical when someone loans someone else money, the *borrower* pays the *lender* interest as a way of saying "thanks" for the use of the money.

If the bank offers a 2% rate of interest for a 1-year CD, how much interest will you earn if you deposit all $5,040 into the account at the end of the first summer? To find this amount, you simply multiply the interest rate (2% = 0.02) by the deposited amount ($5,040), which is $5,040 × 0.02 = $100.80. So, you will earn $100.80 in interest over the year by depositing your money to the CD, meaning your ending balance at the end of the summer after your sophomore year of college will be $5,040 + $100.80 = $5,140.80.

This basic interest computation lies at the foundation of most financial transactions. Let's introduce some very basic notation which will be useful in understanding more complex financial transactions. The letter *i* is often used to denote the interest rate (typically written as a decimal and not as a percent). More precisely, we will use i to denote the **effective rate of interest** for the first time period—which is usually 1 year. K is typically used to indicate the beginning balance, so that $K \times i$, which we will usually abbreviate as Ki, is the interest earned after 1 year.

Think about it

So what is K and what is i for the 1-year CD account you are considering for your summer savings?

In this case, $K = \$5,040$ and $i = 0.02$. Thus,

Amount of money in the CD after 1 year $= K + Ki = K(1 + i)$

In other words, to find the balance in the account after 1 year, take the initial balance ($K = \$5,040$) and add the interest earned ($Ki = \$100.80$), yielding $5,140.80.

Definition

The **effective rate of interest**, often denoted by the letter i, is the number which, when multiplied by the beginning deposit balance, K, yields the dollar amount of the interest earned at the end of the first period. The value for i is typically reported as a decimal, not as a percentage.

Think about it

Why is your ending balance not much bigger than what you started with? What could you do to increase the ending balance?

There are a few reasons why your ending balance isn't really that much bigger than what you started with: You didn't start with much (K is small), the interest rate isn't that big (i is small) and you only left the money in the CD for 1 year (a longer amount of time would have earned more interest). Working two jobs, finding a job that earned more per hour or finding a higher interest rate are all ways you could end up earning more interest and increase how much you have saved by the end of the third summer.

What if you took a second job on the weekends that earned $15/hour for 5 hours of work each weekend. If you did this job for 12 weeks this summer (in addition to your full time job), then you would earn an additional $15 \times 5 \times 12 = \$900$ this summer. So, the CD you opened could start with \$5,940 and the interest earned the first year would be $5,940 \times 0.02 = \$118.80$ instead of \$100.80, meaning you'll end up with \$6,058.80. While this isn't a lot more interest, it is more and it underscores an important idea about interest—the more you save, the more interest you earn. Imagine how much interest you could earn in 1 year if you deposited a million dollars? Or a billion?

Key idea

Because interest earned is computed as a percentage of the initial balance, the more you start with, the more interest you earn at the same rate of interest.

Interest over longer periods

Let's go a step further. You don't need this money at the end of next summer; you need it a full year later. So, what will you do with your savings then? Typically, you will have the ability to roll your money over into a new CD. In other words, you'll have the option to leave your money in the CD for another whole year. If the new CD stays at the same interest rate—how much interest will you earn the second year? What will the total balance be at the end of the summer before your senior year of college?

To calculate these values, we can take the balance at the end of next summer (\$6,058.80) and multiply it by 1.02 (Why?) to get the balance at the end of the following summer, \$6,179.98. The interest earned the second year was \$121.18; this is more interest than you earned the first year (\$118.80). Why did you earn more interest the second year? Because in the second year you earned interest on the interest from the first year. This is called **compound interest**.

The equation below gives a general formula for the amount of money in the CD after 2 years.

Amount of money in CD after 2 years
$$= \text{Initial Balance} + \text{Year 1 Interest} + \text{Year 2 Interest} = K + Ki + (K + Ki)i$$
$$= K + Ki + Ki + Ki^2 = K\left(1 + 2i + i^2\right) = K(1+i)^2$$

In short, if you don't redeposit your interest, the amount you start with at the beginning of the second year doesn't grow, so your interest earned doesn't change (you would only get $Ki = \$118.80$ instead of $(K + Ki)i = \$121.18$).

Compound interest is one of the most powerful financial tools there is because of the power of reinvestment of interest. Albert Einstein reportedly called compound interest the "Eighth Wonder of the World."

Definition

Compound interest is when the amount of interest that is paid grows over time reflecting the fact that interest paid at the end of each period is reinvested in the account. In essence, compound interest means that you are earning "interest on the interest."

If you didn't redeposit your interest in the account, then the amount of interest earned in the second year would be the same as in the first; you wouldn't earn "interest on the interest." This is much less common but is called **simple interest** (e.g., you withdraw the interest annually and put it in a noninterest earning account). Compound interest grows faster because you reinvest (keeping saving) the interest, letting the interest earn interest.

Definition

Simple interest is when the amount of interest that is paid stays the same over time reflecting the fact that interest paid at the end of each period is not reinvested in the account. In essence, simple interest means that you are not earning "interest on the interest" as you are in the case of compound interest.

A general equation for the balance in an account after t years at effective rate of interest i, where the interest is reinvested (compound interest!), is $A(t) = K(1+i)^t$, where we use $A(t)$ to indicate the amount (using A for Amount) in the account after t years, when the account starts with K. Sometimes, people use a lowercase a, as in $a(t)$, to indicate the ending balance of an account that started with $K = 1$, that is, $a(t) = (1+i)^t$,

Key idea

The general equation for the balance in an account with compound interest at annual effective interest rate i after t years, when starting with K, is given as $A(t) = K(1+i)^t$; If $K = \$1$, then we typically use a lower case a, such as $a(t) = (1+i)^t$.

Suppose you did not go on the study abroad program and just left the initial summer earnings in the CD earning 2% each year. Table 1.1 shows how the amount grows over a long period of time.

Table 1.1 The value of $A(t)$ for different values of t when $K = \$5,940$ and $i = 0.02$

$t =$ Number of years	$A(t) =$ Amount in the account after t years (\$)
0	5,940.00
1	6,058.80
2	6,179.98
5	6,429.65
10	7,240.83
20	8,826.53

Notice that after 20 years, you have earned quite a bit of interest! How would this look if the interest rate was even larger? What if $i = 0.08$? With this higher interest rate of 8%, your initial deposit has more than quadrupled after 20 years! (See Table 1.2.)

Try it with Excel

At this point, you may wish to use the **Chapter 1 Excel file** to try to recreate Tables 1.1 and 1.2 yourself. Try it!

Table 1.2 The value of $A(t)$ for different values of t when $K = \$5,940$ and $i = 0.08$

$t =$ Number of years	$A(t) =$ Amount in the account after t years (\$)
0	5,940.00
1	6,415.20
2	6,928.42
5	8,727.81
10	12,824.01
20	27,686.09

Tip

If you've never used Microsoft Excel before, you might want to search online for some basic Microsoft Excel introductory reading or videos. There are many options available. Your instructor can point you to some specific resources if you aren't sure where to begin.

Fig. 1.1 illustrates this growth over time. The fact that the curve is so noticeable for the account at an interest rate of 0.08 illustrates the power of compound interest. Obviously, higher interest rates and longer amounts of time make saving money a very good proposition.

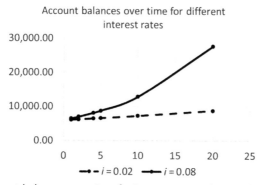

Account balances over time for different interest rates

Figure 1.1 Account balances over time for interest rates of 2% and 8%.

Key idea

When the terms are longer, small changes in interest rates will lead to large changes in the ending balance. This is the power of compound interest.

So, will you have enough to go on the study abroad program? After 2 years of interest, you will only have $6,179.98. But, you can also work next summer, and the summer after that. All told, if you earn a similar amount each year, and deposit all of the money into 2% CDs you will have earned $6,179.98 (first summer total with 2 years of interest earned) + $6,058.80 (second summer total with 1 year of interest) + $5,940 (third summer with no interest earned) = $18,178.78—which is more than the $18,000 you need in order to participate in the program. Of course, if you can get a scholarship to go instead, you could, leave all of your summer earnings in the bank for a while and earn even more interest!

EXPLORATION 1.1. SAVING FOR YOUR FIRST CAR

By the time most students get to college, they've had some time to think about (and hopefully experience!) saving for a major purchase. Maybe it was college, maybe it was a computer, and for some it may have been a car. Let's consider one way this car saving process could work for some students. Knowing that you want to buy a car once you get your driver's license at age 16, you decide to get a summer job at age 15 to save money for your car purchase the next year.

So, what kind of a car will you be able to get if you take your summer earnings, save it in the bank for 1 year, and then withdraw the money to buy a car? Let's assume that you figure that you might be able to find a summer job that pays you, after taxes, $10 per hour.

1. If you work 40 hours a week for 10 weeks at $10 per hour, how much money will you have earned at the summer's end?

When you go to the bank, you will see that there are multiple savings options including basic savings accounts and **certificates of deposit (CDs).**

Definition
A **CD** is a type of savings account that prespecifies the length of time that the deposit will be held by the bank with a prespecified, usually unchanging, interest rate. Penalties are often incurred if money is withdrawn (taken out) sooner.

CDs typically pay more **interest** than a basic savings account so you think maybe you'll put your money in a CD. The banker confirms this for you by saying that since you don't need the money for 1 year this option makes sense (*Note:* CDs often have substantial penalties for taking your money out early).

Definition

Interest is the amount of money the bank or other depositing institution pays you for the privilege of storing (and using!) your money. Usually, interest is paid as a percentage of the amount deposited and is paid at regular, predetermined intervals.

So, what is interest? Interest is what the bank pays you for the privilege of using your money. We usually think of banks as keeping our money safe, and they do, but the reality is that banks are using your money for their own investments and to loan to other people. Another way to think of it is that you are loaning the bank your money and, as is typical when someone loans someone else money, the **borrower** pays the **lender** interest as a way of saying "thanks" for the use of the money.

The most basic interest computation is completed by multiplying the amount of the initial deposit by the interest rate, in order to determine the interest earned.

2. You see that at the bank today, 1-year CDs with a $1,000 minimum deposit have a 3% interest rate. How much interest will you earn by the year's end if you deposit all your summer earnings into a CD at this bank?

This basic interest computation lies at the foundation of most financial transactions. Let's introduce some very basic notation which will be useful in understanding more complex financial transactions. The letter i is often used to denote the interest rate (written as a decimal and not as a percent). More precisely, we will use i to denote the *effective rate of interest* for the first time period—which is usually 1 year. K is typically used to indicate the beginning balance, so that $K \times i$, which we will usually abbreviate as Ki, is the interest earned after 1 year.

3. In the previous question, what is the value of K? What is the value of i?

Definition

The **effective rate of interest**, often denoted by the letter i, is the number which, when multiplied by the beginning deposit balance, K, yields the dollar amount of the interest earned at the end of the first period. The value of i is typically reported as a decimal, not as a percentage.

4. Using only the letters K and i, write a general mathematical formula for how total much money will be in the CD at the end of 1 year.

Amount of money in the CD after 1 year =

5. How much (total) money will be in the CD at the end of the year?

You should have seen in your answer to the previous question that the result is really not that much more than you started with! Why is that? Well, the interest rate, i, is small, the time period is short, and your initial balance, K, isn't too large either. That is why, it doesn't look like you ended up with much more than you started with—just 3% more.

6. Name two ways that you could end up with more money in your account at the end of the first year.

Finding a higher rate investment, working two jobs or finding a job that pays more per hour are ways you could increase how much money you put into your account and, ultimately, increase how much you have at the end.

7. Assume you find a second, part-time job that you will do in the evenings and on Saturday each week, in addition to your regular, full-time summer job. The part-time job lasts 10 weeks, averages 12 hours a week, and earns $15 per hour after taxes.
   a. Now, how much total money will you have at the end of the summer?
   b. If you put the money in the 1-year CD how much interest will you earn?
   c. What will your account balance be at the end of the year?
   d. Compare the amount of interest you earned when working two jobs to what you earned when only working one job. Why is one larger than the other?

While it may seem straightforward, the previous question illustrates an important point. Because interest is computed as a percentage of the initial balance, for any particular interest rate, the more you start with, the more you earn. This principle is a fundamental principle behind the borrower–lender relationship.

Key idea

Because interest earned is computed as a percentage of the initial balance, the more you start with the more interest you earn at the same rate of interest.

Interest over longer periods

Let's say you are successful in finding two jobs, so that you earn approximately $5,800 this summer and put that amount into a 1-year CD that pays 3% interest. Next spring, before the CD matures, you get a letter from the bank asking what you would like to do. You can withdraw the money or you can roll the money over into a new CD. The bank is offering you a new CD with the same terms as the original CD, namely, 3% interest for 1 year.

Obviously, if you want to buy a car, you can withdraw the total amount of money you have ($5,974) and use that money to buy a car. But what would happen if you left the money in the bank and got a new CD? Obviously, you wouldn't have a car! But, what would happen financially? Let's look at the details now.

8. How much interest would you earn in year 2 if you *rolled your CD over* into a new CD with the same terms as the first CD? To answer this question, think about the starting balance and the interest rate. *Note: For the time being, ignore potential additional earnings from your summer job in year 2.*

9. How does this amount compare to the amount of interest you earned in year 1? Larger, smaller, same? Why?

10. What is your balance at the end of year 2?

The interest you earned in year 2 is more than what was earned in year 1 because your starting balance is larger than it was before. Let's compare this to what would happen if you decided to withdraw $174 (the interest earned) at the end of the first year and buy some new clothes. Then you take and deposit the original $5,800 in the new (year 2) CD.

11. If you put a total of $5,800 in the CD for year 2 because you spent the year 1 interest, how much interest will you earn during year 2? How does this compare to the interest earned in the second year if you leave the $174 in the account?

12. If you put a total of $5,800 in the CD for year 2 because you spent the year 1 interest, how much total money will you have at the end of the second year? Again, for the time being, ignore potential additional earnings from your summer job in year 2.

If you don't redeposit your interest, the amount you start with at the beginning of the second year doesn't grow, so your interest earned doesn't change. However, reinvesting the interest, and essentially earning interest on interest, is an example of **compound interest.** This is one of the most powerful financial tools there is because of the power of this reinvestment of interest. Albert Einstein reportedly called compound interest the "Eighth Wonder of the World."

Definition

Compound interest is when the amount of interest that is paid grows over time reflecting the fact that interest paid at the end of each period is reinvested in the account. In essence, compound interest means that you are earning "interest on the interest."

While much less common, **simple interest** is when interest earned does not, itself, accumulate interest (e.g., you withdraw the interest annually).

13. Which kind of account grows faster at the same interest rate: An account with simple interest or an account with compound interest? Why?

Definition

Simple interest is when the amount of interest that is paid stays the same over time reflecting the fact that interest paid at the end of each period is not reinvested in the account. In essence, simple interest means that you are not earning "interest on the interest" as you are in the case of compound interest.

---

14. Come up with a general expression in terms of K and i for the ending balance of the account after 2 years if you reinvest the interest. Plug values into your equation and confirm your answer from above.

Amount of money in the CD after 2 years $=$

Let's assume that after 2 years you still decide you don't need a car and you are able to leave the account alone for 8 more years (for a total of 10). Each year, you reinvest the total amount (including interest) in the same CD which stays at 3%.

15. What is the balance in the account after 10 years?

16. Come up with a general expression (equation) in terms of i and K for the balance in the account after 10 years? Plug the appropriate values for i and K into your equation and confirm your answer from above.

Amount of money in the CD after 10 years $=$

A general equation for the balance in an account after t years at effective rate of interest i, where the interest is reinvested (compound interest!), can be written as $A(t) = K(1+i)^t$, where we use $A(t)$ to indicate the amount (A for Amount!) the account accumulated to after t years, and when the account starts with K. Sometimes, people use a lowercase a, as in $a(t)$, to indicate the ending balance of an account that started with $K = 1$. That is, $a(t) = (1+i)^t$,

---

Key idea

The general equation for the balance in an account with compound interest at yearly effective interest rate i after t years, when starting with K, is given as $A(t) = K(1+i)^t$. If $K = \$1$, then, we typically use a lowercase a, such as $a(t) = (1+i)^t$.

---

17. Use a calculator and the equation above to fill in Table 1.3, which shows the balance of the account at different time points assuming compound interest. You can do this using any calculator.

Table 1.3 The value of $A(t)$ for different values of t when $K = \$5,800$ and $i = 0.03$

$t = $ Number of years	$A(t) = $ Amount in the account after t years
0	
1	
2	
5	
10	
20	

18. How will the values in Table 1.3 change if the interest rate is 6% instead of 3%? Why?

19. Confirm your answer to the previous question by filling in Table 1.4, which shows the value of $A(t)$ when $i = 0.06$.

Table 1.4 The value of $A(t)$ for different values of t when $K = \$5,800$ and $i = 0.06$

$t = $ Number of years	$A(t) = $ Amount in the account after t years
0	
1	
2	
5	
10	
20	

Turning to technology: Excel

While the equation for compound interest is relatively straightforward, there are many more complicated situations where a spreadsheet program, like Excel, will be advantageous to solve financial math problems. Let's start by using Excel to recreate Tables 1.3 and 1.4.

Tip

If you've never used Microsoft Excel before, you might want to search online for some basic Microsoft Excel introductory reading or videos. There are many options available. Your instructor can point you to some specific resources if you aren't sure where to begin.

---

20. Use the **Chapter 1 Excel file** provided, or your own blank worksheet in Excel, to recreate Tables 1.3 and 1.4.

21. Use Excel to generate a graph with time on the x-axis, account balance on the y-axis, and separate curves for $i = 0.03$ and $i = 0.06$.

22. Are the two lines straight or curved? Why? Use financial terms (not mathematical terms) in your explanation.

23. Based on your graph, what can you conclude about the growth of money in an account that earns 3% interest compared to 6% interest?

24. After 20 years, how much more money is in the account that earned 6% interest compared to the account that earned 3% interest?

25. In 20 years, how much money would you have if the CD earned 12%?

Obviously, higher interest rates and longer terms make saving money a very good proposition.

Key idea

When the terms are longer, small changes in interest rates will lead to large changes in the ending balance. This is the power of compound interest.

So, what is our take home message about saving for a car? If you don't need to buy the car—don't! Look at how much you could have later! This is a good general principle—the power of compound interest means that the earlier you start saving, the more money you have. It's a very powerful tool and one that many, if not most, of the most financially savvy individuals use to their benefit regularly. Of course, you might need a car (e.g., to drive to a higher paying job) or you might decide even though you don't need it, you want it and are willing to forgo the benefits of long-term compound interest in order to benefit from the car now. You certainly wouldn't be the first person to make that choice! In the next section, we'll revisit the car savings experiment contrasting a regular savings account paying monthly interest with the annual CD.

SUMMARY

Compound interest is a powerful financial tool. Compound interest means that you earn "interest on the interest." Over time, compound interest can lead to very large and rapid growth in your account—if you are the "saver." As we'll see in later chapters, if you are on the other side of the borrower/lender relationship as the borrower, it is compound interest that can make it challenging to pay back loans. Simple interest is much less common, but is a situation where you don't earn interest on the interest—only gaining the same amount of interest per period over time.

The effective rate of interest is usually stated as a decimal, but can also be stated as a percentage, and is multiplied by the balance in the account to yield the amount of interest earned over a given period of time. While the basic formulas to solve compound interest problems are straightforward, using a financial calculator or Excel can help greatly by evaluating the impact of changing values of the key values of interest (e.g., length of savings; interest rate; initial amount deposited) on the future balance.

Notation and equation summary

$i =$ the effective rate of interest over the first period (often years)

$K =$ the initial balance (\$) in the account

$t =$ the number of periods (often years)

$A(t) =$ the balance on an account at time t that has an initial balance of K

$a(t) =$ the balance on an account at time t that has an initial balance of 1

General formula to compute account balances with compound interest:

$A(t) = K(1+i)^t$

Formula for account balances with starting balance of \$1: $a(t) = (1+i)^t$

HOMEWORK QUESTIONS: SECTION 1.1

Conceptual questions

1. In your own words and using nontechnical language, explain why compound interest leads to substantial growth in account balances over long periods of time.

2. Will the combined balance of two accounts that each start with $1,000 and earn an effective rate of interest of 5% for 1 year be any different than an account that starts with $2,000 and earns 5% effective interest for 1 year? What general conclusion can you draw?

3. In everyday language and without using mathematical formulas, explain the difference between simple and compound interest.

4. Explain how an understanding of compound interest could impact someone's decisions about buying things now vs saving for later.

5. You invest in a 2-year CD that earns 3% compounded annually. Will the amount of interest earned during the second year be less, more, or the same as the amount of interest earned the first year?

6. Suppose you invest $5,000 in a 2-year CD that earns 3% compounded annually. Identify the values of K, t, and i in this situation.

7. What is the difference between $A(t)$ and $a(t)$?

Practice questions

8. At 1% interest, how much interest will you have earned at the end of the year if the starting balance was $1,562.48? What is the ending balance on the account?

9. If you buy a $5,000 CD that earns an annual effective interest of 3%. How much interest will you earn at the end of 1 year? How much will the value of the CD be worth at the end of 1 year?

10. You put $4,000 into a money market account that earns 2.5% compounded annually. If you leave that money in the account for 5 years, how much will the account be worth?

11. Suppose you put $3,500 in a savings account that earns 1% compounded annually. How much will you have in that account if you leave it in for 1 year? Two years?

12. Suppose your parents deposited some money for you in an account that earns 6% interest compounded annually. After 1 year, you find out the value of the account is $3,392. How much did your parents put in the account initially?

13. Suppose your parents deposit $4,500 in an account. After 1 year, the value of the account is $4,644. What was the interest rate earned on the account for the year?

Application questions

14. If you want to have $10,000 to buy a car 1 year from now, how much do you need to deposit today if $i = 0.4\%$? $i = 4\%$? $i = 40\%$?

15. If you want to have $20,000 saved to go to college 4 years from now, how much do you need to deposit today if $i = 0.1\%$? $i = 1\%$? $i = 10\%$? Assume you only deposit money today and no additional times over the next 4 years.

16. If you have $4,000 today and want to have $4,500 1 year from now, what effective rate of interest do you need to earn? What yearly effective rate of interest do you need to earn if you want to have $4,500 in 5 years instead of in only 1 year?

17. If you invest $1,000 today into an account earning 6% effective interest (average for the stock market over last five decades), how much will you have in 40 years (when you are ready to retire)? Assume you only deposit money today and no additional times over the next 40 years.

18. Revisit the exploration, Tables 1.3 and 1.4. Compute these tables for simple interest at 1% and 2%, respectively. Compare and describe the results between simple and compound interest both in the table and by creating the relevant graphs.

Looking ahead

19. At the end of the summer of 2018 (September 1, 2018) you deposit your summer work income into an account earning 3% effective interest. You will also do this each of the next three summers (2019, 2020, and 2021). How much do you have to earn each summer to have $20,000 by September 1, 2021, in time for the start of college?

20. Sometimes, bonds are sold so that the value of the bond is given in terms of what it will be worth in the future (i.e., when it matures) not the value that you have to pay for it. Suppose you want to buy a bond that will be worth $5,000 in 5 years, if it earns 2.5% interest compounded annually. How much will you have to pay for the bond now?

21. Savings bonds are issued by the US government and can be used by individuals to save money while earning interest. In 2017, the rate of interest for one type of savings bond was a "nominal" rate of 1.96% compounded semiannually. This means that every 6 months, interest is added to the bond at a rate of half the 1.96% rate or 0.98%. Suppose you buy a $50 savings bond and keep it for 5 years. How much will it be worth at the end of 5 years if the interest rate remains as it was in 2017?

22. Suppose you invest $1,000 in an account that earns a "nominal" rate of 6% compounded monthly. This means the account will earn 0.5% interest each month. How much will you have in the account after 1 year?

SECTION 1.2. CHANGING THE COMPOUNDING PERIOD: NOMINAL VS EFFECTIVE INTEREST RATES

In the previous section, we explored the power of compound interest—and, how earning interest on interest can lead to very large increases in account balances over time! However, our consideration in the previous section was limited by primarily focusing on certificates of deposit (CDs). In particular, the effective rate of interest, *i*, was used only once each year—computing interest at the end of the year only. While this is the case for a CD, many bank savings accounts (and many other financial instruments), compute interest much more regularly (e.g., monthly). In this section, we will explore what's the same, and what's different, when interest is compounded more regularly.

Learning objectives

By the end of this section, you should be able to
- Comfortably compute compound interest using an effective rate of interest over years, months or other periods of time.
- Use a nominal rate of interest and convert it to an effective rate of interest (and back again) in order to compute account balances over time.

EXAMPLE 1.2. SAVING MONEY TO STUDY ABROAD (REVISITED)

In Example 1.1 we looked at a situation where a student was saving up money to study abroad using CDs. One of the downsides of CDs is that they typically do not allow for early withdrawals without a penalty. A standard savings account is usually more flexible about the number of deposits and withdrawals. Savings accounts often compound interest monthly, not annually like we have considered up until now. Let's explore how it would look if you deposited your summer savings ($5,940) into a savings account with monthly compounding, instead of annual.

When you are given an effective rate of interest for an account (e.g., 0.02 was the effective rate of interest for the CD considered in Example 1.1), you also should know what the compounding period is—that is, how often the interest will be added to the account. If an effective rate of interest is provided, this is often for a 1-year period, but doesn't have to be.

Definition
The **compounding period** is the period over which the savings institution pays interest.

Key idea

When you are provided an effective rate of interest, you should know what the compounding period is. Annually? Monthly? Something else? Most often the effective rate is annually (per year) unless specified otherwise.

Let's assume that you earned 0.001 effective interest *monthly* on a savings account. How much would you have at the end of the first month, if you deposited $5,940 at the start of the month?

To figure this out, we simply multiply the initial balance ($K = \$5,940$) by the effective monthly interest ($i = 0.001$), to find the interest earned ($Ki = \$5.94$), so that the account balance at the end of the month is $5,940 + \$5.94 = \$5,945.94$. The general equation for an account balance for any length period is $A(t) = K(1+i)^t$, where i is the effective interest rate per period and t is the number of periods.

Key idea

The general equation for the balance in an account with compound interest at effective interest rate i per period after t periods, when starting with K, is given as $A(t) = K(1+i)^t$. Note that this is essentially the same as we saw in the previous section but is more flexible by allowing the effective interest rate to be defined over any length period—not just a single year.

If a savings account earns a 0.001 effective interest rate per month, and if the money (initial deposit and accumulated interest) stays in the account all year, what is the effective interest rate for the year? Let's start by considering how much interest will be earned in the account over an entire year. In this case, that would be $\$5,940(1 + 0.001)^{12} = \$6,011.67$. So, the question is what effective annual (yearly) interest rate would leave $6,011.67 in the account at years end? In others words, what is the interest rate, i, so that $\$6,011.67 = \$5,940(1 + i)$? Solving for i, gives us $i = 0.012067$.

Key idea

If the monthly effective rate of interest is j, then the equivalent annual effective rate of interest is found by solving this equation for i:

$$1 + i = (1+j)^{12}$$

As we'll see throughout the text, it is sometimes easier to convert monthly effective rates into their equivalent annual rates in order to more easily and quickly solve financial problems.

The equation above can also be used to find what monthly effective rates of interest are needed in order to yield a particular annual effective rate. For example, if you wanted to yield a 0.02 annual effective rate of interest, you need to earn 0.001652 effective monthly interest with monthly compounding since $(1.02)^{1/12} = 1.001652$.

Nominal versus effective interest rates

So, we've seen that there really isn't much of a difference in how you solve problems with monthly effective rates of interest as compared to effective annual rates of interest. However, in practice, most banks do not report the monthly effective rate of interest—even for a savings account with monthly compounding! Instead, they report something known as the **nominal rate of interest with monthly compounding**, which is also known as the **annual percentage rate (APR)**.

While the APR is a convenient and "quick" way for bank to tell you (sort of) what their interest rate is, it can make it kind of tricky to compute the interest.

If the monthly effective interest rate is j, then the APR is 12 times the monthly rate (APR = $12j$). So, if the monthly effective interest rate is 0.001, then the APR is 0.012 (or 1.2%).

Unfortunately, the notation people use for APR is also kind of tricky. The symbol for APR is $i^{(12)}$ and is pronounced "i upper 12." Note that the 12 in parentheses is not an exponent! Instead, the value in parentheses is a symbol indicating how many compounding periods there are in the year. So, we would say that $i^{(12)} = 0.012$ to indicate that the APR is 0.012. So, how do you find the balance in an account where APR = 0.012? Start by finding the monthly effective rate of interest = 0.012/12 = 0.001. Once you know that you can find account balances at different points in time. For example, as we saw above, $5,940 $(1 + 0.001)^{12} = \$6,011.67$. This also means that an account earning $i^{(12)}$ is earning $i^{(12)}/12$ effective interest per month.

Definition
The **nominal rate of interest with monthly compounding (or APR)**, denoted $i^{(12)}$, and pronounced "i upper 12," is the interest rate such that the effective interest rate for each month is $i^{(12)}/12$. The compounding period for APR will be monthly unless otherwise stated since in practice APR can sometimes to refer to other (nonmonthly) compounding periods. A word of caution, the 12 in parentheses is not an exponent. That is a common mistake—if it was a regular exponent we wouldn't put it in parentheses. The use of parentheses is simply notation.

Alternatively, the APR can be thought of as the interest for the payment period, multiplied by the number of payment periods in the year. For example, if j is the effective interest rate per month, then $12j$ is the APR.

The idea of a nominal rate of interest, however, goes beyond simply monthly compounding (though that is the most common). A nominal rate of interest is possible to state for any compounding period. We will use the letter m to indicate how many compounding periods there are in a year. For example, if $m = 4$, then this is "quarterly compounding" (compounding every 4 months).

Definition

A **nominal rate of interest with m-thly compounding**, denoted $i^{(m)}$, is the interest rate such that the effective interest rate for each period is $i^{(m)}/m$, where there are m periods per year. A word of caution: the m in parentheses is not an exponent. That is a common mistake—if it was a regular exponent we wouldn't put it in parentheses. This is simply notation.

Table 1.5 shows how the end-of-year account balance changes as the number of compounding periods increases. While the changes aren't very large, the ending account balances do increase as the number of compounding periods increases. This should make intuitive sense—the more often you compound the interest the more often the interest gets added to the account, and the more time that interest has time to earn more interest. We also notice that there appears to be a limit to how much additional compounding helps—we'll talk more about this "limiting" idea in Chapter 6, Savings Revisited.

Key idea

For a given nominal rate of interest, as the number of compounding periods (m) increases, the total interest earned per year increases, as does the effective interest rate per year. However, this increase doesn't go on forever—there is a limit.

The general formula that we used to compute the final account balances in Table 1.5 is a modification of the formula we used earlier,

$$A(1) = K\left(1 + \frac{i^{(m)}}{m}\right)^m \quad \text{(balance at end of year 1 if you deposited \$K)}$$

Table 1.5 Changes in end-of-year account balances as the number of compounding periods changes for a nominal rate of interest of 1.2% and opening balance of $5,940

Number of compounding periods, m	Symbol	Period length	Effective interest rate per period $(i^{(m)}/m)$	Effective interest rate per year (APY) $(1 + i^{(m)}/m)^m - 1$	End of year account balance ($)
1 (annually)	$i^{(1)} = 0.012$	1 year	0.012	0.012	6,011.28
2 (semiannually)	$i^{(2)} = 0.012$	6 months	0.006	0.012036	6,011.49
3 (triannually)	$i^{(3)} = 0.012$	4 months	0.004	0.012048064	6,011.57
4 (quarterly)	$i^{(4)} = 0.012$	3 months	0.003	0.012054108	6,011.60
6 (bimonthly)	$i^{(6)} = 0.012$	2 months	0.002	0.01206016	6,011.64
12 (monthly)	$i^{(12)} = 0.012$	1 month	0.001	0.01206622	6,011.67
24 (semimonthly)	$i^{(24)} = 0.012$	~2 weeks	0.0005	0.012069254	6,011.69
52 (weekly)	$i^{(52)} = 0.012$	1 week	~0.0002308	0.012070888	6,011.70
365 (daily)	$i^{(365)} = 0.012$	1 day	~0.0000329	0.012072089	6,011.71

and

$$A(t) = K\left(1 + \frac{i^{(m)}}{m}\right)^{tm} \quad \text{(balance at end of year } t \text{ if you deposited \$}K\text{)}$$

Key idea

The general formula for the ending account balance for an account with a nominal rate of interest of $i^{(m)}$ is given as $A(t) = K\left(1 + \left(i^{(m)}/m\right)\right)^{tm}$. However, it may be easier to first convert nominal rates to effective rates.

Many students find equations and notation for nominal rates of interest to be confusing and tricky. One way to avoid these challenges is to not use them! Instead, most students find it easier to convert nominal rates to effective rates and then use the standard formulas. This is illustrated in Table 1.5 where columns show the effective rate of interest per period and then per year. The annual effective rate of interest is known as the annual percentage yield (APY).

Definition

APY is the annual effective rate of interest.

For example, let's assume that the bank is offering a 0.012 nominal rate of interest with quarterly compounding, that is, $i^{(4)} = 0.012$. To calculate the account balance after 1 year, if we deposit \$5,940 to start, we could first, convert the nominal rate to an effective rate per quarter $(0.012/4 = 0.003)$. Then, we could take the use this effective rate to quickly find the balance by doing $\$5,940(1.003)^4 = \$6,011.60$. This is really no different than what the equation shown earlier does, but may seem more intuitive.

Key idea

If compounding is being done more than once within a year $(m > 1)$ then the APY (effective annual interest rate for the year) will be greater than the annual nominal rate of interest $(i^{(m)})$.

Problem solving tip

Rather than memorizing the direct formula for finding ending balances for nominal interest rate problems, many students start by converting the nominal rate to an effective rate (per period or per year) and then using the "easier" effective rate formula to compute the final balance.

Key idea

Being able to comfortably and quickly move between nominal and effective rates of interest is a key to quickly solve many types of financial problems. You'll want to make sure you are practicing this tricky concept to get comfortable with it as quickly as possible!

Back to the saving for study abroad example

So, now that you know a bit more about interest rates, what will you do with the money you earned this summer? You have $5,940.

You visit the local bank and find out that they have the following savings options:

A. Savings account with a nominal interest rate of 2.4%, compounded monthly (i.e., APR). No withdrawal penalties.

B. 1-year CD with a nominal interest rate of 3.2% with quarterly compounding. All interest is forfeited and a $25 charge is applied for early withdrawals.

C. 2-year CD with a nominal interest rate of 4.3% with semiannual compounding. All interest is forfeited and a $25 charge is applied for early withdrawals. Minimum deposit of $1,000 required.

Think about it

What will you decide to do? What financial and nonfinancial considerations will you take into account?

While there is no specifically "right" or "wrong" answer to the previous question, here are some things we thought of that might be helpful if we were faced with this decision.

For option A, you will have a balance of $6,084.14 after 1 year. For option B, you will have a balance of $6,132.37 after 1 year. For option C, you will have a balance of $6,467.55 after 2 years.

Option B pays more interest than option A, but the difference of $48.23 may not be worth the ability to get at your money whenever you want. Option C pays the most interest, but it ties up your money for two consecutive years and if you withdraw money during year two, you forfeit the interest earned in year one.

EXPLORATION 1.2. SAVING FOR YOUR FIRST CAR (REVISITED)

In the "Exploration 1.1. Saving for Your First Car" section, we began to explore how to save for your first car using a CD. CDs typically allow for limited deposits and withdrawals and have interest computed at the end of the term of the CD. In the "Exploration 1.1. Saving for Your First Car" section, we considered a 1-year CD earning 3% effective interest over the 1-year period of the CD. If you worked two jobs, you thought you could earn $5,800 by the end of the summer. If you deposited the entire amount into the CD, you would earn $174 interest and have $5,974 total 1 year later.

Changing the period over which interest Is computed

Of course, when saving for a car, you may not want to use a CD because of the terms (e.g., penalty for early withdrawal). This is not the case for a regular savings account, though regular savings accounts typically have a lower interest rate than CDs. Additionally, a regular savings account has a slightly more complicated way of computing interest which includes putting interest into the account once a month, instead of once a year.

To begin to understand how *monthly* compound interest works, think about how much interest would be earned after 1 month if the bank offered to pay an effective rate of interest of 0.2% (= 0.002) for the first month.

1. If you start with a balance of $5,800, how much interest will be earned after the first month if you earn 0.2% interest over that month-long period?

Definition
The **compounding period** is the period over which the savings institution pays interest.

Key idea
When you are provided an effective rate of interest, you should know what the compounding period is. Annually? Monthly? Something else? Most often the effective rate is per year unless specified otherwise.

---

2. Let's assume that the interest rate the bank pays monthly is the same for each month for a year (0.2% per month). Assuming you have an initial deposit of $5,800 and keep the money in the bank for the entire year with no withdrawals (including keeping the interest earned in the account), how much money will you have at the end of the year?

Key idea
The general equation for the balance in an account with compound interest at effective interest rate i **per period** after t periods, when starting with K, is given as $A(t) = K(1+i)^t$. Note that this is essentially the same as we saw in the previous section but is more flexible by allowing the effective interest rate to be defined over any length period—not just a single year.

---

3. Is the amount in your answer to the previous question more or less than you would have earned if the bank had paid 3% effective interest for the year, with a single compounding period (i.e., interest is paid once at the end of the year)?

4. Is earning 0.2% effective interest per month with monthly compounding better or worse than earning 2.4% effective interest per year with yearly compounding?

5. Is earning 0.2% effective interest per month with monthly compounding better or worse than earning 2.4265768% effective interest per year with yearly compounding?

6. So, why is 0.2% effective interest per month with monthly compounding the same as 2.4265768% effective interest per year with yearly compounding? *Hint: Use the equation shown above to find* $(1+i)^t = (1+0.002)^{12}$.

Key idea

If the monthly effective rate of interest is j, then the equivalent annual effective rate of interest is found by solving this equation for i:

$$1 + i = (1+j)^{12}$$

As we'll see throughout the text, it is sometimes easier to convert monthly effective rates into their equivalent annual rates in order to more easily and quickly solve financial problems.

As you can see in the key idea box, for any monthly interest rate there is an equivalent annual interest rate. We can also consider the opposite kind of question—for a given annual interest rate, what is the equivalent monthly compounding rate?

7. If the bank wishes to have an effective rate of interest of 1% for the year, but wishes to use monthly compounding, what should the effective rate of interest be each month? *Hint: Use the equation in the key idea box above, but solve for a different unknown value.*

Nominal versus effective interest rates

In the previous questions, we've seen that there really isn't much of a difference in how you solve problems with monthly effective rates of interest as compared to effective annual rates of interest. However, in practice, most banks do not report the monthly effective rate of interest—even for a savings account. Instead, they report something known as the **nominal rate of interest with monthly compounding**, which is also known as the **APR.**

While the APR is a convenient and "quick" way for a bank to tell you (sort of) what their interest rate is, it can make it kind of tricky to compute the actual amount of interest earned.

If the monthly effective interest rate is j, then the APR is 12 times the monthly rate (APR $= 12j$).

8. What is the APR for a monthly effective interest rate of 0.1%? What is the APR for a monthly effective interest rate of 0.2%?

The symbol used for APR is $i^{(12)}$. *Note:* the 12 in parentheses is not an exponent! Instead, the 12 tells you how many compounding periods there are within a year. The symbol $i^{(12)}$ is pronounced "i upper 12."

9. If the APR is reported to be $i^{(12)} = 2\%$, what is the monthly effective rate of interest and what is the annual effective rate of interest? What if the APR is $i^{(12)} = 6\%$?

10. If the bank offers you an APR of 6%, how much money will you have in a savings account with an opening balance of $5,800 after 1 year?

Definition

The **nominal rate of interest with monthly compounding (or APR)**, denoted $i^{(12)}$, and pronounced "i upper 12," is the interest rate such that the effective interest rate for each month is $i^{(12)}/12$. The compounding period for APR will be monthly unless otherwise stated since in practice APR can sometimes to refer to other (nonmonthly) compounding periods. A word of caution: the 12 in parentheses is not an exponent. That is a common mistake—if it was a regular exponent we wouldn't put it in parentheses. The use of parentheses is simply notation.

Alternatively, the APR can be thought of as the interest for the payment period, multiplied by the number of payment periods in the year. For example, if j is the effective interest rate per month, then $12j$ is the APR.

While the APR is the most common "nominal" rate of interest, nominal rates of interest can be defined over any period length. Nominal rates of interest are typically reported as an "annual" rate, but then must also specify how frequently interest is compounded. The compounding frequency per year is denoted by the letter m (e.g., if $m = 2$, there are 2 compounding periods per year—once every 6 months).

11. If the nominal rate of interest is 6% annually, with 6 compounding periods per year, what is m? What is the length of the compounding period? What is the effective rate of interest for each compounding period?

12. If the nominal rate of interest is 6% annually, with 4 compounding periods per year, what is m? What is the length of the compounding period? What is the effective rate of interest for each compounding period?

Definition

A **nominal rate of interest with m-thly compounding**, denoted $i^{(m)}$, is the interest rate such that the effective interest rate for each period is $i^{(m)}/m$, where there are m periods per year. A word of caution: the m in parentheses is not an exponent. That is a common mistake—if it was a regular exponent we wouldn't put it in parentheses. This is simply notation.

---

13. If you deposit $5,800 into an account earning 6% nominal interest with bimonthly compounding (compounding every 2 months), what is the symbol for this nominal interest rate? How much money will you have at the end of 1 year?

14. If you deposit $5,800 into an account earning 6% nominal interest with quarterly compounding (compounding every 3 months), what is the symbol for this nominal interest rate? How much money will you have at the end of 1 year?

15. Compare your answers to the previous two questions. Which is larger? Why? What general rule can you infer from this comparison?

Key idea

For a given nominal rate of interest, as the number of compounding periods (m) increases, the total interest earned per year increases, as does the effective interest rate per year. However, this increase doesn't go on forever—there is a limit.

---

16. If you deposit $5,800 to an account earning 6% nominal interest with daily compounding (compounding 365 days a year), what is the symbol for this nominal interest rate? How much money will you have at the end of 1 year? How does this compare to the previous answers? Is it bigger or smaller than you thought?

The general formula that we used to compute the final account balances is a modification of the formula we used earlier,

$$A(1) = K\left(1 + \frac{i^{(m)}}{m}\right)^m \quad \text{(balance at end of year 1 if you deposited } \$K)$$

and

$$A(t) = K\left(1 + \frac{i^{(m)}}{m}\right)^{tm} \quad \text{(balance at end of year } t \text{ if you deposited } \$K)$$

Key idea

The general formula for the ending account balance for an account with a nominal rate of interest of $i^{(m)}$ is given as $A(t) = K\left(1 + \left(i^{(m)}/m\right)\right)^{tm}$. However, it may be easier to first convert nominal rates to effective rates.

Many students find equations and notation for nominal rates of interest to be confusing and tricky. One way to avoid these challenges is to not use them! Instead, most students find it easier to convert nominal rates to effective rates and then use the standard formulas.

Problem solving tip

Rather than memorizing the direct formula for finding ending balances for nominal interest rate problems, many students start by converting the nominal rate to an effective rate (per period or per year) and then use the "easier" effective rate formula to compute the final balance.

---

17. What is the equivalent effective annual rate of interest for an account earning 6% nominal interest with bimonthly compounding ($i^{(6)} = 0.06$)? Use this to compute the final account balance for a deposit of \$5,800 and show that it is the same you obtained using the direct approach earlier.

The APY is a term used to describe the annual effective rate of interest.

Definition

APY is the annual effective rate of interest.

---

18. What is the equivalent effective annual rate of interest for an account earning 6% nominal interest with quarterly compounding $(i^{(4)} = 0.06)$? Use this to compute the final account balance for a deposit of $5,800 and show that it is the same you obtained using the direct approach earlier.

19. Is this APY (effective annual rate of interest) larger or smaller than the nominal annual rate of interest?

This fact (APY = effective annual rate of interest is greater than the nominal rate of interest) is true if compounding is happening more than once per year.

Key idea

If compounding is being done more than once within a year $(m > 1)$ then the APY (effective annual interest rate for the year) will be greater than the annual nominal rate of interest $(i^{(m)})$.

Key idea

Being able to comfortably and quickly move between nominal and effective rates of interest is a key to quickly solve many types of financial problems. You'll want to make sure you are practicing this tricky concept to get comfortable with it as quickly as possible!

Back to the car example

So, now that you know a bit more about interest rates, what will you do about the money you earned this summer? You have $5,800.

You visit the local bank and find out that they have the following savings options:

A. Savings account with a nominal interest rate of 1.2%, compounded monthly (i.e., APR). No withdrawal penalties.

B. 1-year CD with a nominal interest rate of 1.5% with quarterly compounding. All interest is forfeited and a $25 charge is applied for early withdrawals.

C. 2-year CD with a nominal interest rate of 1.8% with semiannual compounding. All interest is forfeited and a $25 charge is applied for early withdrawals.

20. Consider each of the savings options above by computing the (projected) interest earned and final balance over a relevant time period for buying a car. Consider the various terms of the savings accounts. Use graphs and tables as appropriate. Write a $1-2$ paragraph response that compares the different savings options and provides a conclusion as to what you would likely do and why in this scenario.

SUMMARY

In this section, we explored how compounding does not need to occur only once each year. In practice, interest is often compounded monthly, though any time period can be chosen. Typically, effective interest rates are annual rates (APY), though they can be stated over any period. Banks use the APR, or nominal rate of interest, as a shorthand way to describe the interest rate, but the nominal rate of interest is only an approximation of how much interest will be earned. In fact, the annual nominal rate of interest will always be less than effective rate of interest for the year if compounding occurs more than once a year. While there are direct formulas to directly calculate account balances using nominal rates of interest, many students find it easier to first convert nominal interest rates to effective rates of interest and then compute account balances.

Notation and equation summary

$i^{(12)}$ = the nominal rate of interest with monthly compounding (APR)

$i^{(m)}$ = the nominal rate of interest with m-thly compounding

If j is the effective annual rate of interest each month and interest is compounded monthly, then $1 + i = (1 + j)^{12}$ gives the equivalent effective annual interest rate, i, also known as the APY.

$A(t) = K\left(1 + \left(i^{(m)}/m\right)\right)^{tm}$ is the equation for an account balance at the end of t years with m-thly compounding. Many students do not use this formula directly, they prefer to first convert nominal rates to effective rates and then use the easier $A(t) = K(1+i)^t$ formula we saw earlier. These approaches are equivalent.

HOMEWORK QUESTIONS: SECTION 1.2

Conceptual questions

1. What is the difference between effective and nominal interest rates?

2. What does the notation $i^{(12)}$ mean?

3. Which will result in earning more interest or are they the same: A nominal rate of 6% compounded quarterly or an effective annual rate of 6%? Why?

4. Which will result in earning more interest or are they the same: A nominal rate of 3% compounded quarterly or a nominal rate of 3% compounded daily? Why?

5. Keeping the nominal interest rate constant, as the compounding period gets shorter does the effective annual interest rate increase, decrease or stay the same? Why?

6. Which leads to more interest paid: an effective interest rate of 12%, compounded annually or a nominal interest rate of 12%, compounded monthly? Why?

Practice questions

7. Find the nominal annual interest rate for an account paying 3% effective interest quarterly? Semiannually?

8. Find the nominal annual interest rate for an account paying 6% effective interest quarterly. Semiannually?

9. If the APR for an account is 6%, what is the effective rate of interest each month? Each year? How often will interest be compounded?

10. If the APR for an account is 12%, what is the effective rate of interest each month? Each year? How often will interest be compounded?

11. If you deposit $2,000 into an account earning an APR of 2% what will the ending balance be in 1 year?

Application questions

12. What is the effective annual rate of interest at a 3.25% APR with monthly compounding? What if compounding was done weekly? (*Note:* To find the effective weekly rate use $i^{(52)}/52$.) Extend this idea and find the effective rate of interest with daily compounding, semi-annual compounding, annual compounding and biennial (every 2 years) compounding.

13. If you invest $10,000 today into an account earning 6% nominal interest, how much will you have in 40 years (when you are ready to retire) if that amount is compounded:
    a Annually?
    b Semiannually?
    c Monthly?
    d Daily?

14. Using the formula. $A(t) = K\left(1 + \left(i^{(m)}/m\right)\right)^{tm}$:
    a Explain what the variables K, $i^{(m)}$, m, and t represent.
    b Find the value of the amount in the account when $K = 5,000$, $i = 0.015$, $m = 4$, and $t = 5$.

15. A CD earns 3% compounded monthly. How much would you have to put in the CD now to have it be worth $10,000 in 4 years?

16. You want to invest in a savings plan that will earn you the most amount of interest. Plan A earns 4% compounded annually. Plan B earns 3.95% nominal compounded monthly. Plan C earns 3.92% nominal compounded daily. What is the effective annual rate (APY) for each plan? Which plan yields the highest effective annual interest rate?

Looking ahead

17. Let's explore what happens when we increase the number of compounding periods per year.

    a Find the effective annual interest rate if the nominal annual rate is 10% compounded:

        i. Monthly.

        ii. Daily.

        iii. 10,000 times per year.

        iv. 1,000,000 times per year.

        v. 1,000,000,000 times per year.

    b You should have found that while the effective rate increased as the number of compounding periods increased, it doesn't increase by much and there seems to be a limit to how much it increases. The constant e has the property that $\lim_{m \to \infty} \left(1 + (1/m)\right)^m = e$. (Does the argument of that limit look a bit familiar?) When an interest rate is compounded an infinite number of times a year (which we call compounded continuously), the formula $A(t) = Ke^{it}$ can be used. Using this formula, find the effective annual rate if the nominal rate is 10% compounded continuously. How does it compare to your answers to part a? [*Note:* While compounding continuously might not be used too often in financial mathematics, it is used to model growth in other things, like different kinds of populations that do (almost) grow continuously.]

18. Suppose it is January 1, 2020 and you decide to put $1,000 into an account that earns 2% interest compounded quarterly. You again, put $1,000 into that account on April 1, July 1, and September 1 of that same year. How much money will you have in the account on January 1, 2021?

SECTION 1.3. VALUING ACCOUNTS WITH MULTIPLE TRANSACTIONS

In the previous sections, we explored the basic idea of compound interest, and how to think about and work with interest rates over different length compounding periods. However, we were limited in our analysis because we focused on how to value accounts with a single transaction. Now we will begin to explore how to combine these basic interest rate ideas when considering more complex problems involving multiple deposits and withdrawals, and how to handle all of this in the presence of infrequent changes to the effective rate of interest, i.

Learning objectives

By the end of this section, you should be able to

- Create an account chart to compute the future balance of an account with multiple transactions using the recursive approach.
- Create an account chart using either pencil and paper or a spreadsheet program like Excel.
- Be able to make the account chart using either effective or nominal rates of interest.
- Understand that, if you have a choice, the best time to deposit money to a savings account is as soon as possible to have the deposit gain as much interest as possible.

EXAMPLE 1.3. SAVING FOR A DOWN PAYMENT ON A HOUSE

At some point in your life, and maybe not all that long from now, you may want to buy a house instead of renting an apartment. You know that most people cannot afford to pay all cash for a house and so you plan to take out a mortgage (a specific loan for purchasing a house). Typically, interest rates and mortgage terms are better if you "put money down"— that is, pay a portion of the purchase price in cash and take a loan for the rest, instead of just taking a loan for the entire purchase price.

Let's say that you have looked and seen that houses that are of interest to you are in the $200,000 range and that you've heard you'll get the best deal if you put 10% "down" on the purchase price. This means that you will need to have $20,000 in cash in order to buy the house (and you will take a loan for the remaining amount of $180,000). You've determined that you can put approximately $800/month into a savings account to save for the down payment and the current APR on your savings account is 1.8%. How long will it take you to save $20,000?

Basic account chart

An account chart is a useful way to calculate balances for accounts with multiple transactions.

Definition
When solving problems with multiple deposits and withdrawals and/or changes in effective interest rate, an **account chart** is a useful way to summarize information. An account chart summarizes account balances, interest, deposits and withdrawals over time, usually with one row for each compounding period.

Table 1.6, shows a simple account chart for this savings situation. Notice that the chart has a row for each month since that is the compounding period for this account. The chart indicates the
- prior balance in the account,
- the deposited amount (could be negative for a withdrawal),
- the new balance on day one (after deposit or withdrawal),
- the effective rate over the month ($0.018/12 = 0.0015$ effective/month),
- interest earned during the month (prior balance times interest rate for the month)
- new balance (interest earned plus prior balance)

Notice that to fill in the values in the table you go in order, month-by-month.

Table 1.6 Account chart to save for a down payment with APR 1.8% and $800 deposits

Month	Beginning of month savings ($)	Beginning of month deposit ($)	Total amount in account on day 1 of month ($)	Effective monthly rate of interest ($)	Interest earned during the month ($)	Balance in account on last day of the month ($)
1	0	800	800	0.0015	1.20	801.20
2	801.20	800	1,601.20	0.0015	2.40	1,603.60
3	1,603.60	800	2,403.60	0.0015	3.61	2,407.21
4	2,407.21	800	3,207.21	0.0015	4.81	3,212.02
5	3,212.02	800	4,012.02	0.0015	6.02	4,018.04

Think about it

What would go in the next row of the account table?

The next row of the table would be for month 6 and would have $4,018.04 as the starting balance, $800 as the deposit, $4,818.04 as the new balance on day one of the month, an effective rate of 0.0015, $7.23 of earned interest and a balance at the end of the month of $4,825.27.

Key idea

When using an account chart, you typically go row-by-row (e.g., month by month or year by year), in order to calculate the final/end balance.

So, remember that our question was really about how long it would take in order to save $20,000. So far, we can say that we know it's more than 6 months, but we can't say much more than that! To find the length of time more precisely, we can keep going in the same manner as above (month by month) calculating the new balance until we get to $20,000.

Before we look at a faster method for calculating the balance, let's look at a key relationship present in Table 1.6.

Think about it

What is the total amount that has been deposited to the account over the 5-year period?

The total amount deposited to the account is $800 \times 5 = \$4,000$. Since the ending balance is $4,018.04, this means that there has been $18.04 "added" to the account through interest. This gets us to a key relationship—the total balance in an account is a sum of the total deposits (using negatives for withdrawals) and interest earned.

Key idea

The total account balance is Total Sum of Deposits + Total Interest Earned, where you use negative values for withdrawals.

Creating a dynamic account chart using Excel

While you could keep going, line by line, by hand, there are two important shortcuts to solving this problem. We will explore some other shortcuts soon, but for now, we can use Excel to quickly and easily solve this problem. This is a great situation to use Excel since, once we have the pattern down, it's just doing the same thing over and over. Using Excel will also give us the ability to quickly and easily evaluate small changes to the problem (e.g., What if the interest was a bit higher/lower? What if we could save $900/month instead of $800?) which would otherwise be very tedious to evaluate by hand.

Definition

A **dynamic account chart** uses technology to instantly update all balances in an account chart to alleviate tedious by hand calculations. Microsoft Excel is a popular business tool to create dynamic account charts.

Table 1.7 shows a dynamic account chart created in Excel for our example. You should make sure to go to the **Chapter 1 Excel file** and explore the table above since it's an important skill to be sure that you can make the table yourself. We can see from this table that at the start of the 25th month your deposit of $800 will push the account balance over $20,000—meaning you will have reached your goal and will be able to make the down payment.

How much different is this than if you'd simply hidden your money under your mattress instead of putting it in the bank? If you divided $20,000 by 800 you get 25—meaning that it takes 25 months to accumulate $20,000 under your mattress (no interest!), which isn't any quicker than putting it in this savings account. Why would you put the money in the savings account then? One reason is that savings accounts are often insured, meaning that, unlike cash under your mattress which could get lost or stolen, many bank accounts guarantee that won't happen.

The other reason to use a savings account is to earn some interest.

Think about it

How much total interest will you have earned by the end of the 25-month period?

Table 1.7 Snapshot of a full account chart from Excel

Month	Beginning of month balance ($)	Deposit ($)	Interest earned ($)	End of month balance ($)
1	0.00	800.00	1.20	801.20
2	801.20	800.00	2.40	1,603.60
3	1,603.60	800.00	3.61	2,407.21
4	2,407.21	800.00	4.81	3,212.02
5	3,212.02	800.00	6.02	4,018.04
6	4,018.04	800.00	7.23	4,825.26
7	4,825.26	800.00	8.44	5,633.70
8	5,633.70	800.00	9.65	6,443.35
9	6,443.35	800.00	10.87	7,254.22
10	7,254.22	800.00	12.08	8,066.30
11	8,066.30	800.00	13.30	8,879.60
12	8,879.60	800.00	14.52	9,694.12
13	9,694.12	800.00	15.74	10,509.86
14	10,509.86	800.00	16.96	11,326.82
15	11,326.82	800.00	18.19	12,145.01
16	12,145.01	800.00	19.42	12,964.43
17	12,964.43	800.00	20.65	13,785.08
18	13,785.08	800.00	21.88	14,606.95
19	14,606.95	800.00	23.11	15,430.07
20	15,430.07	800.00	24.35	16,254.41
21	16,254.41	800.00	25.58	17,079.99
22	17,079.99	800.00	26.82	17,906.81
23	17,906.81	800.00	28.06	18,734.87
24	18,734.87	800.00	29.30	19,564.17
25	19,564.17	800.00	30.55	20,394.72
26	20,394.72	800.00	31.79	21,226.51
27	21,226.51	800.00	33.04	22,059.55
28	22,059.55	800.00	34.29	22,893.84
29	22,893.84	800.00	35.54	23,729.38
30	23,729.38	800.00	36.79	24,566.18

By the end of month 25, you will have earned $20,394.72 −
$800 \times 25 = \$20,394.72 - \$20,000 = \$394.72$ in interest. So, even though
putting the $800 in the bank takes the same amount of months to reach
your savings goal as putting the money under your mattress, you do earn
almost $400 in interest by depositing money in the bank.

What if you saved $900/month instead?

Twenty-five months (over 2 years!) is a long time to wait to buy your
house and you might not want to wait that long. If you decided to cut
back on your spending money each month, how much quicker could you
accumulate a down payment if you saved $900/month in the savings
account instead? Obviously, you could do this by hand using the same
approach we saw earlier in this section (filling in an account chart by
hand), but using the **Chapter 1 Excel file** this goes quite quickly—especially if you already set up your Excel spreadsheet to look at the $800/
month case. Table 1.8 demonstrates that by saving $900/month you will
reach your savings goal within 22 months instead of 25.

How much would you need to save each month to reach your goal within 18 months?

Another common type of question people ask when looking at savings
accounts is how much they would need to save to reach a target savings
goal within a given amount of time. For example, if you wanted to have
your down payment saved within 18 months, how much would you need
to save each month to achieve the goal?

Think about it
How could you approximate an answer to this question? *Hint: Ignore the
impact of interest.*

A quick, approximate answer that recognizes the low interest rate on
this savings account, short time frame and relatively small amounts being
saved means that you can ignore the impact of interest to get an approximate answer. For example, simply take the savings goal ($20,000) and
divide it by 18 months, $20,000/18 = \$1,111.11$. So, saving approxi-
mately $1,111/month should get you to your savings goal within 18
months.

A more precise answer can be found using the **Chapter 1 Excel file**.
How? One way is a guess-and-check approach. Guess and check is where

Table 1.8 Snapshot of a full dynamic account chart from Excel

Month	Beginning of Month Balance ($)	Deposit ($)	Interest Earned ($)	End of Month Balance ($)
1	0.00	900.00	1.35	901.35
2	901.35	900.00	2.70	1,804.05
3	1,804.05	900.00	4.06	2,708.11
4	2,708.11	900.00	5.41	3,613.52
5	3,613.52	900.00	6.77	4,520.29
6	4,520.29	900.00	8.13	5,428.42
7	5,428.42	900.00	9.49	6,337.91
8	6,337.91	900.00	10.86	7,248.77
9	7,248.77	900.00	12.22	8,160.99
10	8,160.99	900.00	13.59	9,074.59
11	9,074.59	900.00	14.96	9,989.55
12	9,989.55	900.00	16.33	10,905.88
13	10,905.88	900.00	17.71	11,823.59
14	11,823.59	900.00	19.09	12,742.68
15	12,742.68	900.00	20.46	13,663.14
16	13,663.14	900.00	21.84	14,584.98
17	14,584.98	900.00	23.23	15,508.21
18	15,508.21	900.00	24.61	16,432.82
19	16,432.82	900.00	26.00	17,358.82
20	17,358.82	900.00	27.39	18,286.21
21	18,286.21	900.00	28.78	19,214.99
22	19,214.99	900.00	30.17	20,145.16
23	20,145.16	900.00	31.57	21,076.73
24	21,076.73	900.00	32.97	22,009.70
25	22,009.70	900.00	34.36	22,944.06
26	22,944.06	900.00	35.77	23,879.83
27	23,879.83	900.00	37.17	24,817.00
28	24,817.00	900.00	38.58	25,755.57
29	25,755.57	900.00	39.98	26,695.56
30	26,695.56	900.00	41.39	27,636.95

you set up your spreadsheet to allow for easy manipulation of the payment amount each month and you keep trying different values until you get the right answer.

For example, we know that $1,111.11 is more than we need to deposit each month to be done saving within 18 months because this doesn't account for interest, so maybe our first guess is $1,000. But, using the Excel file we see that saving $1,000/month yields only $18,258.69 by the end of the 18th month—not enough.

Next, let's try $1,050/month. Still not enough. A payment of $1,050 monthly only gets us to $19,171.63. We see that $1,075 isn't enough either ($19,628.10). If we keep going in this manner (Guess, check, guess, check, etc.), eventually, we find that $1,095.37/month yields almost exactly $20,000 at the end of 18 months.

Key idea

When using a dynamic account chart, "guess and check" is a viable approach to solving problems like "How much do I need to save in year X?" or "What kind of interest rate would get me to my savings goal?" Without using a technology-based dynamic chart, which automatically updates all of the balances, it would be a very tedious process to evaluate these questions.

You might be wondering, isn't there a better way? Yes, there is. We'll soon learn some direct, shortcut formulas for valuing accounts where transactions are regular and the same size.

What about an extra deposit?

You currently own a fairly nice car and are debating selling it, buying a cheaper one and, thus, having some extra money available to make the down payment. Ignoring things like car depreciation and anticipated mechanical/repair needs, when is the best time to sell the car? Let's assume that you think you can generate about $5,000 of cash by selling your current car and buying a cheaper one that will still meet your needs.

Think about it

Should you sell your car now or later? Why?

What if you sell your car now and deposit the extra $5,000 into the savings account? This means that the $5,000 will have time to earn interest. For example, over a 1-year period you will earn $90.75 of interest on the money. If you wait to sell your car until later, the $5,000 won't earn any interest. Thus, if you are going to make an extra deposit to a savings account, the best time to do it is as soon as possible.

Key idea

If you are going to make an extra deposit to a savings account, the best time to do it is as soon as possible, so you can earn as much interest as possible.

EXPLORATION 1.3. SAVING FOR COLLEGE

It wasn't long ago that you were probably thinking about how you were going pay for college. In addition to scholarships, help from parents and student loans, using money that you saved was probably something you considered. In the previous sections, we took a *long-term view to investing*—compound interest really starts making money in the long-run. So, a key to saving for college is starting early. Realistically, you probably weren't thinking about getting a job and starting to save for college when you were in kindergarten, but let's assume that you were still ahead of the curve and thought about this when you were in eighth grade before you headed off to high school.

In trying to think about how much you want to have saved for college when you start, you do some approximate calculations to determine that you will need to come up with $40,000 after you earn some scholarships and get some grants. That $40,000 represents $10,000 per year for 4 years. The question is, if you work for each of the next four summers and, each year, put the money into a CD how much money will you have saved before you go to college?

Getting started

Let's assume that you've just finished 8th grade. You have $1,000 in your savings account and you anticipate earning $6,000 this summer at your job.

1. Suppose you deposit all of your summer earnings plus the $1,000 already in your account into a 1-year CD earning an effective annual rate of interest of 3%. How much money will you have in the CD 1 year later? When will this be (end of which summer)?

2. You earn $6,500 the summer after ninth grade and put this money and all prior savings and interest into another 1-year CD which earns 3% effective annual interest. How much money will you have in the CD when the 1-year CD matures (is 1-year old)? When will this be (end of which summer)?

Basic account chart for college savings

We could keep going in this manner—calculating the new amounts saved, but we are essentially doing the same calculations over and over again. Sometimes, an account chart can help organize and simplify the calculations.

Definition

When solving problems with multiple deposits and withdrawals and/or changes in effective interest rate, an **account chart** is a useful way to summarize information. An account chart summarizes account balances, interest, deposits, and withdrawals over time. Usually with one row for each compounding period.

To assist in answering the question "Is it possible to have $40,000 saved for college?" we'll use the following basic account chart. You'll work to fill this in over the next few questions.

The chart makes two basic assumptions:

- Assume you have 5 years to work and save (you've just finished 8th grade). Assume further that you will go to college starting at the end of the summer immediately after your senior year and that you will be in high school for 4 years.
- To ease the computations for now, let's assume that you will get paid at the end of the summer in one lump payment and you will open up a CD with the money you earned that summer, plus whatever is currently in the CD. Later, we'll be able to easily tackle more complex/

frequent/irregular cash flows with ease. But, we'll leave those details aside for now.

Begin filling in the account chart

3. Use the information below to completely fill in the account chart in Table 1.9.

   a. Each of the four, 1-year CDs you will open has an effective annual rate of interest, i, of 3%.

   b. As of right now (just finished 8th grade), you have $1,000 in your savings account that you decide will all go to your college savings, but you won't deposit it into a CD until the end of the summer.

   c. You will have a job this summer (just finished 8th grade) and earn $6,000 (ignore taxes for now).

   d. In year 2, you anticipate getting a small raise and earn $6,500. Same in year 3.

   e. In years 4 and 5, you anticipating being able to save $7,000 each year.

To fill in the chart, it is easiest to follow the account forward in time, that is, start by entering the "opening balance," then new income, compute interest, etc. for year 1, then move on to year 2, going in order line by line. For example, for line 1, the prior savings total is $1,000, your new income is $6,000, and so the total to be deposited into the CD is $7,000. At an annual effective interest rate of 3%, you will earn $210 in interest, so the value of the CD on 8/31 the following year will be $7,210. Do similarly for each subsequent year, in order.

Key idea

When using an account chart, you typically go row by row (e.g., year by year), in order to calculate the final/end balance.

---

4. How much will you have saved for college by the end of year five (8/31) as you start your freshman year of college?

5. How much money will you have deposited during the entire period? *Hint: Add up $1,000 plus the appropriate column in the account chart.*

Table 1.9 Basic account chart

Year (summer)	Prior savings (total by 8/31)	New summer income (total by 8/31)	Total savings to be deposited into CD (8/31)	What is the effective annual interest rate, i for the CD	How much interest will you earn?	What will be the value of the CD on 8/31 of the following year?
1 (after 8th grade)						
2 (after 9th grade)						
3 (after 10th grade)						
4 (after 11th grade)						
5 (after 12th grade)			—[a]	—[a]	—[a]

Total savings on 8/31 as you start your freshman year of college _____.

[a]You need the money by the end of the summer after 12th grade, so we're not interested in the balance at the end of the following year!

6. How much money will you have earned in interest during the entire period? *Hint: Add up the appropriate column in the account chart.*

Key idea

The total account balance is Total Sum of Deposits + Total Interest Earned, where you use negative values for withdrawals.

---

7. Use the key idea box above to verify that your answers to the previous three questions follow the stated relationship (Total Account Balance = Sum of Deposits + Total Interest Earned)

This key idea, that the total of what you deposit, plus what interest you earn (and subtracting any withdrawals!) will total the final account balance, is a handy trick when solving complicated account valuation problems with multiple transactions.

Revisiting nominal rates of interest

In the previous section, we saw that banks often use nominal interest rates (APR) instead of effective rates of interest.

8. How do you need to change Table 1.9 if, instead of earning an annual effective interest rate of 3%, the CDs earn 2% APR? *Hint: Don't add more rows to the chart, just calculate what the equivalent effective annual rate is when you have 2% APR.*

Note:. You don't need to do any computations for this question. Just explain how you would change the table and predict the impact. In the next section, we will compute the interest and balances more precisely.

9. Which CDs will generate more interest 2% APR or 3% effective annually? Why?

Creating a dynamic account chart using Excel

To figure out how much we'd actually end up saving if the CD was at 2% APR, we'd have to redo Table 1.9, which would be rather time consuming. Instead, let's use technology, which is the quickest and most efficient way to solve problems using account charts—especially when you are faced with trying to determine the impact of small changes in interest rates, timing of deposits/withdrawals, etc.

Definition

A **dynamic account chart** uses technology to instantly update all balances in an account chart to alleviate tedious by hand calculations. Microsoft Excel is a popular business tool to create dynamic account charts.

Refer to Exploration 1.3 in the **Chapter 1 Excel file** in order to create an account chart that allows you to change any of the interest rates or amount of money earned, and instantly computes the final account balance. Use your worksheet to answer the following questions. When setting up the chart use the same basic approach we did by hand. That is, compute the values across a row, and then have the next row start with the ending balancing of the previous row.

10. Returning to our original question, if you used 2% APR CDs, what would the total savings be? *Hint: The first step is to convert the 2% APR to an annual effective rate of interest. Then, you can use the Excel sheet you already created.*

11. Returning everything in the spreadsheet to the same as it was originally, find the total amount saved if the annual effective interest rate is 4% instead of 3% in each of the 4 yearlong CDs? What is the total saved if the interest rate was 5%?

12. Make a prediction: If you are going to deposit more into the account in just one of the years than the others, which year would be best to work a lot and deposit a lot into your account? Why?

13. Explore the answer to your prediction by seeing how your account balance changes if you make an extra deposit of $1,500 in year 1 vs an extra deposit of $1,500 in year 5. Was your prediction confirmed?

Key idea

If you are going to make an extra deposit to a savings account, the best time to do it is as soon as possible, so you can earn as much interest as possible.

---

14. Return everything in the spreadsheet to the original conditions (e.g., 3% effective annual interest). If you only change the amount saved in year 3, how much do you need to save in year 3 in order to yield a total amount saved of $40,000? Find your answer to the nearest penny using a "guess-and-check" approach (keep trying values until you get to a final amount saved of $40,000).

Key idea

When using a dynamic account chart, "guess and check" is a viable approach to solving problems like "How much do I need to save in year X?" or "What kind of interest rate would get me to my savings goal?" Without using a technology-based dynamic chart, which automatically updates all of the balances, it would be a very tedious process to evaluate these questions.

---

15. Return everything in the spreadsheet to the same as it was originally. You decide that to reach your goal, you will work very hard in summer 5. How much do you need to earn in summer 5 to reach the savings goal?

16. Saving the amount you found in the previous question in one summer seems a bit unrealistic. Assuming you still earn the same amounts in summers 1−3 as originally ($6,000, $6,500, and $6,500), but decide to work hard in both years 4 and 5, how much would have to be earned both summers 4 and 5 (assume it's the same amount) to reach the savings goal? Use a guess-and-check approach to the nearest penny.

17. With the same original interest rate you started with (0.03 effective annually) and an initial deposit of $1,000, use a guess-and-check approach to find the amount you need to deposit in each of the 5 years, *assuming it is the same amount each year and you wish to have a final amount saved of $40,000.*

18. To still get you to the $40,000 goal, how much would the annual deposit amount change if you found CDs paying 4% effective annually and *the annual deposit amount was the same each year*? Why did it change the way it did?

SUMMARY

In this section, we saw how account charts can be used to calculate account balances over time when you have multiple transactions. Following an account balance forward in time, carefully keeping track of deposits and withdrawals, interest earned and interest rate changes was the key. While this can be done by hand, using a technology tool (like Excel) helped if you wanted to evaluate the impact of changes to the timing of deposits or interest rate changes. Finally, we saw that if you are going to make an extra deposit to a savings account, the best time to do so is as soon as possible, so that the deposited amount has as much time as possible to earn interest.

Notation and equation summary
Account balance = Total deposits + Total interest earned

HOMEWORK QUESTIONS: SECTION 1.3

Conceptual questions

1. If you are going to make a large deposit into an account, is it better to do it sooner or later? Why?

2. What does your answer to Question 1 suggest about saving for any large purchase? Explain your answer in terms of compound interest.

3. If you were able to put $500 a month into a savings account, will you earn more interest if you make deposits each month or if you save the cash and put a lump sum of $6,000 into the account at the end of the year? Or doesn't it matter since will you earn the same amount of interest?

4. Looking at Table 1.7 in Example 1.3, describe two ways to determine the total amount of interest earned during the 25 months.

5. In Table 1.7 in Example 1.3, there are two calculations done to get the end-of-month balance. The balance on day 1 of the month is multiplied by the interest rate. Then that product is added to the balance on day 1. How could you do this in one calculation?

Practice questions

6. For an account earning 3% effective interest, find the "doubling time" (i.e., how long you need to wait for an investment to double). *Note:* You do not need to know the starting amount to solve this problem.

7. Refer to the previous question. What is the doubling time for an account earning 6% effective interest?

8. Refer to the previous two questions. What do your answers suggest about the general relationship between doubling the interest rate and changes to doubling time? (*Hint:* You might want to explore some other interest rates to help you determine this and test your conjecture.)

9. At the beginning of the next 3 months, you put $600 into an account that earns an effective monthly rate of 1.2%. How much will you have in the account at the end of those 3 months? How much interest did you earn during the entire period?

Application questions

10. An account earns 5% nominal interest compounded semiannually. An initial deposit of $2,000 is made to the account on January 1, 2015. A withdrawal of $500 is made on January 1, 2016. A deposit of $3,000 is made on July 1, 2016. What is the fund balance on January 1, 2018?

11. Repeat the previous question but assume that there is an interest rate change to 7.5% nominal interest, compounded semiannually on January 1, 2017.

12. At the beginning of the month for the next 2 years, you put $750 into an account that earns a monthly interest rate of 0.9%. How much will you have in the account at the end of those 2 years? How

much interest did you earn during the entire period? You can either do his by hand or use a dynamic account chart in Excel to help you.

13. Redo the previous question except for the second year you put in $800 per month and the interest rate drops to 0.8% (just for the second year).

14. Write your own question about finding the value of a fund at the end of a period of time. Have at least five transactions (deposits and withdrawals) and at least one change in interest rate. Prepare the question so that it can be given to another student. Write a solution to the problem.

Looking ahead

15. You are starting to save for retirement by putting $200 per month into a mutual fund made up of stocks. While the stock market has no guaranteed rate of return and values of stocks can go up or down drastically, as a whole, you figure your mutual fund (which is made up of many different stocks) will earn APR 8%.
    a. How much will you have in your account after 40 years if you put the money in at the beginning of every month?
    b. How much will you have in your account after 40 years if you put in $200 per month for the first 10 years, $300 per month for the second 10 years, $400 per month for the third 10 years and $500 per month for the last 10 years?

16. Recall the previous question where you are putting money into a mutual fund that you expect to earn 8% compounded monthly. How much do you have to put in each month so you will have $1,000,000 after 40 years?

SECTION 1.4. TIPS AND TRICKS FOR SOLVING CASH FLOW PROBLEMS

In the previous section, we used Excel to quickly and easily answer a series of financial questions. The advantage of Excel or similar spreadsheet-type programs is that they can simultaneously do many, many computations, which allows you to quickly and easily evaluate a range of assumptions about deposit and interest rate changes. We started with Excel so that you could:

- More quickly develop your financial intuition so that when you solve problems "by hand" you can more readily identify egregious mistakes.
- Appreciate an integrated, dynamic spreadsheet tool in solving complex **cash flow problems**.
- Gain experience with a tool used commonly in financial practice.

Definition

A **cash flow problem** is a financial problem where there are multiple deposits and/or withdrawals to an account with a constant or variable rate of interest. Goals of such problems are usually to calculate the total fund balance, find the value of particular deposits or withdrawals given the final fund balance or to find the interest rate needed or total amount of time of the investment to achieve some final fund balance.

That said, there is still some value in knowing how to solve complex cash flow problems by hand—if you're taking actuarial or other professional certification exams or if you're stuck on a desert island with no computer! The two keys to success to the "by hand" approaches are to

- Break the problem into smaller, simpler problems.
- Be precise, since you'll be doing many, many computations and mistakes in any one of the steps will make your final answer incorrect.

In the previous section, you filled in an account chart by hand, going row by row through the chart, essentially computing the balance at the end of 1 year and carrying it forward to the start of another year. This is called a **recursive approach** to finding account balances.

Definition

A **recursive approach** to solving cash flow problems computes account balances by moving forward in time with each transaction. For accounts with many transactions this can be tedious to do by hand, but technology can often speed the process, especially when there are patterns in the transactions (e.g., same deposit amount each period).

Essentially, to find a new account balance you take the balance at the start of the period, add deposits (and subtract withdrawals) and then compute the new balance by calculating the interest earned. You then do the same for each subsequent year, in order. This is the same approach we took in Excel.

In this section, we will look at a few "by-hand" approaches and tricks for solving a variety of problems related to computing account balances with a complex series of cash flows.

Learning objectives

By the end of this section you should be able to
- Calculate an account balance by treating each deposit or withdrawal as if it was in its own account and realize this is equivalent to treating them as if they were in the same account.
- Use guess-and-check approaches in Excel to estimate unknown interest rates and time periods needed to achieve savings goals.
- Accurately make predictions about the impact of changing interest rates, timing of deposits (or withdrawals) and length of time on account balances.

EXAMPLE 1.4. SAVING FOR A DOWN PAYMENT (REVISITED)

In Example 1.3, we examined a situation where you were trying to figure out how long it would take you to save up for a down payment of $20,000 to buy a house. We started by looking at the case of saving $800/month in an account earning 1.8% APR. The recursive approach to figuring out this question is fairly tedious. Table 1.10 shows how to start this computation.

Nonrecursive approach

The time consuming part of doing the recursive approach by hand (like Table 1.10) is that you have to calculate many "intermediate" account balances (e.g., how much money you have in the account in, say, month 12) when you may not really care about that value.

One trick which can, at times, save time if you are doing the calculations by hand is to realize that putting money into separate accounts, at the same interest rate will yield the same balance as combining the money first and putting it into the same account. For example, if I have $5,000 to save, I can open two accounts of $2,500 each or a single account of

Table 1.10 Account chart to save for a down payment

Month	Prior savings (total on day 1 of the month) ($)	Amount that can be deposited on day 1 of the month ($)	Total amount in account on day 1 of month ($)	Effective monthly rate of interest	Interest earned during the month ($)	Balance in account on last day of the month ($)
1	0	800	800	0.0015	1.20	801.20
2	801.20	800	1,601.20	0.0015	2.40	1,603.60
3	1,603.60	800	2,403.60	0.0015	3.61	2,407.21
4	2,407.21	800	3,207.21	0.0015	4.81	3,212.02
5	3,212.02	800	4,012.02	0.0015	6.02	4,018.04

$5,000 and, if all accounts have the same interest rate, they will end up with the same amount whether I use two accounts or a single account.

Key idea

The sum of a series of cash flows (deposits and withdrawals) over time can be computed by valuing each cash flow separately, treating each cash flow as its own "account."

Let's see how this works for the first 3 months of deposits.

Mini account 1—First month's deposit

The first month's deposit is $800. Let's imagine we deposited this in its own savings account. How much will this be worth after 25 months? The effective monthly interest rate is 0.0015 (Why?), and so this is simply $800(1.0015)^{25} = \$830.55$.

Mini account 2—Second month's deposit

The second month's deposit is also $800. Let's imagine we also deposited this to its own savings account. How much will this be worth at the end of 25 months? *Note:* While we want the value at the end of the 25th month from today, this second payment will only receive 24 months of interest, and so the value is $800(1.0015)^{24} = \$829.30$.

Mini account 3—Third month's deposit

Hopefully, by now you are seeing the pattern. The value of the third deposit at the end of the 25th month will be $800(1.0015)^{23} = \$828.06$

If we use Excel to quickly do the rest of the computation we get the following results shown in Table 1.11.

Table 1.11 Valuing monthly deposits of $800 using a nonrecursive (separate accounts) approach

Month	Months of interest	Initial deposit ($)	Ending amount ($)
1	25	800	830.55
2	24	800	829.30
3	23	800	828.06
4	22	800	826.82
5	21	800	825.58
6	20	800	824.35
7	19	800	823.11
8	18	800	821.88
9	17	800	820.65
10	16	800	819.42
11	15	800	818.19
12	14	800	816.96
13	13	800	815.74
14	12	800	814.52
15	11	800	813.30
16	10	800	812.08
17	9	800	810.87
18	8	800	809.65
19	7	800	808.44
20	6	800	807.23
21	5	800	806.02
22	4	800	804.81
23	3	800	803.61
24	2	800	802.40
25	1	800	801.20
		Total	20,394.72

Notice that the final amount saved at the end of the 25th month is computed as $20,394.72—exactly what we saw back in Example 1.3 (Table 1.7)! While this probably didn't save us much time in this case, for accounts with fewer transactions this can sometimes be a faster approach to solving the problem—especially if you don't have access to a spreadsheet program like Excel. This also is an idea we will come back to in future chapters as it leads to a convenient shortcut approach.

Evaluating the impact of a withdrawal

Another way this approach can be helpful is to evaluate the impact of a withdrawal from the account. What if you needed to withdraw $300 at the start of the 21st month for an emergency? How would this impact your final account balance?

If we treat the $300 withdrawal as its own "account," then we can say $300(1.0015)^5 = \$302.26$ to see what this account value is at the end of the 25th month (after 5 months of interest). This account can be thought of as a $300 loan, which accumulates interest at the same 1.8% APR as the deposits.

To find the final account balance simply subtract off the cost of our "loan": $20,394.72 − $302.26 = $20,092.46.

Key idea

When using the nonrecursive approach to valuing accounts, withdrawals can be handled by treating them like any deposit, but then subtracting their value (incorporating interest) to calculate the final balance.

Irregular payments and withdrawals

One limitation to the kinds of problems we've considered so far is that we've always examined the case where the deposit (or withdrawal) was timed to nicely coincide with the changes in interest rate or when compounding of interest occurs. How do you handle situations where that is not the case?

For example, what if you get a gift of an extra $1,000 for your birthday on the 15th of the month and you want to deposit it into your savings account? Do you wait until the end of the month to deposit it? You could, but what if you deposited it on the 15th—halfway through the month?

Most banks will pay interest on money deposited halfway through the month. So, how do you account for this in your calculations? First, you need to know how the bank will pay out interest on this amount. Let's assume that the bank pays a daily interest rate of 0.00003 on any transactions made mid-month. For a month with 30 days, your $1,000 will accumulate to $1,000(1.00003)^{15} = $1,000.45$ by the end of the month. To evaluate the impact on the final savings account balance you could either lump this amount ($1,000.45) in with the next month's payment of $800 (making it $1,800.45), or use the "separate account" method described above and figure out how much the $1,000.45 will accumulate to at the end of the time period of interest (e.g., 12 months later).

Key idea

To value deposits and withdrawals that are not timed with compounding periods, first determine the interest rate (if any) for the fractional period and then roll the amount forward (or back) to the next compounding period.

We now briefly consider two other types of cash flow problems—unknown interest rates and unknown time periods.

Problems involving an unknown interest rate

Sometimes it is helpful to know what kind of interest rate is needed in order to achieve a certain savings goal. For example, if you deposit $800/month, what kind of interest rate would you need in order to have saved $20,000 within 20 months?

First, will this unknown interest rate be larger or smaller than 1.8% APR? It will be larger because at 1.8% APR it took 25 months. If you want to accumulate $20,000 sooner you will have to earn interest faster—meaning a higher rate.

Sometimes problems involving an unknown interest rate can be solved directly using polynomial equations [there are some examples of this in the exercises and Exploration 1.4]. But, most often that is not the case. Some financial programs use Newton's method to estimate this value—but that's really just a fast way of doing guess and check.

You can create a dynamic spreadsheet in Excel to do your own guess and check. We did this and found that an effective interest rate of

0.0208/month (which is an APR of $12 \times 0.0208 = 24.96\%$!!) will achieve \$20,001.04 by the end of the 20th month—a pretty unrealistic interest rate! You'd be much wiser to try to save more each month than to try to find an investment earning that much interest!

Key idea

Many problems with unknown interest rates involve using guess and check (usually in Excel) or a financial calculator to find the interest rate. Only the simplest problems (e.g., one or two periods) will allow direct algebraic computation of the unknown interest rate. More sophisticated "guess-and-check" approaches can be programmed into some financial tools to quickly find (converge to) a solution.

Problems involving an unknown time period

Finally, sometimes you want to find out how long it will take to achieve a certain savings goal. We actually first saw this in the previous section. A recursive solution to this problem means setting up a table and computing each period's account balance until you reach the goal you have in mind. In rare cases you can solve problems searching for an unknown time period directly using logarithms. See the end of Exploration 1.4 and the homework exercises for a few examples of this situation.

EXPLORATION 1.4. SAVING FOR COLLEGE (REVISITED)

In "Section 1.3. Valuing Accounts with Multiple Transactions", we saw how filling out an account chart (table) helped us to compute the value of an account with multiple deposits. We did this *recursively*, by computing the value of the account at the end of each time period (e.g., each month). One problem with this recursive approach is that it is time consuming to compute. One trick to solve problems without using the recursive approach is to treat every account contribution as a separate "account" and then sum the accounts at some future time. Let's see how this approach works.

In Exploration 1.3, we began exploring what it would look like to save for college by saving \$6,000 in summer 1 (plus \$1,000 of savings you already had on hand), \$6,500 in each of years 2 and 3 and \$7,000 in years

4 and 5. We started by assuming that we could earn 3% effective interest each year—but this only got us to $36,087.14 by the time college started—short of our goal of $40,000.

Recursive approach

1. What if you earned 4% effective annual interest each year? Use the recursive approach to fill in the account chart in Table 1.12 "by hand."

2. Now, create a dynamic account chart for this problem and confirm your work about by using Excel.

Nonrecursive approach

One of the time consuming parts of solving complicated cash flow problems by hand is that the recursive approach requires you to compute all of the intermediate account balances (e.g., account balance after year 3) instead of jumping right to the final account balance. Sometimes you are not so interested in the intermediate account balances.

One trick to solving cash flow problems more quickly is to realize that putting money into separate accounts, at the same interest rate will yield the same balance as combining the money first and putting it into the same account. For example, if I have $2,000 to save, I can open two accounts of $1,000 each or a single account of $2,000 and, if all accounts have the same interest rate, they will end up with the same amount whether I use two accounts or a single account.

Key idea
The sum of a series of cash flows (deposits and withdrawals) over time can be computed by valuing each cash flow separately, treating each cash flow as its own "account."

Let's see how this works. We will start by using this approach for the first two summers of earnings by setting up two "accounts," one "account" for the initial contribution (Account 1) and one account for the second contribution (Account 2).

Valuing account 1: Summer 1 earnings + prior savings

Table 1.12 Basic account chart for college savings

Year (summer)	Prior savings (total by 8/31) ($)	New summer income (total by 8/31) ($)	Total savings to be deposited into CD (8/31)	What is the effective annual interest rate, i for the CD	How much interest will you earn?	What will be the value of the CD on 8/31 of the following year?
1 (after 8th grade)	1,000	6,000				
2 (after 9th grade)		6,500				
3 (after 10th grade)		6,500				
4 (after 11th grade)		7,000				
5 (after 12th grade)		7,000		—[a]	—[a]	—[a]

[a]You need the money by the end of the summer after 12th grade, so we're not interested in the balance at the end of the following year!

3. Find the value of the initial deposited amount [$7,000 = $1,000 (prior savings) + $6,000 (summer earnings)] at the end of the second summer. (Remember you are earning 4% effective annual interest each year.)

4. Now find the value of the initially deposited amount ($7,000) that includes the interest added at the end of the second summer as well as the interest added at the end of the third summer.

   Valuing account 2: Summer 2 earnings

5. Find the value of the money you earned the second summer ($6,500) at the end of year 3.

   Combined earnings

6. To find the total fund balance at the end of year 3 sum the value of the initial contribution and the value of the summer 2 earnings at the end of year 3. Confirm this is the same amount as you obtained using the recursive definition earlier in Table 1.12.

   Applying the nonrecursive approach to the entire 5 years

7. Now use this same nonrecursive approach (a separate "account" for each deposit) to find the total fund balance at the end of the 5th summer. Confirm that your answer is the same that you received when using the recursive approach in Table 1.12.

8. Use this same "separate funds" approach to find the value of the account at the end of the 5th summer if you withdrew $1,000 at the end of summer 3. To solve this problem create a separate "account" for the $1,000 withdrawal, find out how large this account would "grow" to by the end of the 5th summer and then subtract this amount from your earlier answer.

Key idea

When using the nonrecursive approach to value accounts, withdrawals can be handled by treating them like any deposit, but then subtracting their value (incorporating interest) to calculate the final balance.

It is important to note that this "nonrecursive" approach would work fine in Excel, but isn't particularly necessary there since the recursive approach is easy to implement and gives comprehensive account balances at all points in time. If you did the nonrecursive approach in Excel you would have to pick a particular time at which you want to know the account balance (e.g., at the end of the savings period), but if you wanted to know the balance at any other point in time you would have to modify the spreadsheet.

Irregular payments and withdrawals

A fairly big assumption of the methods we've used so far is that they assume that the deposits and withdrawals are "timed" to synchronize with changes to the interest rate and any compounding that will take place. Of course, this is an unrealistic assumption! While there are many variations on this theme possible in the types of problems you can see, we will now briefly look at the general approaches you can use to solve these types of problems.

Imagine that on February 28, after the first summer, you get a birthday present of $1,000 from your grandma for college. Let's assume that your account will allow you to make a deposit on that date (*Note:* In reality, CDs don't often allow this), so you decide to deposit the full amount. How does this change your final savings? It depends on whether the bank will give you interest on that money.

9. If the bank does not give you any interest on the extra $1,000 deposited on February 28 what will your account balance be at the end of the second summer?

10. If the bank says that they will give you 2% nominal interest, with semiannual compounding (interest is paid out every 6 months) on the extra $1,000 deposit, what will the account balance be at the end of the second summer (before the next deposit)? *Hint: It may be convenient to use the nonrecursive approach we learned earlier to solve this problem!*

Key idea
To value deposits and withdrawals that are not timed with compounding periods, first determine the interest rate (if any) for the fractional period and then roll the amount forward (or back) to the next compounding period.

Problems involving an unknown interest rate

Sometimes, an investor may wonder what kind of interest rate is needed to obtain a certain future account balance.

11. If you have $7,000 at the end of the first summer and anticipate depositing $6,500 at the end of the second summer, what is effective rate of interest, i, do you need in order to obtain a balance of $15,000 in the account at the end of the third summer (before you deposit your new earnings)? Create a dynamic account sheet and solve this problem by guess-and-check.

12. (extension problem) In the scenario from the previous question, assume i is the same for the first 2 years. Find the interest rate needed to obtain a balance of $15,000 by hand directly (not using guess-and-check or Excel). *Hint: You will need to solve a quadratic equation to answer this question!*

13. (extension problem) For the scenario from #11, write down a polynomial equation that could be solved for i which expresses i in terms of all the account contributions as described at the very beginning of this exploration which yields an account balance of $40,000. You do not need to solve the equation.

As shown in the previous question, questions involving an unknown interest rate are not always easily solvable. In these cases, you can use guess-and-check, Newton's method, or other computational approaches.

14. Use guess and check and your Excel sheet to find the interest rate, i, that would be needed to have $40,000 in savings at the end of the savings period.

15. (extension problem) Why is the problem from the previous question not possible to solve directly using a polynomial equation?

Key idea

Many problems involving unknown interest rates involve using guess and check (usually in Excel) or a financial calculator to find the unknown interest rate. Only the simplest problems (e.g., one or two periods) will allow direct algebraic computation of the unknown interest rate. More sophisticated "guess and check" approaches can be programmed into some financial tools to quickly converge to a solution.

Problems involving an unknown time period

Finally, sometimes an investor might wonder how long he or she will need to invest in order to yield a certain final account balance.

16. Imagine that your grades end up being very good and, as a result, your scholarship money ends up paying for college so the $36,087.14 you saved isn't needed to pay for college. How long will it take for the money to grow to $40,000? Assume the money is invested in an account earning 3% effective interest compounded annually.
    a. Write down the equation that needs to be solved.
    b. Use an Excel spreadsheet and a guess-and-check approach to solve the problem
    c. (extension problem) Guess-and-check would be one approach to solving this problem, but the direct approach to solving a problem with an unknown exponent uses logarithms. Use logarithms to find the unknown amount of time.

Review

Logarithms are a short hand way of describing large numbers. You can think of logarithms as exponents. Logarithms of base 10 are the exponents that 10 needs to be raised to for it to equal some number. For example since $10^2 = 100$ this means $\log_{10}100 = 2$ (the logarithm equals the exponent). What is $\log_{10}1,000$? Hopefully you can see that $\log_{10}1000 = 3$ since $10^3 = 1000$.

Some basic rules for logarithms are:
    i. $\log_b a = c$ is equivalent to $b^c = a$
    ii. $\log ac = \log a + \log c$
    iii. $\log(a/c) = \log a - \log c$
    iv. $\log a^c = c \cdot \log a$
        $\log_e a$ can be written as $\ln a$

---

    d. (extension problem) How many full years does the money need to be left in the bank to be worth at least $40,000 when the money can only be withdrawn at the end of the year?

SUMMARY

In this section, we explored a few alternative ways of solving problems using a mix of by-hand approaches and guess-and-check approaches using technology. Valuing each deposit or withdrawal as a separate account will turn out to be a convenient way to think about account transactions in the next few chapters as we think about loans, annuities and other financial instruments. We saw that technology is often needed to find unknown interest rates or unknown periods of time as these problems can be tricky or impossible to solve directly. Simple versions of these problems can sometimes be solved directly using polynomial equations or logarithms.

HOMEWORK QUESTIONS: SECTION 1.4

Conceptual questions

1. For which approach, recursive or nonrecursive, do you calculate the balance in an account for each time period?

2. For which approach, recursive or nonrecursive, do you treat each deposit (or withdrawal) as its own separate account?

3. If you are using the nonrecursive approach for calculating the amount left in an account as was outlined in this section, how do you handle a withdrawal?

4. How do you handle deposits or withdrawals that are not timed with the compounding periods?

5. Logarithms are useful when solving problems where the unknown value is in what part of an equation?

Practice questions

6. You open up a money market account that earns 2% nominal interest compounded monthly. You put in $500 on January 1, February 1, and March 1. How much will you have in the account on April 1?

7. You open up a money market account that earns 2% nominal interest compounded monthly. You put in $500 on January 1, $600 on February 1, and $700 on March 1. How much will you have in the account on April 1?

8. Recall the previous question. If you change the order of the deposits for January and March (so you put in $700 on January 1 and $500 on March 1) and didn't change February's deposit, how much will you have on April 1?

9. Your parents put $5,000 into an account on the day you were born and again on your first birthday. If that account earns an effective annual rate of 5%, how much will the account be worth on your 18th birthday?

10. Recall the previous question. What effective annual rate (to the nearest tenth of a percent) is needed so the account will be worth $25,000 on your 18th birthday? You can use a guess-and-check method to determine this.

Application questions

11. Your parents put $1,000 into an account on the day you were born and again on your every birthday up until, but still including your 18th birthday.
    a. If that account earns an effective annual rate of 3%, how much is the account worth on your 18th birthday?
    b. How much would your parents have to put into the account on the day you were born, while leaving all other deposits at $1,000, for the account to be worth $30,000 on your 18th birthday?

12. You are saving for a new car and put $500 into a money market account at the beginning of every month. The account earns 1% APR. You make these deposits for 24 months.
    a. At the end of the 24th month, how much do you have in your account?
    b. To the nearest tenth of a percent, what APR would you need to have $15,000 in the account at the end of the 24th month?

13. You are saving for a down payment on a house and put $700 into a money market account at the beginning of every month. The account earns 0.9% APR. You make these deposits for 18 months.
    a. At the end of the 18th month, how much do you have in your account?

    b. How much would you have to put in this account each month so that at the end of the 18th month you had $20,000 for your down payment?

14. You are putting $200 a month into a bond fund to use as a supplement to your retirement account. You start doing this on your 25th birthday and put the last deposit in on your 65th birthday so you have 481 deposits. For estimation purposes, you are assuming the bond fund will earn 5% APR during that time.

    a. Including the last deposit on your 65th birthday, how much will you have in the bond fund at that time?

    b. Suppose you take $10,000 out of this account on your 35th birthday. With this withdrawal, how much will be in your account on your 65th birthday?

    c. Without making any withdrawals, how many total months do you have to contribute to this account until you have $500,000 accumulated?

15. You put $2,000 into an account that earns an annual effective rate of 2% on January 1 of this year. You do this again on January 1 of next year.

    a. How much will you have in the account on January 1 of the year after next?

    b. Using algebra, determine the interest amount needed for you to have $4200 in the account on January 1 of the next year.

16. You deposit $1,000 into an account today and $250 1 year from now. At the end of 2 years, you have $1,500. What is the effective interest rate on the account assuming it is the same for the entire period? Use a polynomial equation to solve.

Looking ahead

17. Instead of depositing money into an account, let's turn things around and look at a loan. Suppose you borrow $15,000 at 4% compounded monthly for a car.

    a. How many months will it take to pay off your loan if you pay $200? (*Hint:* Use Excel. Start with $15,000, calculate the interest for 1 month, subtract $200, and continue to the next month.)

b. Using Excel, and guessing and checking, find the payment, to the nearest dollar, that you would need so the loan is paid off in 60 months.

End of chapter summary

In this chapter, we explored the basics of interest, recognizing that compound interest can lead to substantial gains in an account balance over time by earning interest on the interest. Nominal rates of interest are one short-hand that banks use to summarize rates of interest, but it's usually more convenient to convert nominal rates to effective rates to calculate account balances. Finally, we used technology to compute dynamic account charts and think about more complex problems (e.g., What interest rate is needed? How long do I need to save?) that would be tedious to do by hand. In the next chapter, we will apply what we've learned to loans.

End of chapter review problems

(SOA EXAM FM SAMPLE QUESTIONS May 2000, Question 1)

1. Joe deposits 10 today and another 30 in 5 years into a fund paying simple interest of 11% per year.

   Tina will make the same two deposits, but the 10 will be deposited n years from today and the 30 will be deposited $2n$ years from today. Tina's deposits earn an annual effective rate of 9.15%.
   At the end of 10 years, the accumulated amount of Tina's deposits equals the accumulated amount of Joe's deposits.
   Calculate n.
   A. 2.0
   B. 2.3
   C. 2.6
   D. 2.9
   E. 3.2

(SOA EXAM FM SAMPLE QUESTIONS May 2003, Question 12)

2. Eric deposits X into a savings account at time 0, which pays interest at a nominal rate of i, compounded semiannually.

Mike deposits $2X$ into a different savings account at time 0, which pays simple interest at an annual rate of i.

Eric and Mike earn the same amount of interest during the last 6 months of the 8th year. Calculate i.

A. 9.06%

B. 9.26%

C. 9.46%

D. 9.66%

E. 9.86%

(SOA EXAM FM SAMPLE QUESTIONS May 2005, Question 7)

3. Mike receives cash flows of 100 today, 200 in 1 year, and 100 in 2 years. The present value of these cash flows is 364.46 at an annual effective rate of interest i.

Calculate i.

A. 10%

B. 11%

C. 12%

D. 13%

E. 14%

(SOA EXAM FM SAMPLE QUESTIONS May 2005, Question 13)

4. At a nominal interest rate of i convertible semiannually, an investment of 1,000 immediately and 1,500 at the end of the first year will accumulate to 2,600 at the end of the second year.

Calculate i.

A. 2.75%

B. 2.77%

C. 2.79%

D. 2.81%

E. 2.83%

(SOA EXAM FM SAMPLE QUESTIONS May 2005, Question 18)

5. A store is running a promotion during which customers have two options for payment. Option 1 is to pay 90% of the purchase price 2 months after the date of sale. Option 2 is to deduct X% off the purchase price and pay cash on the date of sale.

A customer wishes to determine X such that he is indifferent between the two options when valuing them using an effective annual interest rate of 8%.

Which of the following equations of value would the customer need to solve?

A. $\left(\frac{X}{100}\right)\left(1 + \frac{0.08}{6}\right) = 0.90$

B. $\left(1 - \frac{X}{100}\right)\left(1 + \frac{0.08}{6}\right) = 0.90$

C. $\left(\frac{X}{100}\right)(1.08)^{\frac{1}{6}} = 0.90$

D. $\left(\frac{X}{100}\right)\left(\frac{1.08}{1.06}\right) = 0.90$

E. $\left(1 - \frac{X}{100}\right)(1.08)^{\frac{1}{6}} = 0.90$

(SOA EXAM FM SAMPLE QUESTIONS May 2005, Question 21)

6. A discount electronics store advertises the following financing arrangement:

"We don't offer you confusing interest rates. We'll just divide your total cost by 10 and you can pay us that amount each month for a year."

The first payment is due on the date of sale and the remaining eleven payments at monthly intervals thereafter. Calculate the effective annual interest rate the store's customers are paying on their loans.

A. 35.1%
B. 41.3%
C. 42.0%
D. 51.2%
E. 54.9%

(SOA EXAM FM SAMPLE QUESTIONS November 2005, Question 7)

7. A bank offers the following choices for certificates of deposit:

Term (in years)	Nominal annual interest rate convertible quarterly
1	4.00%
3	5.00%
5	5.65%

The certificates mature at the end of the term. The bank does NOT permit early withdrawals. During the next 6 years the bank will continue to offer certificates of deposit with the same terms and interest rates.

An investor initially deposits 10,000 in the bank and withdraws both principal and interest at the end of 6 years.

Calculate the maximum annual effective rate of interest the investor can earn over the 6-year period.

A. 5.09%
B. 5.22%
C. 5.35%
D. 5.48%
E. 5.61%

(SOA EXAM FM SAMPLE QUESTIONS Interest Theory, Question 27)

8. Bruce and Robbie each open up new bank accounts at time 0. Bruce deposits 100 into his bank account, and Robbie deposits 50 into his. Each account earns the same annual effective interest rate.

    The amount of interest earned in Bruce's account during the 11th year is equal to X. The amount of interest earned in Robbie's account during the 17th year is also equal to X.

    Calculate X.

    A. 28.00
    B. 31.30
    C. 34.60
    D. 36.70
    E. 38.90

(SOA EXAM FM SAMPLE QUESTIONS Interest Theory, Question 77)

9. Lucas opens a bank account with 1,000 and lets it accumulate at an annual nominal interest rate of 6% convertible semiannually. Danielle also opens a bank account with 1,000 at the same time as Lucas, but it grows at an annual nominal interest rate of 3% convertible monthly.

    For each account, interest is credited only at the end of each interest conversion period.

Calculate the number of months required for the amount in Lucas's account to be at least double the amount in Danielle's account.

A. 276
B. 282
C. 285
D. 286
E. 288

(SOA EXAM FM SAMPLE QUESTIONS Interest Theory, Question 94)

10. A couple decides to save money for their child's first year college tuition.

    The parents will deposit 1,700 n months from today and another 3,400 $2n$ months from today.
    All deposits earn interest at a nominal annual rate of 7.2%, compounded monthly.
    Calculate the maximum integral value of n such that the parents will have accumulated at least 6,500 five years from today.

    A. 11
    B. 12
    C. 18
    D. 24
    E. 25

CHAPTER TWO

Loans: Fundamentals of Borrowing and Lending

Abstract

Saving money is something that we should do more of and, if we did a better job of it and were willing to delay gratification longer, we wouldn't have to take loans. However, loans are a reality for most individuals and organizations to function in the world today. In this chapter, we will explore the basic constructs of a loan—how payments are made, the typical structure of loans and the types of loans available. We will also explore how different strategies for paying back loans impacts how much interest the borrower will pay and the concept of refinancing. Finally, we conclude by exploring sinking funds, which are savings accounts that accumulate money in order to pay back a future loan balance.

Keywords: Sinking funds; loans; borrowing; refinancing; lending

SECTION 2.1. INTRODUCTION TO LOANS

If you haven't already considered taking out a loan, you likely will soon. Whether it's considering the use of student loans to pay for college, a loan for a car, an application for a credit card, or something else, loans are prevalent in our world today. But, how do loans work? In particular, who pays money, who gets money, how much and when? We will explore these questions in this chapter. As you'll soon see, understanding loans is really just about knowing how to value an account with multiple cash flows, much like we looked at in the previous chapter.

Learning Objectives

By the end of this section, you should be able to

- Understand the basic structure of a loan in terms of the borrower—lender relationship, the principal, interest rate, term, and payment frequency.
- Contrast an interest-only loan with an amortized loan.

A Spiral Approach to Financial Mathematics.
DOI: https://doi.org/10.1016/B978-0-12-801580-3.00002-2
© 2018 Elsevier Inc.
All rights reserved.
81

- Set up a basic amortization table in Excel or by hand, and use the recursive approach when filling in the values in the table.
- Use a guess-and-check approach to find the payment size for an amortized loan.

EXAMPLE 2.1. PAYING BACK A STUDENT LOAN

Many students take out loans during college. A Stafford Loan is available to most undergraduate students in the United States and is a low-interest loan to help pay for college.

Definition

A **loan** is when one entity (e.g., a bank) lends money to another entity (e.g., an individual). Typically, the borrower pays back the original amount of the loan plus interest.

Let's assume you determine that you will need a Stafford Loan during your freshman year to help pay for college. An unsubsidized Stafford Loan accumulates interest during the entire time that you are in college, plus the 6 months after you graduate—but you don't have to make any payments during that time.

Let's assume that the Stafford Loan accumulates at 4.5% APR. How much will your loan balance be when you graduate (assuming you don't take any more loans after freshman year)? To calculate this value, we will use an account chart like we have done before. In this chart we assume that you take out a $3,500 loan (Note that this is less than the maximum you could take) on for freshman year (Table 2.1).

Table 2.1 Loan Balance for an Unsubsidized Stafford Loan Taken During Freshman Year Only (Assuming a $3,500 Loan Amount)

Year	Principal Balance (Aug 15) ($)	Interest Accrued (Aug–Jul) ($)	Payment (Jul) ($)	New Loan Balance (Jul) ($)
Freshman	3,500	160.79	0	3,660.79
Sophomore	3,660.79	168.18	0	3,828.97
Junior	3,828.97	175.90	0	4,004.87
Senior	4,004.87	183.89	0	4,188.85

The interest rate of 4.5% APR (compounded monthly) is equivalent to 0.375% effective interest/month $(0.045/12 = 0.00375)$, which is equivalent to $i = 0.04594$ effective interest/year since $(1.00375)^{12} = 1.04594$. This means that during your freshman year of college your loan will accumulate (accrue) $160.79 in interest since $3,500 $\times$ 0.04594 = $160.79. Notice that by not making any payments the interest gets added to the new loan balance. This is called *capitalizing* the interest.

Definition

Capitalizing interest on a loan occurs when no interest payment is made and so the interest on the loan gets added to the loan balance.

Think about it

Why does the interest accrued annually on the loan increase each year?

When loan interest is capitalized (added to the loan balance), the interest in the following years increases because the loan is "earning" interest on the interest. You can think of this as a loan to pay the interest. Thus, the lender is benefitting from the power of compound interest, while, for the borrower, this isn't so nice!

Capitalizing the interest for a loan is fairly rare because lenders are often worried about loan default—the inability of the borrower to pay back the loan. Instead, most lenders want periodic payments from the borrower to pay the interest—reducing the risk of loan default, and giving the lender a steady income stream.

Definition

If a borrower cannot pay back their loan it is called **defaulting** on the loan and the lender may be able to take things the borrower owns (repossession) or garnish wages (take a portion of the borrower's income).

Key idea

Most loans involve making payments over time from the borrower to the lender, instead of leaving the entire loan balance plus interest due at the end of the loan term.

Loan Terminology

There are some key terms to know when talking about loans. The *principal* of the loan is how much the borrower owes the bank at any particular time; sometimes, this is referred to as the loan balance. The initial principal is simply the amount of the loan. In the case of this unsubsidized Stafford Loan, the initial principal freshman year is $3,500.

Definition

The **principal** of a loan is the amount that the borrower owes the lender at any particular time; it is the loan balance.

The *term of the loan* is the length of time the loan contract lasts. In the case of this loan, the initial term is 4 years (while you are in college plus 6 months; a grace period). The actual term will be longer since, when you graduate, you will renegotiate the terms of the loan to begin paying it back.

The *frequency of payments* indicates how often the borrower is contractually obligated to make payments on the loan. Usually, this is timed to coincide with the interest compounding period. To do any calculations involving loans you also need to know the interest rate and frequency of compounding.

Paying Off the Interest Over Time

Based on family income, some students are eligible for a different kind of loan known as a subsidized Stafford Loan. In a subsidized Stafford Loan, the federal government makes the interest payments on your loan for you while you are in college. The maximum amount that you can take on a subsidized Stafford Loan is $3,500 during your freshman year. Table 2.2

Table 2.2 Loan Balance for a Subsidized Stafford Loan Taken During Freshman Year Only ($3,500 Original Loan Amount)

Year	Principal Balance (Aug 15) ($)	Interest Accrued (Aug–Jul) ($)	Payment Made by Federal Government on Your Behalf (Jul) ($)	New Loan Balance (Jul) ($)
Freshman	3,500	160.79	(160.79)	3,500
Sophomore	3,500	160.79	(160.79)	3,500
Junior	3,500	160.79	(160.79)	3,500
Senior	3,500	160.79	(160.79)	3,500

illustrates the principal balance and interest accrued on your loan over the 4-year period of the loan. Notice that because the government is paying the interest that accrues on your loan, the new loan balance never rises above the original amount! This also means that the interest that accrues does not grow over time, which is different than when the interest on the loan is capitalized as we saw above.

Notice that the loan balance when you graduate is quite a bit different for the subsidized loan ($3,500) as compared to the unsubsidized version ($4,188.85). The difference in these amounts is exactly equal to the total interest accumulated on the loan ($160.79 + $168.18 + $175.90 + $183.89 = $688.85).

Amortization

When you graduate college and start working, you will need to start paying back your student loan. At that time, you will work with a student loan servicing company to set up the terms of your repayment. Typically, you will make equal-sized, monthly payments for some predetermined amount of time (e.g., 10 years) at a predetermined, fixed, interest rate.

If your student loan servicing company has a 4.2% APR on a 10-year payback period, how much interest will your loan have accumulated after the first month if it starts with a balance of $4,188.85 (unsubsidized loan from freshman year only)? The effective interest rate/month will be $0.042/12 = 0.0035$. This means that your loan will accumulate $14.66 after the first month.

Think about it

Will your monthly payment be larger or smaller or equal to $14.66 to pay back your loan over 10 years?

If you paid less than $14.66 the loan balance (principal) would grow, and not get paid off in 10 years. If you paid $14.66, the principal would never change. So, you'll have to pay more than $14.66 each month. But how much more?

We can set up a dynamic account chart in Excel to find out. Here is a snippet from the chart we created using **Chapter 2 Excel file** where we explored what would happen if we paid $25 each month (Table 2.3).

Table 2.3 Dynamic Account Chart in Excel for a $25 Monthly Payment

Month	Principal Balance (1st of Month) ($)	Interest Accrued (During the Month) ($)	Payment (Last Day of Month)	New Loan Balance (Last Day of Month) ($)
1	4,188.85	14.66	25	4,178.51
2	4,178.51	14.62	25	4,168.14
3	4,168.14	14.59	25	4,157.72
...	...	...	25	...
120	2,665.94	9.33	25	2,650.27

First, notice that when a payment is made to the loan, the payment is first applied to the interest, and then the remainder is used to reduce the principal. Thus, the principal drops by $25 − $14.66 = $10.34 the first month from $4,188.85 to $4,178.51. The interest accrued each month is dropping which is good. But, notice that after 120 months (10 years) the loan balance is not zero!

Think about it

Will your monthly payment need to be larger or smaller or equal than $25 to payback your loan over 10 years?

Your monthly payment will need to be larger than $25 to pay back the loan after 10 years. We used a guess and check approach in Excel and found the following. *Note:* See the "Exploration 2.1. So, You Want to Buy a Car..." section and **Chapter 2 Excel file** for some details on the PMT function in Excel which is faster than guess-and-check.

Key idea

When paying back a loan, the payments made by the borrower are typically used to pay off the loan's interest first, with the remainder of the payment applied to the loan's principal.

Table 2.4 is called an amortization table because it illustrates how equally sized payments can be used to pay off a loan over time. (The word amortization comes from the Latin root *mortem* which means death; so to amortize a loan literally means to "kill off" the loan.)

Table 2.4 Dynamic Account Chart in Excel for a $42.81 Monthly Payment

Month	Principal Balance (1st of Month) ($)	Interest Accrued (During the Month) ($)	Payment (Last day of Month) ($)	New Loan Balance (Last day of Month) ($)
1	4,188.85	14.66	42.81	4,160.70
2	4,160.70	14.56	42.81	4,132.45
3	4,132.45	14.46	42.81	4,104.11
...	...	...	42.81	...
120	42.57	0.15	42.81	0[a]

[a]Actually, we got a balance of − $0.09. In this case, the bank would charge us $42.72 instead of $42.81 for the final payment to end up with a balance of exactly $0.00. This is called a *drop payment* and is discussed in Chapter 7, Loans Revisited, for now we will ignore this relatively minor issue.

Definition
Amortization is a term used to describe how a debt is paid off with a fixed repayment schedule of equally sized payments.

Definition
An **amortization table** is a table that shows the principal balance, interest accrued and amount of money paid toward principal each period when payments are equally sized.

How much interest will you have paid when you are done paying back your loan after 10 years? To find this you can sum up the appropriate column in the spreadsheet (14.66 + 14.56 + 14.46 + ··· + 0.15). We did this and found a value of $948.26 for the total interest paid during the 10-year payback period. What is the total value of your payments? If you pay $42.81/month, then you will have paid $42.81 each month for 120 months, or $42.81 × 120 = $5,137.20.

Think about it
If you paid $5,137.20 total and $948.26 went to pay for interest, what is the rest going to pay for?

The rest ($5,137.20 − $948.26 = $4,188.94) is going to pay the original loan amount. The only difference between $4,188.94 and the original loan amount of $4,188.85 is the nine-cent difference we noted above in Table 2.4. Thus, an important relationship exists between total interest, total principal, and the sum of all payments made on an amortized loan:

Sum of payments = Total interest + Total Principal

This formula is a nice "shortcut" to calculating total interest paid without calculating the entire amortization table.

Key Idea
The sum of all payments made on an amortized loan equals the principal of the loan plus the total interest paid.

How Much Does Your $3,500 Actually Cost You?

So, when you're done paying off your $3,500 loan from freshman year, what will it end up actually costing you? You accumulated $688.94 in interest while in college and an additional $948.26 while paying back the loan, or $688.94 + $948.26 = $1,637.20 total. Is it worth it? Obviously, investing in education is important for many reasons, but it does show that it doesn't take much of a loan to accumulate a lot of interest payments.

EXPLORATION 2.1. SO, YOU WANT TO BUY A CAR...

To explore loans, we will consider the following situation. Let's assume that you are on the market for a new car. You don't currently have a car, but you just took a job which will require you have one. You have $1,000 in your savings account, but are concerned that for $1,000 you could only afford an unreliable car. You know that once you start your job you will have an increased income so you are considering whether you should take out a short-term loan now in order to buy a reliable car, and pay the loan back over time.

You go to the car dealer and start looking at cars. You see a variety of cars, ranging from $5,000 (for an older midsized) to $27,000 (for a sweet red convertible). Before the salesman comes up to talk to you, let's learn a little bit more about loans.

What is a Loan and How Does It Work?

A loan is when a bank (or another entity) temporarily gives you money, typically to make a major purchase.

Definition

A **loan** is when one entity (e.g., a bank) lends money to another entity (e.g., an individual). Typically, the borrower pays back the original amount of the loan plus interest.

---

1. Let's assume that your parents offer you the following on a $10,000 loan for a car: 5% effective annual interest, compounded annually and with the entire amount of the original loan plus all accumulated interest due in 5 years. How much interest will you end up paying back on the loan? What is the total amount of the payment you will owe your parents 5 years from now?

   This loan capitalizes the interest (add the interest to the loan balance).

Definition

Capitalizing interest on a loan occurs when no interest payment is made and so the interest on the loan gets added to the loan balance.

---

2. As we did in the previous chapter, you can use an account chart to follow the account balance over time. Fill in the account chart below.

Year	Principal Balance (Jan 1) ($)	Interest Accrued (Jan 1–Dec 31) ($)	Payment (Dec 31) ($)	New Loan Balance (Dec 31)
1	10,000	500	0	
2			0	
3			0	
4			0	
5			0	
6		XXX	XXX	XXX

3. Describe some of the pros and cons of this approach to loan repayment for you (the *borrower*).

4. Describe some of the pros and cons of this approach to loan repayment for your parents (the *lender*).

Most loans do not have a lump sum payment that includes the original amount of the loan plus the interest. While this may be initially appealing to borrowers because they have no payments to make in the near future, if they don't start saving on their own they might not save enough to pay back the loan when it is due. When someone doesn't pay back their loan, they default on it and the lender may choose to take ownership of some of the borrower's belongings or take some of their future income (which is called repossession or wage garnishment).

This risk of loan default is potentially concerning for the lender in a loan where no payments are made over time. This is particularly problematic for an asset that loses value over time (depreciating asset—like a car), because if the lender chooses to repossess the asset it may not be worth the value of the loan.

Definition

If a borrower cannot pay back their loan, it is called **defaulting** on the loan and the lender may be able to take things the borrower owns (repossession) or garnish wages (take a portion of the borrower's income).

Key idea

Most loans involve making payments over time from the borrower to the lender, instead of leaving the entire loan balance plus interest due at the end of the loan term.

There are some key terms to know when talking about loans. The *principal* of the loan is how much the borrower owes the bank at a particular time; sometimes this is referred to as the loan balance. The initial principal is simply the amount of the loan. The *term of the loan* is the length of time the loan contract lasts. The *frequency of payments* indicates how often the borrower is contractually obligated to make payments on the loan. Usually, this is timed to coincide with the interest compounding period. To do any calculations involving loans you also need to know the interest rate and frequency of compounding.

Definition

The **principal** of a loan is the amount that the borrower owes the lender at any particular time; it is the loan balance.

If you chose to take the loan from your parents,

5. What is the principal?

6. What is the term of the loan?

7. What is the frequency of payments?

8. What is the interest rate and frequency of compounding?

Paying Off the Interest Over Time

One simple kind of loan which requires payments over time is known as an interest-only loan. While some of the details of interest-only loans vary, the fundamental idea is the same—each compounding period you pay the interest that accumulated (accrued), but don't pay any of the principal. Then at the end of the loan term, the entire amount of the principal is due.

9. How would things change if your parents offered you a $10,000 interest-only loan with 5% effective annual interest, compounding annually with a 5-year term? What sized payment would you make each year? How much total interest will you pay?

10. Would you end up paying more total money to your parents with the interest-only loan or the original loan which paid off all of the accumulated interest and the principal at the end of the loan term? Why?

When you pay off the interest each month, you don't allow the interest to "earn' interest—while that is to the lenders benefit, it hurts the borrower.

Account charts can be used to help visualize what is happening with a loan over time.

11. Fill in the account chart below assuming that you have a 5-year interest-only car loan for $10,000 at 5% annual effective interest, with an annual payment of $500. For convenience, we'll assume that your loan starts on January 1. We've filled in the first row for you to get you started.

Year	Principal Balance (Jan 1) ($)	Interest Accrued (Jan 1–Dec 31) ($)	Payment (Dec 31) ($)	New Loan Balance (Dec 31) ($)
1	10,000	500	500	10,000
2				
3				
4				
5				
6		XXX	XXX	XXX

12. What is the principal balance at the end of the 5-year period? What does that mean in terms of your financial obligations to your parents? Why could this be a problem?

13. What could you do in order to address the problem noted in the previous question?

Amortization

To avoid potentially being stuck with the need to make a very large payment at the end of the term of the loan (and one that, if you aren't very disciplined, you might not be able to pay!) in most loans you pay not only the interest, but also some of the principal with each payment. Let's say that you decide to pay your parents $600 instead of $500 for the first payment. Your parents, like most lenders, apply your payment to the accrued interest first and then apply the rest to the principal.

14. Fill in the first row of an account chart related to this loan payback approach.

Year	Principal Balance (Jan 1)	Interest Accrued (Jan 1–Dec 31)	Payment (Dec 31)	New Loan Balance (Dec 31)
1				

Key idea

When paying back a loan, the payments made by the borrower are typically used to pay off the loan's interest first, with the remainder of the payment applied to the loan's principal.

---

15. If you continue making payments of $600 each year, instead of $500, do you think that you'll end up paying more or less total interest than if you paid the interest ($500/year) only each time? Why?

16. Now, fill in the account chart assuming a $600 payment each year for 5 years and confirm your answer to the previous question.

Year	Principal Balance (Jan 1)	Interest Accrued (Jan 1–Dec 31)	Payment (Dec 31)	New Loan Balance (Dec 31)
1				
2				
3				
4				
5				
6		XX	XX	XX

Unfortunately, $600/year isn't enough and you still have a fairly sizeable loan balance when the loan is due to be paid off.

17. How does the table change if you paid off $1,000 each December 31?

Year	Principal Balance (Jan 1)	Interest Accrued (Jan 1–Dec 31)	Payment (Dec 31)	New Loan Balance (Dec 31)
1				
2				
3				
4				
5				
6		XX	XX	XX

Unfortunately, $1,000 isn't enough either.

18. Create dynamic account chart in Excel using **Chapter 2 Excel file** and use guess-and-check to find the payment amount so that if you pay that exact amount each January 1, the loan will be paid off. Fill in the values in the table below.

Year	Principal Balance (Jan 1)	Interest Accrued (Jan 1–Dec 31)	Payment (Dec 31)	New Loan Balance (Dec 31)
1				
2				
3				
4				
5				
6		XX	XX	XX

The table above is an amortization table because it illustrates how equally sized payments can be used to pay off a loan over time. (The word amortization comes from the Latin root *mortem* which means death; so to amortize a loan literally means to kill off the loan.)

Definition

Amortization is a term used to describe how a debt is paid off with a fixed repayment schedule of equally sized payments.

Definition

The chart above is an **amortization table**, a table that shows the principal balance, interest accrued, and amount of money paid toward principal each period when payments are equally sized.

---

19. How much total interest will you have paid over the course of the loan?

20. How much total principal will you have paid over the course of the loan?

21. How much total will you have paid for the $10,000 car?

An important relationship exists between total interest, total principal and the sum of all payments made on an amortized loan: Sum of payments = Total interest + Total Principal.

Key idea

The sum of all payments made on an amortized loan equals the principal of the loan plus the total interest paid.

---

22. Confirm the key idea above for the 5-year amortized car loan.

23. Compare the total interest paid on the amortized loan vs the interest-only loan vs the "no payments until the end" loan. Which has the most/least interest paid? Why?

24. So, which loan offer from your parents (amortized, interest-only, one big payment at the end) would you take? Why?

Using Excel Functions and Online Loan Calculators to Simplify Loan Computations

The PMT function in Excel is a quick and easy way to calculate the payment size of a loan. Other calculators and online tools do many of these calculations very quickly as well.

The PMT function in Excel takes five entries into the function and returns the payment size. The five entries are:

Rate: Effective interest rate per period

Nper: Total number of periods in the loan payback period

PV: The loan amount (principal)

FV: The amount of principal left at the end of the loan term (0 for a fully paid back loan). This is an optional entry to the formula and can be omitted.

Type: Defaults to "0" which is end of month payments. Can be set to 1 for beginning of the month payments. This is an optional entry to the formula. *Note:* We'll discuss beginning of the month payments more in later chapters.

25. Use the PMT function in Excel to confirm your answer above for the payment needed each month to pay off the loan. Note that an example with the PMT function is shown in **Chapter 2 Excel file**.

If you are wondering how the PMT function works, we'll see short-cut formulas in later chapters which can be used to find payment sizes, and some other quantities for loans, directly. The PMT function is using a shortcut formula.

SUMMARY

In this section, we saw how it is typical to pay back a loan over time instead of waiting to pay only a large lump sum at the end of the term of a loan. An interest-only loan still left a large payment at the end, but paid off the interest along the way, while an amortized loan used equal sized payments that were a mix of interest and principal to pay back the loan over time without leaving a large "lump sum" payment at the end.

As we'll see in the next two sections, there are a few practical considerations with loans we have not considered yet. Next, we'll consider refinancing and a more typical "monthly payment" loan. Later, we'll evaluate the pros and cons of a sinking fund approach to loan repayment which is one method to figure out how much you need to save along the way if you end up with a lump sum payment at the end of your loan term.

Notation and equation summary
Sum of payments = Total interest + Total Principal

HOMEWORK QUESTIONS: SECTION 2.1

Conceptual Questions

1. When paying off a loan, if you have extra money to pay on the loan, you save the most in terms of future interest payments by paying the extra money _____ (sooner/later).

2. Explain the dangers of an interest–only loan.

3. Increasing the monthly payment will _____ (increase/ decrease) the amount paid toward principal each month, _____ (increase/decrease) the amount of interest paid each month, and _____ (increase/decrease) the length of the loan payback period.

4. Increasing the initial loan amount will _____ (increase/ decrease) the loan payback period assuming the interest rate and monthly payment stay the same.

5. Explain the implications of a novel loan payback program where the payment amount is first applied to principal and then to interest.

6. When you pay off a loan according to an amortization schedule, your monthly payments over time will _____(increase/ decrease/stay the same), the amount of interest you pay each month _____(increases/decreases/stays the same), and the amount of the principal balance you pay each month _____ (increases/decreases/stays the same).

Practice Questions

7. Susan takes a $15,000 car loan with payments of $450/month for 4 years (completely paid off after 4 years). Without doing extensive calculations, how much total interest will Susan pay over the life of the loan?

8. Jack takes a $10,000 car loan with monthly payments for 5 years. Without doing extensive calculations, if Jack pays $4,500 in cumulative interest over the course of the loan, how much is his monthly payment?

9. You have a student loan for your freshman year in college where you get $3,000 on September 1 and $3,000 on the following January 1. Your loan will accumulate interest at 4% APR compounded monthly. How much will your total loan balance be (assuming you make no payments) for just your two freshmen-year loans on September 1 after you graduate (4 years after you first received $3,000)?

10. If you take out a 5-year interest-only loan for $8,000 where you pay 6% APR compounded monthly, what are your monthly payments for the life of the loan? How much will you owe at the end of the 5-year period? Use guess-and-check or the PMT function in Excel.

11. Emma finances $100,000 of her new home by taking out a 30-year mortgage at 4.125% APR compounded monthly. Her monthly payments are $484.65. How much of her first payment (after having the loan for 1 month) is interest?

Application Questions

12. In the previous question, we saw that Emma financed $100,000 of her new home by taking out a 30-year mortgage at 4.125% APR. Her payments are $484.65.
   a. How much total interest is she paying over the life of the loan?
   b. How much of her 180th payment (after having the loan for 180 months) is interest?
   c. How much of her 360th payment (after having the loan for 360 months) is interest?

13. Create an amortization schedule for a 36-month car loan taken for $12,000 at an APR of 3.2% with monthly payments.
   a. Find the monthly payment amount using guess and check.
   b. Find the amount of principal in the 10th payment.
   c. Find the amount of interest in the 26th payment.
   d. What is the total principal paid?
   e. What is the total interest paid?
   f. What is the effect on total principal paid, total interest paid, and the loan term of an extra $2000 payment on the loan after the 12th payment (without changing the monthly payment)?

14. Create an amortization schedule for a 60-month home equity loan taken for $25,000 at an APR of 4% with monthly payments.
   a. Find the monthly payment amount using guess and check.
   b. Find the amount of principal in the 20th payment.
   c. Find the amount of interest in the 30th payment.
   d. What is the total principal paid?
   e. What is the total interest paid?

f. What is the effect on total principal paid, total interest paid and the loan term of an extra $3000 payment on the loan after the 24th payment (without changing the monthly payment)?

15. You borrowed $20,000 at 5% APR and are making yearly payments of $3,500.

   a. Complete the following account chart for this loan.

Year	Principal Balance (Jan 1) ($)	Interest Accrued (Jan 1–Dec 31)	Payment (Dec 31) ($)	New Loan Balance (Dec 31)
1	20,000		3,500	
2			3,500	
3			3,500	
4			3,500	
5			3,500	

   b. How much is still owed at the end of the 5 years?

   c. What equal-sized annual payments are needed so the account balance is $0 after 5 years?

16. You borrowed $25,000 at 4.25% annual effective interest and are making yearly payments of $4,000.

   a. Complete the following account chart for this loan.

Year	Principal Balance (Jan 1) ($)	Interest Accrued (Jan 1–Dec 31)	Payment (Dec 31) ($)	New Loan Balance (Dec 31)
1	25,000		4,000	
2			4,000	
3			4,000	
4			4,000	
5			4,000	

   b. How much is still owed at the end of the 5 years?

   c. How much would still be left after 5 years if instead of a $4,000 payment on December 31 of Year 2, you made an $8,000 payment?

d. How much would still be left after 5 years if instead of a $4000 payment on December 31 of Year 4, you made an $8,000 payment?

e. What equal-sized annual payments are needed so the account balance is $0 after 5 years?

Looking Ahead

17. You borrowed $20,000 at 4% annual effective interest and are making yearly payments. We will find payments of equal sized amounts, but **not** through guessing and checking. Suppose you are going to pay off the loan in just two annual payments, one a year after you take out the loan and one 2 years after you take out the loan.

a. Write down an expression for how much you owe on the loan after you make your first payment. Use numbers for everything in your expression except for the payment. Use P for payment.

b. Write down an expression for how much you owe on the loan after you make the second and final payment.

c. Since you should now have your loan paid off, so set your expression from part b equal to 0 and solve for P. That should be your payment.

d. Instead of making two equal-sized payments in 2 years to pay off the loan, suppose you made three equal-sized payments in 3 years. Using a similar process that you used for parts a−c, find the three equal-sized payments.

SECTION 2.2. REFINANCING A LOAN

In the previous section, we were introduced to loan repayment, and learned that amortization uses equally sized payments to pay off a loan over a set period of time. In this section we'll explore the financial implications of refinancing a loan, considering both the borrower and lender's perspectives.

Learning Objectives

By the end of this section you should be able to

- Compute an amortization table and evaluate the proportion of interest (or principal) in each payment.
- Understand the implications of loan refinancing on payment size, total loan term, total interest paid, proportion of interest in each payment, etc.

EXAMPLE 2.2. PAYING BACK A STUDENT LOAN (REVISITED)

In the "Example 2.1. Paying Back a Student Loan" section we looked at aspects of different types of student loans and how they get paid back. In a typical student loan scenario, a student might end up taking a student loan all 4 years that they are in college. Let's assume that by the time a student finishes college they have accumulated $45,000 in student loan debt that needs to be repaid. The amortization table for a 10-year loan payback period for $45,000 in debt at 4.2% APR is shown in Table 2.5. We used guess-and-check in **Chapter 2 Excel file** (you could also use the PMT function) to determine that a payment size of $459.89 monthly will pay back the loan in 10 years.

Table 2.5 Amortization Table for $45,000 Student Loan at 4.2% APR Over 10 Years

Month	Principal Balance (Day 1) ($)	Interest Accrued (During Month) ($)	Payment (31st of Month) ($)	New Loan Balance (31st of Month) ($)
1	45,000	157.50	459.89	44,697.61
2	44,697.61	156.44	459.89	44,394.16
3	44,394.16	155.38	459.89	44,089.65
...	...	...	459.89	...
120	458.68	1.61	459.89	0

Notice that the interest accrued each month in Table 2.5 is decreasing, which means that the amount of payment that is going to pay down the principal is increasing each month.

Table 2.6 shows that the portion of payment going to pay the interest is decreasing. If more rows were shown you could see that these decreases are getting larger and larger. For example, you can see the portion of payment going to interest drops $1.06 between months 1 and 2. Between months 60 and 61 it drops $1.31 and between months 110 and 111 it drops $1.55.

This is further illustrated in Fig. 2.1 which graphs the proportion of each payment which goes to interest over time. The line is not straight, but is slightly curved downward. As you pay more and more toward loan, the interest payments are dropping faster and faster.

Table 2.6 Payment Distribution for $45,000 Student Loan at 4.2% APR Over 10 Years

Month	Payment ($)	Portion of Payment Going to Interest ($)	Portion of Payment Going to Principal ($)	Proportion of Payment Going to Interest
1	459.89	157.50	302.39	0.3424
2	459.89	156.44	303.45	0.3402
3	459.89	155.38	304.51	0.3379
...	459.89	...	...	...
120	459.89	1.61	458.28	0.0035

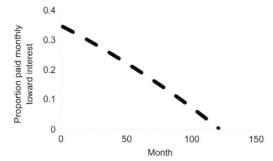

Figure 2.1 Proportion of monthly payment going to interest.

Key idea
The proportion of each payment which is going toward interest declines over time as more and more money goes toward principal. Furthermore, the rate at which interest declines increases (accelerates) over time.

Refinancing

It is common practice for lenders to offer borrowers the option to "refi-nance" their loans part way through a payback period.

Definition
Refinancing involves ending the terms of the original loan and taking the principal balance on the original loan and making that the starting balance on a new loan, with new terms.

What would your payback look like if you refinanced your student loan after paying it back for 5 years? Let's assume that you can refinance at a lower interest rate (3.6% APR) for 10 more years when you refinance. At the end of 5 years, your loan balance will be \$24,849.77. Your new payment will be \$246.89.

Your new payment is more than \$200 lower per month than your original payment—a substantial decrease, but what else is changing?

The total amount paid with the original loan terms is \$459.89 × 120 = \$55,186.80, which means that the total amount paid to interest is \$55,186.80 − \$45,000 = \$10,186.80. In the refinanced loan, the total amount paid to interest will be

- Interest paid first 5 years = Total payments minus total paid to principal = \$459.89 × 60 − (\$45,000 − \$24,849.96) = \$7,443.36.
- Interest paid next 10 years = \$246.89 × 120 − \$24,849.96 = \$4,776.84.

So, the total interest paid will be \$7,443.36 + \$47,76.84 = \$12,220.20—more than the original loan. Why is this the case? First, realize that the refinanced loan increased the loan term. Second, when you refinance the loan, you "reset the clock" on the interest. See Figs. 2.2 and 2.3, which show that while the interest paid per month drops a bit with the refinancing initially (this is because the interest rate is lower), the amount paid per month in interest is soon higher with the refinanced loan than the original loan.

In Fig. 2.3, it is easy to see that as soon as the loan is refinanced the proportion of interest in each payment jumps up.

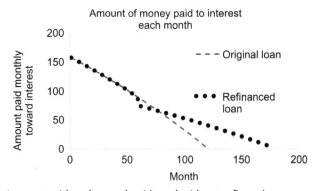

Figure 2.2 Interest paid each month with and without refinancing.

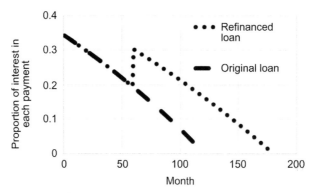

Figure 2.3 Proportion of interest in each payment.

Key idea
Refinancing a loan "resets" the interest-principal proportions in the favor of the lender by reducing the payment size and stretching out the term of the loan.

While refinancing to take advantage of a lower interest can be appealing, caution is needed to ensure that you don't end up paying more interest in the long run by stretching out the loan term well beyond the original terms of loan.

EXPLORATION 2.2. SO, YOU WANT TO BUY A CAR... (REVISITED)

In the "Exploration 2.1. So, You Want to Buy a Car..." section, we started to explore what it would look like to take out a loan for a car. We considered a 5-year loan at 5% effective annual interest with equally sized annual payments on a $10,000 loan. Having equally sized payments on a loan means that the loan is amortized. We used guess and check to find that a payment of $2,309.75 each year was the right size to pay off the loan in 5 years (you could also use the PMT function).

Understanding Amortization
Even though each payment in an amortized loan is the same size, the amount of interest (and, hence, principal) in each payment changes over time.

1. How does the amount of interest in each payment change over time in an amortized loan? Why?

2. How does the amount of principal in each payment change over time an amortized loan? Why?

3. The table below shows how much of each payment goes toward interest. Use this to find the proportion of each payment is going toward interest. To find this proportion, take the amount of the payment going toward interest and divide it by the payment size.

Year	Principal Balance (Jan 1) ($)	Interest Accrued (Jan 1−Dec 31) ($)	Payment (Dec 31) ($)	New Loan Balance (Dec 31) ($)	Proportion of Payment Going to Interest
1	10,000	500	2,309.75	8,190.25	
2	8,190.25	409.51	2,309.75	6,290.01	
3	6,290.01	314.50	2,309.75	4,294.76	
4	4,294.76	214.74	2,309.75	2,199.75	
5	2,199.75	109.99	2,309.75	0	
6	0	XXX	XXX	XXX	

4. How is the proportion of each payment going toward interest changing over time? Is it declining by a constant amount?

Key idea

The proportion of each payment that is going toward interest declines over time as more and more money goes toward principal. Furthermore, the rate at which interest declines increases (accelerates) over time.

---

5. Remember that many banks and lenders are *for profit* companies, which make much of their money off interest on loans. When does the bank make most of their money off a loan? Near the beginning of a loan or near the end of a loan?

6. When are you (the borrower) paying back most of the principal? Near the beginning of a loan or near the end of a loan?

Refinancing

Refinancing is a key approach banks use to maximize interest earned from loans.

Definition

Refinancing involves ending the terms of the original loan and taking the principal balance on the original loan and making that the starting balance on a new loan, with new terms.

Let's look at how refinancing impacts things for you and the lender. Let's assume that, instead of your parents giving you the car loan of $10,000 at 5% effective annual interest with annual payments for 5 years, the bank did.

Now, imagine if you made the first three payments on your loan (on December 31 of Year 1, 2, and 3) and then,

In the beginning of Year 4 you get the following letter in the mail from your bank, etc.

"Would you like to free up some of your hard-earned money? Instead of paying $2,309.75 each year, we can lower your payment to only $991.98, saving you a whopping **$1,317.77** per year starting with your next payment on December 31 of next year (end of Year 4). Don't worry, the interest rate and terms of this refinanced loan are the same as your original loan. (Original loan terms were five years from date of signing at 5% effective interest per year.) You must act today to take advantage of this special offer for our most loyal and trustworthy customers."

7. Think about the above scenario before doing any calculations. What would you do and why?

8. Fill in the table below to view the amortization schedule if you take advantage of the loan refinance offer from the bank.

Year	Principal Balance (Jan 1) ($)	Interest Accrued (Jan 1–Dec 31) ($)	Payment (Dec 31) ($)	New Loan Balance (Dec 31) ($)
1	10,000	500	2,309.75	8,190.25
2	8,190.25			

(*Continued*)

(Continued)

Year	Principal Balance (Jan 1) ($)	Interest Accrued (Jan 1–Dec 31) ($)	Payment (Dec 31) ($)	New Loan Balance (Dec 31) ($)
3				
4				
5				
6				
7				
8				

9. Compare the total amount of principal you pay to the bank in the original loan vs if you take advantage of the refinancing offer.

10. Compare the total amount of interest you pay to the bank in the original loan vs if you take advantage of the refinancing offer. *Hint: A shortcut to compute this is to take the total amount paid on the loan and subtract the principal paid back.*

11. How is the total loan timeframe changing with refinancing?

12. Why is the total interest more when refinancing?

13. Fill in the table below in a manner similar to what you did earlier for the loan before you refinanced.

Year	Principal Balance (Jan 1) ($)	Interest Accrued (Jan 1–Dec 31) ($)	Payment (Dec 31) ($)	New Loan Balance (Dec 31) ($)	Proportion Paid to Interest
1	10,000	500	2,309.75	8,190.25	0.2
2	8,190.25				
3					
4					
5					

(Continued)

(Continued)

Year	Principal Balance (Jan 1) ($)	Interest Accrued (Jan 1–Dec 31) ($)	Payment (Dec 31) ($)	New Loan Balance (Dec 31) ($)	Proportion Paid to Interest
6					
7					
8					

14. What is happening to the amount of interest and principal you pay each month immediately after you decide to refinance? What is happening to the proportion of your payment that goes to interest?

Key idea

Refinancing a loan "resets" the interest-principal proportions in the favor of the lender by reducing the payment size and stretching out the term of the loan.

SUMMARY

In this section, we saw the impact of loan refinancing on the loan payback period (longer), the proportion of interest in the loan (increases) and the total interest paid (increases). We also learned how to update an account chart to consider the implications of refinancing. Certainly, there may be good practical reasons to refinance (e.g., take advantage of lower interest rates or changes in life events) but careful consideration to interest and payback period should be made before agreeing to refinance a loan.

HOMEWORK QUESTIONS: SECTION 2.2

Conceptual Questions

1. With an amortized loan, as time goes on the proportion of the monthly payment going toward the principal _____ (increases, decreases, stays the same) and the proportion of the monthly payment going toward the interest _____ (increases, decreases, stays the same).

2. With an amortized loan, as time goes on the amount of interest in each payment decreases and the amount that it decreases _____ (increases, decreases, stays the same) over time.

3. Suppose a loan is refinanced, with the same interest rate, such that the overall time to pay back the loan increases. Do you pay more, less or the same total amount of interest?

4. Suppose a loan is refinanced, with the same interest rate, such that the overall time to pay back the loan increases. Right after the loan is refinanced will the interest proportion of each payment increase, decrease, or stay the same?

5. Why might a bank offer a lender the opportunity to refinance a loan before it is completely paid off?

6. You are comparing two mortgage loans, one is a 20-year loan and one is a 30-year loan. Both have the same interest rates. The amount of interest paid in the first payment for the 20-year loan will be _____ (higher than, lower than, the same as) the amount of interest paid in the first payment for the 30-year loan. The amount of principal paid in the first payment for the 20-year loan will be _____ (higher than, lower than, the same as) the amount of principal paid in the first payment for the 30-year loan.

Practice Questions

7. You take out a $150,000 mortgage for your home. You pay 3.875% APR on a 20-year loan which gives you a monthly payment of $899.12.
   a. How much of the first payment (1 month after you get the loan) is interest and how much is principal?
   b. What proportion of your payment is going for interest?

8. You take out a $150,000 mortgage for your home. You pay 3.875% APR on a 30-year loan which gives you a monthly payment of $705.36.
   a. How much of the first payment (1 month after you get the loan) is interest and how much is principal?
   b. What proportion of your payment is going for interest?

9. Compute how much total interest you would have to pay over the life of the loan for the two loans in questions 7 and 8. Which loan do you pay more total interest, the 20-year loan or the 30-year loan?

10. Tyler borrows $8,000 from his parents for a car. He is charged 4.125% annual effective interest and will be paying the money back in 5 annual installments of $1,803.33. Complete the following amortization table for Tyler's loan.

Date	Payment ($)	Amount of Payment Going to Interest	Amount of Payment Going to Principal
2018	1,803.33		
2019	1,803.33		
2020	1,803.33		
2021	1,803.33		
2022	1,803.33		

11. Zayra borrows $10,000 from his parents for a car. She is charged 4% annual effective interest and will be paying the money back in 4 annual installments of $2,754.90. Complete the following amortization table for Zayra's loan.

Date	Payment ($)	Amount of Payment Going to Interest	Amount of Payment Going to Principal
2018	2,754.90		
2019	2,754.90		
2020	2,754.90		
2021	2,754.90		

Application Questions

12. You want to borrow $150,000 for a new home. You see a 30-year fixed rate loan at 4% APR will have $716.12 monthly payments and a 20-year fixed rate loan at 3.875% APR will have $899.12 monthly payments.

    a. How much will you pay in interest over the life of the loan for each of these?

    b. How much will you be paying in total to get this $150,000?

    c. Using Excel, verify that the monthly payments are accurate and that the loan truly is amortized.

13. You want to buy a $200,000 home and are in the market for a mortgage. You have $40,000 saved up for a down payment. However, the bank says you only need 10% (or $20,000) for a down payment. So you think you can use the extra $20,000 to buy a new car. But how much is that $20,000 really going to cost you? The APR on the loan is 4.125% whether you put 10% down or 20% down, and the life either loan is 30 years.

    a. Your payment if you put $40,000 down is $775.44 per month. How much interest will you pay during the life of this loan?

    b. Your payment if you put $20,000 down is $872.37 per month. How much interest will you pay during the life of this loan?

    c. How much is holding back $20,000 from the down payment actually going to cost you over the life of the loan?

    d. You should have seen from the previous question that it costs much more than $20,000 to hold back this amount of money and not use it for a down payment. What else could you do with a loan if you still want to use the $20,000 on a new car but don't want to pay that much more in interest? (Assume you can't change the APR on the loan.)

14. You've just taken out a $220,000 mortgage on your new house. The mortgage is for 30 years at 4% APR and the payments are $1,050.31.

    a. Using Excel, make a complete amortization schedule giving how much of each of the 360 payments are going toward the principal and how much is interest.

    b. How much total interest will you be paying over the life of the loan?

   c. You think you can pay $100 more per month, so you plan to make payments of $1,150.31. How long will it take you to pay off the loan this way? How much will you save in interest by making this extra payment over the life of the loan?

   d. What if you pay $200 more per month, so you make payments of $1,250.31. How long will it take you to pay off the loan this way? How much will you save in interest by making this extra payment over the life of the loan compared to the original loan?

15. George buys a new car and finances $20,000 of it at 5% APR for 5 years. His monthly payment is $377.42.

   a. Using Excel, make a complete amortization schedule giving how much of each of the 60 payments are going toward the principal and how much is interest.

   b. How much total interest will George be paying over the life of the loan?

   c. Suppose at the very start of year 3 of the loan (right after the 36th payment), the bank offers George the following refinance offer: "Refinance with us and reduce your interest rate and reduce your monthly payment! For a limited time, we are giving you the opportunity to refinance your loan at 4.875% for 5 years."

      i. How much will George still owe after his 36th payment? (Hence, how much will he have to finance?)

      ii. Use Excel and a guess-and-check method to determine how much George's new monthly payment will be.

      iii. How much total interest would George pay if he refinances? Include both interest from the first 3 years before refinancing and the last 5 after refinancing.

      iv. Will refinancing help George save money?

16. Soma has a 15-year mortgage for $300,000 at 4.25% APR. Her monthly payments are $2,256.84 per month.

   a. Using Excel, make a complete amortization schedule giving how much of each of the 180 payments are going toward the principal and how much is interest.

   b. How much total interest will Soma be paying over the life of the loan?

c. Suppose at the very start of year 6 of the loan (right after the 60th payment), Soma notices that mortgage rates have drop and she finds out she can refinance at 3.75% for a 15-year loan.

i. How much will Soma still owe after her 60th payment? (Hence, how much will she have to finance?)

ii. Use Excel and a guess-and-check method to determine how much Soma's new monthly payment will be.

iii. How much total interest would Soma pay if she refinances? Include both interest from the first 5 years before refinancing and the last 15 after refinancing.

iv. Soma, having already taken a financial math course, knows that the longer the time length of the loan, the more she will pay in interest. So she does refinance, but when she does, she keeps paying her original payment of $2,256.84 per month. How much money does this save Soma over the course of the loan compared to her original arrangement?

Look Ahead

17. In a mortgage, a bank gives you a pile of money and then you repay it over time. What if we turned things around and you give the bank a pile of money and they will repay it to you over time. Of course, they are paying you interest now instead of the other way around. This setup is called an annuity. Usually annuities are for a long time, or even indefinitely, but we will just look at a short term one. Suppose you want to be paid $10,000 by the bank on January 1 of each year for the next 3 years. How much will you have to give the bank on January 1 of the year before your first payment to make this happen? We will assume the bank pays 3% effective annual interest. We will let P be the amount of money you initially put in the bank.

a. What will be the bank balance, in terms of P, 1 year after your deposit right before you get your $10,000 payment? How much will it be right after you get your $10,000 payment?

b. What will be the bank balance, in terms of P, 2 years after your deposit right before you get your $10,000 payment? How much will it be after you get your $10,000 payment?

    c. What will be the bank balance, in terms of P, 3 years after your deposit right before you get your \$10,000 payment? How much will it be after you get your \$10,000 payment?

    d. To make sure you put just enough money in the bank initially, you bank balance from part c after you got your payment should be 0. Set your expression from part c to 0 and solve for P. How much will you have to put in the bank to get your three annual \$10,000 payments?

SECTION 2.3. SINKING FUNDS

    In the last two sections, we explored loans primarily using an amortization approach—equal payments made over the life of the loan until it is paid off. Once the complete amortization schedule is available (say, using Excel), it is rather straightforward to solve most problems related to loan repayment (e.g., How much interest is paid over the course of the loan? How much principal or interest is in a particular payment?). However, not all loans are amortized. We saw how for interest-only and "no payments needed until the end" loans, a large lump-sum was due at the end of the loan term. This "lump sum" loan was a bit concerning for the borrower since it requires disciplined saving over the life of the loan in order to ensure that sufficient funds are saved to payback the lump sum. In this section we will explore strategies to save for a lump sum payment using a "sinking fund." Along the way, we'll learn a "shortcut" formula to calculate the future value (FV) of a sinking fund.

Learning Objectives

By the end of this section you should be able to
- Evaluate when a sinking fund may be advantageous or not advantageous as compared to a standard amortized loan.
- Determine the sinking fund payment size through a guess-and-check or PMT function approach in Excel.
- Use a formula to calculate the sinking fund payment size.

EXAMPLE 2.3. PAYING BACK A PERSONAL LOAN

When you were in the process of moving into your first apartment, buying a car, and starting your first job, you were short of cash. Rather than taking a conventional loan from a bank to put down a deposit on the apartment and buy a car, your parents gave you $10,000 and said they would like it paid back in 3 years. They said they didn't want/need interest on the money. You decided this was a nice option (interest free loan!) and went for it.

Think about it

What general strategy should you use so that you have $10,000 in 3 years?

Every month you should likely be putting some money into a savings account with the expressed purpose of accumulating enough money, so that in 3 years you will have the $10,000 to needed to pay back the loan. When a fixed amount of money is regularly saved in a dedicated account for a future purpose (often to pay back a debt/loan), it is called a sinking fund.

Definition

A **sinking fund** is a fund that receives regular payments from the borrower to accumulate value, so it can be used later for some other purpose—for example, against the principal on an interest-only loan. Sometimes the entire approach of an interest-only loan combined with a sinking fund is called the sinking fund approach to paying back a loan. Typically, sinking funds receive regular payments, at a fixed rate of interest with a goal of accumulating the principal balance at the end of the loan term.

Let's start with a relatively straightforward question—how much should you save in the account monthly so that you can accumulate the $10,000 after 3 years? One approximate approach is to take $10,000 and divide it by 36 (the number of months in 3 years), which is $277.78/ month.

Think about it

Is the actual amount you need to save each month more or less than $277.78?

The actual amount you need to save will end up being a little bit less than $277.78—if you put your money into an account earning interest!

If a savings account at a local bank pays 2.4% APR on their money, then we used **Chapter 2 Excel file** and a guess-and-check approach (or you could use the PMT function in Excel) to calculate that saving $268.18 each month will get you to your savings goal. (See Table 2.7.)

Table 2.7 Sinking Fund Account Chart

Month	Savings Account Balance on 1st of Month ($)	Interest Earned During Month at 2.4% APR ($)	Payment to Savings Account Made on 31st of Month ($)	New Savings Account Balance ($)
1	0	0	268.18	268.18
2	268.18	0.54	268.18	536.90
3	536.90	1.07	268.18	806.15
...	...	...	...	...
36	9712.57	19.43	268.18	10,000.17

So, that's not a real huge difference (less than $10 per month), but the interest rate is fairly low and the savings plan only takes place over 3 years. That said, the total interest earned over the entire 3-year period isn't completely inconsequential. We can find that the total interest earned (calculated either by summing the interest earned column in Excel or subtracting all the payments from the ending balance, $10,000 − $268.18 × 36) is $345.69.

Importantly, if you decided to pay your parents back directly month-to-month you would need to pay them $277.78 each month. This is an example of an important point, when interest rates are higher in the sinking fund than for the corresponding loan, it is advantageous to use the sinking fund instead of paying back the loan. Of course, the opposite is true also, as we'll now see.

Interest Rate Comparisons Between Sinking Funds and Amortized Loans

What if your parents were unable to make the $10,000 you needed so you went to a bank and took out a more conventional loan over a 3-year period at 3.6% APR. Using guess-and-check in Excel (or the PMT function; use **Chapter 2 Excel file**) you can find that the payment amount is $293.46. Note that this is higher than the interest-free loan payment amount of $277.78 you would have had to pay your parents monthly.

Should you use a sinking fund in this case to save money? More specifically, if you first capitalize the interest on your bank loan and just make one payment at the end of the 3 years (in practice, a bank may or may not allow you to do that), should you use a sinking fund to save money to pay off your loan balance in 3 years? Intuitively, since the interest rate in your savings account is lower (only 2.4%), hopefully you can see that the answer is no, but let's run the numbers to confirm.

Your loan balance will be $10,000(1 + 0.036/12)^{36} = $11,138.68$ at the end of 3 years. Using Excel, we find that this means we'll have to deposit $298.72 into your savings account each month to get to $11,138.68 after 3 years.

Notice that this is more than we would have to pay monthly if we paid the loan back directly ($298.72 > $293.46). As you might expect, if the interest rates on your savings account and the loan are the same, then the methods (paying loan directly or capitalizing interest and use sinking fund) are equivalent.

Key idea

The sinking fund and amortization approaches to loan repayment are equivalent when all accounts earn the same effective rate of interest.

Key idea

When a loan and the corresponding sinking fund that is used to repay the loan are at different interest rates, the two approaches are no longer equivalent. When the interest rate on a sinking fund is larger than the corresponding loan, the sinking fund approach is advantageous as compared to an amortized loan. When the interest rate is lower on the sinking fund, then the amortized loan is advantageous.

A Direct (Shortcut) Formula to Compute Sinking Fund Payment Sizes

Up until now we've focused on using a guess-and-check or PMT function approach to find payment sizes for sinking funds, but there is a shortcut "by-hand" formula which can find this value quickly. It's actually the formula that the PMT function is using.

To see why the formula makes sense, let's consider the sinking fund earning 2.4% APR to pay back the $10,000, interest-free loan after 3 years that we looked at earlier in this example. Recall how in the last chapter we used a "separate funds" approach to solving some interest problems—essentially, we pretended that each deposit was in its own account.

Here is how that approach works for this sinking fund, with a payment of $268.18 each month.

Month 1 payment accumulates to $268.18(1.002)^{35} = \$287.61$ at the end of 3 years

Month 2 payment accumulates to $268.18(1.002)^{34} = \$287.03$ at the end of 3 years

Month 3 payment accumulates to $268.18(1.002)^{33} = \$286.46$ at the end of 3 years

... And so on. You can sum up the 36 separate accumulated values and get to $10,000.

This example illustrates how you can directly find the size of a payment to a sinking fund, where is the effective interest rate per period and a payment of size P is made each period.

$$\text{Sinking Fund Goal} = P(1+i)^{n-1} + P(1+i)^{n-2} + \cdots + P(1+i) + P$$

Key idea

You can directly calculate the size of the Payment, P for a sinking fund by using the "separate accounts" approach.

But, even this equation is a bit tricky and time consuming to calculate. It turns out that this formula is a *geometric series* and can be written even more simply like this:

$$\text{Sinking Fund Goal} = (P)\left(\frac{(1+i)^n - 1}{i}\right) = (P)s_{\overline{n}|i}$$

There is a special word for of the last symbol in the above equation. The $s_{\overline{n}|i}$ (pronounced "s-angle-n") is the accumulated value of a sinking fund (account) into which $1 is deposited at the end of each of n periods where each period earns an effective rate of interest of i.

Definition

The **accumulated value** of a series of payments of $1 at effective interest rate i, over n payment periods, each payment happening at the end of the period, is equal to $s_{\overline{n}|i}$, pronounced "s-angle-n."

To see how we can use $s_{\overline{n}|i}$ to quickly find the monthly payment size for a sinking fund, recall that the Sinking Fund Goal was $10,000. The effective rate per month is $i = 0.002$ and n (the number of payment periods) is 36. This gives the following:

$$\text{Sinking Fund Goal} = \$10,000 = (P)s_{\overline{n}|i} = (P)\left(\frac{(1+0.002)^{36} - 1}{0.002}\right) = (P)37.28904$$

Solving for P means that, $P = \$268.18$, which is the same as we obtained when using guess-and-check (or PMT function) earlier.

EXPLORATION 2.3. BUYING A HOUSE WITH AN INTEREST-ONLY LOAN

In the early 2000s, prior to the housing crisis of 2008, many people took out interest-only loans on their homes. While these types of loans are rare due to their dangerous financial assumptions and risk, let's explore such a situation, and one way to improve the potentially devastating financial impact such a loan could have on personal finances.

1. Compute the monthly payment amount for a $100,000 *interest-only* mortgage (a loan used to purchase a home) at a 6% APR. *Hint: Start by computing the effective monthly rate.* Note in this loan scenario, no principal is paid back—only interest each month.

2. If the loan term is 15 years, how much:
   a. Total interest will have been paid over the course of the loan?

   b. Total principal will have been paid over the course of the loan?

   c. What will be the size of the loan due at the end of 15 years?

3. What expectations are there about the value of the house and the ability of the borrower to make payments over the 15-year period?

Let's assume that a young family, not knowing much about loans and excited to own their first home takes out the interest-only loan described above. Quickly, however, they realize that this approach carries with it the assumption that their house will not lose value and they will continue to have good jobs so that they can make payments. While they hope these two things are true, they decide to set up another fund, called a *sinking fund*, where they can accumulate money to pay off the loan balance at some point in the future.

Definition

A **sinking fund** is a fund that receives regular payments from the borrower to accumulate value, so it can be used later for some other purpose—for example, against the principal on an interest-only loan. Sometimes the entire approach of an interest-only loan combined with a sinking fund is called the sinking fund approach to paying back a loan. Typically, sinking funds receive regular payments, at a fixed rate of interest with a goal of accumulating the principal balance at the end of the loan term.

A Sinking Fund Savings Account

How much should the family set aside each month? Let's think about how to approach that question.

4. Using **Chapter 2 Excel file** and a guess-and-check approach (or PMT function), determine how much the family should deposit into their "sinking fund" savings account each month if they get the same interest on the savings account as they pay on the loan. They want to accumulate the loan balance in 15 years (a "typical" home loan length), and they make a deposit to the sinking fund monthly (starting one month from now)?

While the sinking fund approach is sometimes used, the amortization approach is more typical. For a 15-year loan for $100,000 at a 6%

nominal annual rate of interest with monthly compounding, we used Excel to find that the monthly payment is $843.86.

5. Compare the monthly payment for an amortized loan to the sum of the interest payment you found earlier plus the sinking fund payment amount you just computed above.

6. Explain why your answer to the previous question makes sense.

The sinking fund and amortization approaches are equivalent when the two funds have the same effective interest rate because each payment using the amortization approach consists of principal and interest. In the sinking-fund approach these two aspects of each payment are separated. However, as we saw earlier (in Section 1.2) the sum of a series of cash flows over time can be computed by valuing each cash flow separately.

Key idea

The sinking fund and amortization approaches to loan repayment are equivalent when all accounts earn the same effective rate of interest.

Sinking Funds With Different Terms

7. How would the monthly amount deposited in the sinking fund change if the family wanted to accumulate the principal in 10 years instead of 15?

8. How would the monthly amount deposited in the sinking fund change if the family could only earn 3% APR instead of 6%?

9. Given a choice, between an amortized loan at 6% and an interest-only loan at 6% with sinking fund at 3% over the same loan term, which would you choose? Why?

10. How would the monthly amount deposited in the sinking fund change if the family could earn 12% APR in their savings instead of 6%?

11. Given a choice, between an amortized loan at 6% and an interest-only loan at 6% with sinking fund at 12% over the same loan term, which would you choose? Why?

Key idea

When a loan and the corresponding sinking fund that is used to repay the loan are at different interest rates, the two approaches are no longer equivalent. When the interest rate on a sinking fund is larger than the corresponding loan, the sinking fund approach is advantageous as compared to an amortized loan. When the interest rate is lower on the sinking fund, then the amortized loan is advantageous.

A Direct (Shortcut) Formula to Compute Sinking Fund Payment Sizes

Up until now we've focused on using a guess-and-check approach to find payment sizes for sinking funds, but there is a shortcut formula which can find this value quickly. In fact, this is the formula used by the PMT function in Excel.

To see how this formula works, let's consider a very simple sinking fund that makes two payments—one at the end of each of the next 2 years into an account earning 5% effective annual interest, with a goal of accumulating $1,000 2 years from now.

12. Will the size of the payments into the sinking fund be more, less, or equal to $500? Why?

The equally sized payments will be less than $500 because the account will earn interest. But, how much less than $500? In the previous chapter, we learned a trick to solving some financial problems that treated each payment like its own separate account.

13. Let's say that each payment is of size P. How much will the first payment be worth at the end of the second year? *Hint: How many years of interest will it earn? Your answer will be something multiplied by P.*

14. How much will the second payment be worth at the end of the second year?

So, if we want $1,000 total after both payments are made, then we want $1.05P + P$ to be equal to $1,000.

15. Solve this equation to find P. This is the size of the payment to the sinking fund.

Key idea

You can directly calculate the size of the Payment, P for a sinking fund by using the "separate accounts" approach.

This mini-example illustrates how you can directly find the size of a payment to a sinking fund. Here is a more general version where P is the size of the equally sized payments which are made n times with an effective rate of interest of i each period. *Note:* We assume that the first payment is made at the end of the period and that the last payment is made at the same time we reach the sinking fund goal.

$$\text{Sinking Fund Goal} = P(1+i)^{n-1} + P(1+i)^{n-2} + \cdots + P(1+i) + P$$

But, even this equation is a bit tricky and time consuming to calculate. It turns out that this formula is a geometric series and can be written even more simply like this:

$$\text{Sinking Fund Goal} = (P)\left(\frac{(1+i)^n - 1}{i}\right) = (P)s_{\overline{n}|i}$$

There is a special word for of the last symbol in the above equation. The $s_{\overline{n}|i}$(pronounced "s-angle-n") is the accumulated value of a sinking fund (account) into which $1 is deposited at the end of each of n periods where each period earns an effective rate of interest of i.

Definition

The **accumulated value** of a series of payments of $1 at an effective interest rate of i, over n payment periods, with each payment happening at the end of the period, is equal to $s_{\overline{n}|i}$, pronounced "s-angle-n."

16. Use the formula above to confirm the monthly payment size for a sinking fund to accumulate $100,000 in 15 years at a 6% APR which you calculated earlier.
    a. What is the value of n?
    b. What is the value of i?
    c. What is the value of $s_{\overline{n}|i}$? Interpret this value.
    d. Now find the payment size, P, by solving the following equation:

$$\text{Sinking Fund Goal} = (P)s_{\overline{n}|i}$$

SUMMARY

In this section, we explored how sinking funds can be used to help structure savings accounts to get ready for a large "lump sum" payment in the future. Sinking funds are equivalent to amortized loans, when the interest rates are the same, but can be better (or worse) depending on whether the interest rate is better (or worse) on the sinking fund account than the loan. While a guess-and-check approach is possible using Excel, we learned a direct formula for the payment size of a sinking fund.

Notation and equation summary

$$\text{Sinking Fund Goal} = (P)\left(\frac{(1+i)^n - 1}{i}\right) = (P)s_{\overline{n}|i}$$

$s_{\overline{n}|i}$ is the FV of a payment of \$1 made at the end of each of n equally spaced periods earning an effective rate of i each period

---

HOMEWORK QUESTIONS: SECTION 2.3

Conceptual Questions

1. **True or False.** If the interest rates are the same, then a sinking fund approach to loan repayment and an amortization approach are equivalent.

2. **True or false.** If the interest rate on a sinking fund is 8% and the interest rate on the corresponding interest-only loan is 6%, the combined payments to the two funds will be less than an amortized loan at 6% with the same initial principal.

3. Three friends, Alli, Beth, and Carmen, are saving for retirement and are putting money into the Retirement Ready account for 30 years. The account pays 5% compounded monthly. Alli deposits P dollars at the end of every month. Beth deposits $12P$ dollars at the end of every year. Carmen deposits $3P$ dollars every quarter. Who will have the most amount of money after 30 years, or will they all be the same? Explain.

4. Explain what $s_{\overline{n}|i}$ (s-angle-n) means.

5. If you know the sinking fund goal and the value of $s_{\overline{n}|i}$, how do you compute the payment?

Practice Questions

6. You want \$20,000 available to you in 10 years. You find a money market account that pays 2% APR. How much will your monthly payment have to be to achieve your goal?

7. You would like to have \$40,000 set aside for your newborn son's college education. You find a college savings account that will earn 4% effective annual interest. How much will your annual payments have to be for you to have \$40,000 in the account in 18 years?

8. You are paying \$400 a month into a sinking fund that is earning 1.875% APR. How much will your account be worth in 5 years?

9. If a sinking fund earns 3% APR for 5 years, what is the value of $s_{\overline{n}|i}$ if there are monthly payments?

10. If $s_{\overline{n}|i} = 40.26$ and the sinking fund goal is \$30,000, what payment is needed?

Application Questions

11. Parents want \$40,000 available to them in 15 years to help pay for their young child's college education. They invest in college savings account that earns 3.625% APR for the 15-year period.
    a. Using Excel, use a guess-and-check method to determine how much they will have to invest each month to reach their goal.
    b. These parents understand that they will be earning more in the future so making a monthly payment of say \$500 now might be difficult, but in 10 years it may be easy. Using Excel and a guess-and-check method, find payments such that during the first 5 years they will put in P dollars per month, the next 5 years they will put in $1.2P$ dollars per month, and the last 5 years they will put in $1.5P$ dollars per month. What are the values of P, $1.2P$, and $1.5P$?

12. Suppose you have a business loan that will have a payment of $50,000 due in 3 years and your goal is to set up a sinking fund that will cover the cost.
    a. If you can put $1,000 per month into the sinking fund, what kind of interest rate do you need to obtain your goal?
    b. If you find a sinking fund that will pay 2.625% APR, how much will your monthly payments have to be in order to reach your goal?

13. You have a sinking fund goal of $20,000. If you deposit $500 a month into a sinking fund that earns 2.4% APR, how long will it take you to attain your goal? (*Hint:* Since the unknown value is in the exponent, you will have to use logarithms to solve this.)

14. Three friends, John, Jack, and Jill, are saving for retirement while their friend Jane is not (though she had some help from her parents). Let's see how they are investing.
    a. John deposits $1,200 at the end of every year for 40 years into a retirement account. Find the accumulated amount in the account at the end of year 40 assuming an annual effective rate of interest of 6%.
    b. Jack deposits $100 at the end of every month for 40 years into a retirement account. Find the accumulated amount in the account at the end of year 40 assuming an annual effective rate of interest of 6%.
    c. Jill deposits $100 at the end of every month for 40 years into a retirement account. Find the accumulated amount in the account at the end of year 40 assuming an annual nominal rate of interest of 6% compounded monthly.
    d. Provide intuitive explanations of the difference in accumulated value between John, Jack, and Jill's accounts.
    e. While still a child, Jane's parents deposit $2,000 a year at the end of each year for 10 years into an account earning 6% effective interest. Jane then leaves the money in the account for 40 years (never depositing into her retirement account) earning 6% effective interest per year. What is the accumulated value of Jane's retirement account?
    f. Compare Jane's account accumulation to John, Jack, and Jill. Who has the most saved for retirement? What fundamental savings principle is this illustrating?

15. One of the authors of this text had 85 months left on his mortgage when the mortgage rates dropped and made refinancing enticing. As we saw in this chapter, refinancing will sometimes increase the overall amount of money you pay out. But there are ways to use it to your advantage. You could take the amount you save each month in your monthly payment and invest that. If that investment earns a higher rate of interest, you can come out ahead. Here are the two scenarios the author faced. (A) Keep paying his monthly payment of $786 per month for 85 months or (B) Refinance his mortgage for 10 years (120 months) and pay $578 per month.

   a. How much will it cost him to pay off his home under these two scenarios?

   b. Let's look a little bit more into option B. If he refinances, he thought he could put the difference in his retirement account (which was a stock mutual fund) and he might make more money this way. If he invests the difference in his retirement fund, which has been earning about 10% per year (you can treat this as a nominal rate, compounded monthly), how much will this difference total up to after 120 months?

   c. Treating his total loan cost for option B as a negative and his retirement fund increase from part b as a positive, how much is he ahead or behind after the 120 months?

   d. Now let's go back to option A. Once he has paid off the mortgage, he can now take the entire $786 payment he was making and invest that in his retirement for the remaining 35 months (so we get to the same point in time as option B). Using the same parameters for a return on investment as in part b, how much will be added to his retirement by investing an additional $786 for 35 months?

   e. Treating his total loan cost for option A as a negative and his retirement fund increase from part d as a positive, how much is he ahead or behind after the 120 months?

   f. The author, about 8 years ago, chose option B. Did he make the correct decision?

Prove It! Questions

16. Earlier in the section we said that the sinking fund goal could be written in either two of the following ways.

$$\text{Sinking Fund Goal} = P(1+i)^{n-1} + P(1+i)^{n-2} + \cdots + P(1+i) + P \tag{2.1}$$

$$\text{Sinking Fund Goal} = (P)\left(\frac{(1+i)^n - 1}{i}\right) \tag{2.2}$$

Let's explore why this is true by transforming Eq. (2.1) into Eq. (2.2).

a. Factor P out of the right side of Eq. (2.1).

b. To help simply our notation through this we, substitute r in for $(1 + i)$ into your answer from part a. (We will change it back at the end.)

c. Multiply your expression from part b by $(1 - r)/(1 - r)$ (which is just a fancy form of 1). Simplify the numerator. Many of the terms in the numerator will cancel each other out.

d. Substitute $(1 + i)$ back in for r and simplify until it looks like the right side of Eq. (2.2) above.

17. We've done guess-and-check methods to calculate the monthly payment on a mortgage or other type of loan. Let's now come up with a formula for that since we are quite close to it with our Sinking Fund Goal formula. Paying into a sinking fund to reach a goal is quite similar to paying for a loan. A big difference, however, is that the sinking fund goal is an amount of money you want in the future while that value of a loan is an amount of money you want now (in the present). Therefore, we can call the sinking fund goal a FV and the loan amount a present value (PV). Because of interest earned or interest paid, these are not the same number. For an effective rate of interest, i, and n payment periods:

$$FV = PV(1+i)^n$$

You have seen this general formula before. But now let's put this into the sinking fund goal formula.

a. Since the sinking fund goal is a FV, substitute $PV(1+i)^n$ in for Sinking Fund Goal in the following formula and solve for P, the payment.

$$\text{Sinking Fund Goal} = (P)\left(\frac{(1+i)^n - 1}{i}\right)$$

b. Your answer to part a should have be one version of the formula for computing the payment needed to repay a loan. Explain (or show) how to do a little more simplification to transform your formula into the following more common version of the formula.

$$P = (PV)\left(\frac{i}{1 - (1+i)^{-n}}\right)$$

c. Use the formula from the previous question to find the monthly payment for a $200,000 mortgage for 30 years at 4.25% APR.

END OF CHAPTER SUMMARY

In this chapter, we explored fundamental behavior of loans. In particular, we saw that amortization is a way to pay off a loan over time by paying a mix of interest and principal each period. Amortized loans are standard for home loans, car loans and student loans, among other types, while interest only loans or loans receiving no payments (which capitalize interest) are sometimes used as well. We explored refinancing loans and so how this approach means that, just like at the beginning of the loan period, a high proportion of each payment will go toward interest instead of principal. Finally, we explored sinking funds which are a strategy for saving money in order to pay off a future debt (e.g., balance on an interest-only loan), and a shortcut formula for finding payment sizes.

END OF CHAPTER REVIEW PROBLEMS

(SOA EXAM FM SAMPLE QUESTIONS May 2005, Question 8)

1. A loan is being repaid with 25 annual payments of 300 each. With the 10th payment, the borrower pays an extra 1,000, and then repays the balance over 10 years with a revised annual payment. The effective rate of interest is 8%.

Calculate the amount of the revised annual payment.
A. 157
B. 183
C. 234
D. 257
E. 383

(SOA EXAM FM SAMPLE QUESTIONS November 2001, Question 12)

2. To accumulate 8,000 at the end of $3n$ years, deposits of 98 are made at the end of each of the first n years and 196 at the end of each of the next $2n$ years.

The annual effective rate of interest is i. You are given $(1 + i)^n = 2.0$. Determine i.
A. 11.25%
B. 11.75%
C. 12.25%
D. 12.75%
E. 13.25%

(SOA EXAM FM SAMPLE QUESTIONS Interest Theory, Question 80)

3. A student takes out a five-year loan of 1,000. Interest on the loan is at an annual effective interest rate of i.

At the end of each year, the student pays the interest due on the loan and makes a deposit of twice the amount of that interest payment into a sinking fund. The sinking fund credits interest at an annual effective rate of $0.8i$. The sinking fund will accumulate the amount needed to pay off the loan at the end of five years.
Calculate i.
A. 7.2%
B. 8.4%
C. 8.7%
D. 10.6%
E. 12.1%

(SOA EXAM FM SAMPLE QUESTIONS Interest Theory, Question 87)

4. An investor wishes to accumulate 5,000 in a fund at the end of 15 years. To accomplish this, she plans to make equal deposits of X at the end of each year for the first ten years. The fund earns an annual effective rate of 6% during the first ten years and 5% for the next five years.

Calculate X.
A. 224
B. 284
C. 297
D. 312
E. 379

(SOA EXAM FM SAMPLE QUESTIONS Interest Theory, Question 96)

5. An investor's retirement account pays an annual nominal interest rate of 4.2%, convertible monthly.

On January 1 of year y, the investor's account balance was X. The investor then deposited 100 at the end of every quarter. On May 1 of year $(y + 10)$, the account balance was $1.9X$.
Determine which of the following is an equation of value that can be used to solve for X.

A. $\dfrac{1.9X}{(1.0105)^{\frac{124}{3}}} + \sum_{k=1}^{42} \dfrac{100}{(1.0105)^{k-1}} = X$

B. $X + \sum_{k=1}^{42} \dfrac{100}{(1.0035)^{3(k-1)}} = \dfrac{1.9X}{(1.0035)^{\frac{124}{3}}}$

C. $X + \sum_{k=1}^{41} \dfrac{100}{(1.0035)^{3k}} = \dfrac{1.9X}{(1.0035)^{124}}$

D. $X + \sum_{k=1}^{41} \dfrac{100}{(1.0105)^{k-1}} = \dfrac{1.9X}{(1.0105)^{\frac{124}{3}}}$

E. $X + \sum_{k=1}^{42} \dfrac{100}{(1.0105)^{k-1}} = \dfrac{1.9X}{(1.0105)^{\frac{124}{3}}}$

(SOA EXAM FM SAMPLE QUESTIONS Interest Theory, Question 108)

6. You are given the following information about an eleven-year loan of
   L to be repaid by the sinking fund method:
   i. The sinking fund earns an annual effective interest rate of 4.70%.
   ii. Immediately following the seventh payment and deposit, the difference between what is owed to the lender on the loan and the
   accumulated value of the sinking fund is 6,241.
   Calculate the sinking fund deposit.
   A. 1,019
   B. 1,055
   C. 1,067
   D. 1,084
   E. 1,104

(SOA EXAM FM SAMPLE QUESTIONS May 2005, Question 2)

7. Lori borrows 10,000 for 10 years at an annual effective interest rate of
   9%. At the end of each year, she pays the interest on the loan and
   deposits the level amount necessary to repay the principal to a sinking
   fund earning an annual effective interest rate of 8%.

   The total payments made by Lori over the 10-year period is X.
   Calculate X.
   A. 15,803
   B. 15,853
   C. 15,903
   D. 15,953
   E. 16,003

(SOA FM EXAM SAMPLE QUESTIONS May 2001, Question 7)

8. Seth, Janice, and Lori each borrow 5,000 for five years at a nominal
   interest rate of 12%, compounded semi-annually. Seth has interest
   accumulated over the five years and pays all the interest and principal
   in a lump sum at the end of five years. Janice pays interest at the end
   of every six-month period as it accrues and the principal at the end of
   five years. Lori repays her loan with 10 level payments at the end of
   every six-month period.

Calculate the total amount of interest paid on all three loans.

A. 8,718
B. 8,728
C. 8,738
D. 8,748
E. 8,758

(SOA EXAM FM SAMPLE QUESTIONS May 2001, Question 4)

9. A 20-year loan of 20,000 may be repaid under the following two methods:

A. amortization method with equal annual payments at an annual effective rate of 6.5%

B. sinking fund method in which the lender receives an annual effective rate of 8% and the sinking fund earns an annual effective rate of j

Both methods require a payment of X to be made at the end of each year for 20 years. Calculate j.

A. $j \le 6.5\%$
B. $6.5\% < j \le 8.0\%$
C. $8.0\% < j \le 10.0\%$
D. $10.0\% < j \le 12.0\%$
E. $j > 12.0\%$

(SOA EXAM FM SAMPLE QUESTIONS May 2003, Question 15)

10. John borrows 1,000 for 10 years at an annual effective interest rate of 10%. He can repay this loan using the amortization method with payments of P at the end of each year. Instead, John repays the 1000 using a sinking fund that pays an annual effective rate of 14%. The deposits to the sinking fund are equal to P minus the interest on the loan and are made at the end of each year for 10 years.

Determine the balance in the sinking fund immediately after repayment of the loan.

A. 213
B. 218
C. 223
D. 230
E. 237

(SOA EXAM FM SAMPLE QUESTIONS November 2000, Question 48)

11. 12-year loan of 8,000 is to be repaid with payments to the lender of 800 at the end of each year and deposits of X at the end of each year into a sinking fund.

Interest on the loan is charged at an 8% annual effective rate. The sinking fund annual effective interest rate is 4%.

Calculate X.

A. 298
B. 330
C. 361
D. 385
E. 411

CHAPTER THREE

Annuities: Fundamentals of Regular Payments

Abstract

In the previous chapter, we learned about loans. Sinking funds are one way to pay back loans. To value a sinking fund, we considered a series of payments of similar size paid to a fund over a period of time, governed by a constant effective rate of interest. The sinking fund account is a type of annuity—a series of equally sized payments over time. In this chapter, we will focus in on annuities and learn more about how to calculate their present and future values, as well as give consideration to a perpetuity—an infinitely long string of payments.

Keywords: Annuity; perpetuity; sinking funds; present value; future value

SECTION 3.1. PERPETUITIES

If something goes on forever, we say it lasts in perpetuity. In financial circles, a perpetuity is a series of payments that goes on forever. How is this possible? We will explore that question and how to put a price tag on a perpetuity in this section. Perhaps surprisingly, it doesn't cost an infinite amount of money to buy a set of payments that goes on infinitely long.

Learning Objectives

By the end of this section, you should be able to

- Explain how it is possible to have an infinitely long set of equally sized payments (perpetuity) without having it cost you an infinitely large amount of money.
- Calculate the payment size, account balance (present value), or interest rate for a perpetuity if two of the three values are provided.

A Spiral Approach to Financial Mathematics.
DOI: https://doi.org/10.1016/B978-0-12-801580-3.00003-4
© 2018 Elsevier Inc.
All rights reserved.

EXAMPLE 3.1. LIVING ON THE INTEREST: PERPETUITIES IN RETIREMENT

As we've seen earlier in the course, if you start saving for retirement early enough, you can ensure you have enough money for your retirement. But, how much should you save by the time you retire?

Think about it

What information would you want to know in order to figure out how much you should try to have saved by the time you retire?

You'll probably want to know a whole variety of things like: At what age do you anticipate retiring? What do you anticipate wanting/needing your monthly (or annual income) to be? How long do most people live? How much "cushion" do you want in your plan? Do you plan to have money left over when you die to give away/leave to heirs?

Answers to these questions can help to clarify how much money will be needed for retirement. The question about how long people live is complex. Sophisticated methods that take into account the probability that someone dies at any given time are used by actuaries to provide retirement payments that are guaranteed to pay out as long as someone is alive (these are called whole life annuities) but require more sophisticated probability calculations.

Let's consider a simpler approach. Is there a way to guarantee that we will have enough money to live on each month as long as we live? While nothing in life is guaranteed, surprisingly, there is a way that gets pretty close.

Imagine that you have managed to accumulate $1 million by the time you retire (you must have started saving early—great work!) at age 65.

What if you immediately go out and buy a $1 million boat to sail around the world—how much money will you have left to live on? OK, so that doesn't work. What if you spend $100,000 the first year instead? That will leave you with $900,000. That's better than spending all the money in the first year!

Think about it

What if you continue spending $100,000/year for 10 years. How much money will you have left?

Tricky question. Did you think the answer was $0? Well, maybe. If you hid all $1 million under your mattress and then took out $100,000 per year for 10 years, then yes, you would be broke in 10 years. But, what if you invested your money? If you invested your money, then the money sitting in the investment would be earning interest while you spent the money you withdrew. This means that if you invested the $1 million at some interest rate, then you won't run out of money in 10 years if you spend $100,000/year—it will be longer than that. How much longer? We use the account chart in Table 3.1 to figure this out. We'll assume you can earn a 5% effective annual interest on your retirement funds. We used **Chapter 3 Excel file** to assist in creating this table.

Table 3.1 Account Chart If You Invest $1 Million at 5% Interest With $100,000 Withdrawals at the End of Each Year

Year	1 Jan ($)	31 Dec ($)	After $100,000 Withdrawal ($)
1	1,000,000	1050,000	950,000
2	950,000	997,500	897,500
3	897,500	942,375	842,375
4	842,375	884,493.80	784,493.80
5	784,493.80	823,718.40	723,718.40
6	723,718.40	759,904.40	659,904.40
7	659,904.40	692,899.60	592,899.60
8	592,899.60	622,544.60	522,544.60
9	522,544.60	548,671.80	448,671.80
10	448,671.80	471,105.40	371,105.40
11	371,105.40	389,660.60	289,660.60
12	289,660.60	304,143.70	204,143.70
13	204,143.70	214,350.90	114,350.90
14	114,350.90	120,068.40	20,068.40
15	20,068.40	210,71.82	− 78,928.20

From the results in Table 3.1, we can see you don't run out of money until year 15. While that's not great if you live past age 80, this is better than the "hide the money under the mattress" strategy which only got you to age 75!

What if you want your $1 million retirement savings to last longer? Don't spend as much each year! Obviously, if you didn't spend anything, your retirement savings would continue to grow and grow and grow, but that's not practical—you will need money to eat, pay health insurance, etc. But, what if you only spent $24,000/year—that works out to be just $2,000/month. Maybe, if you have your house paid off, that's just enough for food, health insurance, food, property taxes, and a few other essentials. Look at what happens to your money then in Table 3.2.

Table 3.2 Account Chart If You Invest $1 Million at 5% Interest With $24,000 Withdrawals at the End of Each Year

Year	1 Jan ($)	31 Dec ($)	After $24,000 Withdrawal ($)
1	1,000,000	1,050,000	1,026,000
2	1,026,000	1,077,300	1,053,300
3	1,053,300	1,105,965	1,081,965
4	1,081,965	1,136,063	1,112,063
5	1,112,063	1,167,666	1,143,666
6	1,143,666	1,200,850	1,176,850
7	1,176,850	1,235,692	1,211,692
8	1,211,692	1,272,277	1,248,277
9	1,248,277	1,310,691	1,286,691
10	1,286,691	1,351,025	1,327,025
11	1,327,025	1,393,376	1,369,376
12	1,369,376	1,437,845	1,413,845
13	1,413,845	1,484,538	1,460,538
14	1,460,538	1,533,564	1,509,564
15	1,509,564	1,585,043	1,561,043
...	...	...	...

So, if you only withdraw $24,000/year, what is happening to your account balance over time? It is growing larger, and larger, and larger. This means that if you only spend $24,000/year, when you die you will have more than $1 million in the bank. That may be what you want to do, but if $100,000/year makes you run out and $24,000/year makes you grow indefinitely, is there some "sweet spot" of withdrawals so that you never run out, but that your balance doesn't grow indefinitely either? Phrased another way, what is the maximum amount that you can withdraw each year so that you never run out of money—no matter how long you live?

The key to answering this question is to think about how much interest you earn each year. Table 3.3 shows your account balance if you withdraw $50,000/year—exactly how much interest you earned that year.

Table 3.3 Account Chart If You Invest $1 Million at 5% Interest With $50,000 Withdrawals at the End of Each Year

Year	1 Jan ($)	31 Dec ($)	After $50,000 Withdrawal ($)
1	1,000,000	1,050,000	1,000,000
2	1,000,000	1,050,000	1,000,000
3	1,000,000	1,050,000	1,000,000
4	1,000,000	1,050,000	1,000,000
5	1,000,000	1,050,000	1,000,000
6	1,000,000	1,050,000	1,000,000
7	1,000,000	1,050,000	1,000,000
8	1,000,000	1,050,000	1,000,000
9	1,000,000	1,050,000	1,000,000
10	1,000,000	1,050,000	1,000,000
11	1,000,000	1,050,000	1,000,000
12	1,000,000	1,050,000	1,000,000
13	1,000,000	1,050,000	1,000,000
14	1,000,000	1,050,000	1,000,000
15	1,000,000	1,050,000	1,000,000

Definition

A **perpetuity** is a series of payments that continues forever. When organizations or individuals "live off the interest"—never spending any of the balance—this amounts to a perpetuity.

In general, the key idea is to live off the interest and never touch the main balance in the account (the principal). This means that a general equation for the size of the annual payment that can be obtained from a perpetuity is

Perpetuity payment (P) = account balance $(B) \times$ interest rate (i)

In this case, this means that

Perpetuity payment (P) = $\$1,000,000 \times 0.05 = \$50,000$

If you're thinking, "haven't we already done this?" you'd be partially correct. Earlier, we explored interest-only loans. In an interest-only loan, the borrower is only paying off the interest, while in a perpetuity, you are only spending the interest. Similar ideas, but in one case you have a loan and in the other an investment.

Rearranging this formula means that you can quickly and easily find the account balance needed for any payment size and interest rate.

$$\frac{\text{Perpetuity payment } (P)}{\text{Interest rate } (i)} = \text{account balance } (B)$$

So, if you'd like to know how large of a retirement savings you need if you want to have an income of $\$60,000$/year in retirement and you anticipate being able to earn 4% effective annually, then you need to have $\$60,000/0.04 = \$1,500,000$ when you retire.

Before we finish, let's quickly address one more practical consideration. First, it is not impossible to get a guaranteed, fixed rate of interest, but it may be tough. If you invest your retirement savings in something like the stock market—some years you may have interest income, some years not. Other investment strategies (e.g., bonds—which we'll explore in a future chapter) may be a more practical option. If you have a variable rate of interest investment, you can still have something act like a perpetuity by trying to never spend anything but the interest—it's just that, in this case, in some years, you'll have more money to spend—and in some years, less.

EXPLORATION 3.1. LIVING ON THE INTEREST: PERPETUITIES AT COLLEGE

A college advancement (fundraising) office is trying to improve the long-term financial viability of the college by working with potential donors on their estate plans. When the potential donor passes away, a large sum of money will be transferred to the college endowment (a large, financial investment fund). A particular donor wishes their money to be used to support student scholarships.

1. The donor anticipates leaving a $400,000 gift to the college and the money will be invested for 1 year at 5% effective interest (annually) before any scholarships are paid out. Using this money, how many $5,000 scholarships can the college pay out (if they use the entire investment)?

2. If you are a student who receives one of these $5,000 scholarships next year, what practical concern might you have about this scholarship money? *Hint: Think about your tuition bill the following year.*

3. To plan ahead so that scholarship money is available over multiple years, the college decides to issue $5,000 scholarships for 2 years. If the college wants to offer the same number of scholarships 1 year from now and then the same number again 2 years from now, how many scholarships can they offer? Note: Whatever money they don't spend this year can continue to be invested in an account earning 5% effective annual interest in the meantime. *Hint: You can solve this using a guess-and-check approach or a direct algebraic formula/equation. Either way you will end up with a fraction of a scholarship.*

4. If you take the number of $5,000 scholarships paid out this year and add it to the number of $5,000 scholarships paid out next year (these are the same number!), how many total $5,000 scholarships (year 1 plus year 2) will be paid out?

5. Why is your answer to the previous question more than what you obtained when all the scholarship money was paid out in the first year?

6. If the college decides to issue scholarships of $5,000 per year for 4 years with the money invested at 5% effective annually, make an educated guess as to the number of scholarships the college can give out annually. Use a spreadsheet program or calculator to find the exact value (Note: Your answer will include a fraction of a scholarship!).

7. How will the number of scholarships the college can pay out each year change if the college increases the length of time that it can pay out scholarships?

Obviously, the less money the college spends out of the donation now (fewer scholarships per year), the more money sits in the bank and earns interest and the more (total) scholarship money can be paid out over time. Colleges and many organizations often like to maximize the duration with which a gift can "keep giving" to the college. One way to do this would be to leave the money in the bank forever and never spend any of it. However, then the college is not recognizing any financial benefits of the gift. An alternative is to set up a **perpetuity**—a number of scholarships that will stay constant over time—forever.

8. How many $5,000 scholarships can the college pay out each year indefinitely assuming a 5% effective rate of interest? Assume now that the first scholarship money is paid out after the account has had one full year to earn interest. *Hint: How much money should be left in the bank be each year in order for the number of scholarships to stay the same forever?*

Each year the account will earn $20,000 of interest. If the college only uses the interest ($20,000/year) to pay out scholarships, then the balance in the account will always be $400,000. This means that if the college can earn 5% effective interest annually, then they can pay out four scholarships of $5,000 indefinitely as well.

Definition

A **perpetuity** is a series of payments that continues forever. When organizations or individuals "live off the interest"—never spending any of the balance—this amounts to a perpetuity.

In general, the key idea is to live off the interest and never touch the main balance in the account (the principal). This means that a general equation for the size of the annual payment that can be obtained from a perpetuity is

Perpetuity payment (P) = account balance $(B) \times$ interest rate (i)

If you're thinking, "Haven't we already done this?" you'd be partially correct. Earlier, we explored interest-only loans. In an interest-only loan, the borrower is only paying off the interest, while in a perpetuity, you are only spending the interest. Similar ideas, but in one case you have a loan and in the other an investment.

9. If a donor leaves $600,000 to the college, how many annual $5,000 scholarships can be paid out in perpetuity? How would this change if the interest rate was only 2.5% effective annually? You may wish to use **Chapter 3 Excel file** to help you answer this question.

10. A donor is curious how large of a gift they need to give in order to yield ten $5,000 scholarships per year in perpetuity (forever). Assume in this case that the account earns interest for exactly one full year before any scholarships are awarded and that the effective rate of interest is 5% annually. How much does the donor need to give?

Rearranging the formula, we showed earlier, you can find the account balance needed for any given payment size and interest rate. This means that a general equation for the size of the annual payment that can be obtained from a perpetuity is

$$\frac{\text{Perpetuity payment } (P)}{\text{Interest rate } (i)} = \text{account balance } (B)$$

11. If the goal is to pay out ten $5,000 scholarships per year, will the account balance need to increase or decrease if the interest rate is only 2.5% annually instead of 5%? Why?

What about investments in variable interest accounts? Practically speaking, investments of endowed funds (what colleges usually call the account balance for a perpetuity) are often in variable interest investments. For example, investments could be in the stock market, real estate, bonds, etc. In this case, it is harder to predict how many scholarships are available each year—since it will be dependent upon the actual interest rate of the investments. One common strategy is to use a moving average of recent interest rates, but being willing to change the number of scholarships available from year to year somewhat. Variable interest rates are practically important but are generally beyond what we discuss in this text.

> ## SUMMARY

One strategy to have a steady stream of payments continue indefinitely is to "live off the interest." For a fixed interest rate over time, the payments will remain the same size over time—a situation which we call a perpetuity. In the next section, we will explore how to have same sized (level) payments continue for a finite amount of time, which is called an annuity.

Notation and equation summary

$$\frac{\text{Perpetuity payment } (P)}{\text{Interest rate } (i)} = \text{account balance } (B)$$

Perpetuity payment (P) = account balance $(B) \times$ interest rate (i)

> ## HOMEWORK QUESTIONS: SECTION 3.1

Conceptual Questions

1. A large amount of money is deposited to a fund and earns interest each year.
   a. If the amount of money withdrawn each year exceeds the interest earned, the fund will eventually_____.
   b. If the amount of money withdrawn each year is exactly the interest earned, the fund balance will_____.
   c. If the amount of money withdrawn each year is less than the interest earned, the fund balance will_____.

2. Part b of the previous question describes a_____.

3. A perpetuity is set up so that it generates $40,000 payments each year. To keep it a perpetuity, what happens to the annual payments if the interest rate:
   a. Drops?
   b. Increases?

4. Interest-only loans and perpetuities.
    a. You take out an interest-only loan of $100,000 at 5% effective annual interest. How large is your annual payment?
    b. You deposit $100,000 into a fund earning 5% effective annual interest. How much can you take out annually to make the account pay in perpetuity?
    c. Explain the relationship between an interest-only loan and a perpetuity.

5. Suppose you set up a perpetuity for retirement where you take out a set amount of money at the end of each year and you do so for 5 years. At the beginning of the sixth year, you decide you don't want to wait until the end of the year for your money and decide to take out 1/12 of that set amount of money at the end of each month. Is this still a perpetuity? Why or why not?

Practice Questions

6. If the account balance in an endowed scholarship fund set up as a perpetuity is $1,500,000 and the annual effective interest rate is 4%, how much money can be given in scholarships each year?

7. If the account balance in an endowed scholarship fund set up as a perpetuity is $2,400,000 and $105,600 is given annually in scholarships from this fund, what interest rate is the fund earning?

8. What is the account balance in an endowed scholarship fund set up as a perpetuity if the annual effective interest rate is 3.2% and the fund pays out $80,000 in scholarships each year?

9. You have $800,000 saved up for retirement and you have it in an account that is earning 5.125% effective annual interest. How many annual withdrawals of $80,000 can you take until the money is all gone? Assume you withdraw money at the beginning of the year (so your initial investment doesn't have any time to grow before the first payment) and include the last payment even though it may not equal the entire $80,000.

10. Repeat the previous question, but assume the first withdrawal comes after the money sits in the account for a year earning interest.

Application Questions

11. If an organization has a $20,000 endowment, how much can the organization spend each year to keep the endowment its current size (yielding payments in perpetuity)? Assume yearly withdrawals from the fund.

    a. If the effective annual interest rate is 4%.

    b. If the effective annual interest rate is 7.5%.

12. An individual is planning for retirement and hopes to save up a large enough "nest egg" so that she can live on the interest alone each year until she dies and then leave the nest egg for her children. Find the value of the nest egg (how much she should have saved for retirement) under the following scenarios.

    a. 3% effective annual interest, yearly withdrawals, annual living expenses of $50,000 per year

    b. 6% effective annual interest, yearly withdrawals, annual living expenses of $50,000 per year

    c. Part a with expenses of $75,000 per year

    d. Part b with expenses of $75,000 per year

13. Recall the previous question about the retiree that wants a large enough nest egg so she can live on just interest from it. She plans to take out $50,000 each year for expenses, but she is doing it monthly, so she is withdrawing $50,000/12 = $4,167.67 per month. Find the value of the nest egg (how much she should have saved for retirement) under the following scenarios.

    a. 3% effective annual interest with monthly withdrawals

    b. 6% effective annual interest with monthly withdrawals

    c. Monthly withdrawals and a nominal annual interest rate of 3% compounded monthly

    d. Monthly withdrawals and a nominal annual interest rate of 6% compounded monthly

14. You have $900,000 saved up for retirement and you have it in an account that is earning 4.75% effective annual interest. Your first withdrawal will be at the end of the first year.

    a. If you withdraw $75,000 each year, how long will your investment last?

    b. If you withdraw $60,000 each year, how long will your investment last?

    c. If you withdraw $45,000 each year, how long will your investment last?

    d. How much can you withdraw each year for your investment to last forever?

15. You want to set up a perpetuity such that you will be paid $50,000 per year and you will make your first withdrawal at the end of the first year.

    a. If you find an account that earns 5% annual effective interest, how much will you have to deposit in this account?

    b. If you find an account that earns 4% annual effective interest, how much will you have to deposit in this account?

    c. If you find an account that earns 5% annual effective interest, but you predict that it will drop to 4% annual effective interest in 10 years, how much will you have to deposit in this account?

Looking Ahead

16. Suppose your parents are looking ahead toward retirement and since you are studying financial mathematics, they are seeking your advice. They would like to withdraw $75,000 from their retirement account at the end of each year. Currently, that account is earning about 6% effective annual interest per year and you will assume that it will continue to do so.

    a. How much should their total investment in the retirement fund be so it will be a perpetuity?

    b. How much should their total investment in the retirement fund be so it lasts 35 years? (You might want to set up an Excel spreadsheet to help you determine the answer.)

    c. How much should their total investment in the retirement fund be so it lasts 25 years?

    d. How much should their total investment in the retirement fund be so it lasts 20 years?

SECTION 3.2. BASIC ANNUITIES

In the previous section, we explored perpetuities—a series of equally sized payments that continues indefinitely because only the interest earned on the fund balance is used each year, keeping the fund balance constant over time. However, if the series of payments does not continue indefinitely, the stream of payments is known as an annuity. We will consider annuities in this section.

Learning Objectives

- Be able to explain the differences and similarities between an annuity and a perpetuity.
- Use an Excel spreadsheet to guess-and-check your way to identify the initial account balance, payment size, and/or interest rate given two of the three values.
- Use the formula for the present value of an annuity to calculate present value or payment size of an annuity.

EXAMPLE 3.2. PLANNING FOR RETIREMENT

In the "Example 3.1. Living on the Interest: Perpetuities in Retirement" section, we saw how you could use a perpetuity to generate an infinite set of equally sized payments, enabling you to live on the interest and have a nice "lump sum" left over when you are done. For example, if you were able to have saved $1 million when you retired at age 65 and you were able to get a 5% effective annual return on your investment, then you could have $50,000 payouts annually (the interest on $1 million) indefinitely and have a $1 million lump sum left over when you die.

However, we also saw that if you withdrew more than $50,000/year, the funds would eventually run out. We set up an account chart and found that $100,000 annual withdrawals would "run out" in year 15 (see Table 3.4 and **Chapter 3 Excel file**). An annuity is the name for a series of (typically) equally sized (level), equally spaced payments which eventually stop. A perpetuity is similar, except the payments continue on indefinitely.

Table 3.4 Account Chart If You Invest $1 Million at 5% Interest With $100,000 Withdrawals at the End of Each Year

Year	1 Jan ($)	31 Dec ($)	After $100,000 Withdrawal ($)
1	1,000,000.00	1,050,000.00	950,000.00
2	950,000.00	997,500.00	897,500.00
3	897,500.00	942,375.00	842,375.00
4	842,375.00	884,493.80	784,493.80
5	784,493.80	823,718.40	723,718.40
6	723,718.40	759,904.40	659,904.40
7	659,904.40	692,899.60	592,899.60
8	592,899.60	622,544.60	522,544.60
9	522,544.60	548,671.80	448,671.80
10	448,671.80	471,105.40	371,105.40
11	371,105.40	389,660.60	289,660.60
12	289,660.60	304,143.70	204,143.70
13	204,143.70	214,350.90	114,350.90
14	114,350.90	120,068.40	20,068.40
15	20,068.40	21,071.82	− 78,928.20

Definition

An **annuity** is a series of often equally sized (level) payments which continue for a finite amount of time. Unless otherwise specified, you can assume that the payments are equally sized and spaced equally apart.

You figure that it's highly unlikely that you will live past age 100. How much can you withdraw annually if you have $1 million in savings at age 65 and invest it at 5% effective annually? Assume you make equally sized withdrawals at the end of each year. We used a guess-and-check approach in Excel and found that you can withdraw $61,071.71 annually until you are 100 years old before you run out (see Table 3.5).

Table 3.5 Account Chart If You Invest $1 Million at 5% Interest With $61,070.71 Withdrawals at the End of Each Year

Year	Age	Beginning of Year Balance ($)	Interest ($)	Withdrawal ($)	End of Year Balance ($)
1	65	1,000,000.00	50,000.00	61,071.71	988,928.29
2	66	988,928.29	49,446.41	61,071.71	977,302.99

(Continued)

Table 3.5 (Continued)

Year	Age	Beginning of Year Balance ($)	Interest ($)	Withdrawal ($)	End of Year Balance ($)
3	67	977,302.99	48,865.15	61,071.71	965,096.43
4	68	965,096.43	48,254.82	61,071.71	952,279.55
5	69	952,279.55	47,613.98	61,071.71	938,821.81
6	70	938,821.81	46,941.09	61,071.71	924,691.19
7	71	924,691.19	46,234.56	61,071.71	909,854.04
8	72	909,854.04	45,492.70	61,071.71	894,275.04
9	73	894,275.04	44,713.75	61,071.71	877,917.08
10	74	877,917.08	43,895.85	61,071.71	860,741.22
11	75	860,741.22	43,037.06	61,071.71	842,706.57
12	76	842,706.57	42,135.33	61,071.71	823,770.19
13	77	823,770.19	41,188.51	61,071.71	803,886.99
14	78	803,886.99	40,194.35	61,071.71	783,009.63
15	79	783,009.63	39,150.48	61,071.71	761,088.40
16	80	761,088.40	38,054.42	61,071.71	738,071.11
17	81	738,071.11	36,903.56	61,071.71	713,902.96
18	82	713,902.96	35,695.15	61,071.71	688,526.40
19	83	688,526.40	34,426.32	61,071.71	661,881.01
20	84	661,881.01	33,094.05	61,071.71	633,903.35
21	85	633,903.35	31,695.17	61,071.71	604,526.80
22	86	604,526.80	30,226.34	61,071.71	573,681.43
23	87	573,681.43	28,684.07	61,071.71	541,293.79
24	88	541,293.79	27,064.69	61,071.71	507,286.77
25	89	507,286.77	25,364.34	61,071.71	471,579.40
26	90	471,579.40	23,578.97	61,071.71	434,086.66
27	91	434,086.66	21,704.33	61,071.71	394,719.29
28	92	394,719.29	19,735.96	61,071.71	353,383.54
29	93	353,383.54	17,669.18	61,071.71	309,981.01
30	94	309,981.01	15,499.05	61,071.71	264,408.35
31	95	264,408.35	13,220.42	61,071.71	216,557.06
32	96	216,557.06	10,827.85	61,071.71	166,313.20
33	97	166,313.20	8,315.66	61,071.71	113,557.15
34	98	113,557.15	5,677.86	61,071.71	58,163.30
35	99	58,163.30	2,908.16	61,071.71	− 0.25

A Direct (Shortcut) Formula to Compute Account Balances and Payment Sizes for Annuities

While the approach using Excel arrives at the correct answer using a guess-and-check approach, there is a shortcut formula, which can value annuities quite quickly. Recall that in Section 2.3, we valued sinking funds using a shortcut formula.

The approach here is quite similar—we will first treat each withdrawal as a separate account.

Account 1. First withdrawal of $61,071.71 (1 year from now).

(Retirement savings needed to make first payment) $\times (1 + 0.05)$

$= \$61,071.71$

Thus, you need to have $\$61,071.71/(1 + 0.05) = \$58,163.53$ today to have $61,071.71 1 year from now.

Account 2. Second withdrawal of $61,071.71 (2 years from now).

(Retirement savings needed to make first payment) $\times (1+0.05)^2$

$= \$61,071.71$

Thus, you need to have $\$61,071.71/(1 + 0.05)^2 = \$55,393.84$ today to have $61,071.71 2 years from now.

Account 3. Third withdrawal of $61,071.71 (3 years from now).

(Retirement savings needed to make first payment) $\times (1+0.05)^3$

$= \$61,071.71$

Thus, you need to have $\$61,071.71/(1 + 0.05)^3 = \$52,756.04$ today to have $61,071.71 3 years from now.

. . ..

So, to calculate how much you need to have today, you simply add up all of the amounts you need in each account today, in order to have enough later to make each payment.

(Retirement savings needed today to make all 35 payments)

$$= \frac{\$61,071.71}{(1 + 0.05)} + \frac{\$61,071.71}{(1+0.05)^2} + \frac{\$61,071.71}{(1+0.05)^3} + \ldots + \frac{\$61,071.71}{(1+0.05)^{35}}$$

This is still quite tedious to compute, but it turns out that this formula can be shortened by recognizing that it is a geometric series.

In particular, this means that

(Retirement savings needed today to make all 35 payments)

$$= \frac{\$61,071.71}{(1+0.05)} + \frac{\$61,071.71}{(1+0.05)^2} + \frac{\$61,071.71}{(1+0.05)^3} + \ldots + \frac{\$61,071.71}{(1+0.05)^{35}}$$

$$= \$61,071.71 \left(\frac{1 - \left(1/(1+0.05)\right)^{35}}{0.05} \right) = \$1,000,000.05$$

While it's kind of a messy and complicated formula, it's certainly quite quick compared to calculating each payment separately or using a guess-and-check approach in a spreadsheet. (You will be guided through how this shortcut formula can be derived in the exercises.)

A more general version of this formula for any interest rate, i, number of payments, n, and payment size, P is

$$\text{Amount needed today} = P a_{\overline{n}|i} = P \left(\frac{1 - \left(1/(1+i)\right)^n}{i} \right)$$

In this formula, the symbol $a_{\overline{n}|i}$ represents the present value of a series of payments of 1 over n periods at an effective interest rate of i each period.

Definition

The **present value** of a series of payments of 1 at an effective interest rate of i, over n payment periods, with each payment happening at the end of the period, is equal to $a_{\overline{n}|i}$, pronounced "a-angle-n." If $n = \infty$, then this is a perpetuity.

Key idea

$a_{\overline{n}|i}$ is used for present value and $s_{\overline{n}|i}$ is used for future value.

Suppose instead of getting $61,071.71 payments for 35 years, you would like to get $75,000 payments for 20 years (we will still assume 5% effective annual interest). We can calculate how much we would need using the shortcut formula.

$$\text{Amount needed today} = P a_{\overline{n}|i} = P\left(\frac{1 - \left(1/(1+i)\right)^n}{i}\right)$$

$$= \$75,000\left(\frac{1 - \left(1/(1+0.05)\right)^{20}}{0.05}\right) = \$934,665.78$$

Essentially, the tradeoff between slightly higher payments (\$75,000) but a shorter amount of time (20 years vs 35 years) yields a retirement plan that needs a bit less than \$1 million (\$935k) at age 65.

Discount Factor

In this section, we've been looking at the *present value* of an annuity—how much we would have to invest now (in the present) to receive a series of equally sized payments. In general, the *discount factor* is a convenient way of expressing an interest rate when thinking about present values.

Definition

The **discount factor**, represented by the Greek letter nu (v), but sometimes called "v" in practice, is the present value of \$1 paid in 1 year at an effective annual rate of interest, i. Thus, $v = 1/(1 + i)$ since $v(1 + i) = 1$.

So, for an interest rate of 5% effective, annually, the discount factor is $1/1.05 = 0.952381$. In other words, you need slightly more than \$0.95 today to have \$1 one year from now at 5% effective annual interest.

We can use the discount factor to quickly compute how much we need today to have any specific amount 1 year (or period) from now, by taking the future value and multiplying it by the discount factor. For example, if our investment will earn 5% annual effective interest and we want \$70,000 one year from now, simply compute $\$70,000v = \$70,000(0.952381) = \$66,666.67$.

This idea generalizes further to find the amount needed today for any future amount at any future time. For example, if we want \$70,000 five years from now, this is simply $\left(\$70,000/(1+i)^5\right) = \$70,000v^5 = \$70,000(0.952381)5 = \$54,846.83$.

Key idea

The present value of a future payment of size P, n periods in the future, in an account earning an effective interest rate i (and corresponding discount factor is $v = 1/(1 + i)$) is present value $= P/(1+i)^n = Pv^n$.

We can rewrite the formula for the present value of annuity in terms of the discount factor as well.

$$\text{Amount needed today} = Pa_{\overline{n}|i} = P\left(\frac{1 - \left(1/(1+i)\right)^{n}}{i}\right) = P\left(\frac{1 - v^{n}}{i}\right)$$

EXPLORATION 3.2. USING A LIFE INSURANCE PAYOUT AS A BASIC ANNUITY

To plan for his family's future in the event he passes away, John considers buying life insurance but doesn't know how much he needs. John goes through the following thought process:

a. He would like to buy enough insurance so that his wife and children can replace his income (currently $60,000 per year) for 20 years after his death.

b. He figures by that time (20 years after his death) his children will have grown up and his wife will have had opportunity to seek a higher paying job than she currently has to make up for the lost income and/ or adjust her lifestyle accordingly.

c. He figures his wife/children will invest the lump-sum insurance payout at 5% effective annual interest and make annual withdrawals of the same amount for 20 years, starting 1 year after the insurance money is paid.

Before we help John figure out how much life insurance he needs, let's consider a simpler problem to develop your intuition and see how to approach the problem.

1. How much insurance does John need if he wants the $60,000 payments to continue in perpetuity and he assumes the money is invested at 5% effective annual interest?

2. How much insurance does John need if he only assumes a 3% effective annual interest rate?

John determines that while $1.2–$2 million in life insurance would be nice, it will be quite expensive to buy that much insurance now and is probably more than his family/wife need.

3. Imagine if John only wants enough insurance so that his family receives two payments of $60,000. How much insurance should he purchase if the effective annual interest rate is 5%? Note: The payments are of equal size occurring at the end of year 1 and the end of year 2.

These two equally sized payments of $60,000 payments are an example of an annuity.

Definition

An **annuity** is a series of often equally sized (level) payments which continue for a finite amount of time. Unless otherwise specified, you can assume that the payments are equally sized and spaced equally apart.

---

4. Set up an Excel spreadsheet (you may wish to start with **Chapter 3 Excel file**) to determine how much life insurance John should purchase if he wishes his family to be able to get equal sized payments from the account for 20 years, assuming a 5% effective interest rate.

A Direct (Shortcut) Formula to Compute Account Balances and Payment Sizes for Annuities

While the approach using Excel arrives at the correct answer using a guess-and-check approach, there is a shortcut formula which can value annuities quite quickly. Recall that in Section 2.3, we valued sinking funds using a shortcut formula. The approach here is quite similar—we will first treat each payment to John's family as a separate account.

Let's start by going back to the case where John only wants $60,000 paid out twice to his family—once a year after his death, and once 1 year after that.

The "trick" to the direct approach is to think of each of the two payments that John wants as a separate account.

5. *First payment.* How much insurance does John need if he wants a payment of $60,000 paid 1 year from now and the money earns 5% effective annual interest for the year?

6. *Second payment.* How much insurance does John need if he wants a payment of $60,000 paid 2 years from now, and the money earns 5% effective annual interest for both years? Will this amount be larger or smaller than the amount needed to make the first payment? Why?

7. Using your answers from the previous two questions, how much total insurance does John need when he dies to have enough money to pay out $60,000/year for 2 years?

We can write out the work you just did in the previous questions as an equation

(Insurance needed to make first payment) $\times (1 + 0.05) = \$60,000$

(Insurance needed to make second payment) $\times (1 + 0.05)^2 = \$60,000$

Rearranging these formulas and combing gives this

$$\text{Total insurance needed} = \frac{\$60,000}{1 + 0.05} + \frac{\$60,000}{(1+0.05)^2}$$

8. Following this same approach (separating out the payments into separate "accounts" and adding them together), write down an equation for how much insurance John needs today to make 20 years' worth of $60,000 annual payments. You don't need to find the sum of the terms in your equation!

Obviously, this equation is still tedious, but using a mathematical formula for a geometric series, it turns out that

$$\text{Total insurance needed} = \frac{\$60,000}{1 + 0.05} + \frac{\$60,000}{(1+0.05)^2} + \dots + \frac{\$60,000}{(1+0.05)^{20}}$$

$$= \$60,000 \left(\frac{1 - \left(1/(1+0.05)\right)^{20}}{0.05} \right)$$

While that's kind of a messy and complicated formula, it is probably quicker to use it then to do a separate calculation for each payment as we were doing before. (You will be guided through how this shortcut formula can be derived in the exercises.)

9. Confirm that you get the same amount of total insurance needed when you use the formula as you obtained before when using a guess-and-check approach using a spreadsheet.

A more general version of this formula for any interest rate, i, number of payments, n, and payment size, P, is

$$\text{Amount needed today} = Pa_{\overline{n}|i} = P\left(\frac{1 - \left(1/(1+i)\right)^n}{i}\right)$$

In this formula, the symbol $a_{\overline{n}|i}$ represents the present value of a series of payments of $1 over n periods at an effective interest rate of i each period.

Definition

The **present value** of a series of payments of $1 at an effective interest rate of i, over n payment periods, with each payment happening at the end of the period, is equal to $a_{\overline{n}|i}$, pronounced "a-angle-n." If $n = \infty$, then this is a perpetuity.

Key idea

$a_{\overline{n}|i}$ is used for present value and $s_{\overline{n}|i}$ is used for future value.

---

10. How much insurance will John need if he only assumes 3% effective annual interest over the 20 payments?

11. Explain intuitively why your answer to the previous question is smaller or larger than the insurance needs if the interest rate is 5%.

12. How much insurance does John need if he decides to only have payments of $40,000 per year (instead of $60,000) but assumes a 5% effective annual interest rate?

13. Explain, intuitively, why your answer to the previous question is smaller or larger than the insurance needs if the payment size is $60,000 per year.

Discount Factor

In this section, we've been looking at the *present value* of an annuity—how much we would have to invest now (in the present) to receive a series of equally sized payments. In general, the *discount factor* is a convenient way of expressing an interest rate when thinking about present values.

Definition

The **discount factor**, represented by the Greek letter nu (v), but sometimes called "v" in practice, is the present value of \$1 paid in 1 year at an effective annual rate of interest, i. Thus, $v = 1/(1 + i)$ since $v(1 + i) = 1$

---

14. What is the value of the discount factor if the interest rate is 5% effective annually?

15. How much do you need today if you want to have \$60,000 one year from now at 5% effective annually? Use the discount factor to find this value.

Key idea

The present value of a future payment of size P, n periods in the future, in an account earning an effective interest rate i (and corresponding discount factor is $v = 1/(1 + i)$) is present value $= P/(1+i)^n = Pv^n$.

We can rewrite the formula for the present value of annuity in terms of the discount factor as well.

$$\text{Amount needed today} = Pa_{\overline{n}|i} = P\left(\frac{1 - \left(1/(1+i)\right)^n}{i}\right) = P\left(\frac{1 - v^n}{i}\right)$$

SUMMARY

In this section, we've seen that annuities are streams of equally sized, equally spaced payments over time. Unlike perpetuities, annuities do end at some point, instead of continuing forever. We saw that, by using the discount factor (v, the present value of \$1 today), we can find the present value of all of the future payments of an annuity and, thus, obtain a short cut formula for finding the payment size or present value of an annuity.

Notation and equation summary

$$\text{Amount needed today} = Pa_{\overline{n}|i} = P\left(\frac{1 - (1/(1+i))^n}{i}\right) = P\left(\frac{1 - v^n}{i}\right)$$

$$v = \frac{1}{1+i} \text{ is the present value of \$1 today}$$

$a_{\overline{n}|i}$ is the present value of \$1 paid out for n periods earning an effective rate of i each period.

HOMEWORK QUESTIONS: SECTION 3.2

Conceptual Exercises

1. An annuity paid out over 20 years will have _____ (larger/smaller) payments than a perpetuity that earns the same annual effective rate of interest and has the same initial (present) value.

2. As the number of years of an annuity increases, the present value of the annuity_____. (increases/decreases)

3. As the interest rate increases, the present value of an annuity_____. (increases/decreases)

4. As the size of the payment increases, the present value of an annuity _____. (increases/decreases)

5. As an interest rate increases, the discount factor _____. (increases/decreases)

6. Explain the difference between $a_{\overline{n}|i}$ and $s_{\overline{n}|i}$.

7. Explain intuitively what $a_{\overline{\infty}|i}$ means and what special term we use for this kind of annuity.

Practice Exercises

8. Find the present value of an annuity that pays $5,000 annually for 10 years at an effective annual rate of interest of 5%. The first payment is 1 year from now.

9. Repeat question 8, but for an annuity that pays out for 20 years.

10. Repeat question 8 but use an annual effective rate of interest of 10%.

11. Find the present value of an annuity that pays $500 monthly for 30 years at a nominal annual rate of 6% compounded monthly. The first payment is 1 month from now.

12. Repeat question 11 but use an annual effective rate of interest of 6%.

13. Determine the effective annual discount factor on an investment that earns 3.125% APR.

14. If the discount factor on an investment is 0.98512. What is the investment's effective annual interest rate? What is the investment's APR?

Application Exercises

15. After making your fortune, you decide to give back to your college by setting up a scholarship fund. You would like to donate $2 million and it will be invested at an effective annual interest rate of 5% with the first scholarship given out in 1 year.
   a. How many $10,000 scholarships can be given out if you would like the money to last 10 years?
   b. How many $10,000 scholarships can be given out if you would like the money to last 20 years?
   c. How many $10,000 scholarships can be given out if you would like the money to last 40 years?
   d. How many $10,000 scholarships can be given out if you would like the money to last in perpetuity?

16. Beth saved up $500,000 and has put it in an annuity for her retirement.

    a. If she finds a fund that will pay 4% annual effective interest, how much will her annual payments be if she would like the fund to last 20 years?

    b. If she finds a fund that will pay 4% APR, how much will her monthly payments be if she would like the fund to last 20 years?

    c. If she would like annual payments of $40,000 for 20 years, what effective annual interest rate would she need to achieve this?

17. Allan saved up $900,000 and has put it in an annuity for his retirement.

    a. If he finds a fund that will pay 4.5% annual effective interest and would like to receive annual payments of $40,000, how many years will he get full payments of $40,000?

    b. If he finds a fund that will pay 4.5% APR and would like to receive monthly payments of $4,000, how many months will he get full payments of $4,000?

    c. Allan decides he can work part time for 5 years and let his $900,000 accumulate interest in an account earning 4.5% APR. After that time he would like to receive monthly payments of $4,000, how many months will he get full payments of $4,000 now?

18. You are saving for retirement and want to put that money into a 20-year annuity.

    a. If you find a fund that earns 3.5% APR and would like to receive monthly payments of $5,000, how much money will you need to invest?

    b. If you find a fund that earns 3.5% APR and would like to receive yearly payments of $60,000, how much money will you need to invest?

    c. If you find a fund that earns 3.5% annual effective interest and would like to receive yearly payments of $60,000, how much money will you need to invest?

    d. If you find a fund that earns 3.5% annual effective interest and would like to receive monthly payments of $5,000, how much money will you need to invest?

19. Jack agrees to pay Jill $100 monthly for the next 36 months, starting 1 month from now. They agree to a 3% nominal annual rate of interest with monthly compounding.

   a. How much should Jill pay Jack for this privilege? That is, what is the present value of the payments?

   b. If Jill immediately takes each payment and invests it at 6% nominal annual interest compounded monthly, how much will Jill have at the end of the 36-month period? Use a formula from the previous chapter to answer this question.

   c. Answer part b assuming Jill invested the money at 3% nominal annual rate of interest with monthly compounding.

   d. What if, instead of Jill paying Jack now, getting payments, and reinvesting them, Jill simply put her money (your answer to part a) in the bank at 3% nominal interest, compounded monthly for 36 months. How much would she have at the end of the 36-month period?

   e. Compare your answers to parts c and d. Explain why this is the case.

   f. Write a general equation relating the present value and future value of an annuity that are invested at the same rate of interest.

20. A financial services firm is trying to value a series of investment options for clients and has come to you for help. To do this, they would like to know the present value (how much they can/should charge) for a series of different investment options they would like to offer. Help them out and find the present value of the following.

   a. Fund 1. A $60,000 payment in 1 year at 5% annual effective interest.

   b. Fund 2. Two $30,000 payments, one at the end of year 1 and one at the end of year 2 at 6% effective interest.

   c. Fund 3. Six $10,000 payments, one at the end of each of the next 6 years at 5.5% effective interest.

   d. Fund 4. $1,000 payments at the end of each month for the next 5 years at an annual nominal interest rate of 6% with monthly compounding.

   e. Fund 5. A $40,000 payment at the end of year 1, an additional deposit of $20,000 into the fund by the investor at the end of year 2, and a payment of $40,000 at the end of year 4 at 6% effective annual interest.

Prove It!

21. In this section, we saw that the amount needed today (present value) for an annuity that will give payments of P dollars over n periods of time (e.g., years or months) with an effective interest rate of i over that same period can be determined using the following formula. (We have substituted A in for "amount needed today" just to have the notation nice and simple.)

$$A = \frac{P}{(1+i)} + \frac{P}{(1+i)^2} + \frac{P}{(1+i)^3} + \ldots + \frac{P}{(1+i)^n}$$

a. Explain what each term in the above formula represents. (*Hint: How did we derive each term?*)

b. We also gave a shortcut version of the formula. We will now guide you through how that can be derived using the above formula.

   i. Multiply both sides of the equation above by $(1+i)$. Make sure you multiply each term on the right side by $(1+i)$ and simplify each term.

   ii. Subtract the equation above from the equation you created in part b(i). To do this, subtract the left side of one equation from the other and subtract the right side of one equation from the other. You should now have a new equation that includes a term or terms with A in them on the left side and a term or terms with P and i in them on the right side.

   iii. Simplify both sides of the equation so the left side is just Ai and the right side consists of just two terms where each contains P.

   iv. Factor the P out of the right side and then divide both sides by i and you should have the following shortcut formula we presented in this section.

$$S = P\left(\frac{1 - \left(1/(1+i)\right)^n}{i}\right)$$

END OF CHAPTER SUMMARY

Annuities and perpetuities are steady streams of payments, which either end at some point in time (annuities) or continue indefinitely (perpetuities). Perpetuities, a stream of payments which continues forever, may seem like a financial impossibility; however, when we think of them as a way of "living off the interest," they become more intuitive. The idea of "living off the interest" is also at the heart of shortcut formulas to value perpetuities. A similar approach, living off the interest—plus more, is at the heart of annuities. We used the discount factor, the present value of $1 today, to value annuities.

END OF CHAPTER EXERCISES

(SOA EXAM FM SAMPLE QUESTIONS May 2000, Question 39)

1. Sally lends 10,000 to Tim. Tim agrees to pay back the loan over 5 years with monthly payments payable at the end of each month.

   Sally can reinvest the monthly payments from Tim in a savings account paying interest at 6%, compounded monthly. The yield rate earned on Sally's investment over the five-year period turned out to be 7.45%, compounded semiannually.

   What nominal rate of interest, compounded monthly, did Sally charge Tim on the loan?
   A. 8.53%
   B. 8.59%
   C. 8.68%
   D. 8.80%
   E. 9.16%

(SOA EXAM FM SAMPLE QUESTIONS May 2001, Question 5)

2. A perpetuity-immediate pays X per year. Brian receives the first n payments, Colleen receives the next n payments, and Jeff receives the remaining payments. Brian's share of the present value of the original perpetuity is 40%, and Jeff's share is K.

   Calculate K.
   A. 24%
   B. 28%
   C. 32%
   D. 36%
   E. 40%

(SOA EXAM FM SAMPLE QUESTIONS May 2001, Question 17)

3. At an annual effective interest rate of i, $i > 0\%$, the present value of a perpetuity paying 10 at the end of each 3-year period, with the first payment at the end of year 6, is 32.

At the same annual effective rate of i, the present value of a perpetuity-immediate paying 1 at the end of each 4-month period is X.

Calculate X.

A. 38.8

B. 39.8

C. 40.8

D. 41.8

E. 42.8

(SOA EXAM FM SAMPLE QUESTIONS May 2001, Question 50)

4. The present values of the following three annuities are equal:

   i. Perpetuity-immediate paying 1 each year, calculated at an annual effective interest rate of 7.25%

   ii. 50-year annuity-immediate paying 1 each year, calculated at an annual effective interest rate of j%

   iii. n-year annuity-immediate paying 1 each year, calculated at an annual effective interest rate of $j - 1$%

   Calculate n.

   A. 30

   B. 33

   C. 36

   D. 39

   E. 42

(SOA EXAM FM SAMPLE QUESTIONS May 2003, Question 33)

5. At an annual effective interest rate of i, $i > 0$, both of the following annuities have a present value of X:

   i. A 20-year annuity-immediate with annual payments of 55

   ii. A 30-year annuity-immediate with annual payments that pays 30 per year for the first 10 years, 60 per year for the second 10 years, and 90 per year for the final 10 years.

   Calculate X.

   A. 575

   B. 585

   C. 595

   D. 605

   E. 615

(SOA EXAM FM SAMPLE QUESTIONS May 2005, Question 1)

6. Which of the following expressions does NOT represent a definition for $a_{\overline{n}|i}$?

   A. $v^n \times \frac{(1+i)^n - 1}{i}$

   B. $\frac{1 - v^n}{i}$

   C. $v + v^2 + \ldots + v^n$

   D. $\frac{v(1 - v^n)}{1 - v}$

   E. $\frac{s_{\overline{n}|}}{(1+i)^{n-1}}$

(SOA EXAM FM SAMPLE QUESTIONS May 2005, Question 4)

7. An estate provides a perpetuity with payments of X at the end of each year. Seth, Susan, and Lori share the perpetuity such that Seth receives the payments of X for the first n years and Susan receives the payments of X for the next m years, after which Lori receives all the remaining payments of X.

   Which of the following represents the difference between the present value of Seth's and Susan's payments using a constant rate of interest?

   A. $X\left(a_{\overline{n}|} - v^n a_{\overline{m}|}\right)$

   B. $X\left(\ddot{a}_{\overline{n}|} - v^n \ddot{a}_{\overline{m}|}\right)$

   C. $X\left(a_{\overline{n}|} - v^{n+1} a_{\overline{m}|}\right)$

   D. $X\left(a_{\overline{n}|} - v^{n-1} a_{\overline{m}|}\right)$

   E. $X\left(v a_{\overline{n}|} - v^{n+1} a_{\overline{m}|}\right)$

(SOA EXAM FM SAMPLE QUESTIONS May 2005, Question 24)

8. An annuity pays 1 at the end of each year for n years. Using an annual effective interest rate of i, the accumulated value of the annuity at time $(n + 1)$ is 13.776. It is also known that $(1 + i)^n = 2.476$.

   Calculate n.
   A. 4
   B. 5
   C. 6
   D. 7
   E. 8

(SOA EXAM FM SAMPLE QUESTIONS November 2000, Question 55)

9. Iggy borrows X for 10 years at an annual effective rate of 6%. If he pays the principal and accumulated interest in one lump sum at the end of 10 years, he would pay 356.54 more in interest than if he repaid the loan with 10 level payments at the end of each year.

   Calculate X.
   A. 800
   B. 825
   C. 850
   D. 875
   E. 900

(SOA EXAM FM SAMPLE QUESTIONS November 2001, Question 6)

10. A 10-year loan of 2,000 is to be repaid with payments at the end of each year. It can be repaid under the following two options:
   i. Equal annual payments at an annual effective rate of 8.07%.
   ii. Installments of 200 each year plus interest on the unpaid balance at an annual effective rate of i.

   The sum of the payments under option (i) equals the sum of the payments under option (ii).
   Determine i.
   A. 8.75%
   B. 9.00%
   C. 9.25%
   D. 9.50%
   E. 9.75%

(SOA EXAM FM SAMPLE QUESTIONS November 2001, Question 24)

11. David can receive one of the following two payment streams:
   i. 100 at time 0, 200 at time n, and 300 at time $2n$
   ii. 600 at time 10

   At an annual effective interest rate of i, the present values of the two streams are equal.

Given $v'' = 0.75941$, determine i.

A. 3.5%

B. 4.0%

C. 4.5%

D. 5.0%

E. 5.5%

(SOA EXAM FM SAMPLE QUESTIONS November 2005, Question 13)

12. For 10,000, Kelly purchases an annuity-immediate that pays 400 quarterly for the next 10 years.

Calculate the annual nominal interest rate convertible monthly earned by Kelly's investment.

A. 10.0%

B. 10.3%

C. 10.5%

D. 10.7%

E. 11.0%

(SOA EXAM FM SAMPLE QUESTIONS November 2005, Question 25)

13. The parents of three children, ages 1, 3, and 6, wish to set up a trust fund that will pay X to each child upon attainment of age 18, and Y to each child upon attainment of age 21. They will establish the trust fund with a single investment of Z.

Which of the following is the correct equation of value for Z?

A. $\dfrac{X}{v^{17} + v^{15} + v^{12}} + \dfrac{Y}{v^{20} + v^{18} + v^{15}}$

B. $3\left(Xv^{18} + Yv^{21}\right)$

C. $3Xv^3 + Y\left(v^{20} + v^{18} + v^{15}\right)$

D. $(X + Y)\dfrac{v^{20} + v^{18} + v^{15}}{v^3}$

E. $\left(v^{17} + v^{15} + v^{12}\right) + Y(v^{20} + v^{18} + v^{15})$

(SOA EXAM FM SAMPLE QUESTIONS Interest Theory, Question 29)

14. At an annual effective interest rate of i, $i > 0\%$, the present value of a perpetuity paying 10 at the end of each 3-year period, with the first payment at the end of year 3, is 32.

    At the same annual effective rate of i, the present value of a perpetuity paying 1 at the end of each 4-month period, with first payment at the end of 4 months, is X.
    Calculate X.
    A. 31.6
    B. 32.6
    C. 33.6
    D. 34.6
    E. 35.6

(SOA EXAM FM SAMPLE QUESTIONS Interest Theory, Question 49)

15. Happy and financially astute parents decide at the birth of their daughter that they will need to provide 50,000 at each of their daughter's 18th, 19th, 20th, and 21st birthdays to fund her college education. They plan to contribute X at each of their daughter's 1st through 17th birthdays to fund the four 50,000 withdrawals. They anticipate earning a constant 5% annual effective interest rate on their contributions. Let $v = 1/1.05$.

    Determine which of the following equations of value can be used to calculate X.
    A. $X\sum_{k=1}^{17} v^k = 50,000(v + v^2 + v^3 + v^4)$
    B. $X\sum_{k=1}^{16} 1.05^k = 50,000(1 + v + v^2 + v^3)$
    C. $X\sum_{k=0}^{17} 1.05^k = 50,000(1 + v + v^2 + v^3)$
    D. $X\sum_{k=1}^{17} 1.05^k = 50,000\left(1 + v + v^2 + v^3\right)$
    E. $X\sum_{k=0}^{17} v^k = 50,000(v^{18} + v^{19} + v^{20} + v^{21} + v^{22})$

(SOA EXAM FM SAMPLE QUESTIONS November 2001, Question 47)

16. Project P requires an investment of 4,000 at time 0. The investment pays 2,000 at time 1 and 4,000 at time 2.

    Project Q requires an investment of X at time 2. The investment pays 2,000 at time 0 and 4,000 at time 1.
    Using the net present value method and an interest rate of 10%, the net present values of the two projects are equal.
    Calculate X.
    A. 5400
    B. 5420
    C. 5440
    D. 5460
    E. 5480

(SOA EXAM FM SAMPLE QUESTIONS Interest Theory, Question 9)

17. A 20-year loan of 1,000 is repaid with payments at the end of each year.

    Each of the first ten payments equals 150% of the amount of interest due. Each of the last ten payments is X.
    The lender charges interest at an annual effective rate of 10%.
    Calculate X.
    A. 32
    B. 57
    C. 70
    D. 97
    E. 117

(SOA EXAM FM SAMPLE QUESTIONS May 2003, Question 39)

18. A 30-year loan of 1,000 is repaid with payments at the end of each year.

    Each of the first ten payments equals the amount of interest due. Each of the next ten payments equals 150% of the amount of interest due. Each of the last ten payments is X.

The lender charges interest at an annual effective rate of 10%. Calculate X.

A. 32
B. 57
C. 70
D. 97
E. 117

CHAPTER FOUR

Stocks and Bonds: Fundamentals of Investment Strategies

Abstract

In previous chapters, we explored basic concepts of interest, loans, and annuities. However, we saved discussion of two of the most common investment mechanisms (stocks and bonds) until now, since an understanding of annuities makes understanding stocks and bonds much easier. In this chapter, we will explore how to value bonds by applying pricing rules and formulas for annuities since, as we will see, bonds are very closely related to annuities. While stock pricing is a highly complex process, in part, because it relies on consumer/investor perceptions; at the end of this chapter, we will explore a basic and simple way to think about stock pricing.

Keywords: Stocks; bonds; premium; discount; coupon; zero-coupon

SECTION 4.1. BONDS

If your organization needs money to launch a new product, build a new building, or initiate some other new endeavor that requires a large amount of money now, there are a variety of financial mechanisms that you have available. Earlier, we looked at loans as one way to get (borrow) money. After you get the money from a loan, you pay back the loan (typically with a series of payments incorporating both principal and interest) over the time.

Bonds are another method for a company to raise funds. Bonds often come with fewer strings attached than loans and can be an attractive option for companies and municipalities (e.g., cities and towns) to raise funds for projects.

Learning objectives

By the end of this section, you should be able to:

- Find the present value of a zero-coupon or coupon bond, using annuity formulas as appropriate.

A Spiral Approach to Financial Mathematics.
DOI: https://doi.org/10.1016/B978-0-12-801580-3.00004-6
© 2018 Elsevier Inc.
All rights reserved.

- Understand basic bond terminology including face value, redemption value, yield rate, coupon rate and coupon size.
- Understand why a company may choose to issue bonds instead of taking out a bank loan.

EXAMPLE 4.1. INVESTING $1 MILLION

You just found out that your long-lost uncle left you a large sum of money. Your tax advisor tells you that, after taxes, you are likely to have ~$1 million. Congratulations! But sorry to hear about your uncle. What are you going to do with the money? Obviously, you have lots of choices and lots of people will likely want to give you their opinion as to the best options. Aside from spending it or giving it away, what savings options do you have?

If you go to the bank and put the money in CDs or put the money in a standard savings account, you may not earn a very large rate of interest. At 2% effective interest per year you will have "only" $1.22 million after 10 years, $1.49 million after 20 years, and $1.81 million after 30 years, even with compounded interest. Are there any better options? You're probably aware of investing in the stock market (we will come back to that later in this chapter), but another option for investing is bonds.

Bonds are similar to loans, but typically are issued by a company (the borrower) directly to an investor (e.g., a private individual or another company; the lender) instead of a bank and can be structured with an interest rate and terms that the company thinks are reasonable instead of what a bank dictates.

Definition

A **bond** is a formal agreement between the borrower (the bond issuer—often a company or government) and the lender (the bond purchaser—often an individual or another company) for the borrower to pay the lender certain amounts at future dates.

A bond can specify that it will pay back the entire amount of the loan at a single future date or spread it out over the time and at an interest rate determined by the bond issuer.

Zero-coupon bonds

For example, you might find a company offering a bond that will pay out $1.22 million in 5 years. If you go to a bond market (a place where you can buy and sell bonds), you might find that bond being issued today and selling for $1 million.

Think about it

Does this bond appear to be a better deal than the savings account option paying 2% effective interest annually? Why?

The bond will pay you $1.22 million in 5 years for a $1 million investment today, whereas the savings account option we looked at earlier took 10 years to reach a value of $1.22 million—twice as long. Thus, the bond seems to be the better option. Of course, there's a reason that the interest rate is higher—a company is not as "secure" as an investment as a bank—a bank is less risky. A higher rate of interest is paid because of the higher risk of the investment. But, what is the annual effective interest rate associated with this bond?

To find out, we can solve the following equation: $1,000,000(1 + i)^5 = \$1,220,000$ for i. Solving this equation yields $i = 0.04057$. This makes sense since the rate is higher than the rate paid on the savings account (2% annually).

It's helpful to start learning the language of bonds and be a bit more precise about why this kind of bond is called a zero-coupon bond. The **term** of a bond is the length of time from the time the bond is issued until the final payment is made. In this case, the bond term is 5 years.

Definition

The **term** of a bond is the length of time from the time the bond is issued until the final payment is made.

The **redemption value** of the bond is the amount that is paid from the bond issuer to the bondholder at the end of the bond term. Usually, the letter C is used to denote the redemption value of the bond. For this bond, $C = \$1.22$ million.

Definition

The **redemption value** of the bond is the amount that is paid from the bond issuer to the bondholder at the end of the bond term.

The **yield rate** (or yield to maturity) of a bond, typically denoted from i, is the interest rate earned by the investor. Thus, as we showed above, the yield rate, i, is 0.04057 for this bond.

Definition

The **yield rate** (or yield to maturity) of a bond is the interest rate earned by the investor.

As we'll soon see, in many practical situations yield rates are stated as a nominal, semiannual compounding rate, because many bonds pay out **coupons** semiannually (twice a year). Coupons are periodic payments made from the bond issuer to the investor throughout the loan term and are usually paid out in addition to a lump sum at the end (the redemption value).

Definition

Coupons are periodic payments made from the bond issuer to the investor throughout the loan term and are usually paid out in addition to a lump sum at the end of the term (the redemption value).

Thus, the loan we considered above is called a zero-coupon bond because it does not pay out coupons—it only has a $1.22 million redemption value, 5 years from now.

Think about it

Why do you think bonds often pay a higher interest rate than savings accounts?

Bonds often pay a higher rate of interest than savings accounts because there is more risk involved. Banks often will guarantee your money is safe, whereas a company issuing bonds often provides fewer assurances that your money is safe (e.g., if the company goes out of business your money is gone).

A bond with coupons

Some bonds are issued with coupons—periodic payments from the bond-seller (the company) to the bond-buyer (the investor). Let's assume that this $1.22 million bond you are considering also pays out $24,400 "coupons"—that is, $24,400 payments between now and the time that the bond is redeemed for $1.22 million in 5 years.

Typically, coupons are paid out every 6 months, with the final coupon paid out on the redemption date. In this case, there would be 10 coupon payments.

Think about it

How much do you think you will need to pay for a 5-year, $1.22 million bond with $24,400 semiannual coupons yielding an effective rate of 4.057% annually? More than $1 million? Why? How can you calculate the value exactly?

If it costs $1 million today to buy a $1.22 million bond without coupons yielding 4.057%, it will cost more for the same bond, if the bond is also paying out coupons. The key to figuring out the new price of the bond is to realize that the coupons being paid out are acting like an annuity. In this case, the coupon payments are an annuity that pays $24,400 every 6 months for 5 years at an effective rate of interest of 4.057% annually.

To find the cost of the bond, we first convert 4.057% to an effective semiannual interest rate. To do that, we solve $(1+i)^2 = 1.04057$ for i to get $i \approx 0.02008$. We then calculate the present value (price) of the coupon payments as

$$Pa_{\overline{n}|i} = 24,400 \left(\frac{1 - \left(1/(1+0.02008)\right)^{10}}{0.02008} \right) = \$219,083.36$$

Thus, the total cost (present value) of the $1.22 million bond with $24,400 coupons is $1,219,083.36 today.

Key idea

To find the present value of a bond with coupons, first find the present value of the coupons using annuity formulas, and then add the present value of the redemption value.

Let's review what we just did. We first looked at a zero-coupon bond that would pay $1.22 million in 5 years for an initial investment of $1 million. With that, we learned, we would be earning an effective annual interest rate of 4.057%, which converts to a semiannual effective interest rate of 2.008%. We did this conversion to semiannual because we then threw in coupons that were being added to the bond and they paid out semiannually. We then added the present value of the coupons ($219,083.36) to our initial present value of the bond ($1 million) to get the present value of this bond with coupons ($1,219,083.36).

Now, remember that you only had $1 million left to you by your long-lost uncle so you can't afford this bond. Let's look at one more concept, yield rate, before we do some adjustments to get a bond with a present value that you can afford.

Coupon rate

While bond terms are set by the bond issuer, bonds typically don't specify a coupon size directly (e.g., $24,400). Instead, they specify a **coupon rate**, r, which can be used to find the coupon size. The coupon size is found by multiplying the coupon rate by the **face value** (or par value of the bond). In almost all typical situations, the face value of the bond (denoted F) is equal to the redemption value.

Definition
Coupon rate is the value that is multiplied by the face value of the bond to find the coupon size. Most coupon rates are stated as a nominal coupon rate with semiannual compounding.

Definition
The **face value** (par value) of the bond is the value multiplied by the coupon rate of the bond to find the coupon size. Typically, the face value is equal to the redemption value.

Key idea
You can assume that a bond's face value equals its redemption value ($F = C$) unless otherwise specified.

As we noted earlier, most bonds pay coupons semiannually. Thus, most coupon rates are stated as a nominal coupon rate with semiannually compounding. This nominal coupon rate can be used to find the coupon size.

If the bond issuer decides to issue semiannual coupons at a 4% nominal rate with semiannual compounding, this amounts to a coupon rate of $r = 2\%$. Thus, the coupon size is 0.02 times the face value of the bond. In our situation, the face value (or redemption value) of the bond is $1.22 million and 2% of $1.22 million is $24,400. So, the coupons will be $24,400 each. (Note: This is the same $24,400 we seemed to pull out of a hat earlier in this example!)

Important note: Usually, bond yield rates are reported as nominal rates with semiannual compounding. Thus, this bond, which is yielding an annual effective interest rate of 4.057%, is equivalent to a semiannual effective interest rate of 2.008% or 4.016% nominal with effective compounding.

There's a lot going on here, so let's summarize. We can describe our bond as one that

a. Has a face value of $1,220,000

b. Has semiannual coupons that are 2% of face value each ($24,400)

c. Based on the price it is currently selling for on the bond market ($1,219,083.36), it is yielding 4.016% nominal, with semiannual compounding (which is equivalent to 4.057% effective annually or 2.008% effective semiannually).

A formula for bond pricing

This all can be summarized in the following formula, where F is the face value, j is the effective yield rate semiannually, r is the coupon rate, and $Fra_{\overline{n}|j}$ is the present value of the series of coupon payments.

$$\text{Current bond price} = \frac{F}{(1+j)^n} + Fra_{\overline{n}|j}$$

In this case, this means

$$\text{Current bond price} = \frac{1,220,000}{(1+0.02008)^{10}} + 24,400\left(\frac{1 - \left(1/(1+0.02008)\right)^{10}}{0.02008}\right)$$
$$= \$1,000,040.30 + \$219,083.36 = \$1,219,123.67$$

Important note: This is slightly different than what we had above due to rounding.

What size bond can you actually afford?

Of course, the present value of this bond is more money than you have! What size bond can you afford that has 4% semiannual coupons, yielding 4.057% effective annual interest? To determine this, we can use the same formula as above, but we will let the face value be unknown and the present value is $1 million.

$$\frac{F}{(1+j)^{10}} + Fra_{\overline{n}|j} = \frac{F}{(1+0.02008)^{10}} + F(0.02)\left(\frac{1 - \left(1/(1+0.02008)\right)^{10}}{0.020008}\right)$$
$$= \$1,000,000$$

This simplifies to $0.9992828F = \$1,000,000$ or $F = \$1,000,718.82$. So, you have enough money to be able to purchase a bond with a face value of just over $1 million, paying 4% coupons semiannually and yielding 4.016% nominal semiannually. (Note that the coupon size is now $20,000 instead of $24,000 since the coupon rate stayed the same and the face value of the bond changed.) One other thing to note in the above calculation is that the face value ($1,000,040.30) and cost of the bond ($1 million) are almost the same. This is because the coupon rate (4% nominal, semiannually) and the yield rate (4.016% nominal, semiannually) were almost the same. In the exercises, you will be asked to show that when the coupon rate and yield rate are identical, the face value and cost of the bond are also identical. We will explore this topic further in the next section as well.

EXPLORATION 4.1. LAUNCHING A NEW PRODUCT LINE

Let's assume that your start-up company has decided to launch a new product line and determines it needs $500,000 to finalize the product, market it, and produce initial inventory for sale. How will you raise this money? Taking a bank loan is one option.

1. Because you are a new start-up company, the bank considers you to be a high-risk investment. Thus, they will give you a 5-year, $500,000 loan at 8% APR. If you took the loan, what will your monthly payment be? How much total interest will you pay back with this scenario?

Practically, as a start-up company, it may be hard for you to pay over $10,000/month—since you won't necessarily be selling any product in the first couple of years while you get the product ready for market. Furthermore, you will end up spending over $100,000 in interest expense over the course of the loan—which is a lot for a small, start-up business. Finally, most banks are unlikely to even consider giving you a loan like this unless your company has tangible assets that they can hold as collateral against the loan (Note: Collateral is something of value that the bank can take as "payment" if your company goes out of business). Instead of loans, many companies choose to use bonds (or stocks—we'll look at stocks later in this chapter) to raise funds.

Bonds are similar to loans, but typically are issued from a company directly to an investor (e.g., a private individual) instead of a bank and can be structured with an interest rate/terms that the company thinks are reasonable vs what a bank dictates.

Definition

A **bond** is a formal agreement between the borrower (the bond issuer—often a company or government) and the lender (the bond purchaser—often an individual) for the borrower to pay the lender certain amounts at future dates.

A bond can specify that it will pay back all of the loans at a single future date or spread out over the time and at an interest rate determined by the bond issuer.

2. You feel like bonds are pretty appealing. As the company issuing the bonds, what kinds of bond terms (interest rate and payback time) would be in your best interest?

3. What is the practical issue (problems) with structuring the terms of a bond that is in the extreme best interest of the company?

While your company would like to have a very low-interest rate and very long payback period, the practical issue that a bond is an agreement between two entities—the company "selling" the bond (getting money now) and the investor who "buys" the bond (gives the money now). So, if you structure everything in the company's favor you may not be able to find any investors who want to buy your bonds!

While bonds can be structured in many ways, there are some standards that are commonly used. We'll explore these ways now and learn some bond terminology along the way. Practically speaking, though, there is really nothing new mathematically when evaluating bonds—the mathematics follow the same rules and principles we've explored in the last few chapters.

Zero-coupon bonds

The simplest type of bond is a **zero–coupon bond**. A zero-coupon bond is a simple agreement that indicates a date on which a single, lump sum of money will be paid from the company (bond-seller) to the investor (bond-buyer).

A bond typically specifies two things: the bonds redemption value and the term of the bond.

For example, your company sells a single, zero-coupon bond that indicates that you will pay the bondholder (investor) $600,000 in 5 years.

4. What other financial information do you need to know in order determine if this is a better option for your company than the bank loan?

To evaluate this financial scenario, you need to know how much the investor will give you now, with an expectation of getting $600,000 later. This amount will also tell you something about what the investor desires for an interest rate.

5. If the investor will give you $600,000 now, what is the implied interest rate on the bond if the investor expects to receive $600,000 back in 5 years? That is, what is the annual effective interest rate, i, that the investor going to earn on their money over the 5-year period of the bond?

The interest rate you obtained in #5 should be pretty unrealistic unless you are good friends/relatives with the bond-buyer!

6. If the investor will give you $500,000 now, what is the implied interest rate on the bond if the investor expects to receive $600,000 back in 5 years? That is, what is the annual effective interest rate, i, that the investor going to earn on their money over the 5-year period of the bond?

7. If your company can find an investor who will buy the zero-coupon bond at the terms mentioned above, would you rather sell the bond or take the loan? (Remember the loan rate was 8% APR.) Why?

The effective annual interest rate of 3.7137% from the investor is much better than 8% APR (8.3% effective/year) from the bank. Furthermore, the bank will require monthly payments on the loan, which may be challenging if you are a start-up company with little cash flow. The idea of a lump sum payment of the bond in 5 years may be a little frightening ($600,000 is a lot of money!) but, assuming your product is successful, that is probably more practical than trying to make large monthly payments starting right away.

It's helpful to start learning the language of bonds and be a bit more precise about our definition of a zero-coupon bond.

The **term** of a bond is the length of time from the time the bond is issued until the final payment is made.

Definition

The **term** of a bond is the length of time from the time the bond is issued until the final payment is made.

---

8. What is the term of the zero-coupon bond considered above?

The **redemption value** of the bond is the amount that is paid from the bond issuer to the bondholder at the end of the bond term. Usually, the letter C is used to denote the redemption value of the bond.

Definition

The **redemption value** of the bond is the amount that is paid from the bond issuer to the bondholder at the end of the bond term.

---

9. What is the redemption value of the zero-coupon bond considered above?

The **yield rate** (or yield to maturity) of a bond, typically denoted from i, is the interest rate earned by the investor.

Definition

The **yield rate** (or yield to maturity) of a bond is the interest rate earned by the investor.

---

10. What is the yield rate (stated as effective annual interest) of the zero-coupon bond considered above that sells for \$500,000 today?

11. How would you state the yield rate as a nominal interest rate with semiannual compounding?

As we'll soon see, in many practical situations yield rates are stated as a nominal, semiannual compounding rate, because many bonds pay out **coupons** semiannually (twice a year). Coupons are periodic payments made from the bond issuer to the investor throughout the loan term and are usually paid out in addition to a lump sum at the end (the redemption value).

Definition

Coupons are periodic payments made from the bond issuer to the investor throughout the loan term and are usually paid out in addition to a lump sum at the end of the term (the redemption value).

---

12. Based on this definition of coupons, why do you think the bond we considered above is called a "zero-coupon bond?"

The bond we considered above is a zero-coupon bond because it had no coupons—no payments were made during the term—only a single payment (the redemption value) of \$600,000 at the end of the bond's term (after 5 years).

A bond with coupons

Some bonds are issued with coupons—periodic payments from the bond-seller (your company) to the bond-buyer (the investor).

13. If you modify the bond terms so that your company also pays $12,000 semiannually (every 6 months) to the bondholder, starting 6 months from now, up until (and including) the redemption date, how many coupon payments will you make? What will be the total sum of the coupon payments made? How much total will be paid from your company to the investor?

14. If the investor still wishes to earn a yield rate of 3.7137% effective/year (on both the ten $12,000 coupon payments and final lump sum payment of $600,000), will the amount your company receives today be more or less than they received with the zero-coupon bond ($500,000)? Why?

The amount your company will receive today for the bond with $12,000 coupons will be more than the $500,000 for the zero-coupon bond, if the yield rate (3.7137% effective/year) is the same because the coupon payments are worth something to the investor also.

15. Find the present value of the 10, semiannual coupon payments of $12,000 each. *Hint:* What is the term we use for a series of same-sized payments paid out over the time? Note that you will have to convert the annual effective rate of 3.7137% before you can do this problem!

16. Using your answer to the previous question, how much should the investor pay to the company today for the bond with $12,000 semi-annual coupons and a $600,000 redemption value assuming an annual effective yield rate of 3.7137%?

For a coupon bond, the way to find the present value of the bond is to view the bond as a mix of an annuity (the coupon payments) and the redemption value.

Key idea

To find the present value of a bond with coupons, first find the present value of the coupons using annuity formulas, and then add the present value of the redemption value.

Coupon rate

While bond terms are set by the bond issuer, typically bonds don't specify a coupon size directly; instead, they specify a **coupon rate**, r, which can be used to find the coupon size. The coupon size is found by multiplying the coupon rate by the **face value** (or par value of the bond). In almost all typical situations, the face value of the bond (denoted F) is equal to the redemption value.

Definition
Coupon rate is the value that is multiplied by the face value of the bond to find the coupon size. Most coupon rates are stated as a nominal coupon rate with semiannual compounding.

Definition
The **face value** (par value) of the bond is the value multiplied by the coupon rate of the bond to find the coupon size. Typically, the face value is equal to the redemption value.

Key idea
You can assume that a bond's face value equals its redemption value ($F = C$) unless otherwise specified.

As we noted earlier, most bonds pay coupons semiannually. Thus, most coupon rates are stated as a nominal coupon rate with semiannually compounding. This nominal coupon rate can be used to find the coupon size.

17. If your company decides on a 4% nominal (annual) coupon rate with semiannual compounding, what is the *semiannual* coupon rate, r?

18. Use the coupon rate you calculated in the previous question and a face value of $600,000 to find the coupon size.

So, a 4% nominal coupon rate with semiannual coupons, means paying out 2% coupons, or $12,000 every 6 months on a $600,000 face value bond, along with the $600,000 lump sum payment at the end of 5 years. Earlier in this exploration, you found that the present value (price paid today) for such a bond yielding 3.71% was $608,699.42.

A formula for bond pricing

This all can be summarized in the following formula, where F is the face value, j is the effective yield rate semiannually, r is the coupon rate, and $Fra_{\overline{n}|j}$ is the present value of the series of coupon payments. (Note: Because of rounding we don't quite get a present value of $1 million on the portion of the bond without coupons.)

$$\text{Current bond price} = \frac{F}{(1+j)^n} + Fra_{\overline{n}|j}$$

19. Use this formula to find the selling price for a 5-year, $600,000 bond yielding 3.67987% nominal annually with semiannual compounding, which also pays out 2% coupons semiannually. Note: Compare your answer to what you received earlier.

20. Use the **Chapter 4 Excel file** to confirm your answer to the previous question.

> ## SUMMARY

In this section, we explored some of the basics of bonds. We saw that bonds are an alternative to loans, issued directly from companies to investors. Bonds typically pay a lump sum payment at the end of the loan and may or may not pay coupons between the time that the bond is issued and the end of the bond term (when the lump sum is paid). To value a bond, simply find the present value of the lump sum and, if coupons are paid, add the present value of the coupon payments (an annuity). The yield rate of a bond is just another term for interest rate and is determined by the market, not the company issuing the bond. In the next section, we'll explore more practicalities of buying and selling and bonds.

Notation and equation summary

F = Face value of a bond

C = Redemption value of a bond. Typically, $F = C$.

r = coupon rate

$$\text{Current bond price} = \frac{F}{(1+j)^n} + Fra_{\overline{n}|j}$$

HOMEWORK QUESTIONS: SECTION 4.1

Conceptual questions

1. The par value of a bond is the amount that_____

2. A zero-coupon bond means that the borrower will make _____ payment(s) to the lender, with the payment(s) occurring _____

3. As the coupon rate increases, the price of the bond _____ (increases/decreases)

4. As the yield rate increases the price of the bond _____ (increases/decreases)

5. The present value of a bond with coupons is the sum of what two things?

Practice questions

6. For a $5,000 face value bond, find the coupon size for:
   a. 12% coupons, paid semiannually.
   b. 8% coupons, paid semiannually.

7. For a $5,000 face value bond, find the coupon size for:
   a. 12% coupons, paid monthly.
   b. 8% coupons, paid monthly.

8. For a $1,000 face value bond, find the coupon size for:
   a. 12% coupons, paid semiannually.
   b. 8% coupons, paid semiannually.

9. For a $1,000 face value bond, find the coupon size for:
   a. 12% coupons, paid monthly.
   b. 8% coupons, paid monthly.

10. What is the coupon rate of a $100,000 bond that pays:
    a. $2,135 semiannually?
    b. $437.50 monthly?

11. If the redemption value of a 5-year zero-coupon bond is $1 million and it sells for $750,000 now, what is the effective annual interest rate earned?

12. Find the present value of 12 semiannual coupon payments of $8,000 each with a nominal interest rate of 4% with semiannual compounding.

Application questions

13. Consider a $1,000 two-year bond with 4% coupons paid semiannually bought to yield 3% convertible semiannually.
    a. What should be the selling price?
    b. If this was a 5-year bond instead of a 2-year bond, how much would it sell for?

14. Consider a $1,000 two-year bond with 8% coupons paid semiannually bought to yield 3% convertible semiannually.
    a. What should be the selling price?
    b. If this had a yield rate of 6% instead of 3%, how much would it sell for?

15. Find the price of a $1,000 two-year bond with 4% coupons paid semiannually bought to yield 4% convertible semiannually?

16. A 10-year zero-coupon bond sells for $70,000 now and has a redemption value of $100,000.
    a. What is the annual effective yield rate earned on the bond?
    b. What is the yield rate when it is given as a nominal interest rate with semiannual compounding? Monthly compounding?

17. How much should an investor pay to a company for a 10-year bond with $10,000 semiannual coupons, a $900,000 redemption value, and an annual effective yield rate of 4.5%?

18. How much should an investor pay to a company for a 5-year bond that pays coupons semiannually with a 4% nominal annual coupon rate, a $50,000 face value, and an annual nominal yield rate of 4.5% compounded semiannually?

Prove it!

19. We mentioned at the end of the example from this section that you would be asked in the exercises to show that when the coupon rate and yield rate are identical, the face value and cost of the bond are also identical. Let's do that now. We will let the cost of the bond (or present value) be represented by PV, the face value is F, the yield rate is i, the coupon rate is r, and n is the number of compounding periods. For the sake of simplicity, we will assume annual compounding.

    a. Using the notation given, what is the formula for computing the cost of the bond (on the left) given the yield rate, coupon rate, and number of compounding periods (on the right)?

    b. Now let's make the coupon rate and yield rate the same. To do this, make them both r.

    c. Now show that the right side of your equation simplifies to be just F and that this shows that when the coupon rate and yield rate are the same, the cost of the bond and the face value are also the same.

SECTION 4.2. BUYING AND SELLING BONDS

In the previous section, we learned how bonds were a lot like a loan but were typically issued by a company instead of by a bank. Because bonds are issued by a company and don't have the same insurance/guarantees behind them that a bank does, bonds are typically a riskier investment than a loan and so they pay a higher yield rate. In the last section, we saw that coupon bonds periodically (often every 6 months) pay money to the bondholder, with an amount based on the coupon rate—multiplying the coupon rate times the face value of the bond to give the coupon size. In this section, we'll see how comparisons between the coupon rate and the yield rate tell us something about the pricing of the bond.

Learning objectives

By the end of this section, you should be able to:

- Understand the relationship between a bond selling at a premium and a bond selling at a discount and how these comparisons relate to the coupon rate and yield rate.
- Understand that the coupon rate is determined by the bond issuer and the yield rate is determined by the market.
- Calculate how many bonds need to be issued (or purchased) to achieve a certain fundraising (or investment) goal.

EXAMPLE 4.2. INVESTING $1 MILLION (REVISITED)

In the previous section, we considered a situation where your long-lost uncle left you $1 million after taxes. While putting the money in the bank was one option, we were exploring an alternative option—buying bonds, which had a higher interest rate.

In particular, we were considering a $1.22 million, 5-year bond with 4% nominal, semiannual coupons. Typically, companies do not issue $1.22 million bonds, instead choosing to issue many smaller sized bonds.

Let's assume that the company issuing these bonds decides to issue 122, $10,000 bonds instead of a single $1.22 million bond, using the same terms (5 years, 4% coupon rate, and 4.016% nominal yield rate compounded semiannually). This means that the coupons will be $200 paid semiannually for 5 years, with a lump sum of $10,000 paid out to the bondholder for each bond they own.

To find out how much each bond will cost the bond purchaser today, you can use the general formula for bond pricing that we saw in the previous section:

$$\text{Current bond price} = \frac{F}{(1+j)^n} + Fra_{\overline{n}|j}$$

When applied to this problem, we get:

$$\text{Current bond price} = 10,000\frac{1}{1.02008^{10}} + 10,000(0.02)a_{\overline{n}|j}$$

$$= 8,197.05 + 200\left(\frac{1 - (1/1.02008)^{10}}{0.02008}\right) = 8,197.05 + 1795.77 = \$9,992.82$$

So, each bond will sell for $9,992.82, costing you $1,219,123.67 if you bought all 122 bonds, the same as we saw in the previous section if there was only one (large) $1.22 million bond being sold.

Note that in the formula above, we used 2.008% as the effective interest rate every 6-month. This amount is the yield rate but is typically stated as a nominal interest rate over the year. Thus, the yield rate is 4.016% nominal with semiannual compounding or an effective annual rate of 4.056%.

Key idea

Yield rates for coupon bonds are typically given as a nominal rate with a conversion period equal to the coupon frequency.

Yield rate vs coupon rate

It may seem a bit clunky and cumbersome to have both a yield rate and a coupon rate—which are of two different values and mean two different things. Let's dig a bit deeper into these two values.

It's important to realize that the yield rate is not determined by the bond issuer; it is determined by the investor (the market) and what they want as a return on their investment. On the other hand, the bond issuer determines the coupon rate.

Key idea

The yield rate (interest rate) for a bond is not determined by the bond issuer; it is determined by the market.

Since the yield rate is determined by the investor, let's assume that the investor wants to earn a yield rate of exactly 4% nominal with semiannually compounding. Note: This is slightly different than the 4.016%

nominal interest rate considered above. To find the price of the bonds, we use the bond pricing equation:

$$\text{Current bond price} = 10,000\frac{1}{1.02^{10}} + 200(0.02)a_{\overline{n}|j}$$

$$= 8,203.48 + 200\left(\frac{1 - (1/1.02)^{10}}{0.02}\right) = 8,203.48 + 1,796.52 = \$10,000$$

Note that the price you would pay for the bond today ($10,000) is exactly equal to the face value of the bond! But, with this investment, you also get $200 coupon payments, every 6 months.

To better understand this relationship, remember that a bond is like a loan. In the scenario above, this bond is acting like an interest-only loan at a 2% effective interest rate every 6 months. The lender (you—the investor) gets a $200 interest payment every 6 months and the lump sum (balloon) payment when the loan is done (after 5 years).

The interest payment is of the same size as the coupon payment, and so we can say that a bond with a yield rate equal to its coupon rate is pretty much the same thing as an interest-only loan.

Key idea

If the coupon rate equals the yield rate, the bond can be thought of as an interest-only loan with a lump sum principal payment at the end of the term and interest payments along the way.

Selling at a premium, discount, and par

When a bond's yield rate is equivalent to its coupon rate, it is said to be selling at "par value." This should make sense because, as we saw above, when the yield rate is equivalent to the coupon rate the selling price of the bond was its face (or par) value.

Similarly, earlier in this example, we saw that a bond selling for a 4.016% yield rate cost $9,992.82. Using the same formulas, we can find that the same bond with a 3.98% yield rate costs $10,026.99. We summarize these results in Table 4.1.

Table 4.1 Yield rate, coupon rates, and bond price for a 5-year, $10,000 bond

Coupon rate (%)	Nominal, annual yield rate (%)	Bond price ($)	Bond selling at?
4	3.98	10,008.99	Premium
4	4	10,000.00	Par
4	4.016	9,992.82	Discount

Generalizing these patterns, we see that if the yield rate increases, the present value (selling price) of the bond decreases, and when the yield rate decreases, the present value (selling price of the bond) increases. This is the same idea we saw in the last chapter when we priced annuities—and this should make sense because a bond is really just a special kind of annuity. Some special terms are used to quickly indicate the selling price of a bond. If a bond's selling price is more than the face value, the bond is said to be selling at a **premium**, whereas the bond is selling at a **discount** if its selling price is less than face value. See Table 4.1.

Definitions

If a bond's selling price is more than the face value, the bond is said to be selling at a **premium**, whereas the bond is selling at a **discount** if its selling price is less than face value. A bond is selling at a **par** if the selling price equals its face value.

Thus, we get to the following key idea.

Key idea

If a bond is selling at a premium, then the yield rate is less than the coupon rate. If a bond is selling at a discount, then the yield rate is more than the coupon rate.

These relationships may seem a bit counterintuitive at first, but keep in mind that higher yield rates lead to smaller present values (and vice versa). For example, the present value of $1 paid 1 year from now is $0.98 = $1/1.02$ if the interest rate is 2% and only $0.95 = $1/1.05$ if the interest rate is 5%.

Key idea

As the yield rate (interest rate) increases for a payment in the future, the present value decreases.

It should also make sense that the higher the yield rate, the more advantageous it is for the buyer of the bond. It is also advantageous to be able to buy something at a reduced price (or at a discount).

Bond markets and changing yield rates

The yield rate can be thought of as the current "average" yield rate the market anticipates over the life of the bond. Because bonds can be bought and sold by investors (on a "bond market"), the price a bond sells for can change over the time (and so can the yield rate), reflecting changes to the economy or the perceived risk/profitability of the company that issued the bond as well as the payment of coupons.

It is important to note that these changes to the yield rate really have no bearing on the company's bond directly. The only impact is indirect (e.g., if the market is inferring a lower "market value" of the bond, this implies a higher yield rate and, hence, a riskier investment and may impact the company's ability to issue bonds in the future). As an investor, you may wish to sell a bond (or buy more bonds) at some time based on changes in the yield rate over the time.

EXPLORATION 4.2. STARTING A NEW PRODUCT LINE (REVISITED)

In Exploration 4.1, we explored a situation where a company was considering issuing a $600,000 face value bond with 4% nominal coupons, paid semiannually with a redemption date 5 years from now. Let's revisit this situation and consider a few additional practical considerations.

Selling bonds

1. Name a practical issue with trying to sell a single $600,000 face value bond.

In practice, it may be hard to find a single investor willing to buy this large face value bond and so it may be more practical to sell many smaller bonds, each with the same terms.

2. How many $5000, 5-year bonds with 4% nominal, semiannual coupons will the company have to sell in order to have the equivalent of a single, $600,000 face value bond with similar terms?

Key idea

Yield rates for coupon bonds are typically given as a nominal rate with a conversion period equal to the coupon frequency.

---

3. If the yield rate is 3.71% (annual effective), what is the yield rate in terms of a nominal rate of interest convertible semiannually?

4. What is the coupon size for each of the $5,000 bonds?

5. What is the price that each $5,000 bond will sell for today?

Recall from the previous section that:

$$\text{Current bond price} = Fv^n + Fra_{\overline{n}|j},$$

where j is the effective rate per period (usually 6-month for a bond), n is the number of periods in the term, F is the face value of the bond, and r is the coupon rate per period. Note: This formula assumes that the face value equals the redemption value.

Yield rate vs coupon rate

It may seem a bit clunky and cumbersome to have both a yield rate and a coupon rate—which are of two different values and mean two different things. Let's dig a bit deeper into these two values.

It's important to realize that the yield rate is not determined by the bond issuer; it is determined by the investor (the market) and what they want as a return on their investment. On the other hand, the bond issuer determines the coupon rate.

Key idea

The yield rate (interest rate) for a bond is not determined by the bond issuer; it is determined by the market.

Since the yield rate is determined by the investor, let's assume that the investor wants a yield rate of 4% nominal with semiannually compounding.

6. How does this yield rate compare to the coupon rate?

7. What is the selling price for a $5,000, 5-year bond with 4% nominal coupons paid semiannually?

To better understand why your answer is what it is, consider what it would look like if you took at a $5,000 interest-only loan at 4% nominal, semiannually with semiannual payments, and a 5-year term.

8. How much interest would you pay every 6 months? What would the lump sum payment be on this interest-only loan?

9. How does the interest payment compare to the coupons for the bond? How does the lump sum principal payment compare to the redemption value?

The interest payment is of the same size as the coupon payment, and so we can say that a bond with a yield rate equal to its coupon rate is pretty much the same thing as an interest-only loan.

Key idea

If the coupon rate equals the yield rate, the bond can be thought of as an interest-only loan with a lump sum principal payment at the end of the term and interest payments along the way.

Selling at a premium, discount, and par

When a bond's yield rate is equivalent to its coupon rate it is said to be selling at "par value." This should make sense because, as we saw above, when the yield rate is equivalent to the coupon rate the selling price of the bond was its face (or par) value.

10. If the yield rate the market wants is less than the coupon rate, predict how this will impact the selling price of the bond—will the price increase or decrease? Why?

11. What if the yield rate the market wants is more than the coupon rate, predict how this will impact the selling price of the bond—will the price increase or decrease? Why?

Let's check your predictions.

12. Find the selling price of a $5,000, 5-year bond with 4% nominal, semiannual coupons at a yield rate of 3.5% nominal annually, with semiannual compounding.

13. Find the selling price of a $5,000, 5-year bond with 4% nominal, semiannual coupons at a yield rate of 4.5% nominal annually, with semiannual compounding.

If the yield rate increases, the present value (selling price) of the bond decreases, and when the yield rate decreases, the present value (selling price of the bond) increases. This is the same idea we saw in the last chapter when we priced annuities—and this should make sense because a bond is really just a special kind of annuity. Some special terms are used to quickly indicate the selling price of a bond. If a bond's selling price is more than the face value, the bond is said to be selling at a **premium**, whereas the bond is selling at a **discount** if its selling price is less than the face value.

Definitions
If a bond's selling price is more than the face value, the bond is said to be selling at a **premium**, whereas the bond is selling at a **discount** if its selling price is less than the face value. A bond is selling at a **par** if the selling price equals its face value.

---

14. If the bond is selling for \$5,113.77, is the bond selling at a premium or a discount? Why? Is the yield rate larger or smaller than the coupon rate?

15. If the bond is selling for \$4,889.17, is the bond selling at a premium or a discount? Why? Is the yield rate larger or smaller than the coupon rate?

The previous two questions lead us to the following key idea about the relationships between premium/discount and yield rate vs coupon rate.

Key idea

If a bond is selling at a premium, then the yield rate is less than the coupon rate. If a bond is selling at a discount, then the yield rate is more than the coupon rate.

These relationships may seem a bit counterintuitive at first, but keep in mind that higher yield rates lead to smaller present values (and vice versa). For example, the present value of \$1 paid 1 year from now is \$0.98 = \$1/1.02 if the interest rate is 2% and only \$0.95 = \$1/1.05 if the interest rate is 5%.

Key idea

As the yield rate (interest rate) increases for a payment in the future, the present value decreases.

It should also make sense that the higher the yield rate, the more advantageous it is for the buyer of the bond. It is also advantageous to be able to buy something at a reduced price (or at a discount).

Bond markets and changing yield rates

The yield rate can be thought of as the current "average" yield rate the market anticipates over the life of the bond. Because bonds can be bought and sold by investors (on a "bond market"), the price a bond sells for can change over the time (and so can the yield rate), reflecting changes to the economy or the perceived risk/profitability of the company that issued the bond as well as the payment of coupons.

16. If an investor bought the bond at a discounted price of $4,889.17 (inferred yield rate of 4.5% nominal with semiannual compounding) today and in 6 months (immediately after receiving a $100 coupon) sells it for $5,100, is the new yield rate larger or smaller than the coupon rate? Why? Does this mean that the bond is now selling at a premium or a discount? Why?

It is important to note that these changes to the yield rate really have no bearing on the company's bond directly. The only impact is indirect (e.g., if the market is inferring a lower "market value" of the bond, this implies a higher yield rate and, hence, a riskier investment and may impact the company's ability to issue bonds in the future).

SUMMARY

In this section, we saw how to price bonds using the selling price of a bond with coupons formula. We also saw how the coupon rate (determined by the bond issuer) and the yield rate (determined by the market) told us something about the price of the bond. When they were equal the bond is said to be selling "at par"—so that the coupons are acting just like coupon payments on an interest-only loan. When the yield rate increased, the price of the bond dropped—making it sell at a "discount." Similarly, when the yield rate decreased, the price of the bond increased—making it sell at a "premium."

HOMEWORK QUESTIONS: SECTION 4.2

Conceptual questions

1. What is a yield rate?

2. What is a coupon rate?

3. When the yield rate and the coupon rate are the same, what can you say about the relationship between the face value and selling price of the bond?

4. If a bond is selling at a premium, what can you say about the relationship between the yield rate and coupon rate?

5. If a bond is selling at a discount, what can you say about the relationship between the yield rate and coupon rate?

Practice questions

6. If a company is issuing $5,000 bonds with 5% annual nominal coupons given out semiannually, what is the coupon size?

7. If the semiannual coupon size is $200, what is the coupon rate if the face value of the bond is $10,000?

8. Suppose a bond is selling at par. What is the effective annual yield rate, if the coupon has an annual nominal rate of 3% and the bonds are issued semiannually?

9. If a 7-year bond has a face value of $6,000, a yield rate of 5% compounded semiannually, and a coupon rate of 4%, what is the value of $a_{\overline{n}|j}$? What is the value of $Fra_{\overline{n}|j}$?

10. If a 7-year bond has a face value of $6,000, a yield rate of 5% compounded semiannually, and a coupon rate of 4%, what is the value of v^n? What is the value of Fv^n?

Application questions

11. A 5-year bond has a face value of $4,000, a yield rate of 4% compounded semiannually, and a coupon rate of 5%.
    a. What is the selling price of the bond?
    b. Is the bond selling at a discount, at par, or at a premium?
    c. What is the total amount of money that will be returned to the investor during and at the end of the 5-year period?

12. A 10-year bond has a face value of $7,500, a yield rate of 4.25% compounded semiannually, and a coupon rate of 3%.
   a. What is the selling price of the bond?
   b. Is the bond selling at a discount, at par, or at a premium?
   c. What is the total amount of money that will be returned to the investor during and at the end of the 10-year period?

13. Chuck buys a 5-year par value bond with a $5,000 face value and semiannual coupons paid with a coupon rate of 4%.
   a. What is the selling price of this bond?
   b. What is the dollar value of each coupon?
   c. When Chuck gets his coupons, he immediately invests them in a money market fund where he earns 2% annual nominal interest compounded semiannually. At the end of the 5 years, Chuck collects all his money from the bond and from the money market.
      i. How much money does Chuck collect?
      ii. What effective annual interest rate did Chuck essentially earn on this investment?

14. Chloe buys a 10-year par value bond with an $8,000 face value and semiannual coupons paid with a coupon rate of 4.5%.
   a. What is the selling price of this bond?
   b. What is the dollar value of each coupon?
   c. When Chloe gets her coupons, she immediately invests them in a money market fund where she earns 2% APR (compounded monthly). At the end of the 10 years, Chloe collects all her money from the bond and from the money market.
      i. What effective semiannual interest rate is Chloe earning in her money market account?
      ii. How much money does Chloe collect?
      iii. What effective annual interest rate did Chloe essentially earn on this investment?

15. A bond has a face value of $5,000 and a nominal yield rate of 6% compounded semiannually.
   a. If it is a zero-coupon bond and it is being sold for $3,115.83, what is the term length of the bond?

b. If it is a bond that has semiannual coupons at a rate of 4% annually, and it is being sold for $4,435.20, what is the term length of the bond?

c. If it is a bond that has semiannual coupons at a rate of 6% annually, and it is being sold for $5,000, what is the term length of the bond? (*Hint:* Think about it.)

SECTION 4.3. STOCKS

In the TV show *Shark Tank*, entrepreneurs pitch their ideas to "sharks"—venture capitalists who make creative offers to the entrepreneurs—typically offering cash now for partial ownership in the company. Selling ownership in a company is a popular way to raise money for future projects. Like bonds, the way that ownership in a company can be sold can take many forms. However, one of the most common approaches is via "stock."

Simply put, stock is a partial ownership in a company. As you are probably aware, stock in publicly traded companies can be bought and sold on a stock market. Thus, an investor can buy stock as an investment (hoping to sell it later at a higher price, assuming the company is worth more in the future than it is now), and a company can raise funds by selling partial ownership in the company.

Whereas bonds are like loans, stock is fundamentally different in that it does not necessarily come with any guarantee of future payment, except in the form of dividends—which are fractional portions of company profits.

Learning objectives

By the end of this section, you should be able to:
- Distinguish between common and preferred stock.
- Value preferred stock using the dividend discount model.

EXAMPLE 4.3. INVESTING $1 MILLION IN THE STOCK MARKET

In the previous two sections, we've explored investing $1 million in bonds. How would this look different if you invested in the stock market instead?

First, it is important to realize the primary difference between stocks and bonds. A bond is like a loan issued by an individual to a company. On the other hand, stock is when a company allows an individual to *own* a portion of the company. When the company initially issues stock, they sell partial ownership of the company to the stockholder for a price—thus, the company gets money, and the stockholder now has an investment in the future success of the company.

Stock

Common stock is, as its name implies, the most common type of stock available, with each share usually representing a very small share of ownership in the company. Preferred stock is a type of stock that comes with the right to future dividend payments (usually quarterly). Dividends are payou of a company's profits.

Definitioi
Preferred stc k is part ownership in a company, but comes with the right to regular ʌ ually quarterly) dividend payments. Payments of dividends on preferreα ʻock are guaranteed as long as the company has paid its creditors.

Because common stock does not come with a guarantee of future dividends (cash flows), valuing common stock is quite challenging. Preferred stock, however, can be valued more easily by examining the present value of its future dividend payments using the *dividend discount valuation approach.*

Key idea
The purchase price of the preferred stock is equal to the present value of the future dividends when using the dividend discount valuation approach.

The dividend discount valuation approach is part of a broader class of valuation methods, which computes present value as the present value of the sum of all future cash flows. This is really no different than what we've seen before with annuities and bonds—a series of future cash flows is each valued back to the present time and added together to yield the present value of the annuity.

Key idea

One approach to valuing an investment is to find the present value of future cash flows.

As a simple example of how the dividend discount model of pricing works for preferred stock, consider a preferred stock that pays a nonadjustable $2/share quarterly, indefinitely. Thus, if you own one share of the stock, you will receive $2, every 3 months as long as you own the stock. How much is this stock worth?

We can think of this string of dividend payments as a perpetuity—a never-ending series of payments.

Remember that the pricing of a perpetuity is P/i, where P is the payment size each period and i is the effective interest rate per period. So, if the market is currently paying 3% effective interest annually, how much does the dividend discount model say that the stock is worth?

Three-percent effective annually is equivalent to 0.7417% effective quarterly (you can find this by solving $(1+i)^4 = 1.03$ for i, and so $\$2/0.007417 = \$269.65$ is the predicted price of the preferred stock using the dividend discount model).

Key idea

The predicted price, P, of a preferred stock using the dividend discount model is $P = D/i$, where D is the value of the dividend and i is the effective interest rate per dividend period.

EXPLORATION 4.3. RAISING MONEY BY SELLING OWNERSHIP IN THE COMPANY

In the previous two explorations, we looked at a company considering selling bonds as a way to raise $500,000 and considered the pros and cons of this approach vs a bank loan.

1. What are some downsides and challenges to a start-up company look-ing to sell part ownership of the company?

There are many potential downsides and challenges to a start-up com-pany looking to sell part ownership of the company. For example, the current owners of the company are likely hoping to make money them-selves by keeping their ownership into the future anticipating that the company grows in value. On the flip side, it might be hard to get inves-tors to consider the start-up company valuable enough or promising enough to buy partial ownership at the price and for the ownership frac-tion that the company wants.

Cash flow approach to value investments

2. If you wish to raise $500,000 and you find an investor who values your company at $2 million, what fraction ownership will you be sell-ing if you take their offer?

But, how does a company or an investor value a company? There are many, many approaches out there and many get quite complicated as you might expect. That said, there is one commonly used approach that relies on looking at a company's future cash flows and projecting back to the present time.

3. Let's say that your company anticipates using the $500,000 you raise to make a single, large art sculpture that you plan to sell for $750,000 in 5 years. After paying taxes and some other expenses, you expect to have $600,000 left over. What yield rate does the $500,000 anticipate earning/year?

This overly simplistic example illustrates one basic approach to valua-tion—find the present value of future cash flows and this is the current value. Now, we'll see how this general idea applies to stock valuation.

Key idea
One approach to valuing an investment is to find the present value of future cash flows.

Stock

Common stock is, as its name implies, the most common type of stock available, with each share representing a, usually, very small share of ownership in the company. Preferred stock is a type of stock that comes with the right to future dividend payments (usually quarterly). Dividends are payouts of a company's profits.

Definition

Preferred stock is part ownership in a company, but comes with the right to regular (usually quarterly) dividend payments. Payments of dividends on preferred stock are guaranteed as long as the company has paid its creditors.

Because common stock does not come with a guarantee of future dividends (cash flows), valuing common stock is more challenging. Preferred stock, however, can be valued more easily by examining the present value of its future dividend payments.

Key idea

The purchase price of the preferred stock is equal to the present value of the future dividends.

---

4. If your company decides to issue a preferred stock paying a non-adjustable $0.50/share quarterly, indefinitely, what is the present value of the stock if the market is paying an effective yield rate of 1.5% quarterly? *Hint*: Think of the dividends being paid out as a perpetuity.

5. How many shares of stock should the company sell if they hope to get $500,000?

Key idea

The predicted price, P, of a preferred stock using the dividend discount model is $P = D/i$, where D is the value of the dividend and i is the effective interest rate per dividend period.

In reality, company valuation is a very complex, multifaceted process and shouldn't be entered into lightly. The examples above are meant to provide a very preliminary look at how valuations can be done, but in no way is it comprehensive.

SUMMARY

In this section, we saw how valuations of investments (stocks, bonds, and companies) are like annuities. By finding the present value of the future cash flows, we can get one estimate of the present value of the asset. Applying this to preferred stock with guaranteed dividends, we can use the perpetuity formula to estimate the stock price. Common stock, unlike preferred stock, does not guarantee to pay out dividends but it is more common in practice.

Notation and equation summary
The predicted price, P, of a preferred stock using the dividend discount model is $P = D/i$, where D is the value of the dividend and i is the effective interest rate per dividend period.

HOMEWORK QUESTIONS: SECTION 4.3

Conceptual questions

1. If the yield rate increases, the price of preferred stock will _____. (increase/decrease)

2. How is stock different than a bond? (Not in terms of money or how they are valued, but in terms of what they really are.)

3. How is a preferred stock different than a common stock?

4. When using the dividend discount valuation approach, how is the purchase price of a stock calculated?

5. What are dividends?

Practice questions

6. A company decides to issue preferred stock with a nonadjustable (won't change over the time) dividend amount of $0.83 per share, semiannually indefinitely. What is the present value of a share of the stock at a 6% nominal annual yield (interest) rate, compounded semiannually?

7. Suppose a company decides to issue a preferred stock with the same parameters as in the previous question except with a 6% *effective* yearly rate of interest. What is the present value of a share of the stock?

8. A company decides to issue preferred stock with a nonadjustable (won't change over time) dividend amount of $0.83 per share, semiannually with a redemption time of 10 years. What is the present value of a share of the stock at a 6% nominal annual yield (interest) rate, compounded semiannually?

9. Suppose a company decides to issue a preferred stock with the same parameters as in the previous question except with a 6% *effective* yearly rate of interest. What is the present value of a share of the stock?

10. If the predicted price (present value) of a preferred stock that pays $2.50 dividends per quarter (in perpetuity) is $500, what is the effective quarterly interest rate for the stock?

Application questions

11. A company offers quarterly dividends of $3 per share of stock.
   a. If the stock has an annual effective rate of return of 8%, what is the price of the stock?
   b. If the stock has an annual effective rate of return of 9%, what is the price of the stock?
   c. If the stock has an annual effective rate of return of 10%, what is the price of the stock?
   d. As the effective rate of return increases and the dividends stay the same, how does the price of the stock change?

12. The cost of a share of stock in a company is $52 with quarterly dividends.

a. If the stock has an annual effective rate of return of 6%, what is the value of the quarterly dividend?

b. If the stock has an annual effective rate of return of 7%, what is the value of the quarterly dividend?

c. If the stock has an annual effective rate of return of 8%, what is the value of the quarterly dividend?

d. As the effective rate of return increases and the cost of a share of stock stays the same, how does the value of the dividend change?

13. A company's stock will pay $2 annual dividends for 5 years and then after that will pay $3 annual for the dividends in perpetuity. All with an effective rate of return of 8%.

a. Just focusing on the first part of this, what is the present value of the stock that pays $2 dividends for 5 years?

b. Now just focusing on the second part, what is the value of a stock 5 years from now that pays $3 annually in perpetuity?

c. What is the present value of the portion of the stock you calculated in part b?

d. Combining your answers from parts a and c together, what is the present value of the stock?

14. A company's stock will pay $2.50 annual dividends for 4 years, then pay $3.00 dividends for the next 4 years, and after that will pay $3.50 annual for the dividends in perpetuity—all with an effective rate of return of 7.5%.

a. Just focusing on the first part of this, what is the present value of the stock that pays $2.50 dividends for 4 years?

b. Now just focusing on the second part, what is the value of the stock in 4 years that pays $3.00 dividends for 4 years?

c. What is the present value of the portion of the stock you calculated in part b?

d. Now just focusing on the third part, what is the value of a stock 8 years from now that pays $3.50 annually in perpetuity?

e. What is the present value of the portion of the stock you calculated in part d?

     f. Combining your answers from parts a, c, and e together, what is the present value of the stock?

15. A company's stock has a selling price of $40. It offers annual dividend payments of $2.50 at the end of every year for the first 10 years and payments of P thereafter. The annual rate of return is 7.5% and we want to calculate P.

    a. Find the present value of this stock for just the first part where $2.50 dividends are earned every year for 10 years.

    b. Use your answer from part a to find the present value of the second part of this scenario (beyond the first 10 years).

    c. What is the future value (in 10 years) for your answer to part b?

    d. Use your answer to part c to find the payments beyond 10 years, P.

    e. Another company's stock has a selling price of $50. It offers annual dividend payments of $4 at the end of every year for the first 8 years and payments of P thereafter. If the annual rate of return is 8.5%, what is the value of P?

END OF CHAPTER SUMMARY

In this chapter, we began to learn about methods that companies use to raise money: stocks and bonds, and how the pricing for these financial instruments is done. Bonds, which are a form of a loan directly from a company to investors, pay a fixed amount of money in the future either just in a lump sum (zero-coupon bond) or through coupons (acting like interest payments) and a lump sum (redemption value). Bond prices for bonds with coupons can be at, above, or below face value depending on the relationship between the coupon rate and yield rate—essentially, whether the coupon (interest) payments are at, above, or below the interest that is accruing on the loan. In contrast to bonds, stocks are not loans but, instead, are selling part ownership in the company to investors as a way to raise money. The dividend discount money is a simplistic approach to begin to understand how dividend-paying stocks are valued in the marketplace.

END OF CHAPTER EXERCISES

(SOA EXAM FM SAMPLE QUESTIONS May 2000, Question 29)

1. A firm has proposed the following restructuring for one of its 1,000 par value bonds.

   The bond presently has 10 years remaining until maturity. The coupon rate on the existing bond is 6.75% per annum paid semi-annually. The current nominal semi-annual yield on the bond is 7.40%.

   The company proposes suspending coupon payments for four years with the suspended coupon payments being repaid, with accrued interest, when the bond comes due. Accrued interest is calculated using a nominal semi-annual rate of 7.40%.

   Calculate the market value of the restructured bond.

   A 755
   B 805
   C 855
   D 905
   E 955

(SOA EXAM FM SAMPLE QUESTIONS May 2001, Question 41)

2. Bill buys a 10-year 1000 par value 6% bond with semi-annual coupons. The price assumes a nominal yield of 6%, compounded semi-annually.

   As Bill receives each coupon payment, he immediately puts the money into an account earning interest at an annual effective rate of i.

   At the end of 10 years, immediately after Bill receives the final coupon payment and the redemption value of the bond, Bill has earned an annual effective yield of 7% on his investment in the bond.

   Calculate i.

   A 9.50%
   B 9.75%
   C 10.00%
   D 10.25%
   E 10.50%

(SOA EXAM FM SAMPLE QUESTIONS May 2005, Question 5)

3. Susan can buy a zero-coupon bond that will pay 1,000 at the end of 12 years and is currently selling for 624.60. Instead she purchases a 6% bond with coupons payable semi-annually that will pay 1,000 at the end of 10 years. If she pays X she will earn the same annual effective interest rate as the zero-coupon bond.

Calculate X.
A 1,164
B 1,167
C 1,170
D 1,173
E 1,176

(SOA EXAM FM SAMPLE QUESTIONS November 2005, Question 4)

4. A ten-year 100 par value bond pays 8% coupons semi-annually. The bond is priced at 118.20 to yield an annual nominal rate of 6% convertible semi-annually.

Calculate the redemption value of the bond.
A 97
B 100
C 103
D 106
E 109

(SOA EXAM FM SAMPLE QUESTIONS November 2005, Question 11)

5. An investor borrows an amount at an annual effective interest rate of 5% and will repay all interest and principal in a lump sum at the end of 10 years. She uses the amount borrowed to purchase a 1,000 par value 10-year bond with 8% semi-annual coupons bought to yield 6% convertible semi-annually. All coupon payments are reinvested at a nominal rate of 4% convertible semi-annually.

Calculate the net gain to the investor at the end of 10 years after the loan is repaid.

A 96
B 101
C 106
D 111
E 116

(SOA EXAM FM SAMPLE QUESTIONS November 2005, Question 16)

6. Dan purchases a 1,000 par value 10-year bond with 9% semi-annual coupons for 925. He is able to reinvest his coupon payments at a nominal rate of 7% convertible semi-annually.

   Calculate his nominal annual yield rate convertible semi-annually over the ten-year period.

   A 7.6%
   B 8.1%
   C 9.2%
   D 9.4%
   E 10.2%

   (SOA EXAM FM SAMPLE QUESTIONS November 2005, Question 24)

7. A 30-year bond with a par value of 1,000 and 12% coupons payable quarterly is selling at 850. Calculate the annual nominal yield rate convertible quarterly.

   A 3.5%
   B 7.1%
   C 14.2%
   D 14.9%
   E 15.4%

   (SOA EXAM FM SAMPLE QUESTIONS Interest Theory, Question 74)

8. You are given the following information about two bonds, Bond A and Bond B:
   i Each bond is a 10-year bond with semi-annual coupons redeemable at its par value of 10,000, and is bought to yield an annual nominal interest rate of i, convertible semi-annually.

ii Bond A has an annual coupon rate of $(i + 0.04)$, paid semi-annually.

iii Bond B has an annual coupon rate of $(i - 0.04)$, paid semi-annually.

iv The price of Bond A is 5,341.12 greater than the price of Bond B.

Calculate i.

A 0.042

B 0.043

C 0.081

D 0.084

E 0.086

(SOA EXAM FM SAMPLE QUESTIONS Interest Theory, Question 76)

9. Consider two 30-year bonds with the same purchase price. Each has an annual coupon rate of 5% paid semi-annually and a par value of 1,000.

   The first bond has an annual nominal yield rate of 5% compounded semi-annually, and a redemption value of 1,200.

   The second bond has an annual nominal yield rate of j compounded semi-annually, and a redemption value of 800.

   Calculate j.

   A. 2.20%

   B. 2.34%

   C. 3.53%

   D. 4.40%

   E. 4.69%

(SOA EXAM FM SAMPLE QUESTIONS Interest Theory, Question 90)

10. A 1,000 par value 20-year bond sells for P and yields a nominal interest rate of 10% convertible semi-annually. The bond has 9% coupons payable semi-annually and a redemption value of 1,200.

    Calculate P.

    A 914

    B 943

    C 1,013

    D 1,034

    E 1,097

(SOA EXAM FM SAMPLE QUESTIONS Interest Theory, Question 113)

11. An investor purchased a 25-year bond with semi-annual coupons, redeemable at par, for a price of 10,000. The annual effective yield rate is 7.05%, and the annual coupon rate is 7%.

    Calculate the redemption value of the bond.
    A 9,918
    B 9,942
    C 9,981
    D 10,059
    E 10,083

(SOA EXAM FM SAMPLE QUESTIONS Interest Theory, Question 114)

12. Jeff has 8,000 and would like to purchase a 10,000 bond. In doing so, Jeff takes out a 10-year loan of 2,000 from a bank and will make interest-only payments at the end of each month at a nominal rate of 8.0% convertible monthly. He immediately pays 10,000 for a 10-year bond with a par value of 10,000 and 9.0% coupons paid monthly.

    Calculate the annual effective yield rate that Jeff will realize on his 8,000 over the 10-year period.
    A 9.30%
    B 9.65%
    C 10.00%
    D 10.35%
    E 10.70%

(SOA EXAM FM SAMPLE QUESTIONS Interest Theory, Question 115)

13. A bank issues three annual coupon bonds redeemable at par, all with the same term, price, and annual effective yield rate.

    The first bond has face value 1,000 and annual coupon rate 5.28%.
    The second bond has face value 1,100 and annual coupon rate 4.40%.

The third bond has face value 1,320 and annual coupon rate r. Calculate r.

A 2.46%
B 2.93%
C 3.52%
D 3.67%
E 4.00%

CHAPTER FIVE

Portfolios: Fundamentals of Collections of Assets and Liabilities

Abstract

In this chapter, we begin to explore collections of assets and liabilities—called portfolios. Exploring portfolios requires new ways of thinking about and computing interest rates. The dollar-weighted (or internal) rate of return acts as an "average" rate of return for the portfolio's value over the time, but can be significantly impacted by the timing of cash inflows and outflows. In contrast, the time-weighted rate of return ignores the potentially good or bad timing of cash flows to provide a cash-flow independent measure of portfolio performance over the time. We will see that the Macaulay duration, the weighted time of future cash flows, is one way to quantify interest-rate risk. Finally, we will see that an immunized portfolio is protected against changes in the interest rate via cash-flow matching or duration matching assets and liabilities.

Keywords: Dollar-weighted rate of return; internal rate of return; Macaulay duration; immunization

In this text, our focus so far has been primarily on valuing a single financial instrument with regularly timed payments at a constant interest rate. In practice, however, things are usually much more complicated. Interest rates change, payments aren't always "nicely timed," and accounts may involve both contributions and withdrawals. Our goal in this chapter is to start moving towards more "realistic" scenarios, albeit at a slow pace. One of the most complicated parts of a "realistic" view of interest and investments is modeling frequent, small, and unexpected changes in the interest rate. To do this well, you really need to either (a) use a computer to simulate these changes or (b) use probability theory to look at the long run average behavior as well as the variation in that behavior. For now, those important and realistic ideas are beyond the scope of what we want to accomplish.

That said, there are still some important, practical concepts related to analyzing *portfolios*—collections of investments [or liabilities—money you owe (debts)]—that will help us to better understand investor and lender decisions about deposits, withdrawals, investment choices (Section 5.1), and the impact of interest rate changes (Sections 5.2 and 5.3).

A Spiral Approach to Financial Mathematics.
DOI: https://doi.org/10.1016/B978-0-12-801580-3.00005-8
© 2018 Elsevier Inc.
All rights reserved.

SECTION 5.1. YIELD RATES ON A PORTFOLIO

In the previous chapter on bonds, we saw that the yield rate of a bond could be determined by the bond's present value—how much the bond is selling for on the open market. A bond is a series of previously agreed upon cash flows (coupon payments and the final redemption payment). But, how does the concept of yield rate work when an investor owns multiple bonds? Or a mix of stocks, bonds, annuities, perpetuities, loans, savings accounts, Certificates of deposit (CDs), etc.?

In this section, we'll look at two different ways of thinking about yield rates. First, we'll explore the internal rate of return (IRR) (or dollar-weighted yield rate), which is comparable to the types of yield rates we've been thinking about so far. Then, we'll look at another approach—the time-weighted rate of return—an alternative approach, which is not as sensitive to an investor's choices about when to buy or sell. In both contexts, we'll be considering how these rates of return work when applied to a portfolio of investments, not just a single investment (or liability) at a time.

Learning objectives

By the end of this section, you should be able to:

- Understand the idea that a portfolio is a collection of investments or cash flows.
- Find and interpret the dollar-weighted yield rate (IRR) as a measure of investor performance.
- Find and interpret the time-weighted yield rate as a measure of portfolio performance.
- Contrast when a dollar-weighted rate of return vs time-weighted rate of return would be more appropriate and what it means in terms of investor timing when one rate of return is larger than the other.

EXAMPLE 5.1. TIMING A MARKET INVESTMENT

You have decided to invest some money in the bond market as part of your retirement planning. You buy five, $1,000 face value, 10-year zero-coupon bonds from a local company. The bonds you purchase are currently selling for $781.20 each. We will call this collection of bonds a portfolio—since it is a collection of investments. The current value of your portfolio is $3,906.

Definition

A **portfolio** is a collection of investments (e.g., stocks, bonds, etc.) held by a person or organization. While not necessary, portfolios often span multiple market sectors to spread out investment risk.

Definition

A **liability** is a future debt that is owed. For example, a company issuing a bond views the coupon payments and future redemption as liabilities to be paid in the future.

Think about it

What is the yield rate on the bonds?

Since the bond is a zero-coupon bond, the calculation for yield rate is fairly straightforward. Recall the following equation:

$$\text{Selling price of a bond without coupons} = Fv^n$$
$$\$781.20 = \$1,000v^{10}$$
$$v^{10} = 0.7812$$
$$v = 0.97561$$
$$i = 0.025$$

1 year later

The company issuing the bonds used the money it received from bond sales to buildup inventory of its new product—the sales of which are far exceeding company projections. Hearing this news 1 year after you purchased your bonds you look up the price of the bond on the bond market and see that the bonds are now selling for $937.44 each!

Think about it

What was your effective interest rate over the 1-year period?

Your effective rate of interest over the 1-year period was \$937.44/ \$781.20 = 1.20, or a 20% return! Nice work! The current value of your entire investment is now \$4,687.20 (= \$937.44 × 5).

Think about it

What is the new yield rate on the bonds? Did it go up or down?

The market yield rate on the bond dropped because the price increased. Intuitively, you got a better than expected yield on the bond recently, and since the payoff price of the bond is not changing (\$1,000), the overall yield rate dropped.

To find the new yield rate, solve the following equation for i, where we've accounted for the first year by changing the value n to be 9.

$$\text{Selling price of a bond} = \$937.44 = 1,000v^9$$

Solving this, we found $i \approx 0.721\%$ effective annual yield. Note that the yield rate has declined from 2.5% annually when you bought the bond to 0.72% annually now. Why does this make sense intuitively? You can think of the 2.5% annual yield rate when you bought the bond as the "average" yield. Since the company did well early in the life of the bond, the price went up so that you earned the yield early in the life of the bond. This means that the yield during the rest of the life of the bond cannot be as good, since the bond will only be worth \$1,000 when it is redeemed. There is no way for it to be worth more.

You are pretty excited about this awesome performance from your investment. So, you decide to buy another five bonds from this company, at this new price of \$937.44/bond (an additional investment of \$4,687.20). You now own 10 identical bonds and the value of your port-folio is \$9,374.40.

Another year later

During the next year, the new product the company made has gotten some bad press. There were some accidents with the product and people got hurt. Sales have plummeted. The company is claiming these are isolated incidents and that they've resolved the issues with the next batch of shipments. However, 1 year from the time you first bought the bonds, and with a sick feeling in your stomach, you again look up the price the bond is now selling for on the market. You are somewhat comforted to see that the price has *only* dropped to $781.20—the price you initially paid for the bonds.

Think about it

What was your effective interest rate over the latest year?

Your effective rate of interest over the most recent year was $781.20/ 937.44 = 0.8333$, or a 16.67% loss on each bond. Not great. The current value of your entire investment if you sell now is $7,812 (= $781.20 × 10).

Key idea

To compute an effective interest rate when an investment decreases in value, divide the ending value by the starting value. You will end with a number less than one. Subtract one from this number, and you will end up with a number less than zero representing the effective loss. Note: This is no different than what we do with an investment that has increased in value, the only difference is whether the final answer is less than or greater than one.

Think about it

The price of the bond has changed, so what is the new yield rate on the bonds?

Once again, the yield rate has changed. The new market yield rate is found by solving this equation for i:

$$\text{Selling price of a bond} = \$781.20 = 1,000v^8$$

The new yield rate is 3.13% annually. Notice that this is higher than it was to start with! This is because there is less time for the bond to accumulate to the value of $1,000. It also captures the fact that the market is considering this company a riskier investment than they did initially since higher yield rates are associated with higher risk investments.

Key idea

Higher yield rates are associated with higher risk investments.

Dollar-weighted yield rate

The first 2 years of your investments in the bond market were a bit of a roller coaster. How can you evaluate how you did? What was your "overall" performance?

One way to evaluate your overall performance for the year is to compute the IRR, which is also known as the dollar-weighted rate of return. The dollar-weighted rate of return can be thought of as the yield rate over the entire length of the investment—kind of like an "average" yield rate on the investment.

Definition box

The **dollar-weighted rate of return** (or IRR) is the rate so that if all deposits and withdrawals were subject to the same interest rate over the entire investment time period, the individual transactions would accumulate to the investment's ending balance.

To find the dollar-weighted rate of return, solve the following equation for i, the unknown rate of return.

$$\text{Account ending value} = \sum_{\text{all values of } m} C_m (1+i)^{t_m},$$

where for each of the m different deposits and withdrawals from the account, C_m is the value of the mth deposit (using a minus sign for a withdrawal) and t_m is the length of time from the deposit (or withdrawal) until the account "end date."

To find the dollar-weighted yield rate for this 1-year bond investment, we first record information about the accounts ending value, cash flow amounts, and timing:

Account ending value = $7,812 ($781.20 for 10 bonds)

$C_1 =$ Initial investment of $3,906 (five bonds)

$t_1 = 2$ (2 years is the length of time the initial deposit was in the account)

$C_2 =$ Additional investment of $4687.20 after 1 year (bought five more bonds)

$t_2 = 1$ (1 year is the length of time that the additional deposit was in the account)

Account ending value $= \$7,812 = 3,906(1+i)^2 + 4,687.20(1+i)$

Solving for i, gives a value of $i = -0.0638$. In other words, your average return was a loss of 6.38% annually (or a loss of 13.17% over the 2-year period since $1.0638^2 = 1.1317$).

Think about it

Why is your dollar-weighted rate of return so low when you earned 20% in the first year and lost 16.67% in the second year? Why isn't the average of 20% and -16.67%?

Your overall rate of return is quite low (-6.38%) because of the bad timing of your second bond purchase. In particular, you bought additional bonds right before they substantially dropped in value! You can't just "average" the yield rates together because different amounts of money were in the account at different times and, furthermore, when it comes to yield rates, earning 20% and then losing 20% doesn't get you back to where you started!

Key idea

The IRR is called the dollar-weighted rate of return because the rate takes into consideration how much money is in the investment at any time. Thus, poorly timed deposits or withdrawals (buying high and selling low) will make the value drop and vice versa. Also, note that to compute the dollar-weighted in the equation, the rate of return of each term is multiplied (or weighted) by the size of the deposit.

While lamenting your poor return over the past year, you talk to your friend who also invested in the same bond. Your friend is in a great mood. You ask why, and she says, "Despite all of the turmoil with the company, my annual return was 0%—I'm glad it wasn't worse!" You find out that she bought five bonds, just like you did, a year ago, for $3,906. If she sold the five bonds today, they would still be worth $3,906. Thus, she calculates that her rate of return was 0% for the 2-year period (which is also 0% annually).

You can see this mathematically by realizing that

$$3,906 = 3,906(1+i)^2 \text{ is true when } i = 0.$$

This dollar-weighted rate of return for your friend is different than your dollar-weighted rate of return because your friend timed her transactions better than you did. By not buying and selling at the end of the first year, she didn't experience any gain or loss.

Still looking for someone to feel sorry with, you call a third friend who you also know purchased the bond. He is ecstatic and offers to take you to dinner. Over dinner you find out that he bought 10 bonds a year ago for $781.20 each, and then sold all but have one of them 1 year later for $937.44. He claims to have earned 16.58% for his annual IRR (or $1.1658^2 = 1.3591$; 35.91% over the 2-year period). His ending account value if he sold his remaining bond today is $781.20 (the value of one bond).

You can calculate this rate of return mathematically by realizing that:

$$\text{Account ending value} = \$781.20 = \$7,812(1+i)^2 - \$8,436.96(1+i)$$

Think about it
Why is this annual rate of return (16.58%) so high?

This friend earned 20% over the first year when he had a lot of money in the account, but only a small amount of money in the account when it lost 16.67%. Thus, his overall annual dollar-weighted rate of return was quite good (16.58% annually).

Clearly, the timing of transactions matter! The best investment returns are achieved when you buy low and sell high. Of course, this isn't what you did—you bought high and sold low!

Key idea
The highest rates of return on investments will be earned when you buy low and sell high. Conversely, the lowest rates are when you buy high and sell low.

Time-weighted yield rate
Given the rather fickle nature of the dollar-weighted rate of return to an investor's potentially poorly (or well!) timed deposits and withdrawals,

there is another way to think of a rate of return which does not take transaction choices into account.

The time-weighted yield rate is equivalent to the annual effective yield rate if you had invested all of your money into the account at the beginning, and made no deposits or withdrawals. Thus, the time-weighted yield rate ignores potentially good or bad timing of deposits or withdrawals.

Since this is essentially the strategy taken by your first friend, we know that the time-weighted yield rate is equal to the dollar-weighted yield rate for her—0%.

Key idea

The time-weighted yield rate will equal to the dollar-weighted yield rate when no deposits or withdrawals are made to the account during the life of the account.

But, how do you find the time-weighted yield rate when an account does have transactions? In order to "ignore" the transactions, think of the entire period you earned interest (in the example above, this is 2 years) as broken into a series of smaller periods of time—with "break points" for each transaction. The time-weighted yield rate is simply the product of all of the individual yield rates for each of the smaller periods of time. Here is a formal equation showing this:

$$1 + \text{time-weighted yield rate over entire investment time}$$
$$= (1 + \text{yield rate period 1})(1 + \text{yield rate period 2})\ldots(1 + \text{yield rate period } k)$$
$$= \left(\frac{\text{End balance for period 1}}{\text{Start balance for period 1}}\right)\left(\frac{\text{End balance for period 2}}{\text{Start balance for period 2}}\right)$$
$$\ldots\left(\frac{\text{End balance for period } k}{\text{Start balance for period } k}\right)$$
$$= (1 + \text{annual time-weighted yield rate})^{m}$$

In the above equation, m is the number of years over which the investment is made. Note that the periods do not need to be in years for the equation above to work.

The **Start balance** is after a deposit/withdrawal is made to the account, and the **End balance** is before a deposit or withdrawal is made to the account. You break the total length of time into k periods where each of the "splits" between periods corresponds to the timing of the transaction.

Definition

The **time-weighted yield rate** is an overall measure of an investment's performance, which ignores timing and size of transactions. It is computed as the product of all individual period yield rates.

Let's see how the time-weighted yield rate is computed on your account.

Because you had a transaction at the end of the first year (you bought more bonds), there are two periods to compute a yield rate: the first year and the second year. For the first year, the yield rate is $4,687.2/ $3,906 = 1.2, or 20%. For the second year, the yield rate is $7,812.00/ $9,374.40 = 0.8333. Thus, the time-weighted yield rate is 1.2 $\times$ 0.8333 = 1 + i, or i = 0%. Plugging into the equation directly generates the same answer:

$$1 + \text{time-weighted yield rate} = \left(\frac{\$4,687.20}{\$3,906}\right)\left(\frac{\$7,812}{\$9,374.40}\right) = 1$$

Thus, the 2-year time-weighted yield rate is 0, and so is the annual yield rate.

You can do a similar calculation for your second friend who timed her transactions well,

$$1 + \text{time-weighted yield rate} = \left(\frac{\$9,374.40}{\$7,812}\right)\left(\frac{\$781.20}{\$937.44}\right) = 1$$

And so, again, we find that the time-weighted yield rate is 0% over 2 years (which is also 0%/year).

Thus, the time-weighted yield rate is a better measure of the performance of an investment by itself over the time, whereas the dollar-weighted yield rate measures the performance of the investor by incorporating their decisions about deposits and withdrawals into the equation.

Key idea

In practice, if a portfolio is being managed by a financial professional, and that individual has no control over when investors deposit money or withdrawal money, then the time-weighted yield rate is a better measure of their performance than the dollar-weighted yield rate.

Comparing dollar-weighted and time-weighted yield rates

If you are given the dollar-weighted and time-weighted yield rates for an account, you can use these to figure out whether the timing of deposits/withdrawals was good or bad. Table 5.1 summarizes the transactions and yield rates for the three accounts we've been exploring.

Key idea

When the time-weighted yield rate is larger than the dollar-weighted yield rate, the investor timed their deposits/withdrawals poorly. When the time-weighted yield rate is smaller than the dollar-weighted yield rate, the investor timed their deposits/withdrawals well.

▷ EXPLORATION 5.1. PLAYING THE BOND MARKET

After learning about bonds (Chapter 4: Stocks and Bonds: Fundamentals of Investment Strategies), you are excited to start investing in the bond market. You decide to take some of your summer job earnings and buy some bonds. After checking the bond market, you focus in on two bonds that interest you. Table 5.2 illustrates what you see for selling prices of bonds at two different companies.

1. Find the annual effective yield rate for the bond issued by company A.

2. Find the annual effective yield rate for the bond issued by company B.

3. Why do you think these yield rates are different?

Recall that bond prices are driven by the market, which is incorporating general expectations of economic growth and specific expectations of a company's risk. Since a bond is really just a "direct to market" loan, yield rates are incorporating the markets expectation that a company will be able to pay the loan (bond) when it is due. Another term for a bond (from the issuing company's perspective) is a liability.

Table 5.1 Summary of transactions and yield rates for each account

| Investor | Transactions | | | Yield Rates | | | |
	Initial investment (Jan 1) ($)	Deposit (withdrawal) (after 1 year later) ($)	Ending balance (after 2 years) ($)	Effective rate for first year (%)	Effective rate for second year (%)	Dollar-weighted annual return (%)	Time-weighted annual return (%)
You	3,906.00	4,687.20	7,812.00	20.00	− 16.67	− 6.38	0.00
Friend 1	3,906.00	0.00	3,906.00	20.00	− 16.67	0.00	0.00
Friend 2	7,812.00	9,374.40	781.20[a]	20.00	− 16.67	16.58	0.00

[a]Your friend also has $9,374.40 in another account, which is assumed to have earned 0% interest over the second 6 months.

Table 5.2 Current selling prices for $1,000 face value, zero-coupon bonds

Company	Current selling price ($)	Term (years)
A	942.32	3
B	862.61	5

Definition

A **liability** is a future debt that is owed. For example, a company issuing a bond views the coupon payments and future redemption as liabilities to be paid in the future.

Investment strategy 1

You decide that you would like to earn a higher yield on your investment and are willing to take on some risk to get that yield. With this in mind, you buy two bonds from company B.

4. How much do you pay now to buy two bonds from company B?

You now have two bonds in your **portfolio**. Unfortunately, company B's reputation over the year after you buy your bond is suffering—sales are down, and the company keeps taking on more and more debt. One year after buying the two bonds from company B, you see that the bond is now selling for only $822.70.

Definition

A **portfolio** is a collection of investments (e.g., stocks, bonds, etc.) held by a person or organization. While not necessary, portfolios often span multiple market sectors to spread out investment risk.

---

5. What is the new value of your bond portfolio? Did you lose money or make money?

6. What does this say about the effective interest rate you earned on your investment? Will it be positive or negative? Why?

Since you lost money, the effect interest rate you earned on your investment will be negative.

Key idea

To compute an effective interest rate when an investment decreases in value divide the ending value by the starting value. You will end with a number less than one. Subtract one from this number, and you will end up with a number less than zero representing the effective loss. This is no different than what we do with an investment that has increased in value, the only difference is whether the final answer is less than or greater than zero.

7. What was the effective annual interest rate you earned over the past year on your bond portfolio?

8. Predict whether you think that the market yield rate on company B's bond has increased or decreased based on the current value of the bond? Why?

9. Find the new market yield rate on company B's bond. Hint: Don't forget that the term is different now since it is 1 year later from when the bond was originally issued!

The yield rate on company B's bond has increased, reflecting greater risk that company B will be able to pay the bond back in 4 years when it comes due.

Key idea

Higher yield rates are associated with higher risk investments.

What will you do now?

Let's consider what happens if you react to this drop in price by selling one of the bonds.

10. What will the value of your portfolio be if you sell one of the bonds?

After one more year, 2 years from your original bond purchase, the value of company B's bond is now $889.00.

11. What is the new value of your bond portfolio? Note: Ignore the "cash" you have from your earlier bond sale, just value the portfolio.

12. What annual effective interest rate did your bond portfolio earn in the second year?

Your portfolio (now just a single bond), jumped in price rather dramatically from \$822.70 to \$889.00—an increase of 8.06% in a single year! While you are happy that the bond increased in value, you wonder—how did you really do? What was your rate of return over the last couple of years? And, what about your decision to sell one bond part way through?

Dollar-weighted yield rate

One way to evaluate your overall performance for the year is to compute the IRR, which is also known as the dollar-weighted rate of return. The dollar-weighted rate of return can be thought of as the yield rate over the entire length of the investment—kind of like an "average" yield rate on the investment.

Definition box

The **dollar-weighted rate of return** (IRR) is the rate so that if all deposits and withdrawals were subject to the same interest rate over the entire investment time period, the individual transactions would accumulate to the investment's ending balance.

To find the dollar-weighted rate of return, solve the following equation for i, the unknown rate of return.

$$\text{Account ending value} = \sum_{\text{all values of } m} C_m(1+i)^{t_m},$$

where for each of the m different deposits and withdrawals from the account, C_m is the mth deposit amount (using a minus sign for a withdrawal) and t_m is the length of time from the deposit (or withdrawal) until the account "end date."

13. Let's get the values we need in order to calculate the dollar-weighted yield rate, i.

  a. What is the ending value of your bond portfolio? _____

  b. What was the initial investment amount? _____. This is C_1.

    c. How long was it from the time the initial investment was made until the time of the ending value? _____. This is t_1. This is how long the initial investment could have been in the account if you hadn't made any withdrawals.

    d. What was the amount of the withdrawal from the account? _____. This is C_2. Because this is a withdrawal, make sure that your answer is negative!

    e. How long was it from the time of the withdrawal to the end date?_____. This is t_2.

14. Use the following equation and your answers to the previous question to find the dollar-weighted yield rate, i. (You can use a financial calculator, Excel or a guess-and-check approach.)

$$\text{Account ending value} = C_1(1+i)^{t_1} + C_2(1+i)^{t_2}$$

15. Why do you think that the dollar-weighted yield rate is negative, even though the interest rate earned on the bond was only -4.627% in year 1 and 8.059% in year 2?

Your poorly timed withdrawal (you sold the bond after it dropped in price and before it increased in price!) means that you had more money in the account when the account lost money (negative 4.627% rate), and less money in the account when the account made money (positive 8.059% rate). Thus, the dollar-weighted return is "weighted" more heavily towards the time when the bond lost money.

Key idea

The IRR is called the dollar-weighted rate of return because the rate takes into consideration how much money is in the investment at any time. Thus, poorly timed deposits or withdrawals (buying high and selling low) will make the value drop and vice versa. Also, note that in the equation to compute the dollar-weighted rate of return each term is multiplied (or weighted) by the size of the deposit.

What if. . ..?

What if you had actually bought another bond after the first year, instead of selling one? Thus, owning three bonds from company B in the second year?

16. Make a prediction. Do you think that dollar-weighted rate of return would be larger or smaller in this case? Why?

17. Compute the dollar-weighted rate of return assuming that you bought a third bond at the start of the second year.
    a. What is the ending value of your bond portfolio?
    _____

    b. What was the initial investment amount? _____. This is C_1.
    c. How long was it from the time the initial investment was made until the time of the ending value? _____. This is t_1. This is how long the initial investment could have been in the account if you hadn't made any withdrawals.
    d. What was the amount of the deposit from the account? _____. This is C_2.
    e. How long was it from the time of the withdrawal to the end date?_____. This is t_2.
    f. What is the dollar-weighted yield rate?

The dollar-weighted yield rate is now positive (2.75%) because of the well-timed decision to buy another bond when the bond price was low (end of first year) and before it increased (during the second year).

What if…..?

What if you did nothing after buying the two bonds initially? That is, you didn't react after the first year—you simply bought the two bonds and held on through the price fluctuations?

18. Make a prediction. How do you think the dollar-weighted yield rate will compare to the scenario where you sold a bond after the first year? When you bought a bond after the first year?

19. Compute the dollar-weighted rate of return.
    a. What is the ending value of your bond portfolio?
    _____

    b. What was the initial investment amount? _____.
    This is C_1.

    c. How long was it from the time the initial investment was made until the time of the ending value? _____. This is t_1. This is how long the initial investment could have been in the account if you hadn't made any withdrawals.

    d. What is the dollar-weighted yield rate? (Because there are no deposit or withdrawals there is no C_2 or t_2.)

20. Compare this to the prediction you made. How does it compare to the previous dollar-weighted yield rates we computed? Why does this make sense?

Clearly, the timing of transactions matter! The best investment returns are achieved when you buy low and sell high.

Key idea
The highest rates of return on investments will be earned when you buy low and sell high. Conversely, the lowest rates are when you buy high and sell low.

Time-weighted yield rate
Given the rather fickle nature of the dollar-weighted rate of return to an investor's potentially poorly (or well!) timed deposits and withdrawals, there is another way to think of a rate of return, which does not take transaction timing into account.

    The time-weighted yield rate is equivalent to the annual effective yield rate if you had invested all of your money into the account at the beginning, and made no deposits or withdrawals. Thus, the time-weighted yield rate ignores potentially good or bad timing of deposits or withdrawals.

Key idea
The time-weighted yield rate will equal to the dollar-weighted yield rate when no deposits or withdrawals are made to the account during the life of the account.

    But, how do you find the time-weighted yield rate when an account does have transactions? In order to "ignore" the transactions, think of the entire time period you earn interest (in the example above, this is 2 years), as a series of smaller time periods—with "break points" for each transaction. The time-weighted yield rate is simply the product of all of the individual yield rates for each of the smaller periods of time. Here is a formal equation showing this:

1 + time-weighted yield rate over entire investment time

$$= (1 + \text{yield rate period 1})(1 + \text{yield rate period 2})\dots(1 + \text{yield rate period } k)$$

$$= \left(\frac{\text{End balance for period 1}}{\text{Start balance for period 1}} \right) \left(\frac{\text{End balance for period 2}}{\text{Start balance for period 2}} \right)$$

$$\dots \left(\frac{\text{End balance for period } k}{\text{Start balance for period } k} \right)$$

$$= (1 + \text{annual time} - \text{weighted yield rate})^m$$

In the equation above m is the number of years over which the investment is made. Note that the periods do not need to be in years for the equation above to work.

The **Start balance** is after a deposit/withdrawal is made to the account, and the **End balance** is before a deposit or withdrawal is made to the account. You break the total length of time into k periods where each of the "splits" between periods corresponds to the timing of the transaction.

Definition

The **time-weighted yield rate** is an overall measure of an investment's performance, which ignores timing and size of transactions. It is computed as the product of all individual period yield rates.

---

21. Predict the value of the time-weighted yield rate (effective per year) for the scenario where you sold one of the two bonds you owned after the first year.

22. To find the time-weighted yield rate for this scenario record the following values.
    a. Starting   balance   at   the   beginning   of   year 1_____ Ending balance at the end of year 1 (before you sold the bond)_____
    b. Starting balance at the beginning of year 2 (after you sold the bond) _____

    c. Ending   balance   at   the   end   of   year   2

_____

23. Now, plug into the equation as follows:

$$1 + \text{time-weighted yield rate over entire investment time}$$
$$= \left(\frac{\text{End balance for year 1}}{\text{Start balance for year 1}} \right) \left(\frac{\text{End balance for year 2}}{\text{Start balance for year 2}} \right)$$

What is the time-weighted yield rate over the 2-year investment period?

24. What is the "annualized" effective time-weighted yield rate?

Note that this is the same as the dollar-weighted yield rate of the "buy-and-hold" strategy. The time-weighted yield rate ignores your poorly timed "sell" decision at the end of year 1.

Time-weighted yield rate if you buy another bond

Now, let's compute the time-weighted yield rate for the strategy where you bought another bond at the end of year 1.

25. Predict the value of the time-weighted yield rate (effective per year) for the scenario where you buy an additional bond at the end of the first year.

26. To find the time-weighted yield rate for this scenario record the following values.
    a. Starting   balance   at   the   beginning   of   year
        1_____
    b. Ending balance at the end of year 1 (before you bought the bond)_____
    c. Starting balance at the beginning of year 2 (after you bought the bond) _____
    d. Ending   balance   at   the   end   of   year
        2_____
    e. Now, plug into the equation as follows:

$$1 + \text{time-weighted yield rate over entire investment time}$$
$$= \left(\frac{\text{End balance for year 1}}{\text{Start balance for year 1}} \right) \left(\frac{\text{End balance for year 2}}{\text{Start balance for year 2}} \right)$$

What is the time-weighted yield rate over the 2-year investment period?

f. What is the "annualized" effective time-weighted yield rate?

Key idea

In practice, if a portfolio is being managed by a financial professional, and that individual has no control over when investors deposit money or withdrawal money, then the time-weighted yield rate is a better measure of their performance than the dollar-weighted yield rate.

Comparing dollar-weighted and time-weighted yield rates

If you are given the dollar-weighted and time-weighted yield rates for an account, you can use these to figure out whether the timing of deposits/withdrawals was good or bad. Table 5.3 summarizes the transactions and yield rates for the three accounts we've been exploring.

Key idea

When the time-weighted yield rate is larger than the dollar-weighted yield rate, the investor timed their deposits/withdrawals poorly. When the time-weighted yield rate is smaller than the dollar-weighted yield rate, the investor timed their deposits/withdrawals well.

> ## SUMMARY

In this section, we've explored two ways of evaluating the performance of an investment (or collection of investments—called a portfolio) over the time: the dollar-weighted rate of return and the time-weighted rate of return.

The dollar-weighted rate of return reflects investment performance in a way that takes into account the timing of transactions (deposits and

Table 5.3 Summary of transactions and yield rates for each account

Investor	Transactions			Yield rates			
	Initial investment (Jan 1) ($)	Deposit (withdrawal) (after 1 year later) ($)	Ending balance (after 2 years) ($)	Effective rate for first year (%)	Effective rate for second year (%)	Dollar-weighted annual return (%)	Time-weighted annual return (%)
Buy and hold	1,725.22	$0.00	1,778.00	− 4.63	8.06	1.52	1.52
Sell after year 1	1,725.22	$822.70	889.00	− 4.63	8.06	− 0.52	1.52
Buy more after year 1	1,725.22	$822.70	2,667.00	− 4.63	8.06	2.75	1.52

withdrawals). Thus, well-timed transactions (withdrawing money before investments decrease in value or depositing money before investments increase in value) improve the dollar-weighted rate of return, and poorly timed transactions decrease the dollar-weighted rate of return. The dollar-weighted rate of return is also known as the IRR and is comparable to the way we've computed rates of return earlier in the course.

The time-weighted rate of return is a measure of investment performance that ignores deposits/withdrawals. The time-weighted rate of return is used most commonly by portfolio managers (e.g., financial planners) who have no control over whether investors will give them more money (deposits) or less money (withdrawals) at any given time.

Notation and equation summary

Time-weighted yield rate

$$1 + \text{Time-weighted Yield Rate over entire investment time}$$

$$= \left(\frac{\text{End balance for period 1}}{\text{Start balance for period 1}} \right) \left(\frac{\text{End balance for period 2}}{\text{Start balance for period 2}} \right)$$

$$\cdots \left(\frac{\text{End balance for period } k}{\text{Start balance for period } k} \right)$$

$$= (1 + \text{Annual Time-weighted Yield Rate})^m$$

Dollar-weighted yield rate (IRR)

$$\text{Account ending value} = \sum_{\text{all values of } m} C_m (1+i)^{t_m},$$

where for each of the m different deposits and withdrawals from the account, C_m is the mth deposit amount (using a minus sign for a withdrawal) and t_m is the length of time from the deposit (or withdrawal) until the account "end date."

HOMEWORK QUESTIONS: SECTION 5.1

Conceptual questions

1. How does a time-weighted rate of return compare to a dollar-weighted rate of return if the investor timed the deposits and withdrawals well?

2. Which rate of return, time-weighted or dollar-weighted, ignores the timing of deposits and withdrawals and is simply a measure of investment performance.

3. Suppose you and a friend are investors and you both frequently buy and sell stocks and bonds in an attempt at trying to maximize your rate of return. In comparing who is the better investor between the two of you, should you compare each other's dollar-weighted rate of return or time-weighted rate of return? Explain.

4. If, for the year, your portfolio has a dollar-weighted rate of return of 4.5% and a time-weighted rate of return of 5.5%, did you time the market well for the year?

5. If your portfolio of zero-coupon bonds has no deposits or withdrawals for the year. How will the time-weighted of return compare to the dollar-weighted of return on your portfolio?

Practice questions

6. You invest $1,000 in a stock that earns 3% the first year and 6% the second year.
   a. How much will the stock be worth at the end of the first year?
   b. How much will the stock be worth at the end of the second year?
   c. What is the time-weighted rate of return on the stock over the 2-year period?

7. On the stock from the previous question, what is the annualized time-weighted rate of return?

8. If a stock's time-weighted rate of return is 16.75% over a 3-year period, what is its annualized time-weighted rate of return?

9. Suppose you put $3,000 in a bond fund at the beginning of the year and then added $1,000 to that after 9 months. At the end of the year your fund balance was $4,100. Set up an equation, that could be solved for i, in which i is the dollar-weighted rate of return for the year.

10. You have $2,000 in a mutual fund at the beginning of the year, added $1,000 to that after 6 months, and $1,500 after 9 months. At the end of the year your fund balance was $5,000. Set up an equation, that could be solved for i, in which i is the dollar-weighted rate of return for the year.

Application questions

11. Suppose you buy some shares of a stock for $1,000. During the next year it earns 3% effective annual interest. After that first year, you invest another $2,000 into that stock and during this second year the stock goes up 4%.
    a. What is your total investment worth after these 2 years?
    b. Write down an equation that you can use to determine i, your dollar-weighted rate of (annual) return for your portfolio.
    c. Solve your equation for i using guess-and-check or algebra. [Hint: If you use algebra, this involves the quadratic equation and it will be a bit easier if you let $r = (1 + i)$ and then solve for r and subtract one.]

12. Suppose you buy some shares of a stock for $1,000. During the next year it earns 3% effective annual interest. After that first year you invest another $2,000 into that stock and during this second year the stock goes down 10%.
    a. What is your total investment worth after these 2 years?
    b. Write down an equation that you can use to determine i, your dollar-weighted rate of return (annual) for your portfolio.
    c. Solve your equation for i using guess-and-check or algebra. [Hint: If you use algebra, this involves the quadratic equation and it will be a bit easier if you let $r = (1 + i)$ and then solve for r and subtract one.]

13. You just set up a retirement account where $1,000 is automatically deposited into a mutual fund on the first day of each month. You keep track how much your retirement account is worth on the first and last day of each month in the following table.

	Jan	Feb	Mar	Apr	May	June
First	$1,000	$2,014	$3,030	$4,028	$5,041	$6,066
Last	$1,014	$2,030	$3,028	$4,041	$5,066	$6,054

    a. What is the time-weighted rate of return for the 6-month period?

    b. Convert your answer in the previous question to an annual rate of return.

    c. If you put \$1,500 per month in the retirement account each month instead of \$1,000, would the time-weighted rate of return be different than what you calculated in part (a)? If so, what would it be?

    d. If you made \$10 less the first month (so the January ending balance is \$1,004) but made up for that by making \$10 more the second month (so the February ending balance is \$2,040), would the time-weighted rate of return for the 6-month period be different than what you calculated in part (a)? If so, what would it be?

14. You just set up an investment account where \$500 is automatically deposited into a mutual fund on the first day of each month. You keep track how much your fund is worth on the first and last day of each month in the following table.

	Jan	Feb	Mar	Apr	May	June
First	\$500	\$1,011	\$1,520	\$2,020	\$2,580	\$3,083
Last	\$511	\$1,020	\$1,520	\$2,080	\$2,583	\$3,200

    a. What is the time-weighted rate of return for the 6-month period?

    b. Convert your answer in the previous question to an annual rate of return.

    c. Note that in January the account earned 2.2% and in March the account earned 0%. Suppose these two were switched so the account earned 0% in January and 2.2% in March and the rates of return stayed the same for all the other months. Would the time-weighted rate of return be different than what you calculated in part (a)? If so, what would it be?

    d. Notice that in January the account earned \$11 and in March the account earned \$0. Suppose these two were switched so the account earned \$0 in January and \$11 in March and the rates of return stayed the same for all the other months. Would the time-weighted rate of return be different than what you calculated in part (a)? If so, what would it be?

15. You put $2,000 in the stock mutual fund and after 6 months it is worth $2,250. At that time, you add $3,000 into the fund and leave it in there for the rest of the year. At the end of the year the fund is worth $5,460.

    a. What was the rate of return on the account for the first 6 months?

    b. What was the rate of return on the account for the second 6 months?

    c. What is the time-weighted rate of return of your fund for the year?

    d. Write down an equation that you can use to determine i, your dollar-weighted rate of return (annual) for your portfolio.

    e. Solve your equation from part (d) through some method to determine the dollar-weighted rate of return on your account for the year.

    f. Suppose you would have put $3,000 in the fund at the beginning of the year and added $2,000 after 6 months and the rates of return were the same as what you calculated in parts (a) and (b).

        i. Would the dollar-weighted rate of return change? Why or why not?

        ii. Would the time-based rate of return change? Why or why not?

SECTION 5.2. CHANGING YIELD RATES ON A PORTFOLIO

In the previous section, we explored both the dollar-weighted rate of return and time-weighted rate of return as two different measures of investment performance. Since rates of return on investments are often driven by the market (e.g., the bond market or stock market) instead of by prearranged agreement (e.g., loan or CD), investments have risk. In this section, we will dig into understanding the impact of changing rates of return (yield rates) on investment value and explore ways to measure investment risk.

Learning objectives

By the end of this section, you should be able to:

- Understand that as the interest rate (yield rate) changes, so does the present value.

- Understand that there is a larger impact of yield rate changes today on payments coming further in the future than payments happening sooner. Thus, the risk associated with interest rate changes is higher for payments far into the future.
- Understand that Macaulay duration is a measure of interest-rate risk since it is a weighted average "time of the cash flow."

EXAMPLE 5.2. HOW RISKY IS MY PORTFOLIO?

Suppose you are starting to develop a portfolio of investments to save for the future. To spread out your investment risk you decide to buy three separate bonds.

Bond 1. A $1,000, 5-year bond with semiannual coupons at 4% nominal annually.

Bond 2. A $1,000, 3-year bond with semiannual coupons at 4% nominal annually.

Bond 3. A $1,000, 10-year bond with semiannual coupons at 5% nominal annually.

You pay par value for each of the bonds. Because the bonds sold for par that means that the yield rate for each bond is currently at the nominal coupon rate (4%, 4%, and 5%, respectively).

While the bonds are currently selling at par, you are wondering what will happen if market yield rates change.

Think about it

If the yield rate on Bond 1 increases to 6% nominal annually (semiannual compounding) how will the value of the bond change?

If the yield rate increases, the price decreases. In this case, you can use the bond valuation formula or your calculator or Excel (e.g., the **Chapter 4 Excel file**, which contains a bond worksheet) to find that Bond 1 would decrease in value to $914.70 if the nominal yield rate increased to 6% today. Similarly, if the nominal yield rate dropped to 2%, the price of the bond would increase to $1,094.71. Thus, if market yield rates change by 2% (annual, nominal), the value of your bond will increase or decrease by ∼$90.

Think about it

What if Bond 2 also experiences a 2% change in nominal annual interest rates, do you think it also will change in value by ~$90?

If the nominal yield rate decreases to 2%, the value of Bond 2 will increase to $1,057.97, whereas if the nominal yield rate increases to 6% the value of Bond 2 will decrease to $945.83. Thus, for Bond 2, a change in the yield rate of 2% annually will change the value of the bond by ~$55.

To better understand why similar changes in yield rates lead to different impact on current prices, look at both Table 5.4 (Bond 1) and Table 5.5 (Bond 2).

Table 5.4 Payments and present value for Bond 1

Payment date (from now) [year(s)]	Payment size ($)	Present value of future payment at a given yield rate		
		2% Nominal ($)	4% Nominal ($)	6% Nominal ($)
0.5	20	19.81	19.61	19.42
1	20	19.61	19.22	18.85
1.5	20	19.41	18.85	18.30
2	20	19.21	18.48	17.77
2.5	20	19.03	18.11	17.25
3	20	18.84	17.76	16.75
3.5	20	18.65	17.41	16.26
4	20	18.47	17.07	15.79
4.5	20	18.28	16.74	15.33
5	20	18.11	16.41	14.88
5	1,000	905.29	820.35	744.09
	Total	1,094.71	1,000	914.70

Notice for that both bonds, the first few rows are the same. That is, the present values of the coupon payments are the same for both bonds. The difference comes from the different redemption dates—5 years into the future for Bond 1 and 3 years into the future for Bond 2.

Table 5.5 Payments and present value for Bond 2

Payment date (from now) [year(s)]	Payment size ($)	Present value of future payment at a given yield rate		
		2% Nominal ($)	4% Nominal ($)	6% Nominal ($)
0.5	20	19.81	19.61	19.42
1	20	19.61	19.22	18.85
1.5	20	19.41	18.85	18.30
2	20	19.21	18.48	17.77
2.5	20	19.03	18.11	17.25
3	20	18.84	17.76	16.75
3	1,000	942.05	887.97	837.48
	Total	1,057.96	1,000	945.83

Let's start by looking just at the lump sum payment of $1,000 when the bond is redeemed. For Bond 1, the lump sum payment is worth $820.35 at 4% today, but drops to a present value of $744.09 if the yield rate is 6%—a change of $76.26. For Bond 2, the lump sum payment is worth $887.97 today at 4% yield and drops to $837.48 at 6% yield—a change of only $50.49. To see this mathematically, consider the following equations:

Difference in present values of lump sum for Bond #1 =

$$= \frac{1,000}{(1.02)^{10}} - \frac{1,000}{(1.03)^{10}} = 1,000\left(\frac{1}{(1.02)^{10}} - \frac{1}{(1.03)^{10}}\right)$$
$$= 1,000(0.8203 - 0.7441) = 1,000(0.07626) = 76.26$$

Difference in present values of lump sum for Bond #2 =

$$= \frac{1,000}{(1.02)^6} - \frac{1,000}{(1.03)^6} = 1,000\left(\frac{1}{(1.02)^6} - \frac{1}{(1.03)^6}\right)$$
$$= 1,000(0.8879 - 0.8375) = 1,000(0.05049) = 50.49$$

Thus, we see that the change in interest rates is in the denominator. For larger exponents the difference increases. This idea, while potentially a bit less intuitive, is essentially the same one that we discussed in Chapter 1, Savings: Fundamentals of Interest, when discussing interest rates, in Chapter 2, Loans: Fundamentals of Borrowing and Lending, when discussing loans, and most recently in Chapter 4, Stocks and Bonds: Fundamentals of Investment Strategies, when discussing bonds— changes in the interest rate have bigger impacts on savings accounts or loan repayment the further into the future they are.

Key idea

Changes in interest rate have a bigger impact on the present value of payments that occur further into the future.

For example, if you invest $100 for 3 years at 2% effective every 6 months, you will have $100(1.02)^6 = \$112.62$, but if you invest at 3% effective every 6 months you will have $100(1.03)^6 = \$119.41$, a difference of $6.79. But, the difference is even larger if you look over 5 years: $100(1.02)^{10} = \$121.90$ compared to $100(1.03)^{10} = \$134.39$, a difference of $12.49. This gets even more dramatic if the time frame is even longer. For example, if you are on a 30-year term then $100(1.03)^{60} = \$589.16$ and $100(1.02)^{60} = \$328.10$, a difference of $261.06!

Thus, the 5-year bond is more sensitive to changes in the interest rate than the 3-year bond.

Key idea

Bonds with redemption dates further into the future are more sensitive to market changes in the yield rate than bonds with redemption dates sooner.

Summarizing price sensitivity: Macaulay duration

We've seen that changes in the interest rate impact the current price of payments further into the future more than those happening sooner. The Macaulay duration is one way that people use to compare two different portfolios to understand the portfolio's potential sensitivity to changes in the interest rate.

Definition

The **Macaulay duration** is the weighted average time that future investment payments will occur.

The Macaulay duration is the weighted average time that future payments will occur. Thus, the larger the Macaulay duration is the further
into the future the "average" payment will occur. Hence, as we've just
seen, this means that the larger the Macaulay duration is, the more sensitive the payments are to changes in the interest rate.

Let's revisit Table 5.4 at a yield rate of 4% nominal. To compute the
Macaulay duration, we need to compute the weighting factor for each
cash flow. The weighting factor is the proportion of the total present
value accounted for by a single cash flow. Thus, since the first coupon
payment is worth $19.61 today and the present value of the bond is
$1,000, the first coupon payment accounts for $19.61/1{,}000 = 1.961\%$ of
the total present value. Table 5.6 gives the values for the remaining cash
flows. Note that the majority of the "weight" is assigned to the lump
sum payment (82.0%). To compute the Macaulay duration, we multiply
the time of each payment by the weighting factor (the proportional size
of the cash flow in today's dollars), and then add them up. The final value
here is 4.5811 years. This means that the average cash flow occurs 4.5811
years from now.

More precisely, the equation for Macaulay Duration is

$$
MacD = \sum t\,\frac{PV(C_t)}{PV(All)} = 0.5\left(\frac{19.61}{1{,}000}\right) + 1\left(\frac{19.22}{1{,}000}\right) + 1.5\left(\frac{18.85}{1{,}000}\right)
$$
$$
+ \cdots + 5\left(\frac{820.35}{1{,}000}\right) = 4.5811,
$$

where t is a time index variable, C_t is the cash flow at time t, PV indicates
present value, and All is all future cash flows. Thus, we are summing up
the times of the cash flows, as a weighted average of the size of the cash
flow, in today's dollars.

Table 5.7 illustrates how to find the Macaulay duration for Bond 2.
Also see the **Chapter 5 Excel file**.

The Macaulay duration for Bond 1 is $MacD = 4.58$ and the Macaulay
duration for Bond 2 is 2.86. Thus, Bond 1 has a longer duration and will
be more impacted by changes to the yield rate. Of course, we could have
anticipated this simply by looking at the redemption dates of the bonds.
However, in practice, when you find the combined Macaulay duration
for all of the investments in a portfolio, which could each have different
yield rates, it is not necessarily as obvious. Fig. 5.1 visualizes the

Table 5.6 Macaulay duration for Bond 1

Payment date (from now; t) [year (s)]	Payment size; (C_t) ($)	Present value at a 4% nominal yield rate; $PV(C_t)$ ($)	Percentage of total cash flow [weighting factor; $PV(C_t)/PV(All)$]	Product of time and weighting factor; $tPV(C_t)/PV(All)$
0.5	$20	19.61	$19.61/\$1{,}000 = 0.01961$	$0.5 \times 0.01961 = 0.0098$
1	20	19.22	0.01922	0.0192
1.5	20	18.85	0.01885	0.0283
2	20	18.48	0.01848	0.0370
2.5	20	18.11	0.01811	0.0453
3	20	17.76	0.01776	0.0533
3.5	20	17.41	0.01741	0.0609
4	20	17.07	0.01707	0.0683
4.5	20	16.74	0.01674	0.0753
5	20	16.41	0.01641	0.0820
5	1,000	820.35	0.82035	4.1072
Total		$PV(All) = \$1{,}000$	100%	$MacD = 4.5811$

Table 5.7 Macaulay duration for Bond 2

Payment date (from now; t) [year(s)]	Payment size (C_t) ($)	Present value at a 4% nominal yield rate; $PV(C_t)$ ($)	Percentage of total cash flow [weighting factor; $PV(C_t)/PV(All)$]	Product of time and weighting factor; $tPV(C_t)/PV(All)$
0.5	20	19.61	0.01961	0.0098
1	20	19.22	0.01922	0.0192
1.5	20	18.85	0.01885	0.0283
2	20	18.48	0.01848	0.0370
2.5	20	18.11	0.01811	0.0453
3	20	17.76	0.01776	0.0533
3	1,000	887.97	0.88797	2.6639
	Total	1,000	100%	$MacD = 2.8567$

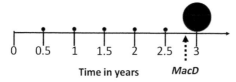

Figure 5.1 Visualizing the Macaulay duration as a weighted average.

Macaulay duration as a weighted average, where the dots on the number line correspond to the weights and the *MacD* is the balance point.

Computing the Macaulay duration for the entire portfolio

To compute the Macaulay duration for the entire portfolio, compute the present values of all of the coupons (from each of the three bonds), the present value of each of the three lump sums and the total present value of the portfolio ($3,000). Then, find the weights for each cash flow by dividing the present values of each cash flow by $3,000. The *MacD* is found by multiplying the time lengths of the cash flows by the appropriate weights and summing all of these as follows:

$$MacD = 0.5\left(\frac{19.61}{3,000}\right) + 0.5\left(\frac{19.61}{3,000}\right) + 0.5\left(\frac{24.39}{3,000}\right)$$
$$+ \cdots = 1.5271 + 0.9522 + 2.663 = 5.1424 \text{ years}$$

From the above, we can see that Bond 1 contributes 1.5271 years to the total *MacD* for the portfolio, Bond 2 contributes 0.9522 years, and Bond 3 contributes 2.663 years. Thus, the *MacD* for the portfolio is 5.1424 years.

Think about it

If you are given an option to buy another bond portfolio with similar present value, but with a *MacD* of 7.235 years, which portfolio has more interest-rate risk, your current portfolio or the new one that you are considering buying?

Since the *MacD* is higher on the new portfolio, it carries with it more interest-rate risk: changes to the yield rate will change the value of the new portfolio more than your current portfolio.

EXPLORATION 5.2. EVALUATING PORTFOLIO RISK

Suppose you are starting to develop a portfolio of investments to save for the future. To spread out your investment risk you decide to buy two separate bonds.

Bond 1. A $1,000, 3-year bond with semiannual coupons at 3% nominal annually.

Bond 2. A $1,000, 1-year bond with semiannual coupons at 4% nominal annually.

1. You pay par value for each bond. How much is your portfolio worth? Why?

2. What are the yield rates for each bond?

You are evaluating how your portfolio value will change if the market determined yield rates will change.

3. What will the value of Bond 1 be if the nominal yield rate changes to 1%? What if the nominal yield rate changes to 5%?

4. Based on your answer to the previous question, what is the approximate average change in value of Bond 1 if interest rates change by 2% (either direction)?

5. How much will Bond 2 be worth if the nominal yield rate changes to 2% and 6%?

6. Based on your answer to the previous question, what is the approximate average change in value of Bond 2 if interest rates change by 2% (either direction)?

7. Based on your answers above, why is the average change in price different for Bond 1 vs Bond 2 when both bonds undergo a similar sized change in yield rate (2% either direction)?

Intuitively, if we were to invest money in the bank, we'd see that a small change in interest rates has little impact in the short-term, but potentially a very large impact into the future.

Key idea

Changes in interest rates have a bigger impact on the present value of payments that occurs further into the future.

Applying this principle to bonds, makes us realize that the further away the redemption time, the more sensitive your bond's price is to market driven interest rate changes.

Key idea

Bonds with redemption dates further into the future are more sensitive to market changes in the yield rate than bonds with redemption dates sooner.

Summarizing price sensitivity: Macaulay duration

We've seen that changes in the interest rate impact the current price of payments further into the future more than those happening sooner. The Macaulay duration is one way that people use to compare two different portfolios to understand their potential sensitivity to changes in the interest rate.

Definition

The **Macaulay duration** is the weighted average time that future investment payments will occur.

Now, let's step through a calculation of the Macaulay duration.

8. Table 5.8 gives a row for each cash flow (C_t) consisting of six coupons and the redemption value. The first step in computing the Macaulay duration is to compute the present value of each cash flow [$PV(C_t)$]. Fill these values into the third column of Table 5.8. Note that the yield rate is 3% nominal, semiannually. Confirm that the sum of your column is $1,000—the current selling price of the bond.

Table 5.8 Macaulay duration for Bond 1

Payment date (years from now; t)	Payment size (C_t) ($)	Present value at a 3% nominal yield rate; $PV(C_t)$ ($)	Percentage of total cash flow [weighting factor; $PV(C_t)/PV(All)$]	Product of time and weighting factor; $tPV(C_t)/PV(All)$
0.5	15	14.78	0.01478	0.007389
1	15			
1.5	15			
2	15			
2.5	15			
3	15			
3	1,000			
	Total	$PV(All) = \$1000$	100%	

9. Which cash flow has the largest present value? Why?

10. The next step in computing the Macaulay duration is to compute the weighting factor for each cash flow. To find this, divide the value in column 3 [present value; $PV(C_t)$] by the present value of the bond (in this case $1,000) and enter these values into column 4 in Table 5.8. Confirm that the column sums to 100% when done.

11. Which cash flow accounts for the majority of the current present value of the bond? What percentage of the present value does it account for?

12. Which cash flow accounts for the lowest proportion of the present value of the bond? What percentage of the present value does it account for? Why does this make sense?

13. The final step in computing the Macaulay duration is to multiply the weighting factors you just computed (column 4 of the table) by the time that the cash flow occurs. Fill in this column completely in Table 5.8 by multiplying the weighting factors by the time that the cash flows occur. What are the units on the values in this column?

14. Compute the sum of the last column in Table 5.8. This the Macaulay duration; sometimes abbreviated *MacD*.

15. Why does it make sense that this value is close to 3 years, but a little less?

Thus, the "average" time that the bond pays money to the owner of the bond is 2.8913 years from now. Recall, that the reason we're computing the Macaulay duration was as a measure of the interest-rate risk.

16. If another bond has a *MacD* value that is smaller than 2.8913, what does this say about the first bond's interest-rate risk compared to this bond.

17. Predict whether you think the *MacD* value will be larger or smaller than 2.8913 for Bond 2. Why?

Here is a more formal equation for the Macaulay duration (*MacD*), where $PV(C_t)$ is the present value of cash flow C_t at time t.

$$MacD = \sum t \frac{PV(C_t)}{PV(All)}$$

18. Compute *MacD* for Bond 2. Use the formula above or the table approach we showed you (e.g., create a table like Table 5.8). Confirm your answer using the **Chapter 5 Excel file**.

As anticipated, the value of *MacD* is smaller for Bond 2 as compared to Bond 1 because the term of the bond is shorter. Thus, Bond 2 has less interest-rate risk than Bond 1. This confirms what we found earlier, which showed that as interest rates changed, the present value of Bond 2 didn't change as much as Bond 1.

Computing the Macaulay duration for the entire portfolio

Admittedly, computing the Macaulay duration for a single bond isn't terribly interesting or helpful. The bond term itself, more or less, tells us what we need to know. But, Macaulay duration becomes more useful when we want to assess the overall interest-rate risk of a portfolio. Let's do this now for our portfolio of two bonds.

19. How many total cash flows will you have as owner of this portfolio? Note: Count the coupon payments from each bond separate, even if they pay out at the same time and count the final coupon payment separate from the redemption value.

20. What is the total present value of your portfolio?

21. Using your answers to the previous questions, plug into the formula directly or use the table approach like we did earlier to find the Macaulay duration of your portfolio.

22. Interpret the Macaulay duration in this context.

23. If another portfolio you are considering purchasing has a *MacD* value of 1.532 years and has a similar present value to your current portfolio, which portfolio has less interest-rate risk? Why?

While the new portfolio may be less impacted by changes to the interest rate, that doesn't, necessarily, mean that you should sell your portfolio and buy the new one. Increases to the yield rate will cause bigger decreases to the present value of your current portfolio than the new one. But, conversely, decreases to the yield rate will cause larger increases in the present value of your current portfolio than the new one. As an investor, you have to decide how much risk you wish to take.

SUMMARY

In this section, we saw that interest rate changes have a greater impact on payments further in the future. Thus, when evaluating how sensitive investments are to changes in the interest rate (interest-rate risk), a measure of how far into the future your investments will payoff will quantify interest-rate risk. The Macaulay duration is a weighted average time of future cash flows and, thus, is a measure of interest-rate risk for a portfolio.

Notation and equation summary

$$MacD = \sum t \frac{PV(C_t)}{PV(All)}$$

HOMEWORK QUESTIONS: SECTION 5.2

Conceptual questions

1. If Bond A has a redemption date further into the future than Bond B is it more or less sensitive to market changes in yield rate?

2. If a bond's yield rate decreases, how does that change its present value?

3. The Macaulay duration is the _____time that _____ will occur.

4. If the Macaulay duration for Bond A is 4.5 and for Bond B is 7.8, which bond is more sensitive to market changes in yield rate?

Practice questions

5. Bond A is a 4-year bond with a face value of $500 and has a yield rate of 4% compounded semiannually. If the yield rate increases to 5% nominal, will its present value increase or decrease? By how much?

6. Bond B is a 6-year bond with a face value of $500 and has a yield rate of 4% compounded semiannually. If the yield rate increases to 5% nominal, will its present value increase or decrease? By how much?

7. A 2-year bond with a face value of $400, a coupon rate and yield rate of 6% nominal per year paid semiannually. Complete the following table to compute the Macaulay duration.

Payment date (from now) [year(s)]	Payment size ($)	Present value ($)	Percentage of total cash flow (weighting factor)	Product of time and weighting factor
0.5	12	11.65	0.029125	0.014563
1				
1.5				
2				
2				
	Total	400	100%	

8. A 2-year bond with a face value of $800, a coupon rate and yield rate of 4% nominal per year paid semiannually. Complete the following table to compute the Macaulay duration.

Payment date (from now) [year(s)]	Payment size ($)	Present value ($)	Percentage of total cash flow (weighting factor)	Product of time and weighting factor
0.5	16	15.69	0.01961	0.09805
1				
1.5				
2				
2				
	Total	800	100%	

Application questions

9. A 2-year bond has a face value of $400 and a coupon rate and yield rate of 10% nominal per year paid semiannually. Find the Macaulay duration for this bond.

10. A 3-year bond has a face value of $800, a nominal annual coupon rate of 8% paid semiannually, and an annual yield rate of 6% nominal paid semiannually. Find the Macaulay duration for this bond.

11. You have a portfolio of two bonds. Bond A is a 3-year bond that has a face value of $800 and a coupon rate and yield rate of 10% nominal per year paid semiannually. Bond B is a 3-year bond that has a face value of $1,000 and a coupon rate and yield rate of 8% effective per year paid annually. Find the Macaulay duration for this portfolio.

Looking ahead

12. Consider a $600 bond selling at par with an 8% yield rate compounded semiannually. If the yield rate decreases to 4%, the bond's present value increases to $645.89 and if the yield rate increases to 12%, the bond's present value decreases to $558.42. Use this information to (a) estimate the change in the price of the bond for a 1% point change in yield rate and then (b) write this estimate as the percent change of the current price of the bond as a function of the yield rate change.

13. Consider a $500 bond selling at par with a 6% yield rate compounded semiannually. If the yield rate decreases to 4%, the bond's present value increases to $519.04 and if the yield rate increases to 8%, the bond's present value decreases to $481.85. Use this information to (a) estimate the change in the price of the bond for a 1% point change in yield rate and then (b) write this estimate as the percent change of the current price of the bond as a function of the yield rate change.

SECTION 5.3. STRATEGIES TO MITIGATE PORTFOLIO RISK

In the previous section, we saw how to quantify interest-rate risk, realizing that interest-rate risk is really about when cash flows occur. The further into the future cash flows are the more sensitive the portfolio is to changes in the interest rate today. Thus, calculating the Macaulay duration for a portfolio allowed us to quantify interest-rate risk by providing us with the weighted average time that future cash flows occurred. While Macaulay duration allows us to compare portfolios to see which is less risky, if we are going to buy a portfolio are there ways to mitigate risk? Of course, a "simple" strategy to mitigate risk is to buy short-term bonds and limit interest-rate risk. However, if interest rates are higher in the bond market and we aren't in the bond market, we've limited risk, but lost the opportunity to grow our money. In this section, we will look at a way to use a portfolio of bonds to take advantage of higher bond market yield rates, while still providing some protection against changes in yield rates.

Learning objectives

By the end of this section, you should be able to:
- Explain the concept of immunization as a way to mitigate interest-rate risk.
- Explain how to cash flow match and duration match as a way to immunize a portfolio.

EXAMPLE 5.3. GETTING READY TO PAYBACK A BOND DEBT

Earlier (see Section 4.1) we looked at a case where a company had issued a large zero-coupon bond as an alternative to a loan. If you are at the company and looking at this looming payment that is coming, how can you prepare for it? In particular, are there ways that protect you from changes in the interest rate?

A few years ago, your company issued zero-coupon bonds totaling $100,000. These bonds are now due to be paid off in exactly 3 years. This means that you have to make sure your company has $100,000 on hand in 3 years. Your company has begun selling some products and has about $94,000 in the bank. What should you do with this money now?

One option is to put the money in the bank. Your local bank is paying 1% annual nominal interest with monthly compounding for a 3-year CD. That doesn't look very appealing, and will only turn your $94,000 into $96,861.52 after 3 years—not enough to pay off your company's debt. You have a general sense that the bond market is paying a higher yield rate and, thus, might be a better investment.

Think about it

Why is the bond market generally paying a higher yield rate than the bank? How does this impact the decision for your company's desire to invest/save money to payback the bond debt?

The bond market is paying a higher interest rate than the bank because the bond market is riskier. Most savings accounts and CDs at the bank are guaranteed by the federal government up to a certain amount. Thus, they can be considered little to no-risk investments. So, your company has a decision to make: get a higher, but riskier, rate of return or take a lower rate of return, but have it be guaranteed.

Looking into investment options in the bond market

You look at current selling prices for zero-coupon bonds and see the following results shown in Table 5.9. Yield rates are between 2% and 3% (better than a CD) and so you can potentially make the company some extra money buying bonds instead of CDs.

Table 5.9 Price of $1,000 zero-coupon bonds

Payoff date (years)	Present value ($)	Yield rate (%)
2	942.60	3
3	942.32	2
4	888.49	3

One thing you may notice is that the yield rate is changing over time. In practice, yield rates are often higher for longer term bonds. However, other patterns are possible based on market expectations and the perceived riskiness of a bond. For example, bonds are graded. While different credit rating services use slightly different scales, generally grade A bonds are less risky than grade B bonds, which are less risky than grade C bonds, etc.

Definition

The **grade** of a bond is measure of its investment risk. Market yield rates are generally higher for more risky bonds.

Thus, the pattern observed in Table 5.9 could be because the 2-year bond being considered is riskier than the 3- and 4-year bonds, contributing to its higher yield rate.

Think about it

How could you calculate the yield rate given the present value of these zero-coupon coupon bonds?

If you know the present value, you can find the yield rate since you know that the future value (redemption value) of the bond is $1,000. In particularly, you can solve that $1,000 = $ Present value$(1 + i)^n$ for i.

Cash-flow matching

One strategy would be to buy 100, 3-year zero-coupon, 2% bonds. This will cost you $94,232.00 today. These bonds will pay off $100,000 ($1,000 $\times$ 100) in 3 years—exactly what you need.

Definition

Cash-flow matching is a strategy where future liabilities are matched exactly by future assets. This means that, regardless of whether or not yield rates change, the liability can be paid off.

The advantage of buying the 3-year bonds is that if yield rates change, it doesn't matter because you will have the money no matter what. Thus, this strategy protects you against yield rate changes and is paying a higher yield than putting the money in a CD. Thus, cash-flow matching is a form of portfolio **immunization.**

Definition

A portfolio is **immunized** if it is protected against interest-rate risk (changing interest rates).

But, look again at Table 5.9. Note that the yield rate for 3-year bonds is currently lower than other terms (i.e., the 2-year and 4-year bonds). So, you wonder, can you save your company even more buy purchasing bonds with shorter or longer payoff times?

Buying 2-year bonds

Let's imagine that you buy 98 of the 2-year bonds. This will cost you $92,374.80 today. They will accumulate to $98,000 in 2 years. If you can invest the balance ($98,000) at 3% (the current yield rate) for the remaining year, you will have $100,940 in 3 years. More than you need, and it will cost less than buying the 3-year bonds!

Of course, the big "if" in this calculation is if you can invest the balance at 3% for that final year. What if you could only invest the balance at 1% for the remaining year, would you have enough? Since $98,000 × 1.01 = $98,980, you would not have enough. On the other hand, if you could invest the balance at 5% for the remaining year, $98,100 × 1.05 = $102,900 you would have come out even better.

Buying 4-year bonds

Alternatively, what if you bought 4-year bonds? You could spend $92,402.96 now (purchasing 104 bonds) and have $100,971.20 in 3 years, under the assumption that the bonds can be sold in 3 years (1 year before they are due to be redeemed) at a yield rate of 3%.

The big "if" here is whether or not the market is still paying 3%. What if the market is now paying only 1%? Then the current value of your bonds will be $104,000/1.01 = $102,970. And what if the market yield has gone up and is now paying 5%? In this case, the current value of your bonds will be $104,000/1.05 = $99,047.60. (See Table 5.10 for a summary of the three strategies with variable yield rates.)

Evaluating interest-rate risk

So, while the 2- and 4-year bond options may be appealing compared to buying the 3-year bond, both strategies carry some risk. In the case of the 2-year bond, the risk is if interest rates drop. In the case of the 4-year bond, the risk is if interest rates increase. This suggests that there may be some "middle-ground."

Table 5.10 Comparison of present value and future value of different bond purchasing strategies

	Buy 100, 3-year bonds ($)	Buy 98, 2-year bonds and reinvest the money for the third year (after bond redemption) ($)	Buy 104, 4-year bonds now and sell at end of third year ($)
Present value (today)	94,232.00	92,374.80	92,402.96
Future value (in 3 years) if rates stay at 3%	100,000.00	100,940.00	100,970.87
Future value (in 3 years) if rates drop to 1%	100,000.00	98,980.00	102,970.30
Future value (in 3 years) if rates rise to 5%	100,000.00	102,900.00	99,047.62

Think about it

What if you bought some 2-year bonds and some 4-year bonds?

If you bought some shorter-term bonds and some longer-term bonds, you might be able to take advantage of the current advantageous interest rates for the 2- and 4-year bonds (3% yield rates), but still protect yourself against interest rate changes—as long as the change in interest rates meant that the loss in value for one type of bond, was offset by the other.

For example, let's say that instead of spending roughly $92,400 on just 2-year bonds or 4-year bonds, you instead decide to spend $46,187.40 on 49, 2-year bonds (at a cost of $942.60 each) and $46,201.48 on 52, 4-year bonds (at a cost of $888.49 each). Your total out of pocket cost today is $92,388.88. We compare this strategy to the other three in Table 5.11.

Let's figure out the future value if interest rates stay at 3%. This means that you redeem the 49, 2-year bonds for $49,000 and invest that cash for 1 more year at 3%, yielding $50,470. You also sell the 52, 4-year bonds for $52,000/1.03 = $50,485.44 at the end of the 3-year period. Thus, your total portfolio value is $50,470 + $50,485.44 = $100,955.40.

If interest rates decrease to 1%, then you will invest the $49,000 at 1%, yielding $49,490 and sell the 4-year bonds for $52,000/1.01 = $51,485.15, for a total portfolio value of $100,975.10. Alternatively, if interest rates increase to 5% then you invest the $49,000 at 5%, yielding

Table 5.11 Comparison of present value and future value of different bond purchasing strategies

	Buy 100, 3-year bonds	Buy 98, 2-year bonds and reinvest the money for the third year (after bond redemption) ($)	Buy 104, 4-year bonds now and sell at end of third year ($)	Buy 49, 2-year bonds (reinvest money for third year) and 52, 4-year bonds (sell at end of third year) ($)
Present value (today)	94,232.00	92,374.80	92,402.96	92,388.88
Future value (in 3 years) if rates stay at 3%	100,000.00	100,940.00	100,970.87	50,470.00 + 50,485.44 = 100,955.44
Future value (in 3 years) if rates drop to 1%	100,000.00	98,980.00	102,970.30	49,490.00 + 51,485.15 = 100,975.15
Future value (in 3 years) if rates rise to 5%	100,000.00	102,900.00	99,047.62	51,450.00 + 49,523.81 = 100,973.81

$51,450 and sell the 4-year bonds for $52,000/1.05 = $49,523.81, for a total portfolio value of $100,973.80. (See Table 5.11 for a summary of this as well as the earlier strategies.)

The great thing about this "mixed" approach is that whether interest rates go up, down, or stay the same, we've still ensured we have over $100,000!

In Table 5.12, we show the net gain over the 3-year period from each of the different investment strategies. Notably the strategy that buys some 2-year and some 4-year bonds has the largest average net gains despite fluctuating interest rates and always yields at least $100,000. The idea of timing payoffs at different times to mitigate risk is an important one and one that we will return to in future sections.

Table 5.12 Net gain by scenario

	Buy 100, 3-year bonds ($)	Buy 98, 2-year bonds and reinvest the money for the third year (after bond redemption) ($)	Buy 104, 4-year bonds now and sell at end of third year ($)	Buy 49, 2-year bonds (reinvest money for third year) and 52 four-year bonds (sell at end of third year) ($)
Initial investment (today)	94,232	92,374	92,402.65	93,146
Net gain after 3 years at $i = 3\%$	5,768.00	8,565.20	8,567.91	8,566.56
Net gain after 3 years at $i = 1\%$	5,768.00	6,605.20[a]	10,567.34	8,586.27
Net gain after 3 years at $i = 5\%$	5,768.00	10,525.20	6,644.66[a]	8,584.93

[a]Investment did not yield $100,000 and so not enough earned to pay off the $100,000 debt.

Key idea

Buying bonds with payoff times that fall on either side of a future liability can maximize investment return and mitigate interest-rate risk.

Duration matching

How did we know to buy 49, 2-year bonds and 52, 4-year bonds? To answer this, calculate the Macaulay duration on this portfolio:

$$MacD = 2\left(\frac{46,187.40}{92,388.88}\right) + 4\left(\frac{46,201.48}{92,388.88}\right) = 3.000$$

Notice that the *MacD* is exactly 3—which is exactly when the liability ($100,000 payment) is due. This is no accident, but is what is called duration matching. **Duration matching** to immunize a portfolio is accomplished by creating a portfolio with a duration equivalent to the time of the liability—in this case 3 years. (Don't worry about the details here; we will address them later in Chapter 10: Portfolios Revisited.)

Definition
Duration matching involves creating a portfolio with a duration equal to the time of the future liability and can create an immunized portfolio.

CONCLUDING REMARKS

Later in this course (Chapter 10: Portfolios Revisited), we will revisit portfolios. At that time, we will more formally illustrate how to design portfolios, digging into related ideas such as convexity, duration, convexity and immunization, among others. The formal mathematical equations we will learn there will give precise "mixes" of bonds and allow us to precisely immunize portfolios.

EXPLORATION 5.3: ANTICIPATING PAYING BACK A LOAN

You are at a company that has issued some large zero-coupon bonds that are coming due in 2 years. In particular, you will owe $1,000,000 in 2 years.

1. As a company, how should we be preparing for the fact that you have zero-coupon bonds due in 2 years?

2. Your company currently has about $950,000 on hand. If you put this money in a CD in the bank and earn 1% effective interest annually, how much will you have in 2 years? Identify advantages and disadvantages of putting the money in the bank.

3. Describe how your company could buy 2-year zero-coupon bonds today instead of a CD in order to prepare to payback the $1 million debt in 2 years. What are advantages and disadvantages of this approach vs using the CD?

4. What effective annual yield rate do you need for 2-year zero-coupon bonds in order to invest the $950,000 in the bond market and hit the $1 million target within 2 years?

Cash-flow matching

5. You look at the bond market and see that highly graded (more financially stable companies) 2-year, zero-coupon bonds are paying 1.5% annual effective yield. If you use all of your current savings to buy these bonds, how much will you have in 2 years when your debt is due?

6. How much are $1,000 face value, 2-year zero-coupon bonds described in the previous question selling for today?

7. How much would you need to invest in 2-year, zero-coupon bonds today in order to hit the $1 million goal? Approximately how many bonds would you need to buy? How many can you actually afford?

The strategy of buying an asset that pays off when a liability comes due is called cash-flow matching.

Definition

Cash-flow matching is a strategy where future liabilities are matched exactly by future assets. This means that, regardless of whether or not yield rates change, the liability can be paid off.

In this case, you don't have enough money on hand to cash-flow match your liability since the 2-year zero-coupon bonds are only yielding 1.5% annually.

8. Let's say you end up buying 978 zero-coupon bonds (all that you can afford today). If yield rates increase to 2.5% on these bonds in the next few months, how much will your bonds be worth in 2 years when they come due? How has their current value changed?

9. How would your answers to the previous question change if the yield rate on the 2-year bonds dropped to 0.5%?

The advantage of the cash-flow matching approach is that if yield rates change, it doesn't matter because you are, more or less, guaranteed to have the face value of the bonds at the time of your debt (liability) payment. Thus, the cash-flow matching strategy protects you against yield rate changes and often pays a higher yield than putting the money in a CD. Thus, cash-flow matching is a form of portfolio **immunization.**

Definition
A portfolio is **immunized** if it is protected against interest-rate risk (changing interest rates).

---

10. Explain how buying 978, 2-year zero-coupon bonds today creates an immunized portfolio.

Buying bonds with different payoff times

Of course, one problem with this approach is that, while immunized, you do not have enough to pay off the debt (you will be $22,000 short). When looking up the yield rate of the two, zero-coupon bonds you notice that the yield rates are better for bonds with different terms. In particular, the yield on 1-year zero-coupon bonds is 2.8% effective annually and for 3-year zero-coupon bonds is also 2.8%.

11. Explain what is appealing about investing in the 1-year and 3-year zero-coupon bonds relative to the 2-year option we were just considering.

12. Fill in Table 5.13 showing the selling prices for the three $1,000 face value zero-coupon bond options you are considering.

Table 5.13 Prices and yield of zero-coupon bonds

Redemption time [year(s)]	Yield (%)	Price
1	2.8	
2	1.5	
3	2.8	

One thing you may note is that the yield rate is changing over time. In practice, yield rates are often higher for longer term bonds. However, other patterns are possible based on market than expectations and the perceived riskiness of a bond. For example, bonds are graded. While different credit rating services use slightly different scales, generally grade A bonds are less risky than grade B bonds, which are less risky than grade C bonds, etc.

Definition

The **grade** of a bond is measure of its investment risk. Market yield rates are generally higher for more risky bonds.

Thus, the pattern observed in Table 5.13 could be because the 2-year bond being considered is less risky than the 1- and 3-year bonds, contributing to its lower yield rate.

13. How many bonds can you buy if you invest all of the $950,000 you have in 1-year zero-coupon bonds?

14. If you buy the bonds as in the previous question, how much cash will you have on hand from these bonds when they pay out? When will you have this cash? What is a practical issue with this approach? Hint: When is the $1 million owed?

15. How much cash will you have on hand if you invest the cash from the previous question in a bank CD paying 1% effective annually for 1-year?

16. If, instead of buying the lowest yielding CD, you again buy 1-year bonds in the bond market, what risk are running? Hint: What if the yield on 1-year bonds in 1 year is only 1.2%?

So, while buying the 1-year bonds with the high yield rate is appealing, there is interest-rate risk. If the yield rate on 1-year bonds drops over the next year, then you may have cash in 1 year, but no good/high–yielding investment options at that time. So, what if you buy 3-year zero-coupon bonds instead?

17. What is a practical issue with investing all of your money in 3-year zero-coupon bonds?

18. If you sell the 3-year bonds in 2 years in order to pay the liability, what risk are you taking? What are you hoping yield rates will be in this scenario—higher or lower?

So, while the higher yield rate on the 1-year and 3-year bonds is appealing, they both come with some interest-rate risk. The risk on the 1-year bond is if rates go down and the risk on the 3-year bonds if rates go up. This suggests that there may be a better way to mitigate risk—by buying some 1-year bonds and some 3-year bonds.

Duration matching

Let's assume that you decide to buy some of each. In particular, you decide to buy 516, 3-year bonds and 488, 1-year bonds

19. How much will you pay today for this bond portfolio?

20. What is the Macaulay duration of your portfolio? How does this compare to the timing of your future liability?

Definition
Duration matching involves creating a portfolio with a duration equal to the time of the future liability and can create an immunized portfolio.

Let's now evaluate how sensitive this bond portfolio is to changing yield rates.

Scenario 1. Yield rates stay constant at 2.8%.

Let's assume that yield rates stay at 2.8% and so (a) after 1 year you can buy more 1-year coupon bonds at 2.8% and (b) you can sell your 3-year bonds after 2-years at 2.8%.

21. What will be your portfolio value after 2 years?

Scenario 2. Yield rates drop to 1.8%.

Let's assume that yield rates drop to 1.8% and so (a) after 1 year you can buy more 1-year coupon bonds at 1.8% and (b) you can sell your 3-year bonds after 2-years at 1.8%.

22. What will be your portfolio value after 2 years?

Scenario 3. Yield rates increase to 3.8%.

Let's assume that yield rates increase to 3.8% and so (a) after 1 year you can buy more 1-year coupon bonds at 3.8% and (b) you can sell your 3-year bonds after 2-years at 3.8%.

23. What will be your portfolio value after 2 years?

Comparing all of the different scenarios

24. Fill in Table 5.14 that compares all of the different interest rate scenarios and investment options. Note: You will have to do a few more computations—we didn't consider all these scenarios earlier.

25. Why is the duration matched option better than the cash-flow matched option in this case? Do you think this will always be the case?

26. Explain why the duration matched option is less risky than buying either 1-year or 3-year bonds, exclusively.

Key idea

Buying bonds with payoff times that fall on either side of a future liability can maximize investment return and mitigate interest-rate risk.

Table 5.14 Comparison of values after 2 years for different interest rate scenarios

	Buy CD ($)	Cash flow matched (2-year bonds) ($)	1-year bonds only ($)	3-year bonds only ($)	Duration matched (mix of 1- and 3-year bonds) ($)
Purchase price (current value)	950,000	949,305 (978 bonds)	949,150 (976 bonds)	949,946 (1,032 bonds)	949,683
Value after 2 years if bond market is 1.8% in 2 years					
Value after 2 years if bond market is 2.8% in 2 years					
Value after 2 years if bond market is 3.8% in 2 years					

CONCLUDING REMARKS

Later in this course (Chapter 10: Portfolios Revisited), we will revisit portfolios. At that time, we will more formally illustrate how to design portfolios, digging into related ideas such as convexity, duration, convexity and immunization, among others. The formal mathematical equations we will learn there will give precise "mixes" of bonds and allow us to precisely immunize portfolios.

SUMMARY

Immunization, the ability to protect a portfolio against changes in the interest rate might seem like wishful thinking; however, cash–flow matching (having future assets directly offset future liabilities) is a simple strategy that immunizes a portfolio. Another approach, duration match-ing, makes some assumptions about assets and liabilities being governed by similar interest rates, but, intuitively, is like cash-flow matching. In short, a duration matched portfolio uses a mix of assets that, in total, has a duration matched to the liability to immunize the portfolio—protecting against interest rate changes.

HOMEWORK QUESTIONS: SECTION 5.3

Conceptual questions

1. With cash-flow matching, what two things are matched?

2. What is a portfolio that is immunized protected against?

3. Suppose you have a future liability to pay off and want to pay it off with a bond purchase. What should you do, in terms of payoff times on the bonds, to maximize the return on investment, and lessen the interest-rate risk?

4. How can having a mixture of different length bonds protect your portfolio against changes in yield rates?

5. When a portfolio is immunized using duration matching, what should be equal to the portfolio's Macaulay duration?

6. Suppose you buy a 5-year bond and want to sell it after 4 years. Also suppose the market yield rate has drops on the bond after 4 years. Is the value of the bond more or less than what it would have been if the market rate remained unchanged for those 4 years?

Practice questions

7. Suppose you buy a zero-coupon bond that has a yield rate of 3% and will pay out $1,000 in 5 years. How much is the bond worth if you sell it in 4 years and:
   a. The yield rate stays at 3%?
   b. The yield rate drops to 2%?

8. Suppose you buy a zero-coupon bond that has a yield rate of 2.5% and will pay out $1,000 in 4 years. How much is the bond worth if you sell it in 2 years and:
   a. The yield rate stays at 2.5%?
   b. The yield increases to 4%?

9. Suppose you buy a zero-coupon bond that has a yield rate of 3% and will pay out $1,000 in 2 years. How much will you have to pay for the bond?

10. What effective annual yield will you need to have for an investment of $43,000 to increase to $50,000 in 5 years?

11. You have $75,000 to invest in the bond market. You are interested in buying some zero-coupon bonds that will pay out $500 in 4 years with a yield rate of 2.625%.
    a. How much each bond cost?
    b. How many of these bonds can you afford to buy?

Application questions

12. You want to invest in the bond market and plan to buy 20, 3-year and 20, 5-year zero-coupon bonds. These bonds have a face value of $1,000 and an effective yield rate of 3%. You will need money from these investments in 4 years so plan to sell your 5-year bonds early and reinvest the money from your 3-year bonds for an extra year.
    a. How much will it cost to buy 20 of the 3-year bonds and 20 of the 5-year bonds?
    b. Suppose that after your 3-year bonds mature, you find another investment that also earns 3% for another year and reinvest in that. The bond rate on your 5-year bonds also stays at 3% when you sell them after 4 years. Under these circumstances, after 4 years, how much will your total portfolio be worth?

13. Using the scenario from the previous question with the 3-year and 5-year bonds answer the following.
    a. Suppose after your 3-year bonds mature, you find another investment that earns 2% for another year and reinvest in that. The

bond rate on your 5-year bonds also drops to 2% when you sell them after 4 years. Under these circumstances, after 4 years, how much will your total portfolio be worth?

b. Now suppose after your 3-year bonds mature, you find another investment that earns 4% for another year and reinvest in that. The bond rate on your 5-year bonds also increases to 4% when you sell them after 4 years. Under these circumstances, after 4 years, how much will your total portfolio be worth?

14. You want to invest in the bond market and plan to buy 20, 4-year and 30, 8-year zero-coupon bonds. These bonds have a face value of $1,000 and an effective yield rate of 4%. You will need money from these investments in 5 years so plan to sell your 8-year bonds early and reinvest the money from your 4-year bonds for an extra year.

   a. How much will it cost to buy 20 of the 4-year bonds and 30 of the 8-year bonds?

   b. Suppose that after your 4-year bonds mature, you find another investment that also earns 4% for another year and reinvest in that. The bond rate on your 8-year bonds also stays at 4% when you sell them after 5 years. Under these circumstances, after 5 years, how much will your total portfolio be worth?

15. Using the scenario from the previous question with the 4-year and 8-year bonds answer the following.

   a. Suppose after your 4-year bonds mature, you find another investment that earns 2% for another year and reinvest in that. The bond rate on your 8-year bonds also drops to 2% when you sell them after 5 years. Under these circumstances, after 4 years, how much will your total portfolio be worth?

   b. Now suppose after your 4-year bonds mature, you find another investment that earns 6% for another year and reinvest in that. The bond rate on your 8-year bonds also increases to 6% when you sell them after 5 years. Under these circumstances, after 5 years, how much will your total portfolio be worth?

16. Bond A is a zero-coupon bond with a redemption value of $1,000 and a yield of 5% that will mature in 10 years. Bond B is a zero-

coupon bond with a redemption value of $1,000 and a yield of 5% that will mature in 5 years.

a. What is the selling price of each bond?

b. Suppose the market yield rate on each of the bonds drops to 3% after 4 years. What is the market value of each of the bonds?

c. How much effective annual interest would have been earned on each bond if they were sold after 4 years and the yield rate dropped to 3%?

17. Bond A is a zero-coupon bond with a redemption value of $1,000 and a yield of 5% that will mature in 10 years. Bond B is a zero-coupon bond with a redemption value of $1,000 and a yield of 5% that will mature in 5 years.

a. What is the selling price of each bond?

b. Suppose the market yield rate on each of the bonds increases to 7% after 4 years. What is the market value of each of the bonds?

c. How much effective annual interest would have been earned on each bond if they were sold after 4 years and the yield rate increased to 7%?

END OF CHAPTER SUMMARY

In this chapter, we began to explore collections of assets and liabilities—called portfolios. Exploring portfolios requires new ways of thinking about and computing interest rates. The dollar-weighted (or internal) rate of return acts as an "average" rate of return for the portfolio's value over time, but can be significantly impacted by the timing of cash inflows and outflows. In contrast, the time-weighted rate of return ignores the potentially good or bad timing of cash flows to provide a cash-flow independent measure of portfolio performance over the time. We also saw that the Macaulay duration, the weighted time of future cash flows, is one way to quantify interest-rate risk. Finally, we saw that an immunized portfolio is protected against changes in the interest rate via cash-flow matching or duration matching assets and liabilities.

END OF CHAPTER EXERCISES

(SOA EXAM FM SAMPLE QUESTIONS May 2005, Question 3)

1. A bond will pay a coupon of 100 at the end of each of the next three years and will pay the face value of 1,000 at the end of the three-year period. The bond's duration (Macaulay duration) when valued using an annual effective interest rate of 20% is X.

   Calculate X.
   A. 2.61
   B. 2.70
   C. 2.77
   D. 2.89
   E. 3.00

(SOA EXAM FM SAMPLE QUESTIONS May 2005, Question 6)

2. John purchased three bonds to form a portfolio as follows:
   i. Bond A has semi-annual coupons at 4%, a duration of 21.46 years, and was purchased for 980.
   ii. Bond B is a 15-year bond with a duration of 12.35 years and was purchased for 1,015.
   iii. Bond C has a duration of 16.67 years and was purchased for 1,000.
   Calculate the duration of the portfolio at the time of purchase.
   A. 16.62 years
   B. 16.67 years
   C. 16.72 years
   D. 16.77 years
   E. 16.82 years

(SOA EXAM FM SAMPLE QUESTIONS May 2005, Question 15)

3. An insurance company accepts an obligation to pay 10,000 at the end of each year for 2 years. The insurance company purchases a combination of the following two bonds at a total cost of X in order to exactly match its obligation:

i. 1-year 4% annual coupon bond with a yield rate of 5%

ii. 2-year 6% annual coupon bond with a yield rate of 5%.

Calculate X.

A. 18,564

B. 18,574

C. 18,584

D. 18,594

E. 18,604

(SOA EXAM FM SAMPLE QUESTIONS November 2005, Question 2)

4. Calculate the Macaulay duration of an eight-year 100 par value bond with 10% annual coupons and an effective rate of interest equal to 8%.

A. 4

B. 5

C. 6

D. 7

E. 8

(SOA EXAM FM SAMPLE QUESTIONS November 2005, Question 10)

5. A company must pay liabilities of 1,000 and 2,000 at the end of years 1 and 2, respectively. The only investments available to the company are the following two zero-coupon bonds:

Maturity (years)	Effective annual yield	Par
1	10%	1,000
2	12%	1,000

Determine the cost to the company today to match the liabilities exactly.

A. 2,007

B. 2,259

C. 2,503

D. 2,756

E. 3,001

(SOA EXAM FM SAMPLE QUESTIONS Interest Theory, Question 30)

6. As of 12/31/2013, an insurance company has a known obligation to pay 1,000,000 on 12/31/2017. To fund this liability, the company immediately purchases 4-year 5% annual coupon bonds totaling 822,703 of par value. The company anticipates reinvestment interest rates to remain constant at 5% through 12/31/2017. The maturity value of the bond equals the par value.

Consider two reinvestment interest rate movement scenarios effective 1/1/2014. Scenario A has interest rates drop by 0.5%. Scenario B has interest rates increase by 0.5%.
Determine which of the following best describes the insurance company's profit or (loss) as of 12/31/2017 after the liability is paid.
A. Scenario A − 6,610, Scenario B − 11,150
B. Scenario A − (14,760), Scenario B − 14,420
C. Scenario A − (18,910), Scenario B − 19,190
D. Scenario A − (1,310), Scenario B − 1,320
E. Scenario A − 0, Scenario B − 0

(SOA EXAM FM SAMPLE QUESTIONS Interest Theory, Question 59)

7. A liability consists of a series of 15 annual payments of 35,000 with the first payment to be made one year from now.

The assets available to immunize this liability are five-year and ten-year zero-coupon bonds.
The annual effective interest rate used to value the assets and the liability is 6.2%. The liability has the same present value and duration as the asset portfolio.
Calculate the amount invested in the five-year zero-coupon bonds.
A. 127,000
B. 167,800
C. 208,600
D. 247,900
E. 292,800

(SOA EXAM FM SAMPLE QUESTIONS Interest Theory, Question 65)

8. Kylie bought a 7-year, 5000 par value bond with an annual coupon rate of 7.6% paid semi-annually. She bought the bond with no premium or discount.

   Calculate the Macaulay duration of this bond with respect to the yield rate on the bond.
   A. 5.16
   B. 5.35
   C. 5.56
   D. 5.77
   E. 5.99

(SOA EXAM FM SAMPLE QUESTIONS Interest Theory, Question 66)

9. Krishna buys an *n*-year 1,000 bond at par. The Macaulay duration is 7.959 years using an annual effective interest rate of 7.2%.

   Calculate the estimated price of the bond, using duration, if the interest rate rises to 8.0%.
   A. 940.60
   B. 942.88
   C. 944.56
   D. 947.03
   E. 948.47

(SOA EXAM FM SAMPLE QUESTIONS Interest Theory, Question 122)

10. Cash flows are 40,000 at time 2 (in years), 25,000 at time 3, and 100,000 at time 4. The annual effective yield rate is 7.0%.

    Calculate the Macaulay duration.
    A. 2.2
    B. 2.3
    C. 3.1
    D. 3.3
    E. 3.4

(SOA EXAM FM SAMPLE QUESTIONS Interest Theory, Question 133)

11. An insurance company wants to match liabilities of 25,000 payable in one year and 20,000 payable in two years with specific assets. The following assets are currently available:

    i. One-year bond with an annual coupon of 6.75% at par

    ii. Two-year bond with annual coupons of 4.50% at par

    iii. Two-year zero-coupon bond yielding 5.00% annual effective

    Calculate the smallest amount the company needs to disburse today to purchase assets that will exactly match these liabilities.

    A. 41,220

    B. 41,390

    C. 41,560

    D. 41,660

    E. 41,750

(SOA EXAM FM SAMPLE QUESTIONS Interest Theory, Question 32)

12. An investor pays 100,000 today for a 4-year investment that returns cash flows of 60,000 at the end of each of years 3 and 4. The cash flows can be reinvested at 4.0% per annum effective.

    Using an annual effective interest rate of 5.0%, calculate the net present value of this investment today.

    A. − 1,398

    B. − 699

    C. 699

    D. 1,398

    E. 2,629

(SOA EXAM FM SAMPLE QUESTIONS November 2005, Question 1)

13. An insurance company earned a simple rate of interest of 8% over the last calendar year based on the following information:

Assets, beginning of the year	25,000,000
Sales Revenue	X
Net Investments income	2,000,000
Salaries paid	2,200,000
Other expenses paid	750,000

All cash flows occur at the middle of the year. Calculate the effective yield rate.
A. 7.7%
B. 7.8%
C. 7.9%
D. 8.0%
E. 8.1%

(SOA EXAM FM SAMPLE QUESTIONS May 2000, Question 16)

14. On January 1, 1997, an investment account is worth 100,000. On April 1, 1997, the value has increased to 103,000 and 8,000 is withdrawn. On January 1, 1999, the account is worth 103,992.

Assuming a dollar weighted method for 1997 and a time weighted method for 1998, the annual effective interest rate was equal to x for both 1997 and 1998.
Calculate x.
A. 6.00%
B. 6.25%
C. 6.50%
D. 6.75%
E. 7.00%

(SOA EXAM FM SAMPLE QUESTIONS May 2003, Question 17)

15. An association had a fund balance of 75 on January 1 and 60 on December 31. At the end of every month during the year, the association deposited 10 from membership fees. There were withdrawals of 5 on February 28, 25 on June 30, 80 on October 15, and 35 on October 31.

Calculate the dollar-weighted rate of return for the year.
A. 9.0%
B. 9.5%
C. 10.0%
D. 10.5%
E. 11.0%

(SOA EXAM FM SAMPLE QUESTIONS May 2005, Question 16)

16. At the beginning of the year, an investment fund was established with an initial deposit of 1,000. A new deposit of 1,000 was made at the end of 4 months. Withdrawals of 200 and 500 were made at the end of 6 months and 8 months, respectively. The amount in the fund at the end of the year is 1560.

Calculate the dollar-weighted (money-weighted) yield rate earned by the fund during the year.
A. 18.57%
B. 20.00%
C. 22.61%
D. 26.00%
E. 28.89%

(SOA EXAM FM SAMPLE QUESTIONS November 2000, Question 27)

17. An investor deposits 50 in an investment account on January 1. The following summarizes the activity in the account during the year:

Date	Value immediately before deposit	Deposit
March 15	40	20
June 1	80	75
October 1	175	75

On June 30, the value of the account is 157.50. On December 31, the value of the account is X. Using the time-weighted method, the equivalent annual effective yield during the first 6 months is equal to the (time-weighted) annual effective yield during the entire 1-year period.

Calculate X.

A. 234.75

B. 235.50

C. 236.25

D. 237.00

E. 237.75

(SOA EXAM FM SAMPLE QUESTIONS November 2001, Question 20)

18. You are given the following information about the activity in two different investment accounts:

Account K			
Date	Fund value before activity	Activity	
		Deposit	Withdrawal
January 1, 1999	100.0		
July 1, 1999	125.0		X
October 1, 1999	110.0	$2X$	
December 31, 1999	125.0		

Account L			
Date	Fund value before activity	Activity	
		Deposit	Withdrawal
January 1, 1999	100.0		
July 1, 1999	125.0		X
December 31, 1999	105.8		

During 1999, the dollar weighted return for investment account K equals the time weighted return for investment account L, which equals i.

Calculate i.

A. 10%

B. 12%

C. 15%

D. 18%

E. 20%

(SOA EXAM FM SAMPLE QUESTIONS Interest Theory, Question 78)

19. On January 1, an investment fund was opened with an initial balance of 5,000. Just after the balance grew to 5,200 on July 1, an additional 2,600 was deposited.

    The annual effective yield rate for this fund was 9.00% over the calendar year.

    Calculate the time-weighted rate of return for the year.

    A. 7.43%

    B. 8.86%

    C. 9.00%

    D. 9.17%

    E. 10.45%

(SOA EXAM FM SAMPLE QUESTIONS Interest Theory, Question 83)

20. On January 1, a fund is worth 100,000. On May 1, the value has increased to 120,000 and then 30,000 of new principal is deposited. On November 1, the value has declined to 130,000 and then 50,000 is withdrawn. On January 1 of the following year, the fund is again worth 100,000.

    Calculate the time-weighted rate of return.

    A. 0.00%

    B. 17.91%

    C. 25.00%

    D. 29.27%

    E. 30.00%

(SOA EXAM FM SAMPLE QUESTIONS Interest Theory, Question 120)

21. On January 1, an investment account is worth 50,000. On May 1, the value has increased to 52,000 and 8,000 of new principal is deposited. At time t, in years, $(4/12 < t < 1)$ the value of the fund has increased to 62,000 and 10,000 is withdrawn. On January 1 of the next year, the investment account is worth 55,000. The dollar-weighted rate of return (using the simple interest approximation) is equal to the time-weighted rate of return for the year.

Calculate t.
  A. 0.411
  B. 0.415
  C. 0.585
  D. 0.589
  E. 0.855

Revisiting Topics in Financial Mathematics

CHAPTER SIX

Savings Revisited

Abstract

In this chapter, we will revisit the basic concepts we introduced in Chapter 1, Saving: Fundamentals of Interest: compound and simple interest, nominal and effective rates, and basic savings concepts. Except now, we will look at some additional detailed and less commonly used techniques of interest theory. For example, we will look at the force of interest (Section 6.1), which can be thought of as what would happen if the compounding period was very, very short. We will also look at the discount rate (Section 6.2), which is when interest is paid at the beginning of the period, instead of the end. In Section 6.3, we will examine discount rate, force of interest, and interest rate simultaneously and see how to solve problems involving moving back and forth between these rates.

Keywords: Discount rate; force of interest; continuous compounding

SECTION 6.1. FORCE OF INTEREST

In Chapter 1, Saving: Fundamentals of Interest, we introduced the idea of a nominal rate of interest. Nominal rates necessarily required specifying the number of compounding periods per year. Savings accounts and bank loans often state APR (a nominal rate with monthly compounding). Bonds typically pay coupons semiannually, so they use nominal rates with semiannual compounding. But, what about more frequent compounding? In highly fluid accounts with lots of money moving in and out of accounts on a daily basis, compounding may happen on a daily basis. You could imagine if you had a billion dollars in an account for a few hours, you might even want hourly compounding of interest! In this section, we will look at what happens to the effective rate of interest earned when the compounding period gets very, very small. It turns out that the approach of nearly instantaneous compounding can be a convenient mathematical model for interest when the compounding periods are small (daily; hourly). The mathematical properties also make this topic a favorite of the folks writing actuarial exams!

A Spiral Approach to Financial Mathematics.
DOI: https://doi.org/10.1016/B978-0-12-801580-3.00006-X
© 2018 Elsevier Inc.
All rights reserved.

Learning objectives

By the end of this section, you should be able to

- Have a strong comfort level with nominal rates of interest.
- Realize that as m (the number of compounding periods) increases at a given nominal rate of interest, the associated effective interest rate does not increase indefinitely but has a limit and that this limit is called the force of interest.
- Be able to compute the value of the third and unknown value when given any two of the following: present value, future value, and force of interest.

EXAMPLE 6.1. WHICH INVESTMENT WILL YOU CHOOSE?

You've just received an inheritance from a long-lost uncle and you now have $100,000 to invest. You are looking for a reasonably secure investment for the next year, while you determine a long-term strategy for the money. Some digging on your part has uncovered the following 1-year CDs available at local and online banks:

CD 1: Nominal rate of 4% with semiannual compounding
CD 2: Nominal rate of 4% with monthly compounding (APR = 4%)
CD 3: Nominal rate of 4% with annual compounding
CD 4: Nominal rate of 4% with daily compounding

Think about it

Which is the best CD to invest your money in, assuming all the terms are the same?

Remember from Chapter 1, Saving: Fundamentals of Interest, that nominal rates are a shorthand way of communicating an interest rate, but they are not directly comparable if the compounding periods are different. One way to make the nominal rates directly comparable is to convert them to an equivalent effective annual rate of interest. While it may be fairly intuitive that more frequent compounding will increase the effective rate, let's see what these effective rates are for the four CDs above.

Recall that the formula for a nominal rate of interest to an effective rate is

$$\left(1 + \frac{i^{(m)}}{m}\right)^m - 1,$$

where $i^{(m)}$ is the nominal rate per year with m compounding (or conversion) periods per year. Table 6.1 shows nominal 4% CDs with different compounding periods. The four CDs we are considering are in the table (along with some other ones) and you can see that the CD with daily compounding has the best effective interest rate, resulting in the largest ending balance for the $100,000 initial deposit—a balance of $104,080.85.

Think about it

Intuitively, does more frequent compounding yield larger balances for nominal rates?

More frequent compounding yields larger balances because you are more frequently earning interest on the interest. This is the m in the exponent of the equation used to convert nominal rates to effective rates. However, it is important to note that in the case of nominal rates, this "growth" in account balances is not infinite because you divide the nominal rate by m before raising the rate to the mth power.

You might have noticed that the growth in account balances (and effective rates) in Table 6.1 seems to be leveling off. In fact, we went further and looked at compounding every hour, every minute, and even every second to see what would happen. As you can see, eventually the change gets so small it essentially isn't really that different. The account balances for compounding every minute and every second are, to the nearest penny, the same.

In Fig. 6.1, we plotted the account balance for different numbers of compounding periods per year up to weekly compounding (52 times per year). We can see this "leveling off" visually as we get closer to 52 weeks, and it would even be more pronounced if we extended the graph out further (e.g., 365 or more). If you've taken calculus or precalculus, this might remind you of the idea of a limit.

Table 6.1 Effective interest rates and end of year account balances for different numbers of conversion periods (m) on a 4% nominal rate of interest

Number of compounding periods, m	Symbol	Period length	Effective interest rate per period ($i^{(m)}/m$)	Effective interest rate per year $(1 + (i^{(m)}/m))^m - 1$	End of year account balance ($)
1 (annually)	$i^{(1)} = 0.04$	1 year	0.04	0.04	104,000.00
2 (semiannually)	$i^{(2)} = 0.04$	6 months	0.02	0.0404	104,040.00
3 (triannually)	$i^{(3)} = 0.04$	4 months	0.0133	0.040537	104,053.57
4 (quarterly)	$i^{(4)} = 0.04$	3 months	0.01	0.040604	104,060.40
6 (bi-monthly)	$i^{(6)} = 0.04$	2 months	0.00667	0.0406726	104,067.26
12 (monthly)	$i^{(12)} = 0.04$	1 month	0.00333	0.0407415	104,074.15
24 (semimonthly)	$i^{(24)} = 0.04$	$\sim$2 weeks	0.00167	0.0407761	104,077.61
52 (weekly)	$i^{(52)} = 0.04$	1 week	0.000769	0.04079477	104,079.48
365 (daily)	$i^{(365)} = 0.04$	1 day	0.00011	0.0408085	104,080.85
8,760 (hourly)	$i^{(8,760)} = 0.04$	1 h	4.57×10^{-6}	0.04081068	104,081.07
525,600 (minutely)	$i^{(525,600)} = 0.04$	1 min	7.61×10^{-8}	0.04081077	104,081.77
31,536,000 (secondly)	$i^{(31,536,000)} = 0.04$	1 s	1.27×10^{-9}	0.04081077	104,081.77

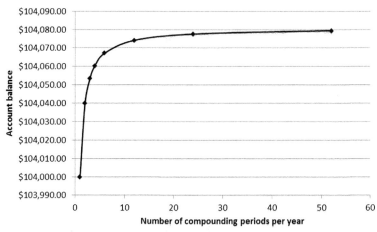

Figure 6.1 Growth in account balances for different number of compounding periods per year at a nominal rate ($i^{(m)}$) of 4%

Definition

The **limit** of a sequence of numbers is the value that the sequence approaches (or converges to) as the sequence continues indefinitely.

One special limit that will help us to determine the limit of our account balance as the number of compounding periods increases indefinitely is $\lim_{m \to \infty} \left(1 + 1/m\right)^m$. We read this as "The limit as m goes to infinity of $\left(1 + 1/m\right)^m$." Table 6.2 shows how this expression increases to some limit as m gets larger and larger.

Table 6.2 As m increases toward infinity, $\left(1 + 1/m\right)^m$ has a limit

m	$\left(1 + 1/m\right)^m$
10	2.5937…
50	2.6915…
100	2.7048…
1,000	2.7169…
10,000	2.7181…
100,000	2.7182…

The number that $\lim_{m \to \infty} \left(1 + 1/m\right)^m$ is approaching is 2.71828... and is commonly known as e. We can use this number e to help determine what the effective annual interest rate as the number of compounding periods per year goes to infinity as follows:

$$\text{Effective annual rate} = \lim_{m \to \infty} \left(\left(1 + \frac{i^{(m)}}{m}\right)^m - 1\right) = e^{i^{(\infty)}} - 1 = e^{\partial} - 1.$$

Besides e in the result, we also have the Greek letter delta ∂, and it represents what is called **force of interest**, which is the nominal interest rate if there is an infinite number of compounding periods per year or what is commonly called continuous compounding. (We will guide you through this limit in the exercises). In our example of a 4% nominal interest rate, we get $e^{\partial} - 1 = e^{0.04} - 1 = 0.04081077$ for our effective annual rate with continuous compounding. Notice this is what we saw in Table 6.1 for minute-by-minute and second-by-second compounding. Thus, in practice, the force of interest is an alternative way to quickly calculate/approximate effective annual rates of interest when there are many compounding periods (e.g., 100 or more) annually.

Definition

The **force of interest**, ∂, is the nominal annual interest rate if there is continuous compounding (infinitely many compounding periods in the year).

Changing the force of interest

Returning to our example, the best possible CD at a 4% nominal rate of interest would be the CD with continuous compounding. Four percent might be a bit ambitious for the interest rate on a CD. What if you found a CD at a 3% force of interest—how much money would you have in the CD at the end of 1 year if you deposited $100,000 now?

A 3% force of interest means that $i^{(\infty)} = \partial = 0.03$, meaning a nominal rate of interest of 3% with continuous compounding. To calculate this balance, we first find the equivalent effective annual rate by $e^{\partial} - 1 = e^{0.03} - 1 = 0.030454534$. This means that a deposit of $100,000 will earn $3,045.45 over the year. So, the account will have an ending balance of $103,045.45 after 1 year.

A common formula (sometimes called the "shampoo formula" because it is pronounced "Pert") is a shortcut to finding balances in accounts with continuous compounding over time.

$$A(t) = Pe^{rt}$$

In this formula, $A(t)$ is the future balance of an account in t years, P is the present value of the account, e is 2.178..., and r is the force of interest (which we typically denote as ∂ but can be indicated by other symbols as well).

Thus, using this formula, you can quickly find the balance in the CD account after 2 years as

$$A(t) = Pe^{rt} = \$100,000e^{0.03(2)} = \$106,183.70$$

Generalizing the idea of force of interest (requires calculus)

It turns out that the idea of force of interest is related to both the idea of derivatives from Calculus and logarithms and is a popular topic on actuarial exams.

The most important relationship to know for actuarial exams is

$$\partial(t) = \frac{a'(t)}{a(t)}$$

where $\partial(t)$ is the force of interest at time t, $a(t)$ is the accumulated amount in the account at time t if you deposited \$1 today, and $a'(t)$ is the derivative of $a(t)$ in terms of t. You can think of $a'(t)$ as an instantaneous measure of how fast the accumulated amount in the account is growing at time t. Thus, $\partial(t)$ is really just a scaled version of the derivative, where the derivative is the slope of the tangent line to the curve (or instantaneous rate of change).

For compound interest, which is what we typically are dealing with in real life, $a(t) = (1+i)^t$ [which means $a'(t) = (1+i)^t \ln(1+i)$] and so

$$\partial(t) = \frac{a'(t)}{a(t)} = \frac{(1+i)^t \ln(1+i)}{(1+i)^t} = \ln(1+i).$$

Changing our resulting logarithmic equation $\partial = \ln(1+i)$ to an exponential equation, we obtain $e^{\partial} = 1+i$, which is what we used earlier when using the force of interest to solve for the equivalent effective interest rate. On the actuarial exam, expect to see some very different looking $a(t)$ functions asking you to compute the force of interest. See the homework exercises and end of chapter exercises to practice.

EXPLORATION 6.1. CHOOSING BETWEEN INVESTMENTS WITH DIFFERENT COMPOUNDING PERIODS

You are saving for a car and want to set your money aside for the next year. You currently have $10,000 and are trying to decide where best to invest it. After doing some looking at investment options, you find the following options:

CD 1: Nominal rate of 2% with semiannual compounding
CD 2: Nominal rate of 2% with monthly compounding (APR = 2%)
CD 3: Nominal rate of 2% with annual compounding
CD 4: Nominal rate of 2% with daily compounding

1. Without doing any calculations, which CD is the best one for you to purchase? Why?

2. Now, do some calculations to justify your answer to the previous question.

CD 4 is the best because the effective rates keep increasing as the number of compounding periods increase. But, does this increase continue forever?

3. Fill in Table 6.3, which includes a variety of additional compounding periods.

4. Does the effective annual interest rate keep growing as you have more and more frequent compounding?

5. Rounded to the nearest penny, does your account balance keep growing with more and more frequent compounding?

We see that with more and more frequent compounding, effective interest rates keep increasing, though the amount they are growing is getting smaller and smaller. In fact, the increases are so small in many cases that the account balance rounded to the nearest penny is essentially the same after a while.

Table 6.3 Effective interest rates and end of year account balances for different numbers of conversion periods (*m*) on a 2% nominal rate of interest

Number of compounding periods, *m*	Symbol	Period length	Effective interest rate per period $(i^{(m)}/m)$	Effective interest rate per year $(1 + (i^{(m)}/m))^m - 1$	End of year account balance if start with $10,000 ($)
1 (annually)	$i^{(1)} = 0.02$	1 year	0.02	0.02	10,200
2 (semiannually)	$i^{(2)} = 0.02$	6 months	0.02	0.0201	10,201
3 (triannually)	$i^{(3)} = 0.02$	4 months			
4 (quarterly)	$i^{(4)} = 0.02$	3 months			
6 (bimonthly)	$i^{(6)} = 0.02$	2 months			
12 (monthly)	$i^{(12)} = 0.02$	1 month			
24 (semimonthly)	$i^{(24)} = 0.02$	~2 weeks			
52 (weekly)	$i^{(52)} = 0.02$	1 week			
365 (daily)	$i^{(365)} = 0.02$	1 day			
8,760 (hourly)	$i^{(8,760)} = 0.02$	1 h			
525,600 (minutely)	$i^{(525,600)} = 0.02$	1 min			
31,536,000 (secondly)	$i^{(31,536,000)} = 0.02$	1 s			

The idea that as m increases the effective interest rate increases, but by smaller and smaller amounts, might remind you of the idea of a limit from Calculus.

Definition

The **limit** of a sequence of numbers is the value that the sequence approaches (or converges to) as the sequence continues indefinitely.

One special limit that will help us to determine the limit of our account balance as the number of compounding periods increases indefinitely is $\lim_{m \to \infty} (1 + 1/m)^m$. We read this as "The limit as m goes to infinity of $(1 + 1/m)^m$." Table 6.4 shows how this expression increases to some limit as m gets larger and larger.

Table 6.4 As m increases toward infinity, $(1 + 1/m)^m$ has a limit

m	$(1 + 1/m)^m$
10	2.5937...
50	2.6915...
100	2.7048...
1,000	2.7169...
10,000	2.7181...
100,000	2.7182...

The number that $\lim_{m \to \infty} (1 + 1/m)^m$ is approaching is about 2.71828... and is commonly known as e. We can use this number e to help determine the effective annual interest rate as the number of compounding periods per year goes to infinity as follows:

$$\text{Effective annual rate} = \lim_{m \to \infty} \left(1 + \frac{i^{(m)}}{m}\right)^m - 1 = e^{i^{(\infty)}} - 1 = e^{\partial} - 1.$$

Besides e in the result we also have the Greek letter delta, ∂. This represents what is called "force of interest" which is the nominal interest rate if there is an infinite number of compounding periods per year or what is commonly called continuous compounding. (We will guide you through this limit in the exercises.)

6. What is the effective annual rate for a new account: CD 5—earning 2% nominal rate of interest with continuous compounding $(m \to \infty)$?

Notice your answer to the previous question is what you saw earlier for minute-by-minute and second-by-second compounding. Thus, in practice, the force of interest is an alternative way to quickly calculate effective annual rates of interest when there are lots of compounding periods annually.

Definition

The **force of interest**, ∂, is the nominal annual interest rate if there is continuous compounding (infinitely many compounding periods in the year).

Changing the force of interest

Returning to our example, the best possible CD at a 2% nominal rate of interest would be the CD with continuous compounding. Let's say you can actually find a CD at a rate that's better than 2% nominal interest— you find one at 2.5% nominal with continuous compounding.

7. How much money will you have in the CD at the end of 1 year if you deposited $10,000 into this new CD (2.5% nominal with continuous compounding)? After 2 years? What is another term for "2.5% nominal with continuous compounding"?

A common formula (sometimes called the "shampoo formula" because it is pronounced "Pert") is a shortcut to finding balances in accounts with continuous compounding over time.

$$A(t) = Pe^{rt}$$

In this formula, $A(t)$ is the future balance of an account in t years, P is the present value of the account, e is 2.178..., and r is the force of interest (which we typically denote as ∂ but can be indicated by other symbols as well).

8. Use the Pert formula to find the value of the CD at the end of 2 years and confirm it matches the answer you obtained above.

Generalizing the idea of force of interest (requires calculus)

It turns out that the idea of force of interest is related to both the idea of derivatives from Calculus and logarithms and is a popular topic on actuarial exams. See a brief note on this at the end of Example 6.1 and in the exercises.

SUMMARY

In this section we saw how for a given nominal interest rate, more and more frequent compounding continues to increase the corresponding effective interest rate. However, there is a limit to the increase. This limit is called the force of interest. The force of interest, essentially representing the idea of continuously compounded interest, can help to quickly approximate frequent (e.g., daily) compounding.

Notation and equation summary

Force of interest for compound interest

$$\lim_{m \to \infty} \left(1 + \frac{i^{(m)}}{m}\right)^m - 1 = e^{i^{(\infty)}} - 1 = e^{\partial} - 1$$

General force of interest for accumulation function $a(t)$

$$\partial(t) = \frac{a'(t)}{a(t)}$$

Generalized formula for future value in terms of a continuously compounded rate, r.

$$A(t) = Pe^{rt}$$

HOMEWORK QUESTIONS: SECTION 6.1

Conceptual questions

1. As the number of compounding periods per year increases for a specific nominal interest rate, the effective interest rate _____(increases/decreases) and does so _____(without bound/by approaching a limit).

2. What is force of interest?

3. What will give you a better rate of return: investing in an account with 4% force of interest or 4% APR?

4. Consider three investments where all will earn you a nominal interest rate of 3%. In investment A, the interest is compounded monthly, in investment B, the interest is compounded quarterly, and in investment C, the interest is compounded continuously. Which will give you the largest return and which will give you the smallest return?

5. Can you increase the number of compounding periods per year so that a nominal rate of 5% can by increased to a 5.2% effective rate of interest? Explain why or why not.

Practice questions

6. You invested $500 into an account where the force of interest is 2%. How much will that account be worth in 1 year?

7. How much money would you need to put into an account where the force of interest is 2.5% and you want to have the account be worth $1,000 in 1 year?

8. You invest $800 into an account where the interest rate is compounded continuously. After 1 year the account is worth $812.09. What was the force of interest on this account?

9. You invest $400 into an account where the interest rate is compounded continuously. After 4 years the account is worth $451. What was the force of interest on this account?

10. Christopher puts $1,000 into an account that earns 3% compounded monthly while Christine puts $1,000 that earns a force of interest of X. After 6 years, the two accounts have the same amount of money. What is the value of X?

Application questions

11. Joaquin invests $100 at the beginning of each week into an account where the force of interest is 1%. How much will his account be

worth at the start of the 20th week just after he makes a deposit? (For this question, we will assume a year has exactly 52 weeks.)

12. You put $10,000 into a crazy account that earns 3% effective interest for the first 3 years, 3% APR for the next 3 years, and 3% force of interest for the next 3 years. How much is your account worth at the end of the 9 years?

13. You put $5,000 into an account that earns 4% APR and after 2 years you add $3,000 to that account. At year 5, the account changes so that it pays out at a force of interest of 3%. At year 7, you add $5,000 more to the account. How much is this account worth at the end of year 10?

14. You put $3,000 into an account that earns 3% APR and after 4 years you add another $3,000 to that account. At year 6, the account changes so that it pays out at a force of interest of 2.5%. At year 7, you take out $2,000 from the account and at year 9 you add $4,000 more to the account. How much is this account worth at the end of year 10?

15. We saw that for a fixed nominal rate of interest, increasing the number of compounding periods has a limited effect on the resulting effective rate of interest and hence return on investment. But what if we fix the effective rate and keep increasing the number of compounding periods? Does this have a limiting effect as well? To answer this, we will suppose the fixed effective rate of interest is 1%.
    a. What is the annual effective interest rate if you earn 1% each quarter?
    b. What is the annual effective interest rate if you earn 1% each month?
    c. What is the annual effective interest rate if you earn 1% each day?
    d. Does there seem to be a limit to the annual effective interest rate as the number of compounding periods per year increases?
    e. Write this situation in the limit notation where the number of compounding periods, m, goes to infinity.

16. If $a(t) = t^2 + 3t + 3$, answer the following questions

    a. What is the force of interest?

    b. What is the account balance after 10 years if $1 is deposited today?

    c. What's a pretty exciting thing about this account if you deposit your money and immediately withdrawal it?

17. There are two versions of a fairly common rule that relates interest rates to the time (in years) needed for an investment to double. One version it is called the "Rule of 72" and the other is the "Rule of 70". These rules state that the interest rate (written as a percentage) multiplied by the time needed to double is equal to 72 (or 70). They are used to determine the doubling time. So, if you are using the rule of 72 and have 6% interest then the doubling time, D, is estimated by solving $6 \times D = 72$ or $D = 72/6 = 12$ years. Let's see where how these rules are determined.

    a. Suppose we start out with P dollars and it is invested at a continuous annual interest rate of i and we want that to turn into $2P$ dollars in t years. Write down an equation for that situation.

    b. Use your equation from part (a) and solve it for ti (the product of t and i).

    c. You should have obtained a number less than one in part b. Multiply this by 100 to convert i to a percentage instead of a decimal. Is it close to 70?

    d. If there were fewer compounding periods in a year (like 12 or 4), would the rule of 70 have to be increased to something like the rule of 72 or decreased? Explain.

Prove it! questions

18. In the section, we said that

$$\text{Effective annual rate} = \lim_{m \to \infty} \left(1 + \frac{i^{(m)}}{m}\right)^m - 1 = e^{i^{(\infty)}} - 1 = e^{\partial} - 1.$$

    Now let's take a closer look at this and show why it's true. The key to this is the idea that $\lim_{x \to \infty} (1 + 1/x)^x = e$. This is one of the ways the number e is defined. Let's make a simple substitution so we can show that the above relationship is true. We will let $x = m/i^{(m)}$.

a. If $x = m/i^{(m)}$, explain why $\lim_{m \to \infty} \left(1 + \left(i^{(m)}/m\right)\right)^m$ can be rewritten as $\lim_{xi^{(m)} \to \infty} \left(\left(1 + \left(1/x\right)\right)^x\right)^{i^{(m)}}$.

b. Since $i^{(m)}$ is a fixed number (we just don't know what it is exactly), as $xi^{(m)}$ goes to infinity, so must x. Use this fact to explain why $\lim_{xi^{(m)} \to \infty} \left(\left(1 + \left(1/x\right)\right)^x\right)^{i^{(m)}} = e^{i^{(m)}}$.

c. Now we need a notation adjustment. Our nominal interest rate $i^{(m)}$ can be rewritten as $i^{(\infty)}$ since we are doing an infinite number of compounding periods. This is just a notation adjustment because the nominal interest rate doesn't change value at all. So $e^{i^{(m)}} = e^{i^{(\infty)}}$. Now explain why $e^{i^{(\infty)}} = e^{\delta}$.

d. Now we have shown that $\lim_{m \to \infty} \left(1 + \left(i^{(m)}/m\right)\right)^m = e^{\delta}$. Explain what is missing to complete the proof.

SECTION 6.2. DISCOUNT RATE

Up until now we've focused most of our time and attention on interest rates (which we sometimes call yield rates or rates of return). It's been a while since we've looked at the fundamental basis of interest. At its most basic level, an interest rate is a percentage of the present value. Interestingly, this is only one way of thinking about interest. While not nearly as common, a discount rate can also be used to compute interest. As we'll see, the idea of a discount rate is related to discounts you might see in a store. For example, if a shoe store is having a 30% off sale, we would say the shoes are discounted 30%. This means that if a pair of shoes originally cost $100, we would get 30% (or $30) off and would only need to pay $70 for the shoes. In this section, we'll see how the discount rate offers an alternative way to pay interest—by paying it at the beginning of the period and as a percentage of the future value, instead of the present value.

Learning objectives

By the end of this section, you should be able to
- Understand discount rate as another way to state an interest rate.
- Understand discount rate as a percentage of the future value, instead of the present value.

- Be able to comfortably move between interest rate and discount rate.
- Distinguish between discount rate and discount factor.
- Evaluate account balances with effective discount rates.
- Given two of the following: present value, future value, and discount rate, be able to find the third.

EXAMPLE 6.2. SAVING MONEY IN U.S. TREASURY BILLS

You have $9,600 to invest for the next year and are evaluating your investment options:

Option 1: 1-year CD paying 3.9% effective annually

Option 2: Zero-coupon bonds yielding 3.95% effective annually

Option 3: 1-year $1,000 Treasury bills (T-bills) selling at a 4% annual effective discount rate

Which is the best investment option?

The first two options are straightforward. If you put the $9,600 in the CD, you will have $9,600(1.039) = $9,974.40 at the end of the year. The zero-coupon bond, however, is even better since the effective yield rate is higher: $9,600(1.0395) = $9,979.20. But what about the T-bill? What is a T-bill? What is a discount rate?

Definition

A **T-bill** is a government financial security, which acts like a short-term loan to the government and like a short-term investment for the lender. An investor buys T-bills today (gives money to the government) for the promise of a payment of a fixed amount sometime in the future. T-bills are typically issued over short terms (e.g., 4, 13, 26, or 52 weeks).

Mini example of a $1,000 T-bill

For example, an investor might buy a 1-year $1,000 T-bill for $990 today, which means that they pay $990 today in order to receive a $1,000 payment, 1 year from now. Before we dig into what the discount rate is, consider that for this example, the interest rate earned on this investment would be $(1,000-990)/990 = 10/990 = 0.010101$, or an effective annual interest rate of 1.0101%. Recall that in this formula, we divide interest earned by the present value of the investment.

The discount rate is an alternative way of stating the rate of interest on an investment, which computes the rate as the interest earned, divided by the future value of the investment.

Definition

The **annual effective discount rate**, d, is an alternative way to communicate how much interest is earned on an investment. In particular, it is computed as interest earned divided by the future value of the account. It is commonly used in financial situations where the future value of the account is predetermined.

We use the symbol d to specify the discount rate, which is computed as

$$d = \frac{\text{Interest earned}}{\text{Future account value}}$$

$$= \frac{\text{Future account value} - \text{Present account value}}{\text{Future account value}} = \frac{A(t_2) - A(t_1)}{A(t_2)}$$

Thus, in the mini example we are exploring, the discount rate is

$$d = \frac{1000 - 990}{1000} = 0.01$$

Back to main example

So, how can we evaluate Option 3—the $1,000 T-bills which are selling at a 4% discount rate? This means that $d = 0.04$. Since the $1,000 T-bills are selling at a 4% discount rate, how much do they cost today? To find the present value, we first multiply the discount rate by the future value—in this case, 4% of $1,000 = $40. This is the interest earned, so the present value is $1,000 − $40 = $960. Here is a more formal equation illustrating this relationship:

$$\text{Present value} = \text{Future value} - \text{Future value} \times d$$

$$\text{Present value} = \text{Future value}(1 - d)$$

or

$$A(t_1) = A(t_2)(1 - d)$$

This means that, with our $9,600, we can buy 10 T-bills, which will accumulate to $10,000 by years end. Since $10,000 is more than either of the future values for Options 1 and 2, the T-bills are paying the most interest and are the best investment.

Relationship between discount rate and interest rate

How do discount rate and interest rate compare? We already noted earlier that the key difference between discount rate and interest rate is what you divide by. In the case of an interest rate, i, you divide the interest earned by the *present value*, whereas in the case of a discount rate, you divide by the *future value*.

Key idea

To compute an interest rate, divide interest earned by the present value and to compute a discount rate, divide interest earned by the future value.

The idea of discount rate may be more intuitive if you think of how you compute a sale price when you shop. When the sale rack at the store says "20% off," you know to multiply 20% times the current price of a $50 pair of pants, and figure out that the discount will be $10, and so you will end up paying $40. The $50 is like the "future value" and the $40 is like the "present value" and the $10 is like the interest in this analogy.

While you can do discount rate problems directly, for some problems, you might find it easier to first convert the discount rate to the equivalent interest rate and then solve. How do you do this? Essentially, we want to determine the relationship between d, the annual effective discount rate, and i, the annual effective interest rate.

We just saw that Present value = Future value$(1 - d)$, which can be rewritten as Future value = Present value$/(1 - d)$, and we know that Future value = Present value$(1 + i)$. We can use these two equations for future value and use a bit of algebra (that we will go to in detail in the exercises) to give us the following relationships:

$$d = \frac{i}{1 + i}$$

$$i = \frac{d}{1 - d}.$$

Thus, in our T-bill example, since $d = 0.04$, the equivalent effective interest rate is $i = 0.04/0.96 = 0.041667$. We also could have calculated this by doing $\$9,600(1 + i) = 10,000$ and solving for i. If you had done this first, you could have seen that the T-bills were the best option since they are paying the highest annual effective interest rate [4.1667% for Option 3 vs 3.9% for Option 1 (CD) and 3.95% for Option 2 (1-year zero-coupon bond)].

Key idea

When solving problems involving a mix of interest rates and discount rates, it may be helpful to convert discount rates to interest rates using the fact that $i = d/(1 - d)$.

Discount rate vs discount factor

You may remember in earlier chapters that there is something called the discount factor, v. It's easy to confuse the discount factor and the discount rate because both terms involve the word discount!

Recall that the discount factor is the present value of $\$1$ paid in the future. For example, for the T-bills described above, the discount factor is 0.96. The T-bill is valued at $\$0.96$ today for every $\$1$ of future value.

Thus, the relationship between discount factor, v, and discount rate, d, is given as

$$d = 1 - v.$$

Recall that earlier we saw $v = 1/(1 + i)$. Using this and the relationship above, we can find the relationship between the discount rate and interest rate we saw earlier.

Key idea

The discount rate, d, and the discount factor, v, are related but distinct ideas. The discount factor is the present value of $\$1$ paid in the future, whereas the discount rate is the interest earned divided by the future value. They are directly related as $d = 1 - v$.

We can relate discount factor back to our 20% off sale rack at a store. In this case, the discount rate was $20\% = 0.20$, which is how much you take off the regular price; the discount factor is $80\% = 0.80$, which is how much of the regular price you have to pay.

Discount rate over multiple periods/fractional periods

We've typically explored the use of interest rates across multiple time periods by compounding. Let's see how this works with discount rates. Let's imagine that we want to invest the $9,600 in a 2-year T-bill that is at annual effective rate of discount of 4%. There are two approaches to find the investment balance after 2 years.

In the first approach, we use the fact that we know that the discount rate of $d = 0.04$ is equivalent to $i = 0.041667$. Thus, the balance after 2 years is simply $9,600(1 + 0.041667)^2 = \$10,416.67$.

In the alternative approach, we use the fact that Future value = Present value$/(1 - d)$ and Future value = Present value $(1 + i)$ to realize that $(1-d)^{-1} = 1 + i$. We can then use this in the following equation which gives the account balance after t years, where d is the annual effective discount rate.

$$a(t) = (1+i)^t = (1-d)^{-t}$$

Thus, $9,600(1 - d)^{-t} = \$9,600(1 - 0.04)^{-2} = \$10,416.67$.

EXPLORATION 6.2. INVESTING IN U.S. TREASURY BILLS

Let's assume you have $950,000 to invest for the next year on behalf of a company you work for. You are evaluating two options. One of which is investing in a 1-year zero-coupon bond (currently yielding 5% effective).

1. If you invest all $950,000 in the 1-year zero-coupon bond, how much will you have at the end of the year?

The other option you are considering is investing in 1-year T-bills that are currently selling at a 5% effective discount rate. But what is a T-bill? And what is a discount rate?

Definition
A **T-bill** is a government financial security which acts like a short-term loan to the government and like a short-term investment for the lender. An investor buys T-bills today (gives money to the government) for the promise of a payment of a fixed amount sometime in the future. T-bills are typically issued over short terms (e.g., 4, 13, 26, and 52 weeks).

Mini example of a $1,000 T-bill

An investor might buy a 1-year $1,000 T-bill for $990 today, which means that they pay $990 today in order to receive a $1,000 payment, 1-year from now.

2. For this mini example, what is the effective interest rate?

The discount rate is an alternative way of stating the rate of interest on an investment, which computes the rate as interest earned divided by the future value of the investment.

The idea of discount rate may be more intuitive if you think of how you compute a sale price when you shop. When the sale rack at the store says "20% off", you know to multiply 20% times the current price of a $50 pair of pants and figure out that the discount will be $10, and so you will end up paying $40. The $50 is like the "future value" and the $40 is like the "present value" and the $10 is like the interest in this analogy.

Definition

The **annual effective discount rate**, d, is an alternative way to communicate how much interest is earned on an investment. In particular, it is computed as interest earned divided by the future value of the account. It is commonly used in financial situations where the future value of the account is predetermined.

We use the symbol d to specify the discount rate, which is computed as

$$d = \frac{\text{Interest earned}}{\text{Future account value}}$$
$$= \frac{\text{Future account value} - \text{Present account value}}{\text{Future account value}} = \frac{A(t_2) - A(t_1)}{A(t_2)}$$

3. What is the discount rate for the T-bill in this mini example?

Back to your $950,000

Let's return now to the $950,000 you are seeking to invest and consider what investment in T-bills would look like.

4. T-bills often come in increments of $1,000. That is, the value they are worth when they are paid out is $1,000. How much are $1,000 T-bills selling for today if the discount rate is 5%?

5. How many T-bills can you buy today if you invest all $950,000 in T-bills?

6. What will be the value of your $950,000 investment in 1 year if you buy T-bills?

7. How does this compare to the zero-coupon bond? Which is a better investment based on future value alone (ignore risk)?

Here is a more formal equation illustrating the relationship between present value and future value for the discount rate, d.

$$\text{Present value} = \text{Future value} - \text{Future value} \times d$$

$$\text{Present value} = \text{Future value}(1 - d)$$

or

$$A(t_1) = A(t_2)(1 - d)$$

RELATIONSHIP BETWEEN DISCOUNT RATE AND INTEREST RATE

How do discount rate and interest rate compare? We already noted earlier that the key difference between discount rate and interest rate is what you divide by. In the case of an interest rate, i, you divide the interest earned by the present value, whereas in the case of a discount rate, you divide by the future value.

Key idea

To compute an interest rate, divide interest earned by the present value, to compute a discount rate divide interest earned by the future value.

While you can do discount rate problems directly, for some problems, you might find it easier to first convert the discount rate to the equivalent interest rate and then solve. How do you do this? Essentially, we want to determine the relationship between d, the annual effective discount rate, and i, the annual effective interest rate.

8. Based on the present value and future value of the T-bill investment, what is the effective interest rate? Compare this to the yield rate on the bond and argue why the T-bills are a better investment.

There are equations to directly relate the discount rate and the interest rate:

We just saw that Present value = Future value $(1 - d)$ which can be rewritten as Future value = Present value$/(1 - d)$ and we know that Future value = Present value $(1 + i)$. We can use these two equations for future value and a bit of algebra (that we will go to in detail in the exercises) to give us the following relationships

$$d = \frac{i}{1 + i}, \text{ or}$$

$$i = \frac{d}{1 - d}.$$

9. Use one of the above equations to convert the discount rate of 5% to the equivalent effective interest rate and confirm your answer is the same as in the previous question.

Key idea

When solving problems involving a mix of interest rates and discount rates, it may be helpful to convert discount rates to interest rates using the fact that $i = d/(1 - d)$.

Discount rate vs discount factor

Recall from earlier chapters, the discount factor, v. The discount factor, v, is distinct from the discount rate, d, but they are related.

10. Define the discount factor v. What is the discount factor for the T-bills?

Key idea

The discount rate, d, and the discount factor, v, are related but distinct ideas. The discount factor is the present value of $1 paid in the future, whereas the discount rate is the interest earned divided by the future value. They are directly related as $d = 1 - v$.

We can relate discount factor back to our 20% off sale rack at a store. In this case, the discount rate was $20\% = 0.20$ (how much you take off the regular price), while the discount factor is $80\% = 0.80$ is how much of the regular price you have to pay.

Discount rate over multiple periods/fractional periods

We've typically explored the use of interest rates across multiple time periods by *compounding*.

11. If you also found a 2-year zero-coupon bond which paid 5% annually, what would your investment be worth after 2 years?

We can also explore account balances for compound discount rates.

12. If you found a 2-year T-bill that pays an effective annual discount rate of 5%, what is the account balance after 2 years? (Hint: Use the formula shown above to convert the discount rate to an interest rate first.)

When finding account balances given discount rates, most students find it preferable to convert a discount rate to an interest rate first. However, there is a direct formula to find account balances with discount rates. We use the fact that Future value $=$ Present value$/(1-d)$ and Future value $=$ Present value $(1+i)$ to realize that $(1-d)^{-1} = 1+i$. We can then use this in the following equation which gives the account balance after t years, where d is the annual effective discount rate:

$$a(t) = (1+i)^t = (1-d)^{-t}$$

13. Use the formula to find the account balance for a 2-year T-bill at 5% discount annually after 2 years. Confirm that your answer is the same as in the previous question.

SUMMARY

In this section, we introduced the idea of the discount rate, which is the interest earned as a percentage of the future value and is in contrast to the interest rate which divides interest earned by the present value. The discount rate is less common than the interest rate but is used in pricing T-bills and in some other financial situations. In practice, converting discount rates to interest rates may make it easier to solve problems involving discount rates.

Notation and equation summary

$$d = \frac{\text{Interest earned}}{\text{Future account value}} = \frac{A(t_2) - A(t_1)}{A(t_2)}$$

$$d = \frac{i}{1+i}$$

$$i = \frac{d}{1-d}$$

$$d = 1 - v$$

$$a(t) = (1+i)^t = (1-d)^{-t}$$

HOMEWORK QUESTIONS: SECTION 6.2

Conceptual questions

1. The discount rate is the interest earned divided by the present value or future value?

2. Discount rates are commonly used when the future or present value of the account is predetermined?

3. Which is the larger value—an effective discount rate or the equivalent effective interest rate?

4. A discount factor and its corresponding discount rate always sum to be what number?

5. If an investment has a 5% effective annual interest rate, the interest rate over a 2-year period would be larger than 5%. If an effective annual discount rate is 5%, is the discount rate over a 2-year period larger than 5% as well?

Practice questions

6. If a discount rate is 4%, what is the corresponding interest rate?

7. If an interest rate is 2.625%, what is the corresponding discount rate?

8. If an annual effective discount rate is 4% on an investment that will be worth $500 in 1 year, what is the present value of that investment?

9. If a $480 investment will turn into $500 in 1 year, what is the discount rate?

10. If a $800 investment has a discount rate of 3%, how much will it be worth in 1 year?

11. If a discount rate is 2%, what is the discount factor?

12. If a discount factor is 0.95, what is the corresponding interest rate?

Application questions

13. You are looking at three investment options. Option 1 will earn 3% APR. Option 2 will earn 3.125% effective annual interest. Option 3 has a discount rate of 3%. Which investment will give the highest rate of return? Which will give the lowest?

14. $2,000 is put into an account. For the first 5 years, the account earns an effective discount rate of 2.5% and thereafter earns an effect interest rate of 3%. What is the accumulated balance in the account after 10 years?

15. $500 is put in a fund at a nominal discount rate of 4%. How much will be in the fund in 2 years if the discount rate is compounded:
   a. Annually?
   b. Semiannually?
   c. Monthly?

16. $1,000 is put into an account today and $1,000 ten years later. For the first 5 years, the account earns a nominal discount rate of 4%

compounded semiannually and thereafter earns a nominal interest rate of 3% compounded quarterly. What is the accumulated balance in the account after 15 years?

17. $500 is put into an account today and $1,000 ten years later. For the first 8 years, the account earns a nominal discount rate of d compounded quarterly and thereafter earns a nominal interest rate of 4% compounded quarterly. If the accumulated balance in the account after 15 years is $2,000, what is the value of d?

Prove it! questions

18. In this question, we want to go through the derivation of the two equations that relate interest rates and discount rates, $i = d/(1 - d)$ and $d = i/(1 + i)$. We start with the two ways to introduce present value and future value in terms of discount rate and interest rate, namely,

$$\text{Present value} = \text{Future value}(1 - d) \tag{6.1}$$

$$\text{Future value} = \text{Present value}(1 + i). \tag{6.2}$$

a. Substitute the right side of Eq. (6.1) in for present value in Eq. (6.2) and show how this simplifies to $1 = (1 - d)(1 + i)$.
b. Show how your result from part (a) can be written as $i = \left(1/(1 - d)\right) - 1$.
c. Now show how the result from part (b) can be written as $i = d/(1 - d)$. (Hint: Get common denominators.)
d. Finally, show that by solving your result from part (c) for the discount rate d, it can be written as $d = i/(1 + i)$.

SECTION 6.3. NOMINAL DISCOUNT RATES

In the previous section, we saw that the discount rate was an alternative way to indicate the amount of interest earned on an investment account. In particular, the discount rate is the ratio of the amount of interest earned to the *future value* of the account. Of course, this approach is in contrast to the more popular approach, the interest rate, which is the ratio of interest earned to the *present value*. While the discount rate is less popular, it does have some applications—particularly, in the statement of interest earned for U.S. T-bills. In the last section of this chapter, we introduce the concept of nominal discount rates (remember nominal interest rates?) and explore how nominal and effective rates relate to each other for interest rates, discount rates, and force of interest.

Learning objectives

By the end of this section, you should be able to

- Understand the concept of a nominal discount rate and how to convert between a nominal discount rate and an effective discount rate.
- Given two of the three following values: present value, future value, and nominal discount rate, find the third.
- Understand how nominal and effective rates of discount and interest relate to each other and the force of interest.

EXAMPLE 6.3. MORE SAVINGS ACCOUNTS

U.S. T-bills are issued over a variety of different terms, including 4, 13, 26, and 52 weeks. As we noted in the previous section, prices for U. S. T-bills are usually stated in terms of the quoted discount rate for the T-bill. Recall the "Example 6.2. Saving money in U.S. Treasury bills" section where you had $9,600 and were considering various investment options. Let's consider some additional options. Table 6.5 shows nominal discount rates for a variety of U.S. T-bills.

Definition

A **nominal rate of discount**, $d^{(p)}$ (pronounced "d upper p"), is like a nominal rate of interest, in that it (typically) gives the annual rate found by multiplying p (the number of compounding periods in a year) by the effective discount rate, d, per period. Note: We use p here for the number of compounding periods when referring to a nominal discount rate, but the idea is the same as the variable m, which we use for nominal interest rates.

Since the terms are all different, an important question to consider is how these rates compare to each other? Obviously, the shorter term T-bills give you flexibility to potentially move your money into a different

Table 6.5 Terms and nominal discount rates for $1,000 U.S. treasury bills

Term (weeks)	P (periods/year)	$d^{(p)}$ Nominal discount rate (%)
4	13	4
13	4	4
26	2	4
52	1	4

account in the future, but the longer term T-bills allow you to "lock in" a particular amount of interest, which also may be appealing.

To compare these rates, as we did when evaluating nominal interest rates, we need to make them effective rates and then put them on the same time scale. To do this here, we will convert each nominal discount rate to an effective annual rate in two steps. We start by dividing the nominal discount rate by p (the number of compounding periods per year) in order to find the effective discount rate, d, per period. We show this in Table 6.6. This also allows us to specify the selling prices for the different T-bills, which are found by multiplying the future value of the T-bill ($1,000) by $1 - d$.

Table 6.6 Terms and nominal discount rates for $1,000 U.S. treasury bills

Term (weeks)	P (periods/ year)	$d^{(p)}$ nominal discount rate (%)	$d = d^{(p)}/p$ effective discount rate/term (%)	Selling price 1000 $(1 - d)$ ($)
4	13	4	0.3077	996.67
13	4	4	1	990.00
26	2	4	2	980.00
52	1	4	4	960.00

Think about it

Does this give you enough information to answer the question of which T-bill is the best to invest in?

This still isn't enough to draw a conclusive answer as to which investment is the best. While the 52-week T-bill yields $40 of interest, it also is over the longest term, so isn't necessarily best. So, how can we evaluate these accounts on a level playing field? To do this, we need to convert the effective discount rates which are currently specified on different terms, to be on the same term. We'll choose to do this for a 1-year period.

The conversion equation between annual effective rate of discount and the nominal rate of discount is given as

$$1 - d = \left(1 - \frac{d^{(p)}}{p}\right)^p$$

Table 6.7 uses this formula to find the effective rate of discount for the year. We also note that we could convert the effective discount rates to effective interest rates first (using the $i = d/(1 - d)$ formula) and then find effective annual interest rates. Table 6.7 illustrates the results of both approaches.

Based on this comparison, notice that the effective annual discount rate is the highest for the 52-week T-bill ($d = 4.0\%$). As expected, this is the T-bill with the highest effective interest rate ($i = 4.1667\%$). Thus, we conclude that the 52-week T-bill is the best. Of course, if you think interest rates (discount rates) might become more favorable in the near future, you might want to not "lock in" your discount for an entire year. Instead, buy the shorter-term T-bill and hope discount rates are higher when your T-bill comes due.

Thus, if you invest your $9,600 in 10, 52-week T-bills, you will have $10,000 at the end of the year.

Trends with more compounding

Think about it

How does the amount of accumulated interest change as the number of compounding periods increases for a constant nominal discount rate? How does this compare to the relationship for nominal interest rate?

For a fixed nominal rate of interest, $i^{(m)}$, the corresponding annual effective rate of interest increases as the number of compounding periods

Table 6.7 Terms and nominal discount rates for $1000 U.S. treasury bills

Term (weeks)	p (periods/ year)	$d^{(p)}$ nominal discount rate (%)	$d = d^{(p)}/p$ effective discount rate/term (%)	Selling price $1000(1-d)$ ($)	Effective annual discount rate $1-(1-d)^p$ (%)	Effective interest rate/term $i = d/(1-d)$ (%)	Effective annual interest rate $(1+i)^p$ (%)
4	13	4	0.3077	996.67	3.927	0.3086	4.0875
13	4	4	1	990.00	3.9404	1.0101	4.102
26	2	4	2	980.00	3.96	2.0408	4.1233
52	1	4	4	960.00	4.00	4.1667	4.1667

per year (m) increases. In fact, we saw earlier in the chapter that the rate increases as a limit approaching the force of interest, delta.

However, for nominal rates of discount, the pattern is different. As the number of compounding periods, p, increases the effective rate of discount decreases.

Key idea

As the number of compounding periods increases for a nominal rate of discount, $d^{(p)}$, the effective annual rate of discount, d, decreases. This is the opposite relationship as compounding has for nominal interest rates.

You can also convert nominal discount rate to the force of interest. When our discount rate is compounded continuously, we have a similar limit and similar result as when the interest rate is compounded continuously. In particular, we can write this in terms of force of interest as follows.

$$\lim_{p \to \infty} \left(1 - \frac{d^{(p)}}{p}\right)^p = 1 - e^{d^{(p)}} = 1 - \delta$$

This means that continuous compounding of a discount rate is the force of interest, the same thing as continuous compounding of an interest rate. From this we can see that if $i = i^{(m)} = \delta = d^{(p)} = d$ (or an annual effective interest rate, a nominal interest rate with m compounding periods per year, the force of interest, a discount rate with p compounding periods per year, and an annual effective discount rate are all equal) then, if K_i represents the amount of interest earned in an account at an effective interest rate of i, the following is true:

$$K_i < K_{i^{(m)}} < K_\delta < K_{d^{(p)}} < K_d,$$

as long as $m > 1$ and $p > 1$ and $i > 0$. In other words, an annual effective discount rate of 4% is better than a nominal discount rate of 4% compounded p times a year, is better than 4% compounded continuously, is better than 4% compounded m times a year, is better than 4% effective annual interest.

EXPLORATION 6.3. SAVING WITH U.S. T-BILLS

In Exploration 6.2, we investigated investment savings options for $950,000 that your company had. We saw that a 1-year US T-bill at 5% discount was better than a 1-year zero-coupon bond yielding 5%.

1. How much will a 1-year, $1,000 T-bill at 5% discount cost now?

2. Explain how many T-bills your company will buy with $950,000, and how much money your company will have after 1 year.

U.S. T-bills are actually issued over a variety of different terms including 4, 13, 26, and 52 weeks.

Let's assume that the nominal discount rate for the 4-, 13-, and 26-week T-bills are also all 5%.

Definition

A **nominal rate of discount**, $d^{(p)}$ (pronounced "d upper p"), is like a nominal rate of interest in which it (typically) gives the annual rate found by multiplying p (the number of compounding periods in a year) by the effective discount rate, d, per period. Note: We use p here for the number of compounding periods when referring to a nominal discount rate, but the idea is the same as the variable m, which we use for nominal interest rates.

---

3. Write the symbol and state the value of the nominal rate of discount for the 4-, 13-, and 26-week T-bills. Note: You'll need to think about the value of p for each T-bill!
   4-week:
   13-week:
   26-week:

The practical question is, which one should we invest in?

4. Ignoring amount of interest earned, explain how interest rate risk might impact your investment decision.

5. Now, let's ignore interest rate risk and think about which investment is best if interest rates didn't change? For example, if we kept buying 4-week T-bills at 5% nominal with 13 compounding periods per year is that better or worse than the 52-week T-bill? Let's explore how to answer this question.

   a. We'll start by finding the effective discount rate, d, for each term, which is simply the nominal rate $d^{(p)}$ divided by p, the number of compounding periods per year. Fill in the 4th column of Table 6.8 to do this.

   b. Now, find the selling price for each T-bill today and fill these values into the 5th column of Table 6.8.

Table 6.8 Terms and nominal discount rates for $1,000 U.S. treasury bills

Term (weeks)	p (periods/ year)	$d^{(p)}$ nominal discount rate (%)	$d = d^{(p)}/p$ effective discount rate/ term	Selling price $1,000(1 - d)$	Effective annual discount rate $1 - (1-d)^p$
4	13	5			
13	4	5			
26	2	5			
52	1	5			

   c. Finally, find the effective rate of discount over the entire year, if the shorter term T-bills kept getting reinvested at the same rate. Fill these values in the last column of Table 6.8 as well.

   Note that the conversion equation between annual effective rate of discount, d, and the nominal rate of discount with p compounding periods, $d^{(p)}$ is given as

$$1 - d = \left(1 - \frac{d^{(p)}}{p}\right)^p.$$

6. Based on the information in Table 6.8, which T-bill is the best investment? Why?

7. Another way to solve this problem would have been to convert discount rates into interest rates first. Do this using Table 6.9.

Table 6.9 Terms and effective interest rates for different term T-bills

Term (weeks)	Effective interest rate/term $i = d/(1 - d)$	Effective annual interest rate $(1 + i)^p$
4		
13		
26		
52		

8. Explain how this table also illustrates that the 52-week T-bill is the best investment option, ignoring interest rate risk.

9. Refer back to Table 6.8. How does the amount of accumulated interest change as the number of compounding periods increases for a constant nominal discount rate?

10. How does the relationship you described in the previous question compare to the relationship between the number of compounding periods and the annual effective interest rate for nominal interest rate?

For a fixed nominal rate of interest, $i^{(m)}$, the corresponding annual effective rate of interest increases as the number of compounding periods per year (m) increases. In fact, we saw earlier in the chapter that the rate increases as a limit approaching the force of interest, delta.

However, for nominal rates of discount, the pattern is different. As the number of compounding periods, p, increases the effective rate of discount decreases.

Key idea

As the number of compounding periods increases for a nominal rate of discount, $d^{(p)}$, the effective annual rate of discount, d, decreases. This is the opposite relationship as compounding has for nominal interest rates.

You can also convert nominal discount rate to the force of interest. When our discount rate is compounded continuously, we have a similar limit and similar result as when the interest rate is compounded continuously. In particular, we can write this in terms of force of interest as follows.

$$\lim_{p \to \infty} \left(1 - \frac{d^{(p)}}{p}\right)^p = 1 - e^{d^{(p)}} = 1 - \delta$$

This means that continuous compounding of a discount rate is the force of interest, the same thing as continuous compounding of an interest rate. From this we can see that if, $i = i^{(m)} = \delta = d^{(p)} = d$ (or an annual effective interest rate, a nominal interest rate with m compounding periods per year, the force of interest, a discount rate with p compounding periods per year, and an annual effective discount rate are all equal) then, if K_i represents the amount of interest earned in an account at an effective interest rate of i, the following is true:

$$K_i \le K_{i^{(m)}} \le K_\delta \le K_{d^{(p)}} \le K_d,$$

as long as $m > 1$ and $p > 1$. In other words, an annual effective discount rate of 4% is better than a nominal discount rate of 4% compounded p times a year, is better than 4% compounded continuously, is better than 4% compounded m times a year, is better than 4% effective annual interest.

SUMMARY

In this section, we saw that a nominal rate of discount could be evaluated using many of the same principles and techniques that we used for nominal rates of interest. In particular, first convert the nominal rate to an effective rate by dividing by the number of conversion periods per year.

Notation and equation summary

$$1 - d = \left(1 - \frac{d^{(p)}}{p}\right)^p$$

$$\lim_{p \to \infty} \left(1 - \frac{d^{(p)}}{p}\right)^p = 1 - e^{d^{(p)}} = 1 - \delta$$

HOMEWORK QUESTIONS: SECTION 6.3

Conceptual questions

1. As the number of compounding periods per year increases for a given annual nominal discount rate, does the effective discount rate increase or decrease?

2. Does a nominal discount rate of 4% compounded monthly give a better or worse rate of return than a nominal discount rate of 4% compounded quarterly?

3. Does a nominal discount rate of 4% compounded monthly give a better or worse rate of return than a 4% interest rate compounded continuously?

4. How does a 4% interest rate compounded continuously compare to a 4% discount rate compounded continuously?

5. True or false: an investment than earns 5% compounded continuously will give a better return than the one that has a discount rate of 5% compounded monthly?

Practice questions

6. What is the selling price for a $5,007 13-week T-bill that has a nominal discount rate of 5%?

7. What is the nominal discount rate for a $500 26-week T-bill that sells for $487.50?

8. What is the future value of a 26-week T-bill that earns a nominal annual interest rate of 3% and can be purchased for $9,850?

9. What is the effective annual discount rate for a nominal discount rate of 6% compounded monthly?

10. What is the force of interest for a 5% discount rate?

Application questions

11. Suppose you invest $500 for 3 months at a nominal discount rate of 2.5%, you take those earnings and invest them at a nominal discount rate of 3% for another 3 months, you take those earnings and invest them at a nominal discount rate of 3.5% for another 3 months, and then finally you take those earnings and invest them at a nominal discount rate of 4% for another 3 months. Assume all nominal discount rates are compounded quarterly.
    a. How much is your investment worth after these 12 months?
    b. What effective annual discount rate did you earn for the entire 12 months?
    c. What effective annual interest rate did you earn for the entire 12 months?
    d. Would your results change if your four different discount rates were earned in a different order than what was given (e.g., 4% first, then 3.5%, then 3%, and finally 2.5%)?

12. $500 is put in a fund at a nominal discount rate of 4%. How much will be in the fund in 2 years if the discount rate is compounded:
    a. Annually?
    b. Semiannually?
    c. Monthly?
    d. Continuously?

13. $1,000 is put into an account today and $1,000 ten years later. For the first 5 years, the account earns a nominal discount rate of 4% compounded semiannually and thereafter earns a nominal interest rate of 3% compounded quarterly. What is the accumulated balance in the account after 15 years?

14. $500 is put into an account today and $1,000 ten years later. For the first 8 years, the account earns a nominal discount rate of d compounded quarterly and thereafter earns a nominal interest rate of 4% compounded quarterly. If the accumulated balance in the account after 15 years is $2,000, what is the value of d?

15. Let A be the accumulated value of $500 invested for 2 years at a nominal annual discount rate d compounded semiannually. Let B be the accumulated value of $500 invested for 1 year at a nominal annual discount rate of d compounded quarterly.
    a. If $A/B = (39/38)^4$ what is the value of d?
    b. What is an equivalent annual effective interest rate for d?

END OF CHAPTER SUMMARY

In this chapter, we explored two additional concepts in interest theory: force of interest and discount rate. Force of interest is a nominal rate of interest with continuous compounding and can be used to approximate the interest earned on accounts with frequent compounding. The discount rate is an alternative way to express interest earnings on an account and is computed as the percentage of interest earned relative to the future value of the account, instead of relative to the present value of the account as is done for interest rates.

END OF CHAPTER EXERCISES

(SOA EXAM FM SAMPLE QUESTIONS May 2001, Question 12)

1. Bruce and Robbie each open up new bank accounts at time 0. Bruce deposits 100 into his bank account, and Robbie deposits 50 into his. Each account earns an annual effective discount rate of d.

   The amount of interest earned in Bruce's account during the 11th year is equal to X. The amount of interest earned in Robbie's account during the 17th year is also equal to X.
   Calculate X.
   A 28.0
   B 31.3
   C 34.6
   D 36.7
   E 38.9

(SOA EXAM FM SAMPLE QUESTIONS May 2001, Question 45)

2. At time $t = 0$, 1 is deposited into each of Fund X and Fund Y. Fund X accumulates at a force of interest $\delta t = \frac{t^2}{k}$. Fund Y accumulates at a nominal rate of discount of 8% per annum convertible semi-annually.

At time $t = 5$, the accumulated value of Fund X equals the accumulated value of Fund Y.
Determine k.

A 100

B 102

C 104

D 106

E 108

(SOA EXAM FM SAMPLE QUESTIONS May 2001, Question 49)

3. Tawny makes a deposit into a bank account which credits interest at a nominal interest rate of 10% per annum, convertible semi-annually.

At the same time, Fabio deposits 1,000 into a different bank account, which is credited with simple interest.
At the end of 5 years, the forces of interest on the two accounts are equal, and Fabio's account has accumulated to Z.
Determine Z.

A 1,792

B 1,953

C 2,092

D 2,153

E 2,392

(SOA EXAM FM SAMPLE QUESTIONS May 2003, Question 1)

4. Bruce deposits 100 into a bank account. His account is credited interest at a nominal rate of interest i convertible semi-annually.

At the same time, Peter deposits 100 into a separate account. Peter's account is credited interest at a force of interest of δ.
After 7.25 years, the value of each account is 200. Calculate $(i - \delta)$.

A 0.12%

B 0.23%
C 0.31%
D 0.39%
E 0.47%

(SOA EXAM FM SAMPLE QUESTIONS May 2003, Question 50)

5. Jeff deposits 10 into a fund today and 20 fifteen years later. Interest is credited at a nominal discount rate of d compounded quarterly for the first 10 years, and at a nominal interest rate of 6% compounded semi-annually thereafter. The accumulated balance in the fund at the end of 30 years is 100.

   Calculate d.
   A 4.33%
   B 4.43%
   C 4.53%
   D 4.63%
   E 4.73%

(SOA EXAM FM SAMPLE QUESTIONS May 2005, Question 19)

6. Calculate the nominal rate of discount convertible monthly that is equivalent to a nominal rate of interest of 18.9% per year convertible monthly.
   A 18.0%
   B 18.3%
   C 18.6%
   D 18.9%
   E 19.2%

(SOA EXAM FM SAMPLE QUESTIONS November 2000, Question 53)

7. At time 0, K is deposited into Fund X, which accumulates at a force of interest $\delta_t = 0.006t^2$. At time m, $2K$ is deposited into Fund Y, which accumulates at an annual effective interest rate of 10%.

At time n, where $n > m$, the accumulated value of each fund is $4K$. Determine m.

A 1.6

B 2.4

C 3.8

D 5.0

E 6.2

(SOA EXAM FM SAMPLE QUESTIONS November 2001, Question 1)

8. Ernie makes deposits of 100 at time 0, and X at time 3. The fund grows at a force of interest $\delta_t = \frac{t^2}{100}, \quad t > 0$.

   The amount of interest earned from time 3 to 6 is X. Calculate X.

   A 385

   B 485

   C 585

   D 685

   E 785

(SOA EXAM FM SAMPLE QUESTIONS November 2001, Question 28)

9. Payments are made to an account at a continuous rate of $(8k + tk)$, where $0 \leq t \leq 10$. Interest is credited at a force of interest $\delta_t = \frac{1}{8+t}$.

   After 10 years, the account is 20,000. Calculate k.

   A 111

   B 116

   C 121

   D 126

   E 131

(SOA EXAM FM SAMPLE QUESTIONS Interest Theory, Question 61)

10. The annual force of interest credited to a savings account is defined by

$$\delta_t = \frac{\frac{t^2}{100}}{3 + \frac{t^3}{150}}$$

With t in years. Austin deposits 500 into this account at time 0.
Calculate the time in years it will take for the fund to be worth 2,000.

A 6.7
B 8.8
C 14.2
D 16.5
E 18.9

(SOA EXAM FM SAMPLE QUESTIONS Interest Theory, Question 79)

11. Bill and Joe each put 10 into separate accounts at time $t = 0$, where t is measured in years. Bill's account earns interest at a constant annual effective interest rate of $K/25$, $K > 0$.

Joe's account earns interest at a force of interest, $\delta_t = \frac{1}{K + 0.25t}$.
At the end of four years, the amount in each account is X. Calculate X.

A 20.7
B 21.7
C 22.7
D 23.7
E 24.7

(SOA EXAM FM SAMPLE QUESTIONS Interest Theory, Question 95)

12. Let S be the accumulated value of 1,000 invested for two years at a nominal annual rate of discount d convertible semi-annually, which is equivalent to an annual effective interest rate of i.

Let T be the accumulated value of 1,000 invested for one year at a nominal annual rate of discount d convertible quarterly.
$S/T = (39/38)^4$.
Calculate i.

A 10.0%

B 10.3%
C 10.8%
D 10.9%
E 11.1%

(SOA EXAM FM SAMPLE QUESTIONS Interest Theory, Question 105)

13. A bank agrees to lend 10,000 now and X three years from now in exchange for a single repayment of 75,000 at the end of 10 years. The bank charges interest at an annual effective rate of 6% for the first 5 years and at a force of interest $\delta_t = \frac{1}{t+1}$ for $t \geq 5$.

Calculate X.
A 23,500
B 24,000
C 24,500
D 25,000
E 25,500

(SOA EXAM FM SAMPLE QUESTIONS May 2000, Question 37)

14. A customer is offered an investment where interest is calculated according to the following force of interest:

$$\delta_t = \begin{cases} 0.02t & 0 \leq t \leq 3 \\ 0.045 & 3 < t \end{cases}$$

The customer invests 1,000 at $t = 0$.
What nominal rate of interest, compounded quarterly, is earned over the first four-year period?
A 3.4%
B 3.7%
C 4.0%
D 4.2%
E 4.5%

CHAPTER SEVEN

Loans Revisited

Abstract

In Chapter 2, Loans: Fundamentals of Borrowing and Lending, we first explored the idea of a loan. Amortization was how you pay off a loan—paying a mix of interest and principal over time until the amount owed equals zero. At that time, early in the text, we had not yet learned about annuities or the formulas associated with them. Now that we have, we will revisit loans and see how the level payments (same payment amount each month or other fixed period) that we make when we pay back a fixed rate-loan can be viewed as an annuity. Thus, it's not too surprising that we can use annuity formulas [e.g., present value ($a_{\overline{n}|i}$) and future value ($s_{\overline{n}|i}$)] to directly calculate payment size, outstanding loan balances, and the amount of principal and interest in a loan. In this chapter, we wi'll explore two different ways to accomplish this: the prospective (looking forward) method and the retrospective (looking backward) method, while reviewing many of the basics of loans that we first saw in Chapter 2, Loans: Fundamentals of Borrowing and Lending, through the lens of annuities.

Keywords: Retrospective method; amortization; prospective method

SECTION 7.1. LOANS AS ANNUITIES

Loans are one of the most common financial transactions you are likely to be involved in as part of your personal financial dealings (e.g., school loans, car loans, home loans, credit cards) as well as in business dealings. In this section, we will see how a loan functions like an annuity and this can help us directly calculate formulas for loan balances. We will do this by viewing loans through the lens of the present value of an annuity, $a_{\overline{n}|i}$.

Learning objectives

By the end of this section, you should be able to

- View a loan as a form of an annuity with level payments and use this to find the level payment size needed to pay back the loan.
- Understand the concept of a drop payment, as a slightly different sized final payment to zero out a loan balance and be able to compute drop payment sizes.

A Spiral Approach to Financial Mathematics.
DOI: https://doi.org/10.1016/B978-0-12-801580-3.00007-1
© 2018 Elsevier Inc.
All rights reserved.

- Use the prospective method of loan valuation to find the outstanding loan balance at any point in time and the amount of principal/interest in any payment.

EXAMPLE 7.1. PAYING BACK A STUDENT LOAN

Earlier, we looked at aspects of different types of student loans and how they get paid back. In a typical student loan scenario, a student might end up taking out a student loan all 4 years they are in college. Once again, let's assume that by the time a student finishes college, they have accumulated $45,000 in debt that needs to be repaid. The amortization table for a 10-year loan payback period for $45,000 in debt at 4.2% APR (compounded monthly) is shown in Table 7.1. We used guess-and-check in Excel (you could also use the PMT function; see the **Chapter 7 Excel file**) to determine that a payment size of $459.89 monthly will pay back the loan in 10 years.

Table 7.1 Amortization table for $45,000 student loan at 4.2% APR over 10 years

Month	Principal balance (day 1) ($)	Interest accrued (during month) ($)	Payment (31st of month) ($)	New loan balance (31st of month) ($)
1	45,000.00	157.50	459.89	44,697.61
2	44,697.61	156.44	459.89	44,394.16
3	44,394.16	155.38	459.89	44,089.65
...	...	...	459.89	...
120	458.68	1.61	459.89	0.00

Notice, that the $459.89 monthly payment is like an annuity in that it is a level payment, which occurs regularly (monthly) and governed by a fixed interest rate (4.2% APR). Thus, we can think of the $459.89 payments as an annuity. This is advantageous, because it allows us to find the payment size for a loan with a single equation.

In this example, the present value of the loan (annuity) is $45,000. The loan will be paid back over 120 months (10 years), and the effective interest rate/month is 4.2%/12 = 0.35%. Thus, we can write

$$\$45,000 = Pa_{\overline{n}|i} = P\frac{1-v^n}{i} = P\left(\frac{1-\left(1/1.0035\right)^{120}}{0.0035}\right) = 97.84891(P)$$

Solving $\$45,000 = 97.84891(P)$ for P gives us $P = \$459.8927$.

In other words, the initial amount of the loan is the present value of all the future level-payments on the loan. This allows us to find that the monthly payment needed is $459.89 to pay off the loan in 120 months. In essence, this is what the PMT function in Excel or your financial calculator is doing.

Key idea

A fixed-rate, amortized loan can be viewed as an annuity with level payments and, so, the present value of a loan is the present value of the future payments of an annuity.

Thus, in general, we have the following relationship:

$$\text{Initial Loan Balance} = Pa_{\overline{n}|i}.$$

Drop payments

Up until now, we've ignored one minor practical issue with loans. Often times, due to rounding and not being able to make payments of fractions of pennies, the actual size of the final payment of the loan will be slightly different than the rest of the payments—this is called a "drop" payment.

Definition

A **drop payment** is the final payment on a loan and is typically of a slightly different size than the rest of the payments in order to make the balance on the loan exactly zero. It is standard practice to set the regular payments through the life of the loan slightly larger, so that the drop payment will be slightly lower than the rest.

Think about it

Earlier we found that the exact "payment size" on the $45,000 student loan should be $P = \$459.8927$. If you pay $459.89 monthly, do you think your final payment will need to be larger or smaller than $459.89 in order to pay off the loan?

Because we rounded the payment size to the nearest penny, which in this case was rounding down, we will end up with a final payment larger than $459.89. Thus, standard practice would instead round up to the nearest penny, in this case, making payments of $459.90 monthly—which would yield a final (drop) payment less than $459.90. Tables 7.2 and 7.3 illustrate this by showing the final payments in bold.

Table 7.2 Amortization table with monthly payments of 459.89 and larger drop payment

Payment number	Balance before payment ($)	Payment size ($)	Interest ($)	Principal ($)	Balance after payment ($)
. . .	. . .	. . .	. . .	. . .	. . .
116	2,275.89	459.89	7.97	451.92	1,823.97
117	1,823.97	459.89	6.38	453.51	1,370.46
118	1,370.46	459.89	4.80	455.09	915.37
119	915.37	459.89	3.20	456.69	458.68
120	458.68	**460.29**	1.61	458.68	0.00

Table 7.3 Amortization table with monthly payments of 459.90 and smaller drop payment

Payment number	Balance before payment ($)	Payment size ($)	Interest ($)	Principal ($)	Balance after payment ($)
. . .	. . .	. . .	. . .	. . .	. . .
116	2,274.48	459.90	7.96	451.94	1,822.54
117	1,822.54	459.90	6.38	453.52	1,369.02
118	1,369.02	459.90	4.79	455.11	913.91
119	913.91	459.90	3.20	456.70	457.21
120	457.21	**458.81**	1.60	457.21	0.00

To find the value of the drop payment using an amortization table, find the loan balance prior to the final payment. Find the interest accrued. The final payment size will simply be the loan balance plus interest.

PROSPECTIVE METHOD OF LOAN VALUATION

The idea that the present value of a loan is the present value of the future payments can also be used to find the outstanding loan balance at any future point in time. Let's say that you are curious to know, after 2 years of making your $459.90 payments, what your loan balance will be? You could, of course, set up the entire amortization schedule, or you could find the value directly by thinking about how many payments will be left at that time.

Think about it

Immediately after the 24th payment (2 years from now), how many payments will remain on the loan?

Since you will make 120 payments over the entire lifetime of the loan, immediately after the 24th payment, you will have 96 payments left to make—95 level payments of $459.90 and the smaller drop payment of $458.81. Thus, the loan balance (immediately after the 24th payment) will be the present value of the level payments plus the present value of the drop payment. To calculate this balance we have

$$\text{Loan balance in 2 years} = Pa_{\overline{n-24-1}|i} + Dv^{96} = 459.90a_{\overline{95}|0.0035} + 458.81v^{96}$$
$$= 459.90(80.7014) + \$328.07 = \$37,442.64.$$

Notice that n is the original number of payments (or 120), 24 is the number of payments that have already been made, and D is the size of the drop payment ($458.81). This balance of $37,442.64 should be the same amount that we would obtain if we completed the entire amortization schedule for the loan.

The general formula for a loan balance after k payments is

$$\text{Loan balance after } k \text{ payments} = Pa_{\overline{n-k-1}|i} + Dv^{n-k}$$

Key idea

The present value of the remaining payments on the loan is equal to the outstanding loan balance. This is called the **prospective method** of finding loan balances.

Amount of principal and interest in any future payment

Knowing the direct formula to find the outstanding loan balance at any future time allows us to find the amount of principal and amount of interest in any future payment. Let's see how much principal and how much interest will be in the 25th payment (of $459.90) which is made on the student loan.

After 24 payments, the loan balance is $37,442.64 as we showed above; thus, the interest accrued is simply $37,442.64(0.0035) = \$131.05$. And so, the amount of interest in the 25th payment is $131.05, leaving $459.90 − $131.05 = \$328.85$ of the payment left to be applied to principal.

This illustration shows that if we know the outstanding loan balance immediately before the payment is made, it is quite straightforward to find the interest and principal amounts in any payment.

Generalizing what we just did, we can see that

Amount of interest in the kth payment $=($Loan balance after $k-1$ payments$)i$

$$= \left(Pa_{\overline{n-k}|i} + Dv^{n-k+1} \right) i = P\left(\frac{1-v^{n-k}}{i} \right) i + iDv^{n-k+1}$$

$$= P\left(1-v^{n-k} \right) + iDv^{n-k+1}$$

Where we note that

$$\text{Loan balance after } k-1 \text{ payments} = Pa_{\overline{n-k}|i} + Dv^{n-k+1}$$

Table 7.4 gives a generic "row" of an amortization schedule for a loan with payment size P, drop payment D, effective interest rate i per period, and a total of n payments made over the term of the loan.

Table 7.4 Generic row of an amortization table[a]

PMT no.	Balance before payment made	PMT size	Interest in payment	Principal in payment	Balance after kth payment is made
k	$Pa_{\overline{n-k}|i}$ $+ Dv^{n-k+1}$	P	$\left(Pa_{\overline{n-k}|i} + Dv^{n-k+1} \right)i$ $= P\left(1-v^{n-k} \right)$ $+ iDv^{n-k+1}$	$P - \left(P\left(1-v^{n-k} \right) + iDv^{n-k+1} \right)$ $= Pv^{n-k} - iDv^{n-k+1}$	$Pa_{\overline{n-k-1}|i}$ $+ Dv^{n-k}$

[a]Applies to all payments except a final drop payment.

Two final points are worth noting:

1. The drop payment makes these formulas messy. If the drop payment isn't necessary, the formulas simplify down further by combining the P and D terms. This is rarely the case in real life.

2. We did not (yet) show you how to calculate the drop payment directly. We will show you this in the next section.

EXPLORATION 7.1. TAKING OUT A CAR LOAN

Let's say that you are considering taking out a 5-year loan on a used car. The loan would be for $15,000 and the interest rate would be fixed at 3.15% APR. In Chapter 2, Loans: Fundamentals of Borrowing and Lending, we determined that the monthly payment on this loan is $270.53.

1. Fill in Table 7.5, a portion of the amortization schedule for this loan.

Table 7.5 Amortization table for $15,000 car loan at 3.15% APR for 5 years

Month	Principal balance (day 1)	Interest accrued (during month)	Payment (31st of month)	New loan balance (31st of month)
1				
2				
3				
...	...	...		...

Remember that setting up the entire amortization schedule in Excel is rather time consuming. If you want to go faster and use the PMT function, you might be wondering "How is the PMT function figuring out the answer?"

One approach is to view your payments as an annuity.

2. Explain how your equally sized monthly payments are like an annuity and indicate the values for each of the following four variables listed below:

Number of payments:

Effective interest per period:

Payment per period:

Present value of the annuity (this is the initial loan amount):

Key idea

A fixed-rate, amortized loan can be viewed as an annuity with level payments and, so, the present value of a loan is the present value of the future payments of an annuity.

Thus, in general, we have the following relationship:

$$\text{Initial loan balance} = Pa_{\overline{n}|i}$$

3. Use the formula above to confirm that the payment size for this loan is $270.53.

Drop payments

Up until now, we've ignored one minor practical issue with loans. Often times, due to rounding and not being able to make payments of fractions of pennies, the actual size of the final payment of the loan will be slightly different than the rest of the payments—this is called a "drop" payment.

Definition

A **drop payment** is the final payment on a loan and is typically of a slightly different size than the rest of the payments in order to make the balance on the loan exactly zero. It is standard practice to set the regular payments through the life of the loan slightly larger, so that the drop payment will be slightly lower than the rest.

---

4. In the previous question, you probably rounded to the nearest penny. Write your answer again giving 5 or 6 values after the decimal point.

5. If you pay $270.53 monthly, do you think your final payment will need to be larger or smaller than $270.53 in order to pay off the loan? Why?

6. Table 7.6 shows all but the last line of the amortization table using a $270.53 monthly payment. Fill in the last row confirming that the final payment will need to be higher to pay off the loan completely. What is the final payment size?

Table 7.6 Amortization table with monthly payments of $270.53 and a larger drop payment

Payment number	Balance before payment ($)	Payment size ($)	Interest ($)	Principal ($)	Balance after payment ($)
. . .	. . .	. . .	. . .	. . .	. . .
56	1,342.15	270.53	3.52	267.01	1,075.14
57	1,075.14	270.53	2.82	267.71	807.44
58	807.44	270.53	2.12	268.41	539.03
59	539.03	270.53	1.41	269.12	269.91
60	269.91				

Because we rounded the payment size to the nearest penny, which in this case was rounding down, we will end up with a final payment larger than $270.53. Thus, it is standard practice to, instead, round up to the nearest penny, in this case, making payments of $270.54 monthly—which should yield a final (drop) payment less than $270.54.

7. Table 7.7 shows all but the last line of the amortization table using a $270.54 monthly payment. Fill in the last row confirming that the

Table 7.7 Amortization table with monthly payments of $270.54 and a smaller drop payment

Payment number	Balance before payment ($)	Payment size	Interest ($)	Principal ($)	Balance after payment ($)
. . .	. . .	. . .	. . .	. . .	. . .
56	1,341.56	270.54	3.52	267.02	1,074.54
57	1,074.54	270.54	2.82	267.72	806.82
58	806.82	270.54	2.12	268.42	538.40
59	538.40	270.54	1.41	269.13	269.27
60	269.27				

final payment will need to be lower to pay off the loan completely. What is the final payment size?

To find the value of the drop payment using an amortization table, find the loan balance prior to the final payment. Find the interest accrued. The final payment size will simply be the loan balance plus interest.

Prospective method of loan valuation

The idea that the present value of a loan is the present value of the future payments can also be used to find the outstanding loan balance at any future point in time.

For example, let's say we want to know how much we will owe on the car loan 1 year from now—after 12 payments (using a monthly payment size of $270.54).

8. Immediately after the 12th payment (1 year from now), how many payments will remain on the loan?

9. What is the present value of the remaining set of payments on the car loan? *Note: Make sure you account for the smaller drop payment size of $269.98.*

Key idea

The present value of the remaining payments on the loan is equal to the outstanding loan balance. This is called the **prospective method** of finding loan balances.

---

10. So, given this key idea, what will the balance on the loan be after 1 year?

The general formula to find the:

$$\text{Loan balance after } k \text{ payments} = P a_{\overline{n-k-1}|i} + D v^{n-k}$$

where n is the total number of payments, k is the number of payments that have occurred so far, P is the level payment, and D is the drop payment.

Amount of principal and interest in any future payment

Knowing a formula to compute the loan balance at any time actually means that we can fairly easily compute the amount of principal and/or interest in any future payment.

11. Use your previous answer to find the amount of interest accrued in the 13th payment.

12. What is the amount of interest paid in the 13th payment?

13. What is the amount of principal paid in the 13th payment?

This illustration shows that if we know the outstanding loan balance immediately before the payment is made, it is quite straightforward to find the interest and principal amounts in any payment.

Generalizing what we just did, we can see that

Amount of interest in the kth payment $=$ (Loan balance after $k-1$ payments)i

$$= \left(Pa_{\overline{n-k}|i} + Dv^{n-k+1} \right) i = P \left(\frac{1-v^{n-k}}{i} \right) i + iDv^{n-k+1} = P \left(1 - v^{n-k} \right) + iDv^{n-k+1}$$

where we note that

$$\text{Loan balance after } k-1 \text{ payments} = Pa_{\overline{n-k}|i} + Dv^{n-k+1}$$

Table 7.8 gives a generic "row" of an amortization schedule for a loan with payment size P, drop payment D, effective interest rate i per period, and a total of n payments made over the term of the loan.

Table 7.8 Generic row of an amortization table[a]

PMT no.	Balance before payment made	PMT size	Interest in payment	Principal in payment	Balance after kth payment is made
k	$Pa_{\overline{n-k}|i}$ $+ Dv^{n-k+1}$	P	$\left(Pa_{\overline{n-k}|i} + Dv^{n-k+1} \right) i$ $= P \left(1 - v^{n-k} \right)$ $+ iDv^{n-k+1}$	$P - \left(P(1 - v^{n-k}) + iDv^{n-k+1} \right)$ $= Pv^{n-k} - iDv^{n-k+1}$	$Pa_{\overline{n-k-1}|i}$ $+ Dv^{n-k}$

[a]Applies to all payments except a final drop payment.

Two final points are worth noting:

1. The drop payment makes these formulas messy. If the drop payment isn't necessary, the formulas simplify down further by combining the P and D terms. This is rarely the case in real life.

2. We did not (yet) show you how to calculate the drop payment directly. We will show you this in the next section.

SUMMARY

In this section, we saw that computing the payment size for a loan is a straightforward application of annuity formulas. Using the prospective method, which says that an outstanding loan balance is the present value of future payments, allows us to quickly and easily find a loan balance at any given point in time, as well as the amount of interest and principal in each payment.

Notation and equation summary

$$\text{Initial loan balance} = Pa_{\overline{n}|i}$$

Generic row of an amortization table[a]

PMT no.	Balance before payment made	PMT size	Interest in payment	Principal in payment	Balance after kth payment is made
k	$Pa_{\overline{n-k}|i}$ $+ Dv^{n-k+1}$	P	$\left(Pa_{\overline{n-k}|i}\right.$ $\left.+ Dv^{n-k+1}\right)i$ $= P\left(1 - v^{n-k}\right)$ $+ iDv^{n-k+1}$	$P - \left(P\left(1 - v^{n-k}\right) + iDv^{n-k+1}\right)$ $= Pv^{n-k} - iDv^{n-k+1}$	$Pa_{\overline{n-k-1}|i}$ $+ Dv^{n-k}$

[a]Applies to all payments except a final drop payment.

HOMEWORK QUESTIONS: SECTION 7.1

Conceptual questions

1. What are level payments?

2. What is a drop payment?

3. Suppose you are amortizing a loan and you round down to the nearest penny when you are calculating the level payments. How will that, most likely, affect the size of the last payment?

4. If you know your loan balance after a given number of payments, your monthly interest rate, and the amount of your payment, how do you calculate the amount of interest you will owe in your next payment? How do you calculate the amount of principal you will owe on your next payment?

5. Rewrite $a_{\overline{n}|i}$ in terms of just n and i.

6. In the formula, Loan balance after k payments $= Pa_{\overline{n-k-1}|i} + Dv^{n-k}$, what does $Pa_{\overline{n-k-1}|i}$ represent? What does Dv^{n-k} represent?

Practice questions

7. Suppose you take out a $100,000 loan at 4.5% APR for 20 years. What are your monthly payments (rounded up to the nearest penny)?

8. You take out a $50,000 loan at 3.75% APR for 10 years. What are your monthly payments (rounded up to the nearest penny)?

9. You are paying off a $15,000 six-year auto loan with a 6% APR. Your monthly payments are $248.60 with a drop payment of $248.02. How much will you owe on your loan right after your 36th payment?

10. Suppose you have a 30-year mortgage for $200,000, and at a 4.5% APR your monthly payments are $1,013.37. How much will you

pay in total over the 30-year period? How much of that will be interest? (Be sure to consider the drop payment)

11. You have a $240,000 mortgage for 30 years at 4.5% APR. Your monthly payments are $1,216.05 with a drop payment of $1,212.06. You want to find the loan balance right after the 180th payment using the formula

    Loan balance after k payments $= Pa_{\overline{n-k-1}|i} + Dv^{n-k}$.

    a. What is the value of $Pa_{\overline{n-k-1}|i}$ and what does it mean?

    b. Dv^{n-k} and what does it mean?

Application questions

12. You are paying off a $10,000 six-year auto loan with a 4.5% APR. Your monthly payments are $158.75 with a drop payment of $157.95.

    a. How much will you owe on your loan right after your 50th payment?

    b. On your 51st payment, how much will be paying interest and how much will be paying off the principal?

13. You are paying off a $250,000 thirty-year mortgage with a 3.75% APR.

    a. What are your monthly payments (rounded up to the nearest penny)?

    b. Your drop payment will be $1,157.11. How much will you owe on your loan right after your 200th payment?

    c. On your 201st payment, how much will be paying interest and how much will be paying off the principal?

14. Suppose you have a $100,000, twenty-year loan at 6% APR, with monthly payments of $716.44 and a final drop payment of $712.31.

    a. Find the amount you will owe right after your
        i. 50th payment.
        ii. 100th payment.
        iii. 150th payment.
        iv. 200th payment.

b. Based on your answers to part (a), is your balance on the loan decreasing linearly? If not, is it decreasing faster early in the life of the loan or later in the life of the loan?

c. Will the amount of interest in each payment be increasing, decreasing, or staying the same through the life of the loan? Explain.

d. Will the amount of principal in each payment be increasing, decreasing, or staying the same through the life of the loan? Explain.

e. Explain how your answer to part (d) relates to your answer to part (b).

15. You are in the process of paying off a \$200,000 mortgage. This mortgage is for 30 years at 4.5% APR.

a. What are the monthly payments on the mortgage rounded up to the nearest penny?

b. After making 120 payments, your bank has a better interest rate and you refinance the balance of your loan at 3.75% APR.

i. What is the balance of your first mortgage after 120 payments? This will become the initial principal of your new mortgage.

ii. What are the monthly payments on your new loan? (rounded up to the nearest penny.)

iii. Assuming all your payments are the same on this new loan (no drop payment), how much did you save over the life of the loan by refinancing?

16. Suppose a 20-year loan has monthly payments of \$578.75 and the interest rate is 3.875% APR. What is the initial principal of the loan?

17. Suppose a 6-year loan has monthly payments of \$135.24 and the initial principal is \$9,000. What is the interest rate?

Prove It! questions

18. Suppose you are paying off a 10-year, 6% APR loan by making \$100 payments each month (no drop payment). The loan balance after x payments would be $100a_{\overline{120-x}|0.005}$.

a. Show that the equation for the loan balance, y, after x payments is $y = 20,000 - \frac{20,000}{1.005^{120}} \times 1.005^x$.

b. What is the shape of the graph of the equation from part (a) as x goes from 0 to 120?

c. Based on the shape of the graph, does the loan balance decrease faster earlier in the life of the loan or later on? In turn, what does that tell you about the amount of interest in each payment as time goes on? Does it increase or decrease? Explain.

d. Using the equation from part (a), what is the balance of the loan after 120 payments?

e. Using the equation from part (a), what is the initial value of the loan?

SECTION 7.2. MORE ABOUT LOANS AS ANNUITIES

In the previous section, we saw how an amortized loan is really just a type of annuity. In that section, we viewed loan calculations through the lens of the present value of an annuity. In this section, we will view loans through the lens of the future value of an annuity, $s_{\overline{n}|i}$, using a method called the retrospective method.

Learning objectives

By the end of this section, you should be able to

- Use the retrospective method of loan valuation to find the outstanding loan balance at any point in time and the amount of principal/interest in any payment.
- Use the retrospective method to find the drop payment size.

EXAMPLE 7.2. PAYING BACK A STUDENT LOAN (REVISITED)

In the previous section, we looked at the amortization schedule for a $45,000 student loan over 10 years at 4.2% APR with level monthly payments.

Another way to directly calculate payment sizes and loan balances at any given point in time is to use the *retrospective method*. It is based on ideas similar to those that we saw earlier for sinking funds.

Think about it

Explain why a sinking fund approach can be used to pay back the student loan. Assume that the lender allows this kind of approach.

A sinking fund approach to pay back a loan lets interest accumulate on the loan balance (or pays down only the interest) and makes regular deposits to a separate account which earns interest with the goal of making a single lump sum payment at the end of the loan term.

While somewhat unrealistic, let's assume that you find a student loan company willing to let you pay back your student loan in a single lump sum at the end of 10 years. If you don't make any payments (not even interest) on the loan, what will the loan balance be after 10 years?

The loan value after 10 years simply $45,000(1.0035)^{120} = \$68,438.07$. Thus, the goal of your sinking fund will be to accumulate $68,438.07 after 10 years. So, how much should you deposit into your sinking fund account monthly? Let's assume that you can also earn 4.2% APR on your sinking fund account. Then, you want to solve the following equation:

$$\$68,438.07 = (P)s_{\overline{120}|0.0035} = (P)\left(\frac{(1+0.0035)^{120} - 1}{0.0035}\right) = \$148.8131P$$

where there are 120 months of equally sized payments of size P to the sinking fund, which earns 4.2% APR. Solving for P gives $459.8927. Notice that this is exactly what we found in Example 7.1 when using the prospective method!

Thus, the retrospective method for finding a loan payment says that

$$B(1+i)^n = Ps_{\overline{n}|i},$$

where B is the initial loan balance and P is the equal size payments. As we discussed in the previous section you should, in general, always round this value up to the nearest penny if you plan on a final drop payment that is slightly smaller than the rest of the level payments. In this case, with a drop payment, the monthly loan payment will be $459.90.

Definition

The **retrospective method** for finding payment sizes and loan balances views loans as a form of a sinking fund where the loan balance accumulates.

We note that this approach relies on an important relationship between $s_{\overline{n}|i}$ (the accumulated value of $1 paid for n periods) and $a_{\overline{n}|i}$ (the present value of $1 paid for n periods).

$$a_{\overline{n}|i}(1+i)^n = s_{\overline{n}|i}$$

which is seen rather easily by recognizing that

$$a_{\overline{n}|i}(1+i)^n = \left(\frac{1 - \left(1/(1+i)^n\right)}{i}\right)(1+i)^n = \left(\frac{(1+i)^n - 1}{i}\right) = s_{\overline{n}|i}$$

This is the intuitive idea behind the retrospective method.

Finding an outstanding loan balance using the retrospective method

The retrospective method also allows us to find the outstanding loan balance at any given time in a rather straightforward manner. In particular, this approach finds the difference in the value of the sinking fund and the value of the loan balance assuming nothing has been paid on it.

Key idea

The **retrospective method** uses the sinking fund approach to find an outstanding loan balance as the difference in the initial loan amount accumulated with no payments, and the value in the sinking fund.

Thus, the outstanding loan balance immediately after the kth payment is

$$\text{Outstanding loan balance after } k\text{th payment} = B(1+i)^k - Ps_{\overline{k}|i}$$

For your student loan, if you are curious how much you will owe on your loan in 2 years, we can apply the formula to see what the balance will be after your 24th monthly payment.

Outstanding loan balance after 24th payment

$$= \$45,000(1+0.0035)^{24} - 459.90 s_{\overline{24}|0.0035}$$

$$= \$45,000(1.0035)^{24} - 459.90 \left(\frac{1.0035^{24} - 1}{0.0035} \right)$$

$$= \$48,936.12 - \$11,493.48 = \$37,442.64$$

which is what we obtained using the prospective approach earlier.

Finding amount of interest and principal in a payment

The retrospective method can also be used to find the amount of interest and principal in a payment. Recall that the amount of interest in the kth payment is simply the effective interest rate (i) times the loan balance before the payment is made.

Thus,

Amount of interest in kth payment $= i \times$ Outstanding loan balance after $(k-1)^{st}$ payment

$$= i \left(B(1+i)^{k-1} - P s_{\overline{k-1}|i} \right)$$
$$= iB(1+i)^{k-1} - P\left((1+i)^{k-1} - 1 \right) = iB(1+i)^{k-1} - P(1+i)^{k-1} + P$$
$$= (1+i)^{k-1}(iB - P) + P$$

Table 7.9 shows a generic row of an amortization table using the retrospective method.

Table 7.9 Generic row of an amortization table[a]

Payment number	Balance before payment made	Payment size	Interest in payment	Principal in payment	Balance after kth payment is made
k	$B(1+i)^{k-1}$ $- P s_{\overline{k-1}|i}$	P	$(1+i)^{k-1}$ $(iB - P) + P$	$(1+i)^{k-1}(iB - P)$	$B(1+i)^{k} - P s_{\overline{k}|i}$

[a]Applies to all payments except a final drop payment.

Thus, the amount of interest in the 25th payment is found by finding the interest accumulated on the loan balance of \$37,442.64, which is

$0.0035(\$37,442.64) = \$131.05$. Using the formula from the table above also gives us this value directly:

$$(1+i)^{k-1}(iB-P) + P = (1+0.0035)^{24}(0.0035(45,000) - 459.90) + 459.90$$
$$= \$131.05$$

Computing the exact value of the drop payment

In the previous section, we mentioned that you can find the value of the drop payment by using an amortization table. Using the retrospective method allows us to compute the drop payment size, D, directly.

The retrospective method says that the loan balance immediately before the final (nth) payment is

$$\text{Loan balance before final payment} = B(1+i)^{n-1} - Ps_{\overline{n-1}|i}$$

For your student loan, this means that the loan balance is

Loan balance before final payment
$$= \$45,000(1+0.0035)^{119} - \$459.90s_{\overline{119}|0.0035}$$
$$= \$45,000(1.0035)^{119} - \$459.90\left(\frac{1.0035^{119} - 1}{0.0035}\right)$$
$$= \$68,19937 - \$67,72.16 =$$
$$= \$457.21$$

Thus, the drop payment will be $\$457.21(1.0035) = \$458.81$.

EXPLORATION 7.2. PAYING BACK A CAR LOAN (REVISITED)

In the previous exploration, we used the prospective method to find payment size, loan balances, and principal/interest amounts for the life of the loan. Now, we illustrate a slightly different.

Recall that you are considering taking a car loan for $15,000 over 5 years, at 3.15% APR which had payments of $270.53/month.

1. Explain how you could use a sinking fund to pay back the car loan (assume that the car loan company is fine with you doing this and that

you don't pay back anything, even accumulated interest on the loan until the payoff date in 5 years).

2. Let's assume you use the sinking-fund approach described in question 1, how much will the $15,000 accumulate to after 5 years? (Assuming you capitalize the interest.)

3. Let's assume that the sinking fund you make deposits into earns 3.15% APR, and you make equally sized payments, monthly, to the account. Use $s_{\overline{60}|0.002625}$ to find the size of the equally sized payments.

4. How does your answer compare to the payment size for a standard, amortized loan?

The retrospective method for finding a loan payment says that

$$B(1+i)^n = Ps_{\overline{n}|i},$$

where B is the initial loan balance and P is the equally sized payments. As we discussed in the previous section, you should, in general, always round the payment size (P) up to the nearest penny if you plan on a final drop payment that is slightly smaller than the rest of the level payments. In this case, with a drop payment, the monthly loan payment will be $270.54.

Definition
The **retrospective method** for finding payment sizes and loan balances views loans as a form of a sinking fund where the loan balance accumulates.

We note that this approach relies on an important relationship between $s_{\overline{n}|i}$ (the accumulated value of $1 paid for n periods) and $a_{\overline{n}|i}$ (the present value of $1 paid for n periods).

$$a_{\overline{n}|i}(1+i)^n = s_{\overline{n}|i}$$

which is seen rather easily by recognizing that

$$a_{\overline{n}|i}(1+i)^n = \left(\frac{1 - (1/(1+i)^n)}{i}\right)(1+i)^n = \left(\frac{(1+i)^n - 1}{i}\right) = s_{\overline{n}|i}$$

This is the intuitive idea behind the retrospective method.

Finding an outstanding loan balance using the retrospective method

The retrospective method also allows us to find the outstanding loan balance at any given time in a rather straightforward manner, by finding the difference in the value of the sinking fund and the loan balance as if nothing had been paid on it.

Key idea

The **retrospective method** uses the sinking fund approach to find an outstanding loan balance as the difference in the initial loan amount accumulated with no payments, and the value in the sinking fund.

Thus, the outstanding loan balance immediately after the kth payment is

$$\text{Outstanding loan balance after } k\text{th payment} = B(1+i)^k - Ps_{\overline{k}|i}.$$

5. Use the retrospective method to find the balance on the car loan after the 12th payment.

Finding amount of interest and principal in a payment

The retrospective method can also be used to find the amount of interest and principal in a payment. Recall that the amount of interest in the $(k+1)$th payment is simply the effective interest rate (i) times the loan balance before the payment is made.

6. How much interest is in the 13th payment?

See Example 7.2 or the summary of this section for a generic row of the amortization table which gives you equations for the interest/principal in any given loan payment for the retrospective method.

Computing the exact value of the drop payment

In the previous section, we mentioned that you can find the value of the drop payment by using an amortization table. Using the retrospective method allows us to compute the drop payment size, D, directly.

7. Use the retrospective method to find the loan balance immediately before the final payment assuming you are paying \$270.54/month.

8. Use the answer to the previous question to find the size of the drop payment, D.

SUMMARY

The retrospective method uses the sinking fund approach to find an outstanding loan balance as the difference in the initial loan amount accumulated with no payments, and the value in the sinking fund. The retrospective method can be used to quickly find loan payment size, outstanding loan balances, and the amount of interest and principal in any payment. Furthermore, and in contrast to the prospective method, the retrospective method can be used to find the drop payment size.

Notation and equation summary

The retrospective method for finding a loan payment says that

$$B(1+i)^n = Ps_{\overline{n}|i}$$

where B is the initial loan balance, and P is the equal size payments

$$a_{\overline{n}|i}(1+i)^n = s_{\overline{n}|i}$$

Generic row of amortization table using retrospective method[a]

Payment number	Balance before payment made	Payment size	Interest in payment	Principal in payment	Balance after kth payment is made
k	$B(1+i)^{k-1}$ $- Ps_{\overline{k-1}|i}$	P	$(1+i)^{k-1}$ $(iB - P) + P$	$(1+i)^{k-1}$ $(iB - P)$	$B(1+i)^k$ $- Ps_{\overline{k}|i}$

[a]Applies to all payments except the final (drop) payment.

HOMEWORK QUESTIONS: SECTION 7.2

Conceptual questions

1. In this section and the previous, we used the notation $a_{\overline{n}|i}$ and $s_{\overline{n}|i}$. What do each of these mean and how are they different?

2. We gave the formula $B(1+i)^n = Ps_{\overline{n}|i}$ in this section, where B was the initial loan balance and P was the amount of a level payment. What does each side represent, and why are they equal?

3. Using the retrospective method to find the loan balance at some time during the life of the loan, you are finding the difference in what two quantities?

4. To find the amount of interest in the 25th payment of a loan, you just need to multiply what two quantities? Knowing the amount of interest in the 25th payment, how do you determine the amount of principal in the payment?

5. To determine the amount of the drop payment, you need to first determine the loan balance after your next-to-last payment. Then, what do you do with that balance and why?

Practice questions

6. Suppose you take out a $100,000 loan at 4.5% APR for 20 years and your monthly payment is $632.65. Use the retrospective method to determine your outstanding loan balance after 120 payments. Do you have more or less than half your loan paid off at that point?

7. You take out a $50,000 loan at 3.75% APR for 10 years and your monthly payment is $500.31. Use the retrospective method to determine your outstanding loan balance after 100 payments?

8. If the loan balance on a 30-year mortgage at 4% APR is $132,722 after the 120th payment, how much interest is in the 121st payment?

9. If the payment on the loan described in the previous question is $634.25, what is the principal amount on the 121st payment?

10. The loan balance on a mortgage right after the next-to-final payment is $787.90 and the interest rate is 4.5% APR, what is the drop payment on the loan?

Application questions

11. You are paying off a $15,000 six-year auto loan with 4.5% APR.
    a. How much are your payments, rounded up to the nearest penny?
    b. What is the amount of your last payment?
    c. On your 51st payment, how much will be paying interest and how much will be paying off the principal?

12. You are paying off a $250,000 thirty-year mortgage with 3.875% APR.
    a. How much are your payments, rounded up to the nearest penny?
    b. What is the amount of your last payment?
    c. On your 100th payment, how much will you be paying interest and how much will you be paying off the principal?

13. You are planning to borrow $220,000, and your bank is offering a 4% APR rate on their loans. You are trying to decide whether to make the length of the loan 20 years or 30 years.
    a. How much will the monthly payments be for each term length (rounded up to the nearest penny)?
    b. How much with the drop payment be on each term length?
    c. How much total interest will be paid on each term length?

14. A 10-year loan with an initial balance of $20,000 and a monthly payment of $204.88 has an outstanding loan balance of $11,056.33 after 5 years (60 monthly payments). What was the loan rate?

15. Allan and Beth each take out $250,000 mortgages for 30 years and each has an effective annual rate of 4.5%.
    a. Allan makes monthly payments
        i. What is Allan's effective monthly interest rate?

      ii. How much are Allan's monthly payments? (round up to the nearest penny.)

      iii. What is the total amount of interest that Allan will pay on his loan? (You don't need to compute any drop payment. Assume all payments are exactly the same.)

  b. Beth makes payments twice a month (semimonthly), once at the beginning and once half way through the month.

      i. What is Beth's effective semimonthly interest rate?

      ii. How much are Beth's semimonthly payments? (round to up to the nearest penny.)

      iii. What is the total amount of interest that Beth will pay on her loan? (you don't need to compute any drop payment. Assume all payments are exactly the same.)

  c. Who pays less interest over the life of their loan, Allan or Beth? Explain why it's lower.

16. You have a 20-year, $200,000 loan at 4% APR.

  a. How much are your monthly payments, rounded up to the nearest penny?

  b. What is the amount of your last payment?

  c. What is the total amount you will have paid over the life of the loan? How much of that total is paying interest?

  d. What is your loan balance after 10 years (i.e., right after 120 payments)?

  e. Suppose starting with your 121st payment you add $200 to each of your monthly payments.

      i. How many months will it take you to pay off the loan now?

      ii. How much will your last payment be?

      iii. How much did adding $200 more a month save you in interest charges?

END OF CHAPTER SUMMARY

    In this chapter, we explored two different ways to accomplish to further look at loan amortization schedules. Using the prospective method, which says that an outstanding loan balance is the present value of future payments, allows us to quickly and easily find a loan balance at any given point in time, as well as the amount of interest and principal in each payment. In contrast, the retrospective method uses the sinking fund approach to find an outstanding loan balance as the difference in the initial loan amount accumulated with no payments, and the value in the sinking fund. Furthermore, and in contrast to the prospective method, the retrospective method can be used to find the drop payment size.

END OF CHAPTER EXERCISES

(SOA EXAM FM SAMPLE QUESTIONS May 2000, Question 10)

1. A bank customer borrows X at an annual effective rate of 12.5% and makes level payments at the end of each year for n years.
    i. The interest portion of the final payment is 153.86.
    ii. The total principal repaid as of time $(n - 1)$ is 6009.12.
    iii. The principal repaid in the first payment is Y.
    Calculate Y.
    A. 470
    B. 480
    C. 490
    D. 500
    E. 510

(SOA EXAM FM SAMPLE QUESTIONS May 2000, Question 24)

2. A small business takes out a loan of 12,000 at a nominal rate of 12%, compounded quarterly, to help finance its start–up costs. Payments of 750 are made at the end of every 6 months for as long as is necessary to pay back the loan.

    Three months before the 9th payment is due, the company refinances the loan at a nominal rate of 9%, compounded monthly. Under the refinanced loan, payments of R are to be made monthly, with the first monthly payment to be made at the same time that the 9th payment under the old loan was to be made. A total of 30 monthly payments will completely pay off the loan.

Determine R.

A. 448

B. 452

C. 456

D. 461

E. 465

(SOA EXAM FM SAMPLE QUESTIONS May 2001, Question 13)

3. Ron has a loan with a present value of $a_{\overline{n}|}$. The sum of the interest paid in period t plus the principal repaid in period in period $t + 1$ is X.

Calculate X.

A. $1 + \frac{v^{n-t}}{i}$

B. $1 + \frac{v^{n-t}}{d}$

C. $1 + v^{n-t}i$

D. $1 + v^{n-t}d$

E. $1 + v^{n-t}$

(SOA EXAM FM SAMPLE QUESTIONS May 2001, Question 37)

4. Seth borrows X for four years at an annual effective interest rate of 8%, to be repaid with equal payments at the end of each year. The outstanding loan balance at the end of the second year is 1,076.82 and at the end of the third year is 559.12.

Calculate the principal repaid in the first payment.

A. 444

B. 454

C. 464

D. 474

E. 484

(SOA EXAM FM SAMPLE QUESTIONS May 2005, Question 25)

5. A bank customer takes out a loan of 500 with a 16% nominal interest rate convertible quarterly. The customer makes payments of 20 at the end of each quarter.

Calculate the amount of principal in the fourth payment.
A. 0.0
B. 0.9
C. 2.7
D. 5.2
E. There is not enough information to calculate the amount of principal.

(SOA EXAM FM SAMPLE QUESTIONS November 2000, Question 12)

6. Kevin takes out a 10-year loan of L, which he repays by the amortization method at an annual effective interest rate of i. Kevin makes payments of 1,000 at the end of each year.

The total amount of interest repaid during the life of the loan is also equal to L.
Calculate the amount of interest repaid during the first year of the loan.
A. 725
B. 750
C. 755
D. 760
E. 765

(SOA EXAM FM SAMPLE QUESTIONS November 2000, Question 34)

7. An investor took out a loan of 150,000 at 8% compounded quarterly, to be repaid over 10 years with quarterly payments of 5,483.36 at the end of each quarter. After 12 payments, the interest rate dropped to

6% compounded quarterly. The new quarterly payment dropped to 5,134.62.

After 20 payments in total, the interest rate on the loan increased to 7% compounded quarterly. The investor decided to make an additional payment of X at the time of his 20th payment. After the additional payment was made, the new quarterly payment was calculated to be 4,265.73, payable for five more years.
Determine X.
A. 11,047
B. 13,369
C. 16,691
D. 20,152
E. 23,614

(SOA EXAM FM SAMPLE QUESTIONS November 2005, Question 18)

8. A loan is repaid with level annual payments based on an annual effective interest rate of 7%. The 8th payment consists of 789 of interest and 211 of principal. Calculate the amount of interest paid in the 18th payment.
   A. 415
   B. 444
   C. 556
   D. 585
   E. 612

(SOA EXAM FM SAMPLE QUESTIONS Interest Theory, Question 63)

9. Tanner takes out a loan today and repays the loan with eight level annual payments, with the first payment one year from today. The payments are calculated based on an annual effective interest rate of 4.75%. The principal portion of the fifth payment is 699.68.

   Calculate the total amount of interest paid on this loan.
   A. 1,239
   B. 1,647
   C. 1,820

D. 2,319

E. 2,924

(SOA EXAM FM SAMPLE QUESTIONS Interest Theory, Question 64)

10. Turner buys a new car and finances it with a loan of 22,000. He will make n monthly payments of 450.30 starting in one month. He will make one larger payment in $n + 1$ months to pay off the loan. Payments are calculated using an annual nominal interest rate of 8.4%, convertible monthly. Immediately after the 18th payment he refinances the loan to pay off the remaining balance with 24 monthly payments starting one month later. This refinanced loan uses an annual nominal interest rate of 4.8%, convertible monthly.

   Calculate the amount of the new monthly payment.
   A. 668
   B. 693
   C. 702
   D. 715
   E. 742

(SOA EXAM FM SAMPLE QUESTIONS Interest Theory, Question 75)

11. A borrower takes out a 15-year loan for 400,000, with level end-of-month payments, at an annual nominal interest rate of 9% convertible monthly.

   Immediately after the 36th payment, the borrower decides to refinance the loan at an annual nominal interest rate of j, convertible monthly. The remaining term of the loan is kept at twelve years, and level payments continue to be made at the end of the month. However, each payment is now 409.88 lower than each payment from the original loan.
   Calculate j.
   A. 4.72%
   B. 5.75%
   C. 6.35 %
   D. 6.90%
   E. 9.14%

(SOA EXAM FM SAMPLE QUESTIONS Interest Theory, Question 88)

12. A borrower takes out a 15-year loan for 65,000, with level end-of-month payments. The annual nominal interest rate of the loan is 8%, convertible monthly.

Immediately after the 12th payment is made, the remaining loan balance is re-amortized. The maturity date of the loan remains unchanged, but the annual nominal interest rate of the loan is changed to 6%, convertible monthly.
Calculate the new end-of-month payment.
A. 528
B. 534
C. 540
D. 546
E. 552

(SOA EXAM FM SAMPLE QUESTIONS Interest Theory, Question 106)

13. A company takes out a loan of 15,000,000 at an annual effective discount rate of 5.5%. You are given:
    i. The loan is to be repaid with n annual payments of 1,200,000 plus a drop payment one year after the nth payment.
    ii. The first payment is due three years after the loan is taken out.
    Calculate the amount of the drop payment.
    A. 79,100
    B. 176,000
    C. 321,300
    D. 959,500
    E. 1,180,300

(SOA EXAM FM SAMPLE QUESTIONS Interest Theory, Question 107)

14. Tim takes out an n-year loan with equal annual payments at the end of each year. The interest portion of the payment at time $(n - 1)$ is equal to 0.5250 of the interest portion of the payment at time $(n - 3)$

and is equal to 0.1427 of the interest portion of the first payment. Calculate n.

A. 18
B. 20
C. 22
D. 24
E. 26

(SOA EXAM FM SAMPLE QUESTIONS Interest Theory, Question 109)

15. On January 1, 2003 Mike took out a 30-year mortgage loan in the amount of 200,000 at an annual nominal interest rate of 6% compounded monthly. The loan was to be repaid by level end-of-month payments with the first payment on January 31, 2003.

    Mike repaid an extra 10,000 in addition to the regular monthly payment on each December 31 in the years 2003 through 2007.
    Determine the date on which Mike will make his last payment (which is a drop payment).
    A. July 31, 2013
    B. November 30, 2020
    C. December 31, 2020
    D. December 31, 2021
    E. January 31, 2022

    (SOA EXAM FM SAMPLE QUESTIONS Interest Theory, Question 110)

16. A 5-year loan of 500,000 with an annual effective discount rate of 8% is to be repaid by level end-of-year payments.

    If the first four payments had been rounded up to the next multiple of 1,000, the final payment would be X.
    Calculate X.
    A. 103,500
    B. 111,700
    C. 115,200
    D. 125,200
    E. 127,500

(SOA EXAM FM SAMPLE QUESTIONS Interest Theory, Question 112)

17. A loan of X is repaid with level annual payments at the end of each year for 10 years.

You are given:
  i. The interest paid in the first year is 3,600; and
  ii. The principal repaid in the 6th year is 4,871.
  Calculate X.
  A. 44,000
  B. 45,250
  C. 46,500
  D. 48,000
  E. 50,000

CHAPTER EIGHT

Annuities Revisited

Abstract

Before this chapter, we'd looked only at a single type of annuity—an annuity with level (equal-sized) payments at the end of the period. In this chapter, we will explore both geometric and arithmetically changing payment sizes and payments at the end of the month. We will focus on the relationships between different types of annuities in order to minimize the number of different equations that are necessary to solve annuity problems.

Keywords: Geometric annuity; arithmetic annuity

SECTION 8.1 GEOMETRICALLY INCREASING AND DECREASING ANNUITIES

One of the most practical considerations with regards to annuities is to adjust the payment size for inflation. Inflation is the continuing decrease in the purchasing power of money. So, if an annuity is being used as income for someone (e.g., in retirement), it is important to consider the fact that an annuity with level payments (same-sized payments over time) will lose its purchasing power over time. To account for this, payments can increase proportionally (e.g., 2% increase/year). In this section, we'll explore the mathematics behind these kinds of annuities.

Learning objectives

By the end of this section, you should be able to:
- Compute present value and initial payment size for geometrically increasing or decreasing annuities and perpetuities.
- State when an increasing perpetuity is possible and when it is not as a function of the relationship between the interest rate and the growth rate of the payments.

A Spiral Approach to Financial Mathematics.
DOI: https://doi.org/10.1016/B978-0-12-801580-3.00008-3
© 2018 Elsevier Inc.
All rights reserved.

EXAMPLE 8.1 BUYING A RETIREMENT ANNUITY ALLOWING FOR INFLATION

You are doing some retirement planning and are evaluating how different retirement savings models will impact your retirement income.

Let's assume that you project you will have $1 million in your retirement savings at age 65 when you plan to retire. If you are able to buy a 30-year, fixed-rate annuity paying 2.4% APR with payments occurring at the end of each month, how much will you receive each month?

To solve this, recall the commonly used formula for the present value of an annuity:

$$\text{Present value} = \text{Payment} \times a_{\overline{n}|i}.$$

Thus,

$$a_{\overline{n}|i} = \frac{1 - v^n}{i} = \frac{1 - \left((1/1.002)\right)^{360}}{0.002} = 256.4488$$

And so, the payment size you will receive is

$$\frac{\$1,000,000}{256.4488} = \$3,899.41.$$

You will receive this same-sized payment at the end of every month for the next 30 years. One downside to this plan is that if you live past age 95, you won't have an income! In practice, you can buy variable-term annuities (e.g., a whole life annuity) which will pay out a monthly payment until you die—but how to value those is beyond the scope of this text.

Think about it

What is a downside to having this payment stay the same size ($3,899.41/month) for 30 years?

While it's possible that your health costs may change over time (e.g., increasing as you get older), you can expect even basic living expenses (e.g., taxes, mortgage/rent, food, utilities, etc.) to increase over the next 30 years due to *inflation*.

Definition

Inflation is the increase in prices and decrease in the purchasing power of money over time.

Historically, the inflation rate has often varied between 1% and 3% in the United States each year, though at times it has been higher and at times lower. In the simplest case, if the inflation rate is 2%, this means that if it costs $1 to buy a loaf of bread this year, it will cost 2% more, or $1.02, next year. Thus, the inflation rate can be thought of as an effective rate, but can also be reported and converted to a nominal rate using standard formulas we've used throughout the course.

Inflation-adjusted annuity

Just like compound interest, inflation can add up! How much purchasing power will your money lose over a 30-year period if the inflation rate is an effective 2% per year? Since $1.02^{30} = 1.811$, this means that it will cost $1.81 in 30 years to buy something that costs $1 now. Thinking of this from the other perspective (current value), you could say that since $1/$1.81 = 0.55, this means that something you pay $0.55, for now, will cost $1.00 in 30 years. This means that a 2% inflation rate will nearly halve your purchasing power over a 30-year period!

Applied to your annuity, the $3,899.41 monthly payment will only be able to buy the equivalent of $3,899.41/1.81 = $2,154.37 worth of goods in today's dollars, in 30 years, after accounting for inflation.

Wouldn't it be nice if your monthly payment increased to keep pace with inflation so that you do not need to change your lifestyle dramatically over the 30-year period of the annuity?

Think about it

By how much should your monthly payment increase each month to "keep pace" with an annual inflation rate of 2% effective per year?

A 2% annual inflation rate is equivalent to a $(1.02)^{1/12} - 1 = 0.001652$ or 0.1652% effective monthly increase. Obviously, if the monthly payment is increasing, this will have an effect on the initial payment size if we are still projecting that the initial (present value) of the annuity is $1,000,000.

Think about it

If the present value of the annuity is $1,000,000 and your monthly payments increase by 0.1652% monthly, will your first payment be less than, more than, or equal to $3,899.41 (our equally sized payments) if the annuity is still "earning" 2.4% APR?

The initial monthly payment will have to be less than $3,899.41. Intuitively, if the payment size grows over time, the "average" payment size will still need to be approximately $3,899.41, and so the early payments will have to be lower to make up for the fact that the payments are growing over time.

Equations for inflation-adjusted annuities

Let's now see how to mathematically calculate payment sizes for an inflation-adjusted annuity.

Recall that $a_{\overline{n}|i}$ is the present value of $1 paid at the end of each period for n periods:

$$a_{\overline{n}|i} = \text{Present value of \$1 paid } n \text{ times} = v + v^2 + v^3 + v^4 + \cdots + v^n = \frac{1 - v^n}{i}$$

Let's now modify this formula so that the first payment is $1 and the size of the payment increase by $k\%$ (e.g., the inflation rate) each period

Present value of $1 paid in one period and $k\%$ increase for n periods

$$= v + (1 + k)v^2 + (1+k)^2 v^3 + (1+k)^3 v^4 + \cdots + (1+k)^{n-1} v^n$$

$$= \frac{1 - \left(\left(1 + k/1 + i\right) \right)^n}{i - k}$$

$$= \frac{1 - (v(1+k))^n}{i - k}$$

Going from the first line (the summation) to the second line (the closed form) in the above equation makes use of rules for finite geometric series that you might have seen in calculus. We also make use of the relationship between v and i. We will guide you through the details of this in the homework exercises.

Let's apply this formula to the retirement plan you are evaluating. If you have $1,000,000 today, the annuity earns 2.4% APR, and payments grow at 2% effective annually, how big will your first payment be? How about your last payment?

$$\$1,000,000 = P\frac{1-(v(1+k))^n}{i-k}$$

$$= P\frac{1-((1/1.002)(1+0.001651581))^{360}}{0.002-0.001651581}$$

$$= P\frac{1-0.8823185}{0.000348}$$

$$= \$337.75875989P$$

Solving $\$1,000,000 = \$337.7588P$ for P we get $P = \$2,960.69$. In other words, the payment size that the annuity will start at is $\$2,960.69/$ month and then will grow by 0.1652% monthly for 30 years to account for inflation. The size of the final payment (360 months from now) is $\$2,960.69(1.001652)^{360} = \$5,363.69$.

What about an increasing perpetuity?

Remember that payments from perpetuities continue indefinitely.

Think about it

Do you think it's possible to have an increasing perpetuity? If so, will there be a limit on how fast the perpetuity can grow?

Intuitively, it may seem hard to believe at first, but it is possible to have a perpetuity that grows over time. However, there is a limit on how fast the perpetuity payments can grow. If you think of a perpetuity as a way to "live off the interest," then as long as you are taking less money from the perpetuity than the amount of interest that has accumulated, you will be okay.

Let's see how this works in practice. To start, let's calculate how big a level payment you can take if you buy a monthly perpetuity paying 2.4% annually with your $\$1,000,000$ savings when you retire. Recall the following relationship for a perpetuity:

$$\$1,000,000 = Pa_\infty = P/i = P/0.002$$

Thus, the level payment you can take on a perpetuity is $\$2,000$. Which means you can take $\$2,000/$month until you die and still have a $\$1,000,000$ lump sum inheritance to leave for your heirs.

Think about it

If you instead by an inflation-adjusted perpetuity, will your monthly payment start at less than or more than $2,000/month?

If you want to adjust for inflation, then you will have to start with a payment size less than $2,000 to ensure that your monthly payments are not lowering the lump sum amount of $1,000,000.

More formally, this means:

$$\text{Initial Balance} = Pv + P(1+k)v^2 + P(1+k)^2v^3 + \cdots = \frac{P}{i-k}$$

This time we use rules about infinite geometric series as well as the relationship between v and i to convert our infinite sum to the closed form above.

In this case, with an initial balance of $1,000,000, you can solve

$$\$1,000,000 = \frac{P}{0.002 - 0.001651581}$$

$$\$1,000,000(0.002 - 0.001651581) = P$$

for P to get a payment of size $P = \$348.42$. But why does this make sense? Put simply, your payment is the difference between the 2.4% (or 0.2% per month) you want to take out and the 2% inflation rate (or an effective rate of 0.1651581% per month). A simplified version of this (ignoring that one rate is nominal and one is effective) is that because 2.4% − 2% = 0.4%, you would get a payment of 0.4% of the $1,000,000 per year or $4,000, which is $333.33 per month. That's pretty small! But, remember, this payment stream will continue indefinitely and is growing indefinitely, so in this case, you must pay a pretty hefty "penalty" in terms of payment size if you choose to go this route.

A few concluding remarks:

1. The general term for these types of annuities/perpetuities is *geometrically increasing*.

Definition

A **geometrically increasing (or decreasing) annuity** (or perpetuity) has the payment grow (decline) by a percentage each period.

2. The value of k can be positive or negative. If it is negative, then it is a geometrically *decreasing* annuity, where k is the percentage decrease per period. When $i = k$, the formulas shown above do not work, since this involves dividing by 0, but valuations can still be made. See homework exercise 16.

3. Perpetuities can also be increasing or decreasing over time. However, you might not be surprised to know that it's tough to have an increasing perpetuity that grows faster than the interest rate!

4. There is a formula for the accumulated value of a geometrically increasing annuity. Here it is:

Future value of geometrically increasing annuity

$$= P\left(\frac{(1+i)^n - (1+k)^n}{i-k}\right)$$

where P is the initial payment size, payments are growing by k each period and the account is governed by an effective rate of i. This formula is a straightforward application of the fact that the future value of an annuity can be obtained by multiplying the present value of an annuity by $(1+i)^n$. Using this formula is something that you can practice in the exercises. Note: It may be not necessary to memorize this formula since you can simply use the $(1+i)^n$ *conversion* to move from present value to future value in a straightforward manner.

EXPLORATION 8.1 LIFE INSURANCE PAYOUT AS AN ANNUITY ALLOWING FOR INFLATION

Back in Chapter 3, Annuities: Fundamentals of Regular Payments, we explored a life insurance analysis. Let's revisit that situation now and evaluate how to keep up with "cost of living" increases.

To plan for his family's future in the event he passes away, John considers buying life insurance but doesn't know how much he needs. John goes through the following thought process:

a. He would like to buy enough insurance so that his wife and children can replace his income (currently $60,000 p/year) for 20 years after his death.

b. He figures by that time (20 years after his death) his children will have grown up and his wife will have had the opportunity to seek a higher paying job than she currently has to make up for the lost income and/or adjust her lifestyle accordingly.

c. He figures his wife/children will invest the lump sum insurance pay-out at 5% effective annual interest and make annual withdrawals of the same amount for 20 years, starting 1 year after the insurance money is paid.

1. Knowing what you know already about annuities, how much life insurance should John buy to meet the criteria outlined above?

2. Describe some downsides of having the annual payout of $60,000 stay the same for 20 years?

The expenses John's family has each year are very likely to increase (e.g., taxes, mortgage/rent, food, utilities, etc.) due to inflation.

Definition

Inflation is the increase in prices and decrease in the purchasing power of money over time.

Historically, the inflation rate has often varied between 1% and 3% in the United States, though at times it has been higher and at times lower. In the simplest case, if the inflation rate is 2% and if it costs $1 to buy a loaf of bread this year, it will cost $1.02 next year. Thus, the inflation rate can be thought of as an effective rate, but can also be reported and converted to a nominal rate using standard formulas we've used throughout the course.

3. If inflation is 2% effective per year, how much *purchasing power* will the $60,000 annual payout have in 20 years, in today's dollars? *Hint: Think of this like any other compound interest problem—what is the present value of $60,000, 20 years from now.*

Inflation-adjusted annuity

You should have seen, from your answer to the previous question, that the purchasing power 20 years from now is quite a bit less than $60,000.

Just like compound interest, inflation can add up. Now one practical option that John can consider is that his family could adjust their living expenses down or adjust their income up over time to make up for inflation. But, wouldn't it be nice if the size of the annual payments increased over time to make up for inflation? That is, the payments grew by 2% annually?

4. If the 20 annual payments from the annuity grow by 2% effective each year, will the starting payment size be more or less than $60,000? Assume that John still buys approximately $750,000 of insurance and the lump sum is invested at 5% effective annually.

Definition
A **geometrically increasing (or decreasing) annuity** (or perpetuity) has the payment grow (decline) by a percentage each period.

Equations for inflation-adjusted annuities

Let's see how we can compute present values associated with annuity payment sizes growing at 2% per year.

5. What if the initial payment from the annuity was $50,000? How big would the next two payments be?

6. Write an equation for the present value of the first three payments from the annuity that starts with a payment of size $50,000 and then payments grow at 2% per year. Don't solve the equation but, instead, write the equation in terms of the discount factor, v.

7. Now, modify the equation you wrote in the previous question using k to represent the growth rate of the annual payments. *Hint: You will only need the number $50,000 and the variables k and v.*

These last couple of questions should give you a sense of how we can write a general formula for the present value of an increasing annuity.

Present value of $1 paid in one period and k% increase for n periods
$$= v + (1+k)v^2 + (1+k)^2 v^3 + (1+k)^3 v^4 + \cdots + (1+k)^{n-1} v^n$$
$$= \frac{1 - \left((1+k/1+i)\right)^n}{i - k} = \frac{1 - (v(1+k))^n}{i - k}$$

Going from the first line (the summation) to the second line (the closed form) in the above equation makes use of rules for finite geometric series that you might have seen in calculus. We also make use of the relationship between v and i. We will guide you through the details of this in a homework exercise.

8. Find the initial payment size if John buys $750,000 of life insurance and wants the annual payments to grow at 2% annually, assuming the $750,000 is invested at 5% effective annually.

9. How much insurance will John have to buy if he wants the first payment to be $60,000 and still have the payments grow at 2% annually?

What about an increasing perpetuity?

What if John prefers to consider buying life insurance so that it could remain a lifelong source of income for his family?

Remember that payments from perpetuities continue indefinitely.

10. Do you think it's possible to have an increasing perpetuity? If so, will there be a limit on how fast the perpetuity can grow?

Intuitively, it may seem hard to believe at first, but it is possible to have a perpetuity that grows over time. However, there is a limit on how fast the perpetuity payments can grow. If you think of a perpetuity as a way to "live off the interest" then, practically, as long as you are taking less money from the perpetuity than the amount of interest that has accumulated you won't ever run out and so can continue forever.

11. If the perpetuity was not increasing, how much insurance would John need if the goal was a payment to his family of $60,000 annually?

12. What is the practical issue with not having the payment size increase over time?

The formula for an increasing perpetuity is essentially the same as for an increasing annuity, except the series never ends:

$$\text{Initial Balance} = Pv + P(1+k)v^2 + P(1+k)^2v^3 + \cdots = \frac{P}{i-k}$$

In the equation above, we use rules about infinite geometric series to find the initial balance in the closed form, $P/(i-k)$ where P is the initial payment size, i is the effective interest rate per period, and k is the inflation rate per period.

13. What will be the size of the initial payment if John buys $1.2 million of life insurance and wants a 2% per year growth in payment size?

14. How does your answer to the previous question compare to the $60,000 initial perpetuity payment size when the payment size does not increase? Why does this make sense?

15. How much insurance will John need to buy if he wants the initial payment size to be $60,000 and to grow at 2% annually?

See the end of Example 8.1 for a few concluding remarks about geometrically increasing and decreasing annuities.

> ## SUMMARY

In this section, we've seen how annuities do not need to keep the same-sized payments over time. In fact, to keep up with inflation, it is quite practical to have payments from an annuity increase over time. Decreasing annuities and increasing or decreasing perpetuities are also possible.

Notation and equation summary

Present value of $1 paid in one period and $k\%$ increase for n periods $= \dfrac{1-(v(1+k))^n}{i-k}$

Present value of increasing perpetuity $= Pv + P(1+k)v^2 + P(1+k)^2v^3 + \cdots = \dfrac{P}{i-k}$

HOMEWORK QUESTIONS: SECTION 8.1

Conceptual questions

1. How do the payouts of an inflation-adjusted annuity differ from a regular annuity?

2. Is it possible to have an annuity set up so it pays in perpetuity and it is also inflation-adjusted (at least for some fixed level of inflation)?

3. Suppose you are setting up a 20-year annuity with level payouts. You then decide to make it an annuity that is adjusted for inflation, which you predict will be 1.5% per year. Will your initial payout be higher or lower in the inflation-adjusted annuity than the one with level payouts?

4. Refer to the previous question. Will your final payout be higher or lower in the inflation-adjusted annuity than the one with level payouts?

5. Suppose you want to set up an inflation-adjusted perpetuity, but the payout percentage matches the inflation rate. (e.g., You want payments of 3% of the balance each year and the inflation rate is also 3%.) This can't be done. Explain why not.

Practice questions

6. How much will you need to put in an annuity if you want it to pay out $1,000 at the end of the first month and then have the payouts grow by 1% effective per year for 20 years? We will assume the annuity earns 4.5% APR.

7. How much will you need to put in an annuity if you want it to pay out $2,500 at the end of the first month and then have the payouts grow by 1.5% effective per year for 30 years? We will assume the annuity earns 4% APR.

8. Suppose $500,000 is put into an annuity that will pay out for 20 years. The payments will grow by 2% effective each year and the annuity earns 4.75% APR. What is the amount of the first payout?

9. In the annuity in the previous question, what is the amount of the final payout?

10. You want to set up a perpetuity that will pay out $500 at the end of the first month and then have the payouts grow by 2% effective per year. Assuming the annuity earns 4.5% APR forever, what is the amount needed for the initial balance?

11. You want to put $2,000,000 into a perpetuity that has payouts grow by 1.5% effective per year. Assuming the annuity earns 4% APR forever, what is the amount of the initial payout?

12. In the perpetuity from the previous question, what is the amount of the 100th payout? 1,000th payout?

Application questions

13. Suppose an annuity earns 5% APR and will pay out monthly for 20 years such that the payouts grow by 1.5% effective per year.
    a. How much will you need to put in an annuity if you want it to pay out $1,000 at the end of the first month?
    b. How much will you need to put in an annuity if you want it to pay out $2,000 at the end of the first month?
    c. How much will you need to put in an annuity if you want it to pay out $3,000 at the end of the first month?
    d. Is there a linear relationship between how much the first payout is and the initial balance in the annuity?

14. Suppose a perpetuity earns 5% APR and will pay out monthly such that the payouts grow by 1.5% effective per year.
    a. How much will you need to put in the perpetuity if you want it to pay out $1,000 at the end of the first month?
    b. How much will you need to put in the perpetuity if you want it to pay out $2,000 at the end of the first month?
    c. How much will you need to put in the perpetuity if you want it to pay out $3,000 at the end of the first month?
    d. Is there a linear relationship between how much the first payout is and the initial balance in the perpetuity?

15. We saw in this section that the series gives the initial balance of a perpetuity:

$$Pv + P(1 + k)v^2 + P(1+k)^2 v^3 + \cdots.$$

a. Explain why the initial balance can also be rewritten as the series:

$$\frac{P}{1 + i} + \frac{P(1 + k)}{(1+i)^2} + \frac{P(1+k)^2}{(1+i)^3} + \cdots.$$

b. Let's assume the interest rate earned on the perpetuity is greater than the rate at which the payments grow (or $i > k$). Specifically, we will assume $P = \$100$, $k = 0.01$, and $i = 0.02$.

  i. What is the value of the 2nd term in the series from part (a)?

  ii. What is the value of the 100th term in the series from part (a)?

  iii. What is the value of the 1,000th term in the series from part (a)?

  iv. As we move further and further out into the series, what value to the terms seem to be approaching?

c. Let's assume the interest rate that is earned on the perpetuity is the same as the rate at which the payments grow (or $i = k$). Specifically, we will assume $P = \$100$, $k = 0.01$, and $i = 0.01$.

  i. What is the value of the 2nd term in the series from part (a)?

  ii. What is the value of the 100th term in the series from part (a)?

  iii. What is the value of the 1,000th term in the series from part (a)?

  iv. As we move further and further out into the series, what value to the terms seem to be approaching?

  v. Explain why, if the series goes on indefinitely, it is impossible to have an initial balance that will cover an infinite number of payments if the growth in the payment matches the return on investment.

d. Is it possible to have a finite initial balance on a perpetuity where $k > i$? Explain.

16. The following expression can be used to determine the initial value of an annuity with payouts of P dollars at the end of each period with a rate of increase of k each period for a total of n periods with a return on investment of i.

$$P \times \frac{1 - \left(\left(1+k/1+i\right)\right)^n}{i-k}$$

a. Explain why this formula cannot be used to determine the initial value of an annuity if $i = k$. (i.e., the rate of return on investment equals the rate of increase in payouts.)

b. This formula can also be given as the series:
$$Pv + P(1 + k)v^2 + P(1+k)^2 v^3 + P(1+k)^3 v^4 + \cdots + P(1+k)^{n-1} v^n.$$
Rewrite this series if $i = k$ by substituting i in for k and $1/1 + i$ in for v and simplify.

c. If there are 120 terms in the series (like it pays out once a month for 10 years), what is the sum of the 120 terms in the series? Is this a finite number?

d. Suppose you want an annuity to pay out \$10,000 at the end of the first year for the next 20 years and these payments grow at by 3% each year. Also, suppose the annuity is invested an effective annual rate of 3%. To accomplish this, what is needed for the initial value of the annuity?

Prove it! questions

17. In this section, we saw the following set of equations and we will now fill in the derivation details.

Present value of \$1 paid in one period and $k\%$ increase for n periods
$$= v + (1 + k)v^2 + (1+k)^2 v^3 + (1+k)^3 v^4 + \cdots + (1+k)^{n-1} v^n$$
$$= \frac{1 - \left(\left(1+k/1+i\right)\right)^n}{i-k}$$
$$= \frac{1 - (v(1+k))^n}{i-k}$$

The first line of the equation above is a finite geometric series with a first term of v and a constant ratio of $(1 + k)v$. Remember that a constant ratio is what each term is multiplied by to get the next term. We will call the present value of \$1 paid in one period and $k\%$ increase for n periods S (for sum) or:

$$S = v + (1 + k)v^2 + (1+k)^2 v^3 + (1+k)^3 v^4 + \cdots + (1+k)^{n-1} v^n. \quad (8.1)$$

   a. Multiply both sides of Eq. (8.1) by the common ratio $(1+k)v$. Call this Eq. (8.2).

   b. Subtract Eq. (8.2) from Eq. (8.1) and show the result can be written as

$$S = \frac{v - (1+k)^n v^{n+1}}{1 - v(1+k)}$$

   c. Factor v out of both the numerator and denominator and then cancel out these terms. (*Hint: When you factor a v out of 1, you get* $1/v$.)

   d. Using the fact that $v = (1/1+i)$ or $1/v = 1+i$. Make these substitutions in your equation from part (c) and simplify so it is written as

$$S = \frac{1 - \left(\left(1+k/1+i\right)\right)^n}{i - k}$$

   e. Finally, explain why your equation from part (d) can be written as

$$S = \frac{1 - (v(1+k))^n}{i - k}$$

SECTION 8.2 ARITHMETICALLY INCREASING AND DECREASING ANNUITIES

In the previous section, we examined geometrically increasing annuities—annuities which increased proportionally to account for inflation and other factors. Now, we will explore a situation where the amount of the change is not changing proportionally, but by a fixed amount.

Learning objectives

By the end of this section, you should be able to:

- Compute the present value and payment size for arithmetically increasing and decreasing annuities and perpetuities.

EXAMPLE 8.2 BUYING A RETIREMENT ANNUITY (REVISITED)

In Example 8.1, we examined a situation where you were planning for retirement and considered what kind of monthly income would be possible if you had saved $1 million by the time of your retirement at age 65. An annuity with level (fixed) payments over time could provide a monthly income of $3,899.41 if the annuity pays 2.4% APR; however, this would mean that you would experience a loss of purchasing power over time due to inflation. To account for an annual 2% inflation rate your initial payment would only be $2,960.69.

This kind of annuity is called a geometrically increasing annuity because it grows by a proportional amount each period. Another type of annuity with changing payment sizes is called an arithmetically increasing (or decreasing) annuity. In this type of annuity, the payment size increases or decreases by a fixed amount each period.

Definition

An **arithmetically increasing (or decreasing) annuity**, increases (decreases) by a fixed amount each period.

For example, instead of growing by 2%/month, the payments might grow by $20/month.

Here is the general equation for an arithmetically increasing annuity. Note the special actuarial notation for this annuity, which uses the letter I to stand for increasing.

Present value of increasing annuity paying $P at the end of the first period

$$
\begin{aligned}
&= \left(I_{P,Q}a\right)_{\overline{n}|i} \\
&= Pv + (P + Q)v^2 + (P + 2Q)v^3 + (P + 3Q)v^4 \\
&\quad + \cdots (P + (n-1)Q)v^n \\
&= Pa_{\overline{n}|i} + \frac{Q}{i}\left(a_{\overline{n}|i} - nv^n\right)
\end{aligned}
$$

The letter P is the initial payment size and Q is the size of the increase each period. If Q is negative then the annuity is a decreasing annuity. This formula can be thought of as consisting of the "base" annuity (based on payment size P—the first term in the equation) and then the increasing portion (based on the increasing amount Q—the second term in the equation).

Calculating initial payment size for an arithmetically increasing annuity that grows by $20/month

Let's return to thinking about retirement scenarios. You have $1 million and are wondering how big of a monthly payment you will start with if you buy a 30-year annuity with monthly payments at 2.4% APR, where payments grow by $20 each month.

This is a straightforward application of the formula shown above. Namely,

$$\$1 \text{ million} = Pa_{\overline{n}|i} + \frac{Q}{i}\left(a_{\overline{n}|i} - nv^n\right) = Pa_{\overline{360}|0.002}$$

$$+ \frac{20}{0.002}\left(a_{\overline{360}|0.002} - 360v^{360}\right)$$

$$= 256.4488P + 10,000\left(256.4488 - 360v^{360}\right)$$

$$= 256.4488P + 810,919.6$$

And, thus, $P = \$737.30$. In other words, if you want your monthly payments to grow by $20/month for 30 years, you will need to start with a payment of $737.30.

Arithmetically increasing perpetuity

Just like there are geometrically increasing perpetuities, there are also arithmetically increasing perpetuities. Here is the formula. See the exercises for a proof and intuition.

Present value of arithmetically increasing perpetuity

$$= Pa_{\overline{\infty}|i} + \frac{Q}{i}\left(a_{\overline{\infty}|i}\right) = \frac{P}{i} + \frac{Q}{i^2}$$

What if you want to consider a perpetuity that has payments grow $20/month forever? Plugging into the formula above gives

$$\$1 \text{ million} = \frac{P}{0.002} + \frac{20}{0.002^2} = \frac{P}{0.002} + \$5 \text{ million}$$

Solving for P we get $-\$8,000$—a negative number! What's going on here? Essentially, the present value of the increasing part of the perpetuity

(Q/i^2) has a present value of \$5 million. Since you only have \$1 million, this is a problem! You can think of this as either (a) not being able to afford such an annuity or (b) starting with $P = -\$8,000$, which means depositing (not taking out) \$8,000 into an account earning 2.4% APR at the end of the first month, and then \$7,980 the second month, \$7,960 the third month, etc.

So, how much can you increase payments by monthly in perpetuity? $1/i^2 = \$250,000$. This means that every \$1 increase in monthly payments costs you \$250,000 today. So, you'll have to increase payments by \$4 or less/month and, if you increase payments by \$4/month your initial payment will be \$0! If you increase payments by \$1/month, then $P = \$1,500$.

Concluding remarks

- There is an equation for the accumulated value of an increasing annuity:

$$\text{Accumulated value of increasing annuity} = Ps_{\overline{n}|i} + \frac{Q}{i}\left(s_{\overline{n}|i} - nv^n\right)$$

Once again this is easily derived by multiplying the present value of an increasing annuity equation by $(1+i)^n$.

- An arithmetically decreasing annuity simply has a negative value for Q in the equations shown above.

EXPLORATION 8.2. LIFE INSURANCE PAYOUT AS AN ANNUITY ALLOWING FOR INFLATION (REVISITED)

In Exploration 8.1, we examined how to have an annuity which grew over time to keep up with inflation. That kind of annuity was called a geometrically increasing annuity because the size of the growth in payments increased as a percentage. However, there is another way to have payments grow over time—arithmetically—that is, as a fixed increase of, say, \$1,000/year.

1. If John buys \$750,000 of insurance and his family will take a level payment annually from the insurance payout for 20 years, and the insurance payout is invested at 5%, what is the annual payment size?

Equations for arithmetically increasing annuity

2. If John wants to allow for increases of $2,400 annually in the payment size his family takes from the account, what will the first three payment sizes be?

3. Write an equation using v, for the present value of the first three annual payments from the account with payments growing at $2,400/year?

4. Now, using only $60,181.94 (the initial payment size), v, and the letter Q (to stand for the annual increase each year), write an equation for the present value of the first three payments.

    Here is the general equation for an arithmetically increasing annuity. Note the special actuarial notation for this annuity, which uses the letter I to stand for increasing.

    Present value of increasing annuity paying P at the end of the first period $= \left(I_{P,Q}a\right)_{\overline{n}|i}$
    $= Pv + (P + Q)v^2 + (P + 2Q)v^3 + (P + 3Q)v^4 + \cdots$
    $+ (P + (n-1)Q)v^n = Pa_{\overline{n}|i} + \dfrac{Q}{i}\left(a_{\overline{n}|i} - nv^n\right)$

Definition
An **arithmetically increasing (or decreasing) annuity**, increases (decreases) by a fixed amount each period.

---

5. What is the size of the first payment if John buys $750,000 worth of insurance and wants his annual payment to increase by $2,400 annually for 20 years?

6. Why does it make sense that the size of the first payment is now less than $60,000?

7. How much insurance does John need if he wants to have payments increase by $2,400 annually, but with the first payment to be $60,000?

8. Explain whether you think an arithmetically increasing annuity or a geometrically increasing annuity is a better long-term strategy to combat inflation? *Hint: You may want to think about how a geometrically*

increasing annuity is like compound interest, and an arithmetically increasing annuity is like simple interest.

Arithmetically increasing perpetuity

Just like there are geometrically increasing perpetuities, there are also arithmetically increasing perpetuities. Here is the formula, see the exercises for a proof and intuition.

$$\text{Present value of arithmetically increasing perpetuity}$$

$$= Pa_{\overline{\infty}|i} + \frac{Q}{i}\left(a_{\overline{\infty}|i}\right) = \frac{P}{i} + \frac{Q}{i^2}$$

9. What is the practical problem if John wants to buy $750,000 in insurance and have the payments grow at $2,400/year indefinitely?

10. How much insurance does John need to buy if he wants payments to start at $60,000 annually and grow at $2,400/year?

See the end of Example 8.2 for some additional comments.

SUMMARY

In this section, we explored arithmetically increasing and decreasing annuities and perpetuities. These annuities and perpetuities changed by a fixed amount each period, in contrast to geometrically increasing or decreasing annuities which change by an amount proportional to the previous payment.

Notation and equation summary

Present value of increasing annuity paying $P at the end of the first period

$$= \left(I_{P,Q}a\right)_{\overline{n}|i}$$

$$= Pv + (P + Q)v^2 + (P + 2Q)v^3 + (P + 3Q)sv^4 + \cdots + (P + (n-1)Q)v^n$$

$$= Pa_{\overline{n}|i} + \frac{Q}{i}\left(a_{\overline{n}|i} - nv^n\right)$$

Present value of arithmetically increasing perpetuity $= Pa_{\overline{\infty}|i} + \frac{Q}{i}\left(a_{\overline{\infty}|i}\right) = \frac{P}{i} + \frac{Q}{i^2}$

HOMEWORK QUESTIONS: SECTION 8.2

Conceptual questions

1. The first four payouts of three different annuities A, B, and C are shown below. Which is increasing arithmetically, which is increasing geometrically, and which is neither?
   a. A: $1,000, $1,100, $1,150, and $1,175
   b. B: $1,000, $1,100, $1,200, and $1,300
   c. C: $1,000, $1,100, $1,210, and $1,331

2. If payments from an annuity grow by $10 each month, are the payouts increasing geometrically or arithmetically?

3. You are considering putting $500,000 into an annuity so it will pay out for 20 years. Annuity A pays out the same amount each month and has a rate of return of 5% APR. Annuity B has payments that increase $10 each month and also has a rate of return of 5% APR. Which annuity will have the highest first payment? Which annuity will have the highest last payment?

4. Will a geometrically increasing annuity or an arithmetically increasing annuity better give payouts that will keep pace with inflation?

5. In an arithmetically decreasing annuity, which of the following symbols from the present value of an annuity would be negative: i, n, P, Q, and v?

6. Suppose you are setting up an annuity with arithmetically increasing payouts and you are calculating the initial balance needed. If you double the first payout, does that double the initial balance needed?

Practice questions

7. If an annuity has a first payout of $1,000 and it increases $20 for each payout, how much is the 5th payout? 6th payout? 106th payout?

8. You want to set up a perpetuity that will pay out $5,000 at the end of the first year and every year after the payout goes up $200. If you can

get 6% effective annual interest on the perpetuity, how much does the initial balance have to be?

9. A donation of $500,000 is given to put into a perpetuity for scholarships. The fund will be earning 6%. We will assume the payout in scholarships will increase by $500 each year. How much can be paid out in scholarships at the end of the first year?

Application questions

10. An annuity has an initial balance of $1,000,000 and will pay out yearly for 20 years. The account will earn 5% effective annual interest and the payouts will increase by $2,000 per year. What is the value of the first payment?

11. You set up an annuity that will pay out $10,000 at the end of the first year and every year after the payout goes up $500 for a total of 20 years. If you can get 4.5% effective annual interest on the annuity, how much is the initial balance.

12. You have $350,000 to put into a 20-year annuity that you want to pay out $20,000 at the end of the first year and every year after the payout is to go up by a certain amount. If you can get 5% effective annual interest on the annuity and you, how much is that certain amount of increase each year?

13. You set up a 30-year annuity that will pay out $10,000 at the end of the next 5 years. After that, the payout goes up $500 each year for the rest of the 30 years. If the annuity earns 5% effective annual interest, how much is the initial balance.

14. An annuity has an initial balance of $1,000,000 and will pay out monthly for 20 years. The account will earn 4% APR and the payouts will increase by $50 per month. What is the value of the first payment?

15. You set up an annuity that will pay out $10,000 at the end of the first year and every year after the payout goes *down* $500 for a total of 20 years. If you can get 4.5% effective annual interest on the annuity, how much is the initial balance?

Prove it! questions

16. In this section, we saw the present value of an arithmetically increasing perpetuity is given by the equation:

$$Pv + (P + Q)v^2 + (P + 2Q)v^3 + (P + 3Q)v^4 + \cdots + = \frac{P}{i} + \frac{Q}{i^2}$$

We will guide you through the derivation of this equation. To start, let's call the left side of the equation X as shown in Eq. (8.3) and our overall goal is to find a closed form for X.

$$X = Pv + (P + Q)v^2 + (P + 2Q)v^3 + (P + 3Q)v^4 + \cdots. \qquad (8.3)$$

a. Multiply both sides of Eq. (8.3) by the common ratio v. Call this Eq. (8.4).

b. Subtract Eq. (8.4) from Eq. (8.3) and show the result can be written as

$$X - Xv = Pv + Qv^2 + Qv^3 + Qv^4 + \cdots. \qquad (8.5)$$

Now consider the right side of Eq. (8.5) above made up of two parts, the Pv and everything else. Let's call everything else Y so we have

$$Y = Qv^2 + Qv^3 + Qv^4 + \cdots. \qquad (8.6)$$

c. Eq. (8.6) is a geometric series. Show that this can be written as $Y = \left(Qv^2/1 - v\right)$.

d. Putting Y back into Eq. (8.5) we should have: $X - Xv = Pv + \left(Qv^2/1 - v\right)$. Solve this for X.

e. Now we need to convert the v's to i's. Given that $v = \left(1/1 + i\right)$, solve this for $1/i$.

f. Using your answers from part d and part e, explain why you should now have shown that

$$Pv + (P + Q)v^2 + (P + 2Q)v^3 + (P + 3Q)v^4 + \cdots = \frac{P}{i} + \frac{Q}{i^2}$$

SECTION 8.3 ANNUITIES WITH PAYMENTS AT THE BEGINNING OF THE PERIOD (ANNUITIES-DUE)

So far in this chapter, we have been exploring alternative kinds of annuities. To this point, our focus has been on annuities with nonlevel payments—payments that are either increasing or decreasing in size over time. In this section, we'll begin exploring another option to the kinds of annuities we can value—the timing of the regular payment. Until now, we've always assumed that the payment occurs at the end of the interest conversion period. Now we'll explore how things look if the payment occurs at the beginning.

Learning objectives

By the end of this section, you should be able to:

- Contrast annuities-immediate and annuities-due
- Compute payment sizes and present values for annuities and perpetuities-due using multiple techniques

EXAMPLE 8.3 BUYING A RETIREMENT ANNUITY (REVISITED)

Earlier in this chapter, we explored using retirement savings of $1 million to purchase a 30-year, monthly annuity at 2.4% APR. Level payments starting 1 month after retiring are $3,899.41 per month for 30-year.

Think about it

One downside to the annuity described above is that it starts at the end of the first month. What will you do for an income during the first month? How will the payment size be impacted if you start your monthly payments immediately (today) with payments continuing on the first day of each month for 30 years?

Obviously, if you start payments today then the payment each month will be slightly lower. You can see this by thinking of an annuity as a form of a loan. The $1 million will have no time to earn interest if the payments start on the first day of the month, whereas if they start at the end of the month they will.

There are a few different ways to think of annuities-due—that is, annuities with payments at the beginning of the period.

Definition

An **annuity-due** is an annuity where the payments occur at the beginning of the period.

This is in contrast to the annuities we've been investigating so far, which are called annuities-immediate.

Definition

An **annuity-immediate** is an annuity where the payments occur at the end of the period.

One way of thinking about the pricing for an annuity-due is to think of buying an annuity-immediate (i.e., an end of period annuity like we've looked at before) with one less payment, since the end of the first month is essentially the same as the beginning of the second month. Then, adding one additional payment of size P now.

For example, first, take a payment of size P from the $1 million. This leaves, $1 million minus P. Buy an annuity-immediate with 359 payments with the $1 million minus P.

We use the notation $\ddot{a}_{\overline{n}|i}$ to represent the present value of an annuity-due (an annuity of n payments of $1, at interest rate i, where the payments occur at the beginning of the month).

Key idea

$\ddot{a}_{\overline{n}|i}$ represents an annuity-due. Note that when we put two dots on top of the variable then the payments come at the beginning of the month.

Thus, we can say the following:

$$\text{Present value for annuity-due} = P\ddot{a}_{\overline{n}|i} = P + Pv + Pv^2 + Pv^3 + \cdots + Pv^{n-1}$$
$$= P + Pa_{\overline{n-1}|i}$$

Thus,

$$\$1 \text{ million} = P\ddot{a}_{\overline{360}|0.002} = P + Pa_{\overline{359}|0.002} = P + 255.9617P = 256.9671P$$
$$P = \$3,891.55$$

And, so the payment size for this annuity is slightly smaller than if the payments started at the end of the month which was $3,899.4.

Perpetuity-due

The intuition in the formula above is similar to that used for a **perpetuity-due**—a special kind of perpetuity where the first payment is made right away.

Definition

A **perpetuity-due** is a perpetuity where the payments occur on the first day of the period.

This is in contrast to the kinds of perpetuities we've investigated so far, where payments occur at the end of the period.

Definition

A **perpetuity-immediate** is a perpetuity where the payments occur on the last day of the period.

We note the following about perpetuities-due:

$$\text{Present value for perpetuity-due} = P\ddot{a}_{\overline{\infty}|i}$$

$$= P + Pa_{\overline{\infty}|i} = P + \frac{P}{i} = P\left(\frac{1+i}{i}\right) = \frac{P}{d}$$

Note that we begin by thinking of a perpetuity-due, as a perpetuity-immediate (end of period payments), with one extra payment at the beginning.

So, how big could payments be if the $1 million was used to purchase a perpetuity-due?

$$\$1 \text{ million} = P\left(\frac{1+i}{i}\right) = P\left(\frac{1+0.002}{0.002}\right) = \$1,996.01$$

Note that this is, once again, slightly lower than the perpetuity-immediate (payments at the end of the period), which would pay $2,000/month ($1 million $\times$ 0.002).

Another shortcut formula for an annuity-due

There is another shortcut formula for an annuity-due. What would happen if you multiplied both sides of the annuity-due formula by v?

$$P\ddot{a}_{\overline{n}|i} = P + Pv + Pv^2 + Pv^3 + \cdots + Pv^{n-1}$$

If you do, you obtain the following:

$$Pv\ddot{a}_{\overline{n}|i} = Pv + Pv^2 + Pv^3 + \cdots + Pv^n$$

Since the right side of the equation is equal to $Pa_{\overline{n}|i}$, we have $Pv\ddot{a}_{\overline{n}|i} = Pa_{\overline{n}|i}$ or since $v = 1/(1 + i)$ we get

$$\text{Present value for annuity-due} = P\ddot{a}_{\overline{n}|i} = (1 + i)Pa_{\overline{n}|i}$$

Key idea

The present value of an annuity-due is equal to the present value of an annuity-immediate with the same number of level payments, but with every payment worth $(1 + i)$ more.

You can use this formula to show that

$$\$1 \text{ million} = (1 + i)Pa_{\overline{n}|i} = (1.002)(256.4488)P.$$

And, once again, $P = \$3,891.55$.

Computing the present value of an annuity-due using the discount rate

Yet another way to compute the present value of an annuity-due is via the discount rate, d, as is shown in the following equation:

$$\ddot{a}_{\overline{n}|i} = (1 + i)a_{\overline{n}|i} = (1 + i)\left(\frac{1 - v^n}{i}\right) = \frac{1 - v^n}{i/(1 + i)} = \frac{1 - v^n}{d}$$

$$\$1 \text{ million} = P\frac{1 - v^n}{d} = P\frac{1 - 0.487102}{0.001996} = 256.9617P.$$

And, once again, $P = \$3,891.55$.

Concluding remarks

1. In addition to the present value formulas we explored above, there is also an "accumulated value" (future value) equation like we've seen before. Here are formulas for the accumulated value in an annuity for $1 payments *into* the annuity-due and a reminder about the equation for an annuity-immediate.

$$\text{Annuity-due:} \; \ddot{s}_{\overline{n}|i} = (1 + i)s_{\overline{n}|i} = \frac{(1+i)^n - 1}{d}$$

$$\text{Annuity-immediate} : \; s_{\overline{n}|i} = \frac{(1+i)^n - 1}{i}$$

2. In practice, annuities-due are commonly used for rent and insurance—two situations where you "prepay."

Key idea

Annuities with payments at the end of the month are the common way of thinking about a loan (e.g., mortgage), whereas annuities with payments at the beginning of the month (annuities-due) are the common way to think about rent and insurance.

---

3. Annuity-due is a funny name, and so is annuity-immediate! In an annuity-due, you are "due" to get a payment right away. The term "immediate" means "the immediate next"—wait a period first. Don't blame us—we didn't pick these terms!

4. The **Chapter 8 Excel file** provides some additional opportunities and ways to check your answers and confirm the structure of annuities-due.

EXPLORATION 8.3 LEAVING MONEY FOR A NEW SCHOLARSHIP

You are working for a college and a wealthy donor has approached you to discuss donating money to the college to support a scholarship for students. The donor indicates having approximately $150,000 ready to donate to the college. Historically, the college has been able to earn 3% effective interest annually.

1. If the scholarship fund is made into a perpetuity, what is the size of the annual scholarship that is made available?

2. If the scholarship fund is set up for only 20 years, what is the size of the annual scholarship that is made available?

Obviously, having the scholarship last forever means that the scholarship amount will be quite a bit less per year compared to it lasting a fixed amount of time.

3. The donor is curious when the first scholarship will be available to be paid out for either the perpetuity or 20-year scholarship scenarios. Using the types of annuities we have been using up to this point, when will the first payment occur?

Because the donor is excited about their gift, they would like the first year's scholarship paid out immediately—before a full year's worth of interest accumulates.

Perpetuities and annuities-due

A **perpetuity-due** is a special kind of perpetuity where the first payment is made right away.

Definition

A **perpetuity-due** is a perpetuity where the payments occur on the first day of the period.

This is in contrast to the kinds of perpetuities we've investigated so far, where payments occur at the end of the period.

Definition

A **perpetuity-immediate** is a perpetuity where the payments occur on the last day of the period.

---

4. If the first scholarship of size P is given now, and then the scholarship is paid out annually in perpetuity at the same amount P, will P be larger or smaller than what you computed earlier for a perpetuity-immediate? Why?

5. In terms of P (the scholarship size), what will the account balance be after the first scholarship is paid out (e.g., tomorrow)?

6. Using your answer to the previous question, write an equation for P and solve it for P. *Hint: Keep in mind that the perpetuity will use the account balance from the previous question as the "lump sum" investment.*

From your answer to the previous question, you should be able to see that we can get the following formulas for the present value of a perpetuity-due:

$$P = (\text{Present Value} - P)i \quad \text{or} \quad \text{Present Value} = P\left(\frac{1+i}{i}\right) = \frac{P}{d}$$

Using notation for the present value of $1 in a perpetuity-due we have:

$$\ddot{a}_{\overline{\infty}|i} = (1+i)a_{\overline{\infty}|i} = \frac{1+i}{i} = \frac{1}{d}$$

Similarly, an annuity-due is an annuity where the first payment occurs immediately.

Definition
An **annuity-due** is an annuity where the payments occur at the beginning of the period.

This is in contrast to the annuities we've been investigating so far, which are called annuities-immediate.

Definition
An **annuity-immediate** is an annuity where the payments occur at the end of the period.

---

7. If the first scholarship is given now, and then the scholarship will be paid out annually for 19 more years (20 total scholarships awards) at the same amount, will the annual scholarship amount be larger or smaller than what you computed earlier for an annuity-immediate? Why?

8. Using P for the scholarship size and v (the discount factor), what symbol(s) will you use for the present value of...
   a. ...The first scholarship?
   b. ...The second scholarship?
   c. ...The third scholarship?
   d. ...The 20th scholarship?

Note that the present value of first scholarship (the one that is paid out immediately!) is P. The rest of the payments, however, look like the kinds of annuities we've seen before (a payment discounted back to the present time). This is because a payment at the end of a period is, essentially, the equal in value to a payment at the start of the next period.

We use the notation $\ddot{a}_{\overline{n}|i}$ to represent the present value of an annuity-due (an annuity of n payments of $1, at interest rate i, where the payments occur at the beginning of the month).

Key idea

$\ddot{a}_{\overline{n}|i}$ represents an annuity-due. Note that when we put two dots on top of the variable then the payments come at the beginning of the month.

Thus, we can say the following:

$$\text{Present value for annuity-due} = P\ddot{a}_{\overline{n}|i}$$
$$= P + Pv + Pv^2 + Pv^3 + \cdots + Pv^{n-1}$$

9. How many separate terms are in the equation? Why does that make sense?

10. Explain why the final term in the equation above (Pv^{n-1}) is raised to the power $n-1$ and not n?

Note, how if you drop the first term of the equation above you have an annuity with $n-1$ payments.

11. Thus, what symbol could we use to represent $Pv + Pv^2 + Pv^3 + \cdots + Pv^{n-1}$?

This leads us to a shortcut formula for an annuity-due:

$$P\ddot{a}_{\overline{n}|i} = P + Pv + Pv^2 + Pv^3 + \cdots + Pv^{n-1} = P + Pa_{\overline{n-1}|i}$$

12. What size scholarship can the donor give annually 20 times if the first scholarship is given out right away?

13. Compare the scholarship size obtained here with what you obtained earlier if the first scholarship is given out 1 year from now.

Another shortcut formula for an annuity-due

14. Below is the formula for an annuity-due, what would happen if you multiplied both sides of it by v? Try it. *Hint:* $v = 1/(1 + i)$.

$$P\ddot{a}_{\overline{n}|i} = P + Pv + Pv^2 + Pv^3 + \cdots + Pv^{n-1}$$

You should recognize the right side of the equation in your answer to the previous question as the formula for an annuity-immediate. This leads to another "shortcut" formula for an annuity-due.

$$\text{Present value for annuity-due} = P\ddot{a}_{\overline{n}|i}$$
$$= P + Pv + Pv^2 + Pv^3 + \cdots + Pv^{n-1} = (1 + i)Pa_{\overline{n}|i}$$

Key idea

The present value of an annuity-due is equal to the present value of an annuity-immediate with the same number of level payments, but with every payment worth $(1 + i)$ more.

This equation reflects the fact that an annuity-due is like an annuity-immediate but with all the payments "shifted" one period sooner.

15. Use this shortcut formula to confirm the scholarship size if the donor wishes to be able to have the scholarship given 20 times.

Computing the present value of an annuity-due using the discount rate

Yet another way to compute the present value of an annuity-due is via the discount rate, d.

16. What is the effective annual discount rate that corresponds to the effective interest rate of 3% annually?

The following formula uses the discount rate to compute the present value of the annuity:

$$\ddot{a}_{\overline{n}|i} = (1 + i)a_{\overline{n}|i} = (1 + i)\left(\frac{1 - v^n}{i}\right) = \frac{1 - v^n}{i/(1 + i)} = \frac{1 - v^n}{d}$$

17. Use the equation above to, again, find the scholarship size if the donor wants their 20 scholarships to begin immediately.

Changing the donation amount

The donor now asks you the following question "If I want to make sure that my gift to the college yields a 'meaningful' scholarship size of $15,000 annually, how much will I need to leave the college?"

18. Find how much money the donor needs to leave the college for four different scenarios: perpetuity-immediate, perpetuity-due, annuity-immediate (20 scholarships), and annuity-due (20 scholarships). Assume 3% effective annual interest and annually issued scholarships.

19. Compare the four donation values you have above and explain intuitively why the largest value is largest and why the smallest value is the smallest.

See the end of Example 8.3 for some concluding remarks.

SUMMARY

In this section, we explored annuities and perpetuities where the payment came at the beginning of the month, instead of the end of the month. Annuities-due have the payment come at the beginning of the month, whereas annuities-immediate have the payment come at the end of the month. One relatively easy way to solve annuity-due problems is to convert the annuity-due to an annuity-immediate, as is reflected in two of the formulas shown in this section.

Notation and equation summary

Present value for annuity-due $= P\ddot{a}_{\overline{n}|i} = P + Pv + Pv^2 + Pv^3 + \cdots + Pv^{n-1} =$

$$P + Pa_{\overline{n-1}|i} = (1+i)Pa_{\overline{n}|i} = \frac{1-v^n}{d}$$

Present value for perpetuity-due $= P\ddot{a}_{\overline{\infty}|i} = P + Pa_{\overline{\infty}|i}$

$$= P + \frac{P}{i} = P\left(\frac{1+i}{i}\right) = \frac{P}{d}$$

HOMEWORK QUESTIONS: SECTION 8.3

Conceptual questions

1. How is an annuity-due different than an annuity-immediate?

2. In general, are the payouts for an annuity-due larger or smaller than that for an annuity-immediate under the same parameters?

3. An annuity-due is like an annuity-immediate with all the payments shifted one period _____ (sooner/later).

4. With identical interest rates and initial balances, order the following in terms of payout sizes from low to high: annuity-due, annuity-immediate, perpetuity-due, and perpetuity-immediate.

5. To find the payout size for a perpetuity-immediate, we simply multiply the present value by the interest rate. To find the payout size for a perpetuity-due, we simply multiply the present value by what?

Practice questions

6. If $500,000 is put into a perpetuity-due and it earns 4% effective annual interest, what is the amount of each annual payout?

7. If $400,000 is put into a perpetuity-due and it earns 3% APR, what is the amount of each monthly payout?

8. If $500,000 is put into a 20-year annuity-due and it earns 4% effective annual interest, what is the amount of each annual payout?

9. What initial balance is needed in an annuity-due to give payouts of $10,000 each year for 10 years with an annual effective interest rate of 3.5%?

10. What initial balance is needed in an annuity-due to give payouts of $2,000 each month for 20 years (240 months) with an APR of 3%?

Application questions

11. $750,000 is put into a 20-year annuity that earns 4% effective annual interest.

   a. What is the amount of each annual payout if it is an annuity-immediate?

   b. What is the amount of each annual payout if it is an annuity-due?

   c. Suppose we switch to monthly payments.

      i. What is the amount of each monthly payout if it is an annuity-immediate? Is the sum of these more or less than that of the annual payout of the annuity-immediate? Explain why that makes sense.

      ii. What is the amount of each monthly payout if it is an annuity-due? Is the sum of these more or less than that of the annual payout of the annuity-due? Explain why that makes sense.

12. An annuity earns 3% effective annual interest and will give 15 annual payments of $6,000.

   a. What initial amount is needed if it is an annuity-immediate?

   b. What initial amount is needed if it is an annuity-due?

   c. Suppose we switch to monthly payments where each monthly payment is $500.

      i. What initial amount is needed if it is an annuity-immediate? Is this more or less than the initial amount needed when there were annual payouts in the annuity-immediate? Explain why that makes sense.

      ii. What initial amount is needed if it is an annuity-due? Is this more or less than the initial amount needed when there were annual payouts in the annuity-due? Explain why that makes sense.

13. A donor wants to give $1,000,000 to a university for scholarships. This donation will be invested at 4% effective annual interest. How much will each payout be if it is:

   a. A 30-year annuity-immediate?

   b. A 30-year annuity-due?

   c. A perpetuity-immediate?

   d. A perpetuity-due?

14. Suppose $500 is being deposited into an annuity at the beginning of each month that earns 1.5% APR. How much will have accumulated in the account at the end of 5 years (60 months)?

15. Suppose $500 is being deposited into an annuity at the end of each month that earns 1.5% APR. How much will have accumulated in the account at the end of 5 years (60 months)?

Prove it! questions

16. Using the fact that $\ddot{a}_{\overline{n}|i} = (1 + i)a_{\overline{n}|i}$ show that $\ddot{a}_{\overline{n}|i} = (1 - v^n)/d$.

Looking ahead

17. $500,000 is put into a 15-year annuity that earns 3% effective annual interest.
   a. What is the amount of each annual payout if it is an annuity-immediate?
   b. Suppose the initial balance is just left in the account earning 3% effective annual interest for 10 years. At the end of the 10th year, the first payout is made and 14 more annual payouts are made. What is the amount of each of these annual payouts?

SECTION 8.4 INCREASING AND DECREASING ANNUITIES-DUE

In this final section of this chapter, we take a brief look at combining the two main themes of this chapter: (1) annuities that change in value over time (increasing or decreasing) and (2) annuities with payments at the beginning of the period instead of the end. So, can we have annuities that change in value over time with payments at the beginning of the period? Sure we can. We'll look at the details now.

Learning objectives

By the end of this section, you should be able to:
• Compute the present value and payment size for annuities-due and perpetuities-due which change in value over time.

EXAMPLE 8.4 RETIREMENT SAVINGS (REVISITED)

We'll return to the retirement savings example one more time in this chapter to illustrate annuities-due that change in value over time. Recall the following monthly payments shown in Table 8.1.

Obviously, the thing missing in Table 8.1 is an evaluation of annuities-due which changes over time.

Table 8.1 Monthly income on a beginning retirement balance of $1 million for annuities at 2.4% aPR

Type of annuity	Length of monthly payments	First monthly payment amount	Payment change?
Due (starts now)	30 years	$3,891.55	None
Immediate (starts next month)	30 years	$3,899.41	None
Due (starts now)	In perpetuity	$1,996.01	None
Immediate (starts next month)	In perpetuity	$2,000	None
Due (starts now)	30 years	?	Increases 0.1652% monthly
Immediate (starts next month)	30 years	$2,960.69	Increases 0.1652% monthly
Due (starts now)	In perpetuity	?	Increases 0.1652% monthly
Immediate (starts next month)	In perpetuity	$348.42	Increases 0.1652% monthly
Due (starts now)	30 years	?	Increases $20/month
Immediate (starts next month)	30 years	$737.30	Increases $20/month
Due (starts now)	In perpetuity	?	Increases $1/month
Immediate (starts next month)	In perpetuity	$1,500.00	Increases $1/month

---

Think about it

Will the monthly payment amounts for the annuities-due which change in value over time be smaller or larger than the monthly payments for the corresponding annuities-immediate?

As we saw for annuities-due with level payments, the payment that is possible will be slightly smaller than for the corresponding annuity-immediate. Let's now run through four separate scenarios to finish filling in Table 8.1.

Scenario 1—annuity-due for 30 years growing 0.1652% per month

Recall that the formula for the present value of a geometrically growing annuity-immediate is $P(1 - (v(1+k))^n)/(i - k)$. To convert between an annuity-immediate and an annuity-due, we can recognize that the first payment P, happens now and so

$$\$1 \text{ million} - P = P(1 + k)\frac{1 - (v(1+k))^{n-1}}{i - k} = P(1 + 0.001652)336.9026$$

$$\$1 \text{ million} = P + 337.4591P$$

And, thus, $P = \$2,954.57$, slightly smaller than, $\$2,960.69$, we obtained for the annuity-immediate. Note: the numerator of the equation above uses $P(1 + k)$ because the second payment is larger than the first payment by a factor of $1 + k$.

Scenario 2—annuity-due in perpetuity growing 0.1652% per month

Recall that the formula for the present value of a geometrically growing perpetuity-immediate is $(P/i - k)$. To convert between a perpetuity-immediate and a perpetuity-due, we again recognize that the first payment P, happens now and so

$$\$1 \text{ million} - P = \frac{P(1 + k)}{i - k} = \frac{P(1 + 0.001652)}{0.002 - 0.001652}$$

$$\$1 \text{ million} = P + 2878.31P$$

And, thus, $P = \$347.31$, slightly smaller than, $\$348.42$, we obtained for the perpetuity-immediate. Note: the numerator of the equation above uses $P(1 + k)$ because the second payment is larger than the first payment by a factor of $1 + k$.

Scenario 3—annuity-due for 30 years growing $20 per month

Recall that the formula for the present value of an arithmetically growing annuity-immediate is $Pa_{\overline{n}|i} + (Q/i)(a_{\overline{n}|i} - nv^n)$. Using the same ideas as above to convert between a perpetuity-immediate and a perpetuity-due, we obtain:

$$\$1 \text{ million} - P = (P + 20)a_{\overline{n-1}|i} + \frac{20}{i}\left(a_{\overline{n-1}|i} - (n - 1)v^{n-1}\right)$$

$$= (P + 20)(255.9617) + 10,000(255.9617 - (359)(0.488077))$$
$$= 255.9617P + 812,541.40$$

Thus, $P = \$729.52$ is the initial payment, again, slightly smaller than, 737.30, we obtained before.

Scenario 4—perpetuity-due growing $1 per month

Recall that we could not afford to grow the perpetuity at $20/month. Also, recall that the formula for the present value of an arithmetically growing perpetuity-immediate is $(P/i) + (Q/i^2)$. Using the same ideas as above to convert between a perpetuity-immediate and a perpetuity-due, we obtain:

$$\$1 \text{ million} - P = \frac{P + 1}{i} + \frac{1}{i^2} = \frac{P + 1}{0.002} + 250,000$$

$$\$750,000 = 501P + 500$$

Thus, $P = \$1\ 496.01$ is the initial payment, again, slightly smaller than, 1500.00, we obtained before.

Concluding remarks

1. While equations do exist for annuities-due and perpetuities-due with changing payment sizes, they may not be worth memorizing if you know how to convert between annuities-due and annuities-immediate, by realizing you can simply "adjust" for the first payment as shown earlier.

2. Another approach not shown above (see Section 8.3) uses $(1 + i)$ to adjust the values. Try this for some of the questions above, confirm

you get the same answer and then see which approach you find more intuitive.

3. Remember another important trick which has to do with accumulated value formulas. To try to remember the accumulated value formulas, as well as the present value formulas, means you will be trying to remember twice as many formulas! This is neither fun nor vary practical. You may be well off simply trying to keep the following relationship in mind.

$$s_{\overline{n}|} = (1+i)^n a_{\overline{n}|}$$

In other words, take the present value and roll it forward n periods of interest and you have the accumulated value! We first saw this in Section 7.2.

4. Actuarial exams sometimes have questions on continuously paying annuities. See homework exercise #16 in this section for an example, as well as the end of chapter exercises.

EXPLORATION 8.4. DONATING MONEY FOR A NEW SCHOLARSHIP

Earlier we examined a situation where a donor wanted to fund a new scholarship at a college. If the donor had $150,000, they had a variety of options for how big the scholarship could be—options which depended on whether the scholarship lasted in perpetuity or for only 20 years, and whether or not the scholarship started this year, or waited a year before starting. Table 8.2 summarizes the different scholarship size options.

Table 8.2 Scholarship amounts for $150,000 gift to college assuming an annual scholarship at 3% effective annual interest rate

Type of scholarship	Length of scholarship	Annual scholarship size
Due (starts now)	20 years	$9,788.70
Due (starts now)	In perpetuity	$4,386.93
Immediate (starts next year)	20 years	$10,082.36
Immediate (starts next year)	In perpetuity	$4,500

While the donor's money will be invested at a 3% effective annual interest rate, the donor is now asking whether the scholarship payouts could grow in size over time to account for inflation. Recall our study of inflation-adjusted annuities and perpetuities earlier in this chapter.

1. What size scholarship could be provided initially if the payment size grows at 2% annually in perpetuity and the donor gives $150,000 at a 3% annual effective rate of return? How does this value compare to the corresponding value of the nonincreasing perpetuity in Table 8.2? (Assume the scholarship starts at the end of the first year and recall that the present value of a perpetuity-immediate of $1 growing at k% annually was $(1/i - k)$.)

2. What size scholarship could be provided at first, if the payment size grows at 2% annually for 20 years? Assume the scholarship starts at the end of the year. How does this value compare to the corresponding value of the nonincreasing annuity in Table 8.2? (Recall that the present value of an annuity-immediate of $1 growing at k% annually was $\left(1 - (v(1+k))^n / i - k\right)$.)

3. If the donor wants his/her scholarship to grow at 2% annually in perpetuity, but to start right away instead of waiting 1 year, what size scholarship can be provided at first? How does this value compare to the corresponding value of the nonincreasing perpetuity in Table 8.2? (Hint: Recall from the previous section that you can think of a perpetuity-due as a perpetuity-immediate plus one additional payment right now.)

4. If the donor wants his/her scholarship to grow at 2% annually for 20 total scholarships, but to start right away instead of waiting 1 year, what size scholarship can be provided at first? How does this value compare to the corresponding value of the nonincreasing annuity in Table 8.2? (Hint: Recall from the previous section that you can think of an annuity-due as an annuity-immediate with one less total payment plus one additional payment right now.)

While you can derive general equations for each of the previous two situations, it's probably not worth trying to derive and then memorize them, when, instead, you can easily convert between annuities-immediate and annuities-due as described above.

Arithmetically increasing and decreasing perpetuities and annuities

The donor is now asking whether the scholarship could grow in size at $100 annually. Recall our study of arithmetically increasing and decreasing annuities and perpetuities earlier in this chapter.

5. What size scholarship could be provided in perpetuity if the payment size grows at $100 annually? Assume the scholarship starts at the end of the year. (Recall the equation for an arithmetically increasing perpetuity is $(P/i) + (Q/i^2)$.)

6. What size scholarship could be provided for 20 years if the payment size grows at $100 annually? Assume the scholarship starts at the end of the year. (Recall the equation for an arithmetically increasing annuity is $Pa_{\overline{n}|i} + (Q/i)\left(a_{\overline{n}|i} - nv^n\right)$.)

7. If the donor wants his scholarships to grow at $100 annually, but to start right away instead of waiting 1 year, what size scholarship can be provided annually in perpetuity? (*Hint: Recall from the previous section that you can think of a perpetuity-due as a perpetuity-immediate plus one additional payment right now.*)

8. If the donor wants his 20 scholarships to grow at $100 annually, but to start right away instead of waiting 1 year, what size scholarship can be provided annually for 20 years? (*Hint: Recall from the previous section that you can think of an annuity-due as an annuity-immediate with one less total payment plus one additional payment right now.*)

Again, while you can derive general equations for each of the previous two situations, it's probably not worth trying to do so and memorize them when you can easily convert between immediate and due type of annuities as described above.

Deferring the start

Finally, the donor asks how big of a scholarship they could give in perpetuity if they deferred the start of the scholarship for 5 years.

9. How big can the scholarship be if it is paid out in perpetuity and starts in 5 years? Use the perpetuity-due formula.

10. How big can the scholarship be if it is paid out in perpetuity and starts in 5 years? Use the perpetuity-immediate formula and confirm that your answer is the same as in the previous question.

Key idea

One way to calculate values for deferred annuities is to first figure out how much the current value of the account will be at the start of the annuity (perpetuity), and then calculate the payment size on this modified amount.

See the end of Example 8.4 for some concluding remarks.

SUMMARY

In this section, we combined ideas from previous sections in this chapter and looked at how to calculate payment sizes and present values for annuities with payments at the beginning of the period, but that also changed over time. In general, we saw that annuities-due have smaller payment sizes than annuities-immediate if the term and present values, and all other aspects of the annuities are equal.

HOMEWORK QUESTIONS: SECTION 8.4

Conceptual questions

1. How is an annuity with arithmetically increasing payments different than one with geometrically increasing payments?

2. What is a geometrically increasing perpetuity-due?

3. A donor to gives money to create an endowment for scholarships and decides that annual scholarships will be given in perpetuity starting 7 years from the donation. If the money will earn a constant annual effective interest rate from the time it is given and in perpetuity,

explain how a perpetuity-due formula can be used to calculate the value of the first payment.

4. In the formula, Present Value $= (P/i) + (Q/i)$, for an increasing annuity, what do the P and the Q represent?

5. In a previous section, we showed that you could not have a perpetuity where the interest rate received on the money invested was smaller than the rate of increase of the payouts. Can this problem be overcome, by deferring the time of the first payment (to some finite amount of time, of course)? Explain.

Practice questions

6. Suppose $100,000 is put in a perpetuity such that the payouts grow by $100 each year and the money is earning 3% effective annually. If the first payout is 1 year from the time the investment is made, what is its amount?

7. Using the parameters given in the perpetuity in the previous question, if the first payout is given at the time the investment is made, what is its amount?

8. An annuity that will give out 20 annual payments has an initial payment of $1,000 and will increase by $100 each year. If it earns 3% effective annual interest and the initial payment is made the day the investment is made, how much is the initial balance?

9. An annuity that will give out 20 annual payments has an initial payment of $1,000 and will increase by 2% each year. If it earns 3% effective annual interest and the initial payment is made the day the investment is made, how much is the initial balance?

Application questions

10. Suppose $100,000 is put into a 20-year annuity-due at a 4% annual effective interest rate.
    a. What is the value of each annual payment if they are all the same amount?
    b. What is the value of the first payment if the payments increase by 2% each year?

   c. What is the value of the first payment if the payments increase by $500 each year?

11. Suppose $200,000 is put into a perpetuity-due at a 3% annual effective interest rate.
    a. What is the value of each annual payment if they are all the same amount?
    b. What is the value of the first payment if the payments increase by 1% each year?
    c. What is the value of the first payment if the payments increase by $300 each year?

12. A 30-year annuity-due is being set up and will earn a 3% annual effective interest rate such that the first payout is $5,000.
    a. What is the value of the initial balance if each payment is the same amount?
    b. What is the value of the initial balance if the payments increase by 2% each year?
    c. What is the value of the initial balance if the payments increase by $200 each year?
    d. What is the value of the initial balance if the first payment is deferred for 5 years and the payments increase by $200 each year?

13. A perpetuity-due is being set up and will earn a 2.5% annual effective interest rate such that the first payout is $3,000.
    a. What is the value of the initial balance if each payment is the same amount?
    b. What is the value of the initial balance if the payments increase by 1.5% each year?
    c. What is the value of the initial balance if the payments increase by $100 each year?
    d. What is the value of the initial balance if the first payment is deferred for 5 years and the payments increase by $100 each year?

14. Lin would like to set up a perpetuity with an initial balance of $200,000. He would like the initial payout to be $3,000 and increase by 2% each year. What interest rate is needed for this to occur if:
    a. Payments begin immediately?
    b. Payments are deferred so the first payment begins in 5 years?

15. Suppose $1,000,000 is being put into a perpetuity for scholarships where the scholarships increase by 2% per year and the money earns an effective annual interest rate of 3.5%.

   a. If the first payout will be made in a year from when the investment was made, how much will it be?

   b. Suppose the payouts were given every 6 months instead of every year and the first payout is made 6 months from when the investment was made.

       i. Convert the annual effective rates of increase and interest to 6-month rates of increase and interest.

       ii. What is the amount of the first payout?

       iii. What is the amount of the second payout?

       iv. Is the sum of the first two payouts more or less than the first-year payout from part (a)? Explain why this makes sense.

   c. Suppose the payouts were given every 6 months instead of every year and the first payout is made 1 year from when the investment was made.

       i. What is the amount of the first payout?

       ii. What is the amount of the second payout?

       iii. Is the sum of the first two payouts more or less than the first-year payout from part (a)? Explain why this makes sense.

16. A continuously paying annuity makes payments continuously. While not practical, like force of interest, it can be a convenient approximation for very frequent annuity payments. Let the present value of a continuously paying annuity which pays a total of $1 per year at a force of interest, ∂, be given as $\overline{a}_{\overline{n}|i} = \left(1 - e^{\partial n}/\partial\right)$. If the force of interest is 2%, what is the present value for an annuity if it pays continuously for 10 years with a total of $1,000 paid per year?

Prove it! questions

17. In the concluding remarks portion of the section, it was mentioned that $s_{\overline{n}|} = (1+i)^n a_{\overline{n}|}$. Show that is true by starting with the right side of the equation and make it equal to the left side.

END OF CHAPTER SUMMARY

Before this chapter, we'd looked only at a single type of annuity—an annuity with level (equal-sized) payments at the end of the period. In this chapter, we explored both geometric and arithmetically changing payment sizes and payments at the end of the month. We focused on the relationships between different types of annuities in order to minimize the number of different equations that are necessary to solve annuity problems.

END OF CHAPTER EXERCISES

(SOA EXAM FM SAMPLE QUESTIONS May 2000, Question 14)

1. A perpetuity paying 1 at the beginning of each 6-month period has a present value of 20. A second perpetuity pays X at the beginning of every 2 years.

   Assuming the same annual effective interest rate, the two present values are equal. Determine X.
   A. 3.5
   B. 3.6
   C. 3.7
   D. 3.8
   E. 3.9

(SOA EXAM FM SAMPLE QUESTIONS May 2000, Question 26)

2. Betty borrows 19,800 from Bank X. Betty repays the loan by making 36 equal payments of principal at the end of each month. She also pays interest on the unpaid balance each month at a nominal rate of 12%, compounded monthly.

   Immediately after the 16th payment is made, Bank X sells the rights to future payments to Bank Y. Bank Y wishes to yield a nominal rate of 14%, compounded semi-annually, on its investment.

What price does Bank X receive?
- **A.** 9,792
- **B.** 10,823
- **C.** 10,857
- **D.** 11,671
- **E.** 11,709

(SOA EXAM FM SAMPLE QUESTIONS May 2000, Question 51)

3. Seth deposits X in an account today in order to fund his retirement. He would like to receive payments of 50 per year, in real terms, at the end of each year for a total of 12 years, with the first payment occurring seven years from now.

The inflation rate will be 0.0% for the next six years and 1.2% per annum thereafter. The annual effective rate of return is 6.3%.
Calculate X.
- **A.** 303
- **B.** 306
- **C.** 316
- **D.** 327
- **E.** 329

(SOA EXAM FM SAMPLE QUESTIONS May 2001, Question 26)

4. Susan invests Z at the end of each year for seven years at an annual effective interest rate of 5%. The interest credited at the end of each year is reinvested at an annual effective rate of 6%. The accumulated value at the end of seven years is X.

Lori invests Z at the end of each year for 14 years at an annual effective interest rate of 2.5%. The interest credited at the end of each year is reinvested at an annual effective rate of 3%. The accumulated value at the end of 14 years is Y.
Calculate $\frac{Y}{X}$.
- **A.** 1.93
- **B.** 1.98
- **C.** 2.03
- **D.** 2.08
- **E.** 2.13

(SOA EXAM FM SAMPLE QUESTIONS May 2003, Question 8)

5. Kathryn deposits 100 into an account at the beginning of each 4-year period for 40 years. The account credits interest at an annual effective interest rate of i.

The accumulated amount in the account at the end of 40 years is X, which is 5 times the accumulated amount in the account at the end of 20 years.
Calculate X.
A. 4,695
B. 5,070
C. 5,445
D. 5,820
E. 6,195

(SOA EXAM FM SAMPLE QUESTIONS May 2003, Question 22)

6. A perpetuity costs 77.1 and makes annual payments at the end of the year.

The perpetuity pays 1 at the end of year 2, 2 at the end of year 3,..., n at the end of year $(n + 1)$. After year $(n + 1)$, the payments remain constant at n. The annual effective interest rate is 10.5%.
Calculate n.
A. 17
B. 18
C. 19
D. 20
E. 21

(SOA EXAM FM SAMPLE QUESTIONS May 2003, Question 26)

7. 1,000 is deposited into Fund X, which earns an annual effective rate of 6%. At the end of each year, the interest earned plus an additional 100 is withdrawn from the fund. At the end of the tenth year, the fund is depleted.

The annual withdrawals of interest and principal are deposited into Fund Y, which earns an annual effective rate of 9%.

Determine the accumulated value of Fund Y at the end of year 10.

A. 1,519

B. 1,819

C. 2,085

D. 2,273

E. 2,431

(SOA EXAM FM SAMPLE QUESTIONS May 2003, Question 45)

8. A perpetuity-immediate pays 100 per year. Immediately after the fifth payment, the perpetuity is exchanged for a 25-year annuity-immediate that will pay X at the end of the first year. Each subsequent annual payment will be 8% greater than the preceding payment.

   Immediately after the 10th payment of the 25-year annuity, the annuity will be exchanged for a perpetuity-immediate paying Y per year. The annual effective rate of interest is 8%. Calculate Y.

   A. 110

   B. 120

   C. 130

   D. 140

   E. 150

(SOA EXAM FM SAMPLE QUESTIONS May 2005, Question 9)

9. The present value of a series of 50 payments starting at 100 at the end of the first year and increasing by 1 each year thereafter is equal to X. The annual effective rate of interest is 9%.

   Calculate X.

   A. 1,165

   B. 1,180

   C. 1,195

   D. 1,210

   E. 1,225

(SOA EXAM FM SAMPLE QUESTIONS May 2005, Question 12)

10. Which of the following are characteristics of all perpetuities?
    I. The present value is equal to the first payment divided by the annual effective interest rate.

II. Payments continue forever.

III. Each payment is equal to the interest earned on the principal.

A. I only

B. II only

C. III only

D. I, II, and III

E. The correct answer is not given by (A), (B), (C), or (D).

(SOA EXAM FM SAMPLE QUESTIONS May 2005, Question 12)

11. An annuity-immediate pays 20 per year for 10 years, then decreases by 1 per year for 19 years. At an annual effective interest rate of 6%, the present value is equal to X.

    Calculate X.

    A. 200

    B. 205

    C. 210

    D. 215

    E. 220

(SOA EXAM FM SAMPLE QUESTIONS May 2005, Question 17)

12. At an annual effective interest rate of i, the present value of a perpetuity-immediate starting with a payment of 200 in the first year and increasing by 50 each year thereafter is 46,530.

    Calculate i.

    A. 3.25%

    B. 3.50%

    C. 3.75%

    D. 4.00%

    E. 4.25%

(SOA EXAM FM SAMPLE QUESTIONS May 2005, Question 20)

13. An investor wishes to accumulate 10,000 at the end of 10 years by making level deposits at the beginning of each year. The deposits earn a 12% annual effective rate of interest paid at the end of each

year. The interest is immediately reinvested at an annual effective interest rate of 8%.

Calculate the level deposit.

A. 541
B. 572
C. 598
D. 615
E. 621

(SOA EXAM FM SAMPLE QUESTIONS November 2000, Question 9)

14. Victor invests 300 into a bank account at the beginning of each year for 20 years. The account pays out interest at the end of every year at an annual effective interest rate of i%.

The interest is reinvested at an annual effective rate of $\left(\frac{i}{2}\right)$%.
The yield rate on the entire investment over the 20-year period is 8% annual effective.
Determine i.

A. 9%
B. 10%
C. 11%
D. 12%
E. 13%

(SOA EXAM FM SAMPLE QUESTIONS November 2000, Question 20)

15. Sandy purchases a perpetuity-immediate that makes annual payments. The first payment is 100, and each payment thereafter increases by 10.

Danny purchases a perpetuity-due which makes annual payments of 180.
Using the same annual effective interest rate, $i > 0$, the present value of both perpetuities are equal.
Calculate i.

A. 9.2%

B. 9.7%

C. 10.2%

D. 10.7%

E. 11.2%

(SOA EXAM FM SAMPLE QUESTIONS November 2000, Question 22)

16. Jerry will make deposits of 450 at the end of each quarter for 10 years.

    At the end of 15 years, Jerry will use the fund to make annual payments of Y at the beginning of each year for 4 years, after which the fund is exhausted.

    The annual effective rate of interest is 7%. Determine Y.

    A. 9,573

    B. 9,673

    C. 9,773

    D. 9,873

    E. 9,973

(SOA EXAM FM SAMPLE QUESTIONS November 2000, Question 44)

17. Joe can purchase one of two annuities:

    Annuity 1: A 10-year decreasing annuity-immediate, with annual payments of 10, 9, 8, ..., 1.

    Annuity 2: A perpetuity-immediate with annual payments. The perpetuity pays 1 in year 1, 2 in year 2, 3 in year 3, ..., and 11 in year 11. After year 11, the payments remain constant at 11.

    At an annual effective interest rate of i, the present value of Annuity 2 is twice the present value of Annuity 1.

    Calculate the value of Annuity 1.

    A. 36.4

    B. 37.4

    C. 38.4

    D. 39.4

    E. 40.4

(SOA EXAM FM SAMPLE QUESTIONS November 2001, Question 5)

18. Mike buys a perpetuity-immediate with varying annual payments. During the first 5 years, the payment is constant and equal to 10. Beginning in year 6, the payments start to increase. For year 6 and all future years, the current year's payment is K% larger than the previous year's payment.

At an annual effective interest rate of 9.2%, the perpetuity has a present value of 167.50. Calculate K, given $K < 9.2$.
  A. 4.0
  B. 4.2
  C. 4.4
  D. 4.6
  E. 4.8

(SOA EXAM FM SAMPLE QUESTIONS November 2001, Question 9)

19. A loan is amortized over five years with monthly payments at a nominal interest rate of 9% compounded monthly. The first payment is 1,000 and is to be paid one month from the date of the loan. Each succeeding monthly payment will be 2% lower than the prior payment.

Calculate the outstanding loan balance immediately after the 40th payment is made.
  A. 6,751
  B. 6,889
  C. 6,941
  D. 7,030
  E. 7,344

(SOA EXAM FM SAMPLE QUESTIONS November 2001, Question 16)

20. Olga buys a 5-year increasing annuity for X.

Olga will receive 2 at the end of the first month, 4 at the end of the second month, and for each month thereafter the payment increases by 2.

The nominal interest rate is 9% convertible quarterly. Calculate X.

A. 2,680

B. 2,730

C. 2,780

D. 2,830

E. 2,880

(SOA EXAM FM SAMPLE QUESTIONS November 2001, Question 35)

21. At time $t = 0$, Sebastian invests 2,000 in a fund earning 8% convertible quarterly, but payable annually.

   He reinvests each interest payment in individual separate funds each earning 9% convertible quarterly, but payable annually.
   The interest payments from the separate funds are accumulated in a side fund that guarantees an annual effective rate of 7%.
   Determine the total value of all funds at $t = 10$.

   A. 3,649

   B. 3,964

   C. 4,339

   D. 4,395

   E. 4,485

(SOA EXAM FM SAMPLE QUESTIONS November 2005, Question 3)

22. An investor accumulates a fund by making payments at the beginning of each month for 6 years. Her monthly payment is 50 for the first 2 years, 100 for the next 2 years, and 150 for the last 2 years. At the end of the 7th year the fund is worth 10,000.

   The annual effective interest rate is i, and the monthly effective interest rate is j.
   Which of the following formulas represents the equation of value for this fund accumulation?

   A. $\ddot{s}_{\overline{24}|i}(1 + i)\left[(1+i)^4 + 2(1+i)^2 + 3\right] = 200$

   B. $\ddot{s}_{\overline{24}|i}(1 + j)\left[(1+j)^4 + 2(1+j)^2 + 3\right] = 200$

C. $\ddot{s}_{\overline{24}|j}(1+i)\left[(1+i)^4 + 2(1+i)^2 + 3\right] = 200$

D. $s_{\overline{24}|j}(1+i)\left[(1+i)^4 + 2(1+i)^2 + 3\right] = 200$

E. $s_{\overline{24}|i}(1+j)\left[(1+j)^4 + 2(1+j)^2 + 3\right] = 200$

(SOA EXAM FM SAMPLE QUESTIONS November 2005, Question 8)

23. Matthew makes a series of payments at the beginning of each year for 20 years. The first payment is 100. Each subsequent payment through the tenth year increases by 5% from the previous payment. After the tenth payment, each payment decreases by 5% from the previous payment.

Calculate the present value of these payments at the time the first payment is made using an annual effective rate of 7%.

A. 1,375

B. 1,385

C. 1,395

D. 1,405

E. 1,415

(SOA EXAM FM SAMPLE QUESTIONS November 2005, Question 9)

24. A company deposits 1,000 at the beginning of the first year and 150 at the beginning of each subsequent year into perpetuity.

In return the company receives payments at the end of each year for-ever. The first payment is 100. Each subsequent payment increases by 5%.

Calculate the company's yield rate for this transaction.

A. 4.7%

B. 5.7%

C. 6.7%

D. 7.7%

E. 8.7%

(SOA EXAM FM SAMPLE QUESTIONS November 2005, Question 12)

25. Megan purchases a perpetuity-immediate for 3,250 with annual payments of 130. At the same price and interest rate, Chris purchases an annuity-immediate with 20 annual payments that begin at amount P and increase by 15 each year thereafter.

Calculate P.
A. 90
B. 116
C. 131
D. 176
E. 239

(SOA EXAM FM SAMPLE QUESTIONS November 2005, Question 14)

26. Payments of X are made at the beginning of each year for 20 years. These payments earn interest at the end of each year at an annual effective rate of 8%. The interest is immediately reinvested at an annual effective rate of 6%. At the end of 20 years, the accumulated value of the 20 payments and the reinvested interest is 5,600.

Calculate X.
A. 121.67
B. 123.56
C. 125.72
D. 127.18
E. 128.50

(SOA EXAM FM SAMPLE QUESTIONS November 2005, Question 23)

27. The present value of a 25-year annuity-immediate with a first payment of 2,500 and decreasing by 100 each year thereafter is X.

Assuming an annual effective interest rate of 10%, calculate X.
A. 11,346
B. 13,615
C. 15,923
D. 17,396
E. 18,112

B. 1.56
C. 1.60
D. 1.74
E. 1.94

(SOA EXAM FM SAMPLE QUESTIONS Interest Theory, Question 89)

33. College tuition is 6,000 for the current school year, payable in full at the beginning of the school year. College tuition will grow at an annual rate of 5%. A parent sets up a college savings fund earning interest at an annual effective rate of 7%. The parent deposits 750 at the beginning of each school year for 18 years, with the first deposit made at the beginning of the current school year. Immediately following the 18th deposit, the parent pays tuition for the 18th school year from the fund.

The amount of money needed, in addition to the balance in the fund, to pay tuition at the beginning of the 19th school year is X. Calculate X.
A. 1,439
B. 1,545
C. 1,664
D. 1,785
E. 1,870

(SOA EXAM FM SAMPLE QUESTIONS Interest Theory, Question 93)

34. Seth has two retirement benefit options.

His first option is to receive a lump sum of 374,500 at retirement.
His second option is to receive monthly payments for 25 years starting one month after retirement. For the first year, the amount of each monthly payment is 2,000. For each subsequent year, the monthly payments are 2% more than the monthly payments from the previous year.
Using an annual nominal interest rate of 6%, compounded monthly, the present value of the second option is P.

Determine which of the following is true.

A. P is 323,440 more than the lump sum option amount.

B. P is 107,170 more than the lump sum option amount.

C. The lump sum option amount is equal to P.

D. The lump sum option amount is 60 more than P.

E. The lump sum option amount is 64,090 more than P.

(SOA EXAM FM SAMPLE QUESTIONS Interest Theory, Question 99)

35. Jack inherited a perpetuity-due, with annual payments of 15,000. He immediately exchanged the perpetuity for a 25-year annuity-due having the same present value. The annuity-due has annual payments of X.

All the present values are based on an annual effective interest rate of 10% for the first 10 years and 8% thereafter.

Calculate X.

A. 16,942

B. 17,384

C. 17,434

D. 17,520

E. 18,989

(SOA EXAM FM SAMPLE QUESTIONS Interest Theory, Question 101)

36. A 30-year annuity is arranged to pay off a loan taken out today at a 5% annual effective interest rate. The first payment of the annuity is due in ten years in the amount of 1,000. The subsequent payments increase by 500 each year.

Calculate the amount of the loan.

A. 58,283

B. 61,197

C. 64,021

D. 64,257

E. 69,211

(SOA EXAM FM SAMPLE QUESTIONS Interest Theory, Question 102)

37. A woman worked for 30 years before retiring. At the end of the first year of employment she deposited 5,000 into an account for her retirement. At the end of each subsequent year of employment, she deposited 3% more than the prior year. The woman made a total of 30 deposits.

She will withdraw 50,000 at the beginning of the first year of retirement and will make annual withdrawals at the beginning of each subsequent year for a total of 30 withdrawals. Each of these subsequent withdrawals will be 3% more than the prior year. The final withdrawal depletes the account.
The account earns a constant annual effective interest rate.
Calculate the account balance after the final deposit and before the first withdrawal.
A. 760,694
B. 783,948
C. 797,837
D. 805,541
E. 821,379

(SOA EXAM FM SAMPLE QUESTIONS Interest Theory, Question 103)

38. An insurance company purchases a perpetuity-due providing a geometric series of quarterly payments for a price of 100,000 based on an annual effective interest rate of i. The first and second quarterly payments are 2000 and 2010, respectively.

Calculate i.
A. 10.0%
B. 10.2%
C. 10.4%
D. 10.6%
E. 10.8%

(SOA EXAM FM SAMPLE QUESTIONS Interest Theory, Question 104)

39. A perpetuity provides for continuous payments. The annual rate of payment at time t is

$$\begin{cases} 1 & \text{for } 0 \leq t \leq 10, \\ (1.03)^{t-10} & \text{for } t \geq 10. \end{cases}$$

Using an annual effective interest rate of 6%, the present value at time $t = 0$ of this perpetuity is x.

Calculate x.

A. 27.03

B. 30.29

C. 34.83

D. 38.64

E. 42.41

(SOA EXAM FM SAMPLE QUESTIONS Interest Theory, Question 125)

40. Stocks F and J are valued using the dividend discount model. The required annual effective rate of return is 8.8%. The dividend of Stock F has an annual growth rate of g and the dividend of Stock J has an annual growth rate of $-g$.

The dividends of both stocks are paid annually on the same date. The value of Stock F is twice the value of Stock J. The next dividend on Stock F is half of the next dividend on Stock J.

Calculate g.

A. 0.0%

B. 0.8%

C. 2.9%

D. 5.3%

E. 8.8%

(SOA EXAM FM SAMPLE QUESTIONS May 2005, Question 23)

41. The stock of Company X sells for 75 per share assuming an annual effective interest rate of i. Annual dividends will be paid at the end of each year forever.

The first dividend is 6, with each subsequent dividend 3% greater than the previous year's dividend.
Calculate i.
A. 8%
B. 9%
C. 10%
D. 11%
E. 12%

(SOA EXAM FM SAMPLE QUESTIONS November 2000, Question 30)

42. A 1,000 par value 20-year bond with annual coupons and redeemable at maturity at 1,050 is purchased for P to yield an annual effective rate of 8.25%.

The first coupon is 75. Each subsequent coupon is 3% greater than the preceding coupon.
Determine P.
A. 985
B. 1,000
C. 1,050
D. 1,075
E. 1,115

(SOA EXAM FM SAMPLE QUESTIONS November 2005, Question 20)

43. The dividends of a common stock are expected to be 1 at the end of each of the next 5 years and 2 for each of the following 5 years. The dividends are expected to grow at a fixed rate of 2% per year thereafter.

Assume an annual effective interest rate of 6%.

Calculate the price of this stock using the dividend discount model.

A. 29

B. 33

C. 37

D. 39

E. 41

(SOA EXAM FM SAMPLE QUESTIONS November 2000, Question 38)

44. Chuck needs to purchase an item in 10 years. The item costs 200 today, but its price inflates 4% per year.

To finance the purchase, Chuck deposits 20 into an account at the beginning of each year for 6 years. He deposits an additional X at the beginning of years 4, 5, and 6 to meet his goal.

The annual effective interest rate is 10%. Calculate X.

A. 7.4

B. 7.9

C. 8.4

D. 8.9

E. 9.4

(SOA EXAM FM SAMPLE QUESTIONS Interest Theory, Question 86)

45. A loan of 10,000 is repaid with a payment made at the end of each year for 20 years. The payments are 100, 200, 300, 400, and 500 in years 1 through 5, respectively. In the subsequent 15 years, equal annual payments of X are made.

The annual effective interest rate is 5%.

Calculate X.

A. 842

B. 977

C. 1,017

D. 1,029

E. 1,075

(SOA EXAM FM SAMPLE QUESTIONS Interest Theory, Question 97)

46. Five deposits of 100 are made into a fund at two-year intervals with the first deposit at the beginning of the first year.

The fund earns interest at an annual effective rate of 4% during the first six years and at an annual effective rate of 5% thereafter.
Calculate the annual effective yield rate earned over the investment period ending at the end of the tenth year.
A. 4.18%
B. 4.40%
C. 4.50%
D. 4.58%
E. 4.78%

(SOA EXAM FM SAMPLE QUESTIONS Interest Theory, Question 98)

47. John finances his daughter's college education by making deposits into a fund earning interest at an annual effective rate of 8%. For 18 years he deposits X at the beginning of each month.

In the 16th through the 19th years, he makes a withdrawal of 25,000 at the beginning of each year.
The final withdrawal reduces the fund balance to zero.
Calculate X.
A. 207
B. 223
C. 240
D. 245
E. 260

(SOA EXAM FM SAMPLE QUESTIONS May 2000, Question 47)

48. Jim began saving money for his retirement by making monthly deposits of 200 into a fund earning 6% interest compounded monthly. The first deposit occurred on January 1, 1985.

Jim became unemployed and missed making deposits 60 through 72. He then continued making monthly deposits of 200.

How much did Jim accumulate in his fund on December 31, 1999?

A. 53,572

B. 53,715

C. 53,840

D. 53,966

E. 54,184

CHAPTER NINE

Bonds Revisited

Abstract

In Chapter 4, we introduced bonds as a way for a company or organization to raise money beyond a traditional bank loan. In this chapter, we will dig deeper into bonds. In particular, we will explore how to compute the amortization schedule for bonds, allowing a company to compute a "book value" (or current valuation of bond debt) for their company's balance sheet. We then will see how a company can make decisions about whether or not to call a bond early based on the market-yield rates, call premiums and the calling rules for the bond they have issued. Finally, we will take a look into a bit more about how market yield rates for bonds are really dollar-weighted yield rates (IRR), but these average yield rates can be thought of as a function of spot rates and forward rates.

Keywords: Book value; amortization; IRR; spot rates; forward rates; callable; European; Bermuda; American

SECTION 9.1. FINDING BOND VALUES AT ANY POINT IN TIME

When we first looked at bonds, we focused on the selling price of the bond, which is determined by the yield (interest) rate. But, how should a company think about the value of their outstanding bonds (liabilities) after issue? This is not only an important question for tax purposes, but also, as we'll see later in this chapter, an important question when it comes to considering refinancing.

Learning objectives

By the end of this section, you will be able to
- Determine the amount of premium or discount on a bond.
- Understand what the book value of a bond is.
- Find the book value of a bond at any point in time.
- Compute a bond's amortization schedule and understand amortization of premium and discount.

A Spiral Approach to Financial Mathematics.
DOI: https://doi.org/10.1016/B978-0-12-801580-3.00009-5
© 2018 Elsevier Inc.
All rights reserved.

EXAMPLE 9.1. VALUING A $10 MILLION BOND ISSUE

Last year, the company you worked for issued 10,000, $1,000 bonds in order to raise capital for a new plant. The bonds were issued with semiannual coupons of 3% each (coupon rate is 6% nominal, convertible semiannually), and the market yield on the bonds was 4% convertible semiannually at the time of issue on the 2-year bonds.

Think about it

Were the bonds issued at a premium or discount? Find the selling price of the bonds.

Recall from Chapter 4, Stocks and Bonds: Fundamentals of Investment Strategies that a bond sells at a *premium* if it's selling price is more than the face value of the bond (in this case $1,000) and is selling at a *discount* if its selling price is less than the face value of the bond. We also saw that by comparing the yield rate and the coupon rate, we could quickly determine whether the bond is selling at a premium or discount. Intuitively, we can think of bonds like loans, with the coupon payments acting like interest payments. Thus, when the coupon rate equals the yield rate, the coupon payments are exactly equal to the interest accrued—and the bond acts like an interest only loan and is selling at par.

In this case, the coupons are paying 6% nominal interest convertible semiannually, but the yield is only 4% convertible semiannually. Thus, each coupon payment is more than just interest. To account for this additional value, the bond must have sold for more than $1,000—in other words, it sold at a premium.

To find the exact selling price of the bond, recall the following formula, where the first part of the sum is the present value of the lump sum (redemption value) and the second part is the present value of the coupons:

$$\text{Selling price of a bond with coupons} = Fv^n + Fra_{\overline{n}|j} = Fv^n + Fr\left(\frac{1 - v^n}{j}\right),$$

where j is the effective rate per period (usually 6 months for a bond), n is the number of periods in the term, F is the face value of the bond, and r

is the coupon rate per period. *Note:* This formula assumes that the face value equals the redemption value.

In this example, $F = \$1{,}000$, $j = 0.02$, $r = 0.03$, and $n = 4$. Thus,

$$\text{Selling price of the bond with coupons} = Fv^n + Fra_{\overline{n}|j}$$

$$= 1{,}000\left(\frac{1}{1.02}\right)^4 + 1{,}000(0.03)a_{\overline{4}|0.02}$$

$$= \$923.85 + (30)3.807729 = \$1{,}038.08$$

This confirms what we predicted above—the bond is selling at a premium because the coupon payments of $30 every 6 months are paying more than the accrued interest of $\sim\$20$ every 6 months. Because the bond sold for $38.08 above face value, we say that the amount of premium for the bond is $38.08.

Definition

The **amount of premium (or discount)** is the absolute value of the difference between the selling price of the bond and the face value of the bond.

Think about it

How much capital did your company raise last year? How is the bond issue like taking out a loan and when payments will need to be made?

Since the company sold 10,000 bonds at $1,038.08 each, the company raised $10,380,800. This was like taking a loan, because the company needs to make payments of $300,000 every 6 months, three separate times (first three coupon payments; like interest payments), and then a payment of $10,300,000 at the end of the 2-year period (the lump sum payment and final coupon).

Book value of a bond

Since it's been 1 year since the bond was issued, an important question your company might be asking is how much of a liability the bonds are to your company currently. This **book value** is important for accounting purposes (e.g., for the company's balance sheet). The book value of the bonds can be thought of as the present value of the future coupon payments, plus the present value of the redemption price, calculated at the original yield rate at the time the bond was sold.

Definition

The **book value** of a bond is the present value of the future coupon payments, plus the present value of the redemption price calculated at the original yield rate at the time the bond was sold. It is the amount shown on the issuing company's balance sheet or "books" (hence the name "book" value).

Thus, the book value of the bond today (1 year after the bond was issued, and immediately after paying the second coupon) can be calculated as

$$\text{Book value 1 year after issue} = 1,000(0.03)a_{\overline{2}|0.02} + 1,000\left(\frac{1}{1.02}\right)^2$$

$$= \$1,019.42$$

Note that this is using the prospective method to value the bond.

Key idea

The prospective method can be used to find the book value of a bond at any point in time.

Think about it

Why is the book value on the bond lower than the price it sold for at issuance (\$1,038.08)?

The book value of the bond is less than the issuing price because it was issued at a premium. Thus, each coupon payment contains a mix of "interest" and "principal" and is *writing down the bond*.

Definition

Writing down a bond is when a bond sold at a premium has its book value decrease over time until it reaches par value when the bond is redeemed. Conversely, when a bond is sold at a discount, the coupon payments do not cover interest, and so the bond **is written up** until it reaches par value when the bond is redeemed.

The book value decreases only in the case for bonds sold at a premium. In Exploration 9.1 and the exercises, you will see that when a bond is sold at a discount, the book value increases—a process called *writing up the bond*. Table 9.1 shows the book values of the bond over time for the life of the bond.

Table 9.1 Book values of the bond every 6 months from issue until redemption

Half-year	Coupon payment	Book value ($)
0	—	1,038.08
1	30	1,028.84
2	30	1,019.42
3	30	1,009.80
4	30	1,000.00

Bond amortization schedule

Because a bond is like a loan where coupon payments act as payments on the loan, for a bond selling at premium, each coupon payment is paying a mix of interest earned and principal—just like a more typical fixed interest rate, amortized loan. Thinking of coupon payments in this way means that we can compute a complete amortization table for the bond—representing each coupon payment by the amount of interest earned and the "principal" paid down for a bond selling at premium.

To start, we can compute that the interest accrued in the first 6 months of the bond as $1,038.08 (0.02) = $20.76. Thus, the first coupon payment is paying off the $20.76 in interest, and then the remaining amount $30 − $20.76 = $9.24 is reducing the principal (book value). Thus, the new book value is $1,038.08 − $9.24 = $1,028.84. We continued this process to fill in the rest of Table 9.2—showing the complete

Table 9.2 Amortization of bond every 6 months from issue until redemption

Half-year	Coupon payment	Interest accrued ($)	Amortization of premium ($)	Book value ($)
0	—	—	—	1,038.08
1	30	20.76	9.24	1,028.84
2	30	20.58	9.42	1,019.42
3	30	20.39	9.61	1,009.80
4	30	20.20	9.80	1,000.00

amortization of the bond. You may also wish to use **Chapter 9 Excel file** to recreate this table on your own.

Thus, we can give the following formulas for the interest, book value, and amortized premium (or discount) immediately after any given coupon payment as

Half-year	Coupon payment	Interest accrued	Amortization of premium	Book value
k	Fr	jB_{k-1}	$Fr - jB_{k-1}$	$B_k = F(v)^{n-(k+1)} + Fra_{\overline{n-(k+1)}|j}$

A few remaining considerations are worth mentioning:

1. For a bond that sold at discount, the amortization of discount amount is called the **accumulation of discount** and will be a negative number using the formula shown above. The book value will increase in this scenario. See Exploration 9.1 and the homework exercises for details.

2. In practice, some companies use a straight-line method for computing book values rather than the formulas shown above. In essence, this approach reduces the book value by a fixed amount over-time (hence the name "straight-line"). In the example above, this would mean reducing the book value of the bond by $38.08/4 = 9.52 every 6 months.

3. Book value is not equivalent to market value—the price that the company could get for the bonds if they sold the loan (bonds) to someone else today. We'll tackle this issue in the next section.

EXPLORATION 9.1. VALUING A $1 MILLION BOND ISSUE

Two years ago, your small company issued 1,000, $1,000 face value bonds to raise capital to develop production-ready manufacturing processes for a new product. Your company issued the 3-year bonds to pay semiannual coupons at 2% nominal annual interest with semiannual compounding.

1. Approximately, how much money was the company hoping to raise? How big are the coupon payments?

Because your business is a small start-up and viewed as fairly risky by investors, the bonds sold at a yield of 4% nominal semiannually.

2. Will the bonds sell for a premium or discount? Why?

3. Find the selling price of the bonds and the amount of capital raised by the company.

The difference between the face value of a bond and the selling price of the bond is called the **amount of premium** or **amount of discount**.

Definition

The **amount of premium (or discount)** is the absolute value of the difference between the selling price of the bond and the face value of the bond.

---

4. What is the amount of discount for these bonds?

Book value of a bond

Since it's been 2 years since the bond was issued, an important question your company might be asking is how much of a liability the bonds are to your company currently. This book value is important for accounting purposes (e.g., for the company's balance sheet). The **book value** of the bonds can be thought of as the present value of the future coupon payments plus the present value of the redemption price, calculated at the original yield rate at the time the bond was sold.

Definition

The **book value** of a bond is the present value of the future coupon payments plus the present value of the redemption price calculated at the original yield rate at the time the bond was sold. It is the amount shown on the issuing company's balance sheet or "books" (hence the name "book" value).

---

5. Let's find the book value of the bond immediately after the fourth coupon payment was made (2 years after issue).

   a. First, use the yield rate (4% nominal, convertible semiannually) to find the present value of the remaining coupon payments.

   b. Then, use the yield rate to find the present value of the redemption price (lump sum).

   c. Add the present value of the coupon payments to the present value of the redemption price to find the book value of the bond.

This approach to finding book values of bonds is treating a bond like a loan and using the prospective method to find its book value.

Key idea

The prospective method can be used to find the book value of a bond at any point in time.

---

6. Why does it make sense that the book value of the bond is larger now than the issuing price?

The book value of the bond is more than the issuing price because it was issued at a discount. Thus, each coupon payment is not enough to cover the interest on the bond, and so the value of the bond (loan and debt) increases over time.

Definition

Writing down a bond is when a bond sold at a premium has its book value decrease over time until it reaches par value when the bond is redeemed. Conversely, when a bond is sold at a discount, the coupon payments do not cover interest and so the bond **is written up** until it reaches par value when the bond is redeemed.

The book value increases in the case for bonds sold at a discount. In Example 9.1 and the homework exercises, you can see that when a bond is sold at a premium, the book value decreases—a process called *writing down the bond*.

7. Find the two remaining book values by filling the missing values in Table 9.3. We've filled in the rest for you.

Table 9.3 Book values of the bond every 6 months from issue until redemption

Half-year	Coupon payment	Book value ($)
0	—	943.99
1	10	952.87
2	10	961.92
3	10	
4	10	980.59
5	10	
6	10	1,000.00

Bond amortization schedule

Because a bond is like a loan where coupon payments act as payments on the loan, for a bond selling at discount the coupon payment can be considered as not paying enough to cover the interest accrued. Thus, the interest capitalizes to the book value (loan value) over time. For a bond selling at a premium (see Example 9.1 and the homework exercises), the coupon payments are a mix of principal and interest.

Thinking of coupon payments as interest payments means that we can compute a complete amortization table for the bond—representing each coupon payment by the amount of interest earned and the "principal" paid down or capitalized for the bond.

8. If we view the $943.99 initial bond price as a loan to the company, and the yield rate as the interest rate on the loan, how much interest will accrue during the first 6 months of the loan?

9. If the $10 coupon payment gets applied toward the interest which accrued in the first 6 months, how much interest will need to be "capitalized" (added to the loan balance)?

10. Confirm that the amount of capitalized interest from the first half-year plus the selling price of the bond is equal to the book value of the bond after the first half-year (see Table 9.3).

11. Following the process, find the amount of interest which accrued during the second 6-month period (interest accumulated on the book value at the end of the first 6-month period), the capitalized interest and the book value at the end of the second 6-month period.

We could continue this process for the remainder of the bond term to compute the full amortization schedule for the bond. We've done this in Table 9.4. You should consider doing this yourself or further exploring bond book values by using the **Chapter 9 Excel file**.

Table 9.4 Amortization of bond every 6 months from issue until redemption

Half-year	Coupon payment	Interest accrued ($)	Accumulation of discount ($)	Book value ($)
0	–	–	–	943.99
1	10	18.88	8.88	952.87
2	10	19.06	9.06	961.92
3	10	19.24	9.24	971.16
4	10	19.42	9.42	980.59
5	10	19.61	9.61	990.20
6	10	19.80	9.80	1,000.00

Thus, we can give the following formulas for the interest, book value, and amortized premium (or discount) immediately after any given coupon payment as

Half-year	Coupon payment	Interest accrued	Accumulation of discount[a]	Book value
k	Fr	jB_{k-1}	$Fr - jB_{k-1}$	$B_k = F(v)^{n-(k+1)} + Fr a_{\overline{n-(k+1)}|j}$

[a]A negative number for a discount bond. The book value increases by the absolute value of the accumulation of discount.

A few remaining considerations are worth mentioning and are summarized at the end of Example 9.1.

SUMMARY

When a company issues bonds, the bonds act like a loan, with periodic coupon payments acting like interest payments on the loan. When a bond sells at a premium, the coupon payments are more than the interest accrued, and so a portion of the coupon payment goes toward the "principal" balance (book value) of the loan. When a bond sells at a discount, the coupon payments are not enough to cover the interest accrued and so the book value of the loan increases over time as the remaining interest is capitalized to the book value. If a bond sells at par, coupon payments exactly match the interest, and so the bond acts like an interest only loan. Importantly, the interest rates used when computing bond book values are the market yield rate at the time of issue and, so, since market yield rates can change during the life of the loan the market value of the bonds may not equal the book value.

Notation and formula summary

Thus, we can give the following formulas for the interest, book value, and amortized premium (or discount) immediately after any given coupon payment as

Half-year	Coupon payment	Interest accrued	Amortization of premium	Book value
k	Fr	jB_{k-1}	$Fr - jB_{k-1}$	$B_k = F(v)^{n-(k+1)} + Fr a_{\overline{n-(k+1)}|j}$

HOMEWORK QUESTIONS: SECTION 9.1

Conceptual questions

1. If a bond sells at par, its selling price is _____ (more than, less than, same as) the face value. If a bond sells at a premium, its selling price is _____ (more than, less than, same as) the face value. If a bond sells at a discount, its selling price is _____ (more than, less than, same as) the face value.

2. When a bond is sold at a premium, does its book value increase or decrease over time? Does the same thing happen when a bond is sold at a discount?

3. The book value of a bond consists of the sum of what two things?

4. The coupon payment consists of the sum of what two things?

5. A $1,000 bond is selling at par with $20 coupons each 6 months. How much is the amortization of the premium for the first coupon payment?

Practice questions

6. A 3-year $1,000 face value bond is issued with semiannual coupons at 4% convertible semiannually with a market yield of 5% convertible semiannually. What is the selling price of the bond?

7. In the bond described in the previous question, what is the book value of the bond after 2 years?

8. Suppose a bond has a book value of $1,025 after 1 year and was issued with semiannual coupons of 5% convertible semiannually with a market yield of 4% convertible semiannually. What is the accrued interest after 1.5 years? If the coupon payment is $25, what is the amortization of the premium?

9. Suppose the face value of a bond is $1,000. What is the amount of premium if it has $30 coupons and sells for $1,050?

10. A 2-year $1,000 face value bond is issued with semiannual coupons at X% convertible semiannually with a market yield of 5% convertible semiannually. The book value after 6 months is $957.16. What is the value of X?

Application questions

11. A 3-year $1,000 face value bond is issued with semiannual coupons at 4.5% convertible semiannually with a market yield of 5% convertible semiannually.

a. What is the selling price of the bond?
b. What is the book value after 1 year?
c. How much is a coupon payment?
d. For the coupon payment made after 1.5 years, how much of it is accrued interest and how much is the accumulation of discount?

12. A 3-year $1,000 face value bond is issued with semiannual coupons at 6% convertible semiannually with a market yield of 4% convertible semiannually.
a. What is the selling price of the bond?
b. What is the book value after 1 year?
c. How much is a coupon payment?
d. For the coupon payment made after 1.5 years, how much of it is accrued interest and how much is the amortization of premium?

13. A 3-year $1,000 face value bond is issued with semiannual coupons at 5% convertible semiannually with a market yield of 5% convertible semiannually.
a. What is the selling price of the bond?
b. What is the book value after 1 year?
c. How much is a coupon payment?
d. For the coupon payment made after 1.5 years, how much of it is accrued interest and how much is the accumulation of the discount?

14. A 2-year $1,000 face value bond is issued with semiannual coupons at 4% convertible semiannually with a market yield of 5% convertible semiannually. Complete the following table for the amortization of this bond.

Half-year	Coupon payment	Interest accrued	Accumulation of discount	Book value
0				
1				
2				
3				
4				$1,000

15. A 2-year $1,000 face value bond is issued with semiannual coupons at 5% convertible semiannually with a market yield of 4% convertible semiannually. Complete the following table for the amortization of this bond.

Half-year	Coupon payment	Interest accrued	Amortization of premium	Book value
0				
1				
2				
3				
4				$1,000

16. A 2-year $1,000 face value bond is issued with semiannual coupons at 4% convertible semiannually with a market yield of 4% convertible semiannually. Complete the following table for the amortization of this bond.

Half-year	Coupon payment	Interest accrued	Accumulation of discount	Book value
0				
1				
2				
3				
4				$1,000

SECTION 9.2.PRICING CALLABLE VS NONCALLABLE BONDS

Certain bonds, known as callable bonds, can be paid off early by the bond issuer. This is like paying off a loan early. When is this advantageous? How can calling a bond act like refinancing debt? We'll take these questions into consideration in this section.

Learning objectives

By the end of this section, you should be able to
- Distinguish between callable and non-callable bonds.
- Determine if it's financially advantageous to call a bond and reissue at a new interest rates and after paying a call premium.
- Distinguish between European, Bermuda, and American call options.

EXAMPLE 9.2. VALUING A $10 MILLION BOND ISSUE (CONTINUED)

In Example 9.1 we examined a situation where a company had issued 10,000, $1,000 bonds. We saw this 2-year bond paid 6% semiannual coupons and was sold to yield 4% nominal, semiannually. The full amortization of the bond, showing book values and interest is in Table 9.5.

Table 9.5 Amortization of bond every 6 months from issue until redemption

Half-year	Coupon payment	Interest accrued ($)	Amortization of premium	Book value
0	—	—	—	1,038.08
1	30	20.76	9.24	1,028.84
2	30	20.58	9.42	1,019.42
3	30	20.39	9.61	1,009.80
4	30	20.20	9.80	1,000.00

Bond strategies when interest rates change

As you can see above, after 1 year, the book value of this bond is $1,019.42. One reason the company was interested in evaluating this bond more closely is that interest rates have changed. Interest rates have dropped to 3.6% nominal, semiannually—a fairly big decline. What can the company do about their bonds (debt) which currently has a yield (interest rate) of 4%?

With a standard loan, a company may choose to refinance their debt to a lower interest rate to save the amount of interest they pay over time. For bonds, a similar strategy exists, but only if bond rules allow.

Some bonds are known as *callable bonds*. A **callable bond** is a bond with rules that allow for the issuer (e.g., company) to pay the bond off early.

Definition

A **callable bond** is a bond with rules that allow for the issuer (e.g., company) to pay the bond off early.

There are three standard options (ways) that a callable bond can be "called" (paid off early). The bond can have a **European option** (one specific date that the issuer can choose to redeem the bond), a **Bermuda option** (multiple specific dates that the issuer can choose to redeem the bond), or an **American option** (a range of dates that the issuer can choose to redeem the bond). Typically, an American option will have a range consisting of any date after an initial **lockdown period** and before the redemption date. Typically, if a callable bond is **called** (redeemed early), the issuer pays a higher price than if they wait until the standard redemption date. The price is higher because the issuer not only pays out the redemption value but also pays an additional amount called the **call premium**.

Definition

Callable bonds typically come with one of three options: **European** (one call date), **Bermuda** (multiple call dates), or **American** (range of call dates after an initial **lockdown period** where the bond cannot be called). The bond is called when it is redeemed early and is typically redeemed for a higher price—the redemption value plus the call premium.

Let's assume that the company has issued this bond with a European option giving them a single potential call date, which is 1 year from date the bond is issued. The call premium is $20, which means the early redemption price is $1,020. Recall, we assumed that because interest rates have dropped, the company believes it could issue new bonds today at a yield rate of 3.6% nominal semiannually, which is quite a bit less than the 4% nominal, semiannual yield rate on their current bonds and, thus, could potentially save the company money.

Should the company exercise their European call option?

Since the company has the option to call their bond, the question is, should they?

Think about it

What factors do you think should go into the company's decision to exercise their call option?

The change in interest rates is certainly a big factor that might impact the company's decision to call or not call their bond. Another factor could include the time/expense of calling the bonds which include paperwork, writing checks, mailing, etc. These transaction costs are real and important but are beyond the scope of this text. We'll assume they are $0, even though in reality they are not. Another factor could be whether or not the debt is needed any longer. For example, if the bond money was used to start a new plant and that plant is already profitable enough to payback the debt, the company may want to pay back the debt now instead of paying interest for another year. Finally, it's possible that a company's financial stability has changed enough that their credit rating is better which could impact the anticipated yield rate on the bonds. So, there are a number of reasons why a company might choose to call their bond.

Let's now look at the financial implications of calling the bond so that the company can make an informed decision about whether or not to call the bond.

What if the company does nothing?

If the company does nothing, they have two more coupon payments and the redemption payment left to make. Since they've issued 10,000 bonds and the coupon payments are $30 each and the redemption price is $1,000, this means that they have a $300,000 payment due 6 months from now and a $10,300,000 payment due 1 year from now, for a total of $10,600,000.

What if the company calls the bond?

If the company calls the bond, they have a $10,200,000 payment due today since the early payoff price is $1,020 for each of the 10,000 bonds.

In order to evaluate whether the company should call the bond or not, the company needs to know the terms of the refinance needed to raise $10,200,000 today. If the company is looking to refinance their debt, how many bonds will the company need to sell to do the refinance?

Earlier we said that yield rates today were 3.6% nominal, semiannually. If the company again does $30 coupons for 1 year and a 1-year redemption (so the redemption time is the same as originally scheduled), the current selling price of the new bonds is

$$\text{Selling price of reissued bond} = \$30v + \$1,030v^2 = \frac{\$30}{1.018} + \frac{\$1,030}{1.018^2}$$
$$= \$1,023.37$$

Thus, the company needs to sell $10,200,000/$1,023.37 $\approx$ 9,967 bonds today in order to pay off the original bonds and "refinance" their debt.

To determine whether or not this is a better deal for the company than holding their original bond, we evaluate the total out-of-pocket costs for the company at the 3rd and 4th half-years under each scenario in Table 9.6.

Table 9.6 Out-of-pocket costs for the company over time—call premium $20

Time	Keep original bond (10,000 bonds sold) ($)	Refinance (9,967 bonds sold) ($)	Savings (loss) ($)
3rd half-year	300,000	299,010	990
4th half-year	10,300,000	10,266,010	33,990
Total	10,600,000	10,565,020	34,980

Table 9.6 shows that the company saves approximately $35,000 by refinancing their debt through the new bond issue. Thus, the company should issue the new bonds.

Does refinancing always make sense?

While refinancing makes sense for the company in this scenario, what if the call premium was $25? Would it still make sense to refinance? In this modified scenario, the company will need to raise $10,250,000 at the time it reissues bonds, meaning that it will need to sell $10,250,000/ $1,023.37 $\approx$ 10,016 new bonds.

Table 9.7 shows that the company loses approximately $16,960 refinancing their debt through the new bond issue if the call premium is $25 per bond. Thus, with the higher call premium, it doesn't make sense to refinance.

Table 9.7 Out-of-pocket costs for the company over time—call premium $25

Time	Keep original bond (10,000 bonds sold) ($)	Refinance (10,016 bonds sold) ($)	Savings (loss) ($)
3rd half-year	300,000	300,480	(480)
4th half-year	10,300,000	10,316,488	(16,480)
Total	10,600,000	10,616,960	(16,960)

Notice in our first scenario with a $20 call premium, the number of bonds that needed to be sold was less than that of the original 10,000. However, in the second scenario with a $25 call premium, the number of bonds that needed to be sold was more than that of the original 10,000. This leads to an important key idea about bond refinancing. If the terms are the same as the original (same coupon size and redemption date), then if the number of bonds that need to be sold is less than the number currently issued, refinancing will be advantageous; if it is more, it won't be advantageous.

Key idea

When considering a bond refinance, if the terms are the same as the original (same coupon size and redemption date), then if the number of bonds that need to be sold is less than the number currently issued, refinancing will be advantageous; if it is more, it won't be advantageous.

EXPLORATION 9.2. VALUING A $1 MILLION BOND ISSUE (CONTINUED)

In the previous section, we examined a situation where a small company had issued 1,000, $1,000, 3-year bonds at a discount (2% nominal semiannual coupons; 4% nominal, semiannual yield rate).

The full amortization of the bond showing book values and interest is shown in Table 9.8.

Bond strategies when interest rates change

After 2 years, the book value of the bond is $980.59. One reason the company was interested in evaluating this bond more closely is that the

Table 9.8 Amortization of bond every 6 months from issue until redemption

Half-year	Coupon payment	Interest accrued ($)	Accumulation of discount ($)	Book value ($)
0	—	—	—	943.99
1	10	18.88	8.88	952.87
2	10	19.06	9.06	961.92
3	10	19.24	9.24	971.16
4	10	19.42	9.42	980.59
5	10	19.61	9.61	990.20
6	10	19.80	9.80	1,000.00

company is on more solid financial footing now and market interest rates have dropped. Thus, they believe that they can probably get a lower yield rate now than compared to when they issued the bonds 2 years ago. In particular, they believe that they can now get a yield rate of 2.4% nominal, semiannually—a fairly large decline.

1. If this was a bank loan instead of a bond issue, what might the company do to potentially take advantage of this lower interest rate?

If the company had taken a standard loan, they would likely approach the bank about refinancing their debt. A similar strategy is available for certain types of bonds.

Some bonds are known as *callable bonds*. A **callable bond** is a bond with rules that allow for the issuer (e.g., company) to pay the bond off early.

Definition

A **callable bond** is a bond with rules that allow for the issuer (e.g., company) to pay the bond off early.

There are three standard options (ways) that a callable bond can be "called" (paid off early). It can have a **European option** (one specific date that the issuer can choose to redeem the bond), a **Bermuda option** (multiple specific dates that the issuer can choose to redeem the bond), or an **American option** (a range of dates that the issuer can choose to redeem the bond). Typically, an American option will have a range consisting of any date after an initial **lockdown period** and before the redemption date. Typically, if a callable bond is **called** (redeemed early), the issuer pays a higher price than if they wait until the standard redemption date. The price is higher because the issuer not only pays out the redemption value but also pays an additional amount called the **call premium**.

Definition

Callable bonds typically come with one of three options: **European** (one call date), **Bermuda** (multiple call dates), or **American** (range of call dates after an initial **lockdown period** where the bond cannot be called). The bond is called when it is redeemed early and is typically redeemed for a higher price—the redemption value plus the call premium.

Let's assume that the company has issued this bond with a European option giving them a single potential call back time of 1 year from bond issue. The call premium is $20, which means the early redemption price is $1,020.

Should the company exercise their European call option?

2. What factors do you think should go into the company's decision to exercise their call option?

3. If the company does nothing, what payments are still due on the bond issue? When? What is the total value of the payments?

4. If the company calls the bond using their European option today, what payments are needed on the bonds? When? What is the total value of the payments?

Since the company does not have enough cash on hand to pay off the bonds today, they will need to issue new bonds and use that money to call (pay off) the existing bonds.

5. If the company issues a 1-year bond with $10 coupons, face value $1,000, and at a yield rate of 2.4% nominal, semiannually, what is the selling price of the bond? Will the bond sell at a discount or premium? Why?

6. How many bonds will the company need to sell today in order to cover the cost of calling the original bonds?

7. What payments will be due on the newly issued bonds? When? What is the total value of the payments?

8. Fill in Table 9.9, which compares the payments (totaled across 1,000 bonds) for the original bond and the payments (totaled across 1,024 bonds) for the newly issued bond. Compare these values in the third column.

Table 9.9 Out-of-pocket costs for the company over time—call premium $20; yield rate 2.4%

Time	Keep original bond (1,000 bonds sold) ($)	Refinance (1,024 bonds sold)	Savings (loss)
5th half-year	10,000		
6th half-year	1,010,000		
Total	1,020,000		

9. Based on the savings/loss that will be incurred by the company, do you believe that the company should refinance (call the original bonds and reissue) or stick with the original bonds? Why?

While not advantageous in this scenario, if the call premium was lower or the interest rate was lower, it might be advantageous to reissue bonds.

Now, let's assume that the call premium is only $5 per bond and the yield rate is 0.8% nominal with semiannual compounding, while the face value of the bond stays at $1,000 with $10 coupons. Let's evaluate whether the company should call the and reissue the bonds in this scenario

10. If the company calls the bond, what is the total cost of paying off the bonds? What is the issuing price of the new bonds? How many bonds will the company need to issue in this scenario?

11. Fill in Table 9.10 comparing refinancing via a new bond issue to keeping the original bond.

Table 9.10 Out-of-pocket costs for the company over time—call premium $5; nominal yield rate 0.8%

Time	Keep original bond (1,000 bonds sold) ($)	Refinance (993 bonds sold)	Savings (loss)
5th half-year	10,000		
6th half-year	1,010,000		
Total	1,020,000		

12. Is it advantageous for the company to reissue the bonds in this new scenario (call premium of $5 and 0.8% yield rate)? Why?

Notice in our first scenario with a $20 call premium, the number of bonds that needed to be sold was more than the original 1,000. However, in the second scenario with a $5 call premium, the number of bonds that needed to be sold was less than the original 1,000. This leads to an important key idea about bond refinancing. If the terms are the same as the original (same coupon size and redemption date), then if the number of bonds that need to be sold is less than the number currently issued, refinancing will be advantageous; if it is more, it won't be advantageous.

Key idea

When considering a bond refinance, if the terms are the same as the original (same coupon size and redemption date), then if the number of bonds that need to be sold is less than the number currently issued, refinancing will be advantageous; if it is more, it won't be advantageous.

SUMMARY

Some bonds are callable, meaning that the company issuing the bonds has the option to pay off (call) the bonds early much like a standard bank loan where a company has the option to pay off the loan early. One reason to call a bond is to take advantage of a lower interest rate to refinance the debt and save money in the long run. Different rules for calling bonds exist including the timing of when the bond can be called, and, potentially, a premium that must be paid from the company (borrower) to the investor (lender) for the privilege of calling the bond early.

HOMEWORK QUESTIONS: SECTION 9.2

Conceptual questions

1. What does it mean for a bond to be callable?

2. What is the difference between the European option, Bermuda option, and American option when it terms of callable bonds?

3. In what direction do interest rates have to change for it to be possible to be financially advantageous for a company to call their bonds?

4. What two things does a company have to pay to the owner of a bond when the bond is called?

5. Because of an interest rate change, a company is considering calling 5,000 bonds. They calculate that they will have to sell 5,045 new bonds at the same price, coupon size, and redemption rate to cover the cost of calling them. Is it financially advantageous for them to call their original 5,000 bonds?

Practice questions

6. A company sold 1,000 bonds that had a redemption value of $500. These bonds pay 4% semiannual coupons, yield 3% convertible semi-annually, have a $10 call premium, and a redemption time of 2 years. If these bonds are called after 1 year, what is the payoff price? How much would it cost the company to call all the bonds?

7. Suppose it costs a company to $765,000 to call 750 bonds after a year on the market. The new bonds will pay 4% semiannual cou-pons, yield 3% convertible semiannually, have a redemption value of $1,000, and a redemption time of 1 year. What is the selling price of

the new bonds? How many will have to be sold to cover the cost to call the original bonds?

8. Suppose it costs a company $1,020,000 to call 1,000 bonds after a year on the market. The new bonds will pay 5% semiannual coupons, yield 4% convertible semiannually, have a redemption value of $1,000, and a redemption time of 1.5 years. What is the selling price of the new bonds? How many will have to be sold to cover the cost to call the original bonds?

9. A company sold 1,000 bonds that had a redemption value of $500. These bonds pay 4% semiannual coupons, yield 3% convertible semiannually, have a $10 call premium, and a redemption time of 1 year. What is the out-of-pocket cost for the company after 6 months? 1 year?

10. A company sold 5,000 bonds that had a redemption value of $1,000. These bonds pay 3% semiannual coupons, yield 4% convertible semiannually, have a $20 call premium, and a redemption time of 1 year. What is the out-of-pocket cost for the company after 6 months? 1 year?

Application questions

11. A company sold 1,000 bonds that had a redemption value of $500. These bonds pay 4% semiannual coupons, yield 3% convertible semiannually, have a $10 call premium, and a redemption time of 2 years.

   a. If these bonds are called after 1 year, what is the payoff price? How much would it cost the company to call all the bonds?

   b. The market rate drops to 2.5% and the company is considering selling new bonds with the same coupon rate as before and a redemption time of 1 year. How much would these bonds sell for?

   c. How many bonds need to be sold to cover the total cost to call them?

   d. To determine whether or not it is in the best interest of the company to call the bonds, complete the following table for the out-of-pocket costs for the company during the second year of the original bonds (or the first year of the new ones).

Time	Keep original bond (1,000 bonds sold)	Refinance (??? bonds sold)	Savings (loss)
3rd half-year			
4th half-year			
Total			

    e. What is the total savings or loss for the company if they call the bonds and sell new ones?

12. A company sold 5,000 bonds that had a redemption value of $1,000. These bonds pay 3% semiannual coupons, yield 4% convertible semi-annually, have a $25 call premium, and a redemption time of 2 years.
    a. If these bonds are called after 1 year, what is the payoff price? How much would it cost the company to call all the bonds?
    b. The market rate drops to 3.75% and the company is considering selling new bonds with the same coupon rate as before and a redemption time of 1 year. How much would these bonds sell for?
    c. How many bonds need to be sold to cover the total cost to call them?
    d. To determine whether or not it is in the best interest of the company to call the bonds, complete the following table for the out-of-pocket costs for the company during the second year of the original bonds (or the first year of the new ones).

Time	Keep original bond (5,000 bonds sold)	Refinance (??? bonds sold)	Savings (loss)
3rd half-year			
4th half-year			
Total			

    e. What is the total savings or loss for the company if they call the bonds and sell new ones?

13. A company sold 10,000 bonds that had a redemption value of
    $1,000. These bonds pay 4% semiannual coupons, yield 3% convert-
    ible semiannually, have a $20 call premium, and a redemption time
    of 2 years.
    a. If these bonds are called after 1 year, what is the payoff price?
       How much would it cost the company to call all the bonds?
    b. The market rate drops to 2.75% and the company is considering
       selling new bonds, raising the coupon rate to 5%, and having a
       redemption time of 1 year. How much would these bonds sell
       for?
    c. How many bonds need to be sold to cover the total cost to call
       them?
    d. To determine whether or not it is in the best interest of the com-
       pany to call the bonds, complete the following table for the out-
       of-pocket costs for the company during the second year of the
       original bonds (or the first year of the new ones).

Time	Keep original bond (1,000 bonds sold)	Refinance (??? bonds sold)	Savings (loss)
3rd half-year			
4th half-year			
Total			

    e. What is the total savings or loss for the company if they call the
       bonds and sell new ones?
    f. One of the key ideas of this section was that if the number of
       bonds that need to be sold is less than the number currently
       issued (under certain circumstances), refinancing will be advanta-
       geous. Was refinancing advantageous in this case? What circum-
       stances were not met here?

14. A company sold 10,000 bonds that had a redemption value of
    $1,000. These bonds pay 4% semiannual coupons, yield 3% convert-
    ible semiannually, have a $15 call premium, and a redemption time
    of 3 years.
    a. If these bonds are called after 1 year, what is the payoff price?
       How much would it cost the company to call all the bonds?

b. The market rate drops to 2.75% and the company is considering selling new bonds with the same coupon rate as before and a redemption time of 2 years. How much would these bonds sell for?

c. How many bonds need to be sold to cover the total cost to call them?

d. To determine whether or not it is in the best interest of the company to call the bonds, complete the following table for the out-of-pocket costs for the company during the second year of the original bonds (or the first year of the new ones).

Time	Keep original bond (10,000 bonds sold)	Refinance (??? bonds sold)	Savings (loss)
3rd half-year			
4th half-year			
5th half-year			
6th half-year			
Total			

e. What is the total savings or loss for the company if they call the bonds and sell new ones?

15. Suppose you had the same parameters as in the previous question: what would be the total savings or loss for the company if they call the bonds after 2 years and reissue new bonds for 1 year?

SECTION 9.3. SPOT AND FORWARD RATES

In this final section of Chapter 9, we dig deeper into the concept of a bond yield rate. As we've discussed, the yield rate is determined by many market factors and is not determined by the company issuing the bond. While an in-depth treatment of ways to compute/estimate yield rates is beyond the scope of this text, in this section, we will see how the idea of a yield rate can be viewed as a function of other interest rates known as spot rate and future rates.

Learning objectives

By the end of this section, you should be able to
- Understand the terms spot rate and forward rate.
- Compute spot rates from forward rates and vice versa using the arbitrage principal.

EXAMPLE 9.3. MAKING BOND PRICING DECISIONS

As an investor, you are looking at the bond market and notice that the yield rates for two bonds are not the same (see Table 9.11).

Table 9.11 Yield rates for two grade a, $1,000 bonds with annual 1% coupons

Bond	Term (year)	Yield (effective annual) (%)	Selling price ($)
A	1	1	1,000.00
B	2	2	980.58

Since the bonds have similar grades (this means that the perceived risk of default by the company is the same), this doesn't explain why the yield rates are different.

Think about it
Why might the yield rates be different?

In this case, the most likely explanation for the yield rates being different is that the marketplace perceives that the economy will improve over time and so a higher yield rate for the longer term bond makes sense. Up until now, we've computed bond yield rates as an internal rate of return (dollar-weighted yield rate), which ignores the fact that the marketplace (which is driving yield rates) is typically anticipating changes in interest rates over time.

Key idea
Bond yield rates are dollar-weighted rates of return and, thus, are "average" market yield rates over the term of the bond, averaged over the various coupon payments and the redemption payment.

Spot rates

To help get a somewhat more realistic sense of how the marketplace is arriving at a given overall "average" yield rate, it is helpful to define a spot rate.

Definition

A **spot rate**, s_t, is the annual effective rate of interest earned by money invested now for a period of t years.

The 1-year bond (Bond A) can be viewed as an amount of money invested for 1 year, since there is only a single cash flow 1 year from now. This bond pays $1,010 one year from now and is currently selling for $1,000. Thus, the spot rate, s_1, is 0.01 since

$$\$1,000 = \frac{\$1,010}{1 + s_1}$$

So, in this case, the spot rate equals the yield rate. This is because the 1-year bond with annual coupons only has a single cash flow. This also means that all zero-coupon bonds will have spot rates equal to their yield rates.

Key idea

Spot rates equal yield rates for zero-coupon bonds because there is only a single cash flow.

But, what is the 2-year spot rate, s_2? It's not simply 2%. Bond B has two cash flows and the 2% is the dollar weighted rate of return (average) yield rate across both cash flows. To find s_2, consider the following equation relating the present value of the bond to both its future cash flows in terms of the two spot rates (instead of the "average" dollar weighted rate of return).

$$\$980.58 = \frac{\$10}{1 + s_1} + \frac{\$1,010}{(1 + s_2)^2} = \frac{\$10}{1 + 0.01} + \frac{\$1,010}{(1 + s_2)^2}$$

Thus, $s_2 = 0.020053$. In other words, the market is currently paying 2.0053% annually on money invested today that pays out in 2 years that has a similar amount of market risk (e.g., is at a similar grade).

Using spot rates to compute zero-coupon bond prices

Based on the key idea above, if you know that the 2-year spot rate is 2.0053%, then you can easily compute the price of a similarly graded 2-year, zero coupon bond. For example, a $1,000 2-year zero-coupon bond will be selling for $\$1,000/(1+s_2)^2 = \$1,000/(1+0.020053)^2 = \$961.07$.

Think about it

Why is the present value of the 2-year zero coupon bond less than the present value of the 2-year coupon bond?

The difference in price is due to the coupons and the fact that that the first coupon is governed by a different spot rate than the second coupon and redemption price.

Using spot rates to compute yield rates

We've used yield rates to compute spot rates, but how about the other way around? What if you are told that the 3-year spot rate is 2.2% effective annually? What is the yield rate on a similarly graded 3-year, $1,000 bond with 1% annual coupons? To start, we can find the selling price for the bond as

$$
\begin{aligned}
\text{Selling price} &= \frac{\$10}{1+s_1} + \frac{\$10}{(1+s_2)^2} + \frac{\$1,010}{(1+s_3)^3} \\
&= \frac{\$10}{1+0.01} + \frac{\$10}{(1+0.020053)^2} + \frac{\$1,010}{(1+0.022)^3} \\
&= \$965.68
\end{aligned}
$$

Realizing that the yield rate is a dollar-weighted rate of return (or internal rate of return), we can find the yield rate on the bond, i, by solving the following equation:

$$
\$965.68 = \frac{\$10}{1+i} + \frac{\$10}{(1+i)^2} + \frac{\$1,010}{(1+i)^3}
$$

Using the IRR function in Excel, or guess-and-check yields a value of i equal to 0.021946. Thus, this 3-year bond has a 2.1946% yield rate.

Forward rate

Spot rates give you some information about the anticipated future market performance, but a 3-year spot rate (e.g., $s_3 = 0.022$ above) is still "averaged" over the entire 3-year period. A spot rate doesn't tell you what the market anticipates happening just in year 3.

Definition
A **forward rate**, f_{t_1,t_2} is the anticipated market interest rate on money invested at time t_1 and held until time t_2.

Spot rates can be thought of as a function of forward rates. For example:

$$(1+s_2)^2 = (1 + f_{0,1})(1 + f_{1,2})$$

In other words, the rate of return on money invested for 2 years can be thought of as the product of the growth factor in the first year times the growth factor in the second year. For the bonds we have been investigating here, this means that

$$(1+s_2)^2 = 1.020053^2 = 1.040508 = (1 + f_{0,1})(1 + f_{1,2}) = (1.01)(1 + f_{1,2}).$$

Noticed we used the fact that the 1-year spot rate, s_1, is the same as $f_{0,1}$ so $1 + f_{1,2} = 1.030206$ or $f_{1,2} = 0.030206$. This means that it is anticipated that the market will not do as well this coming year (1% yield) as compared to the following year (3.0206% yield).

These relationships hold in general as shown in the following equations:

1. $(1+s_n)^n = (1 + f_{0,1})(1 + f_{1,2})\ldots(1 + f_{n-1,n})$

2. $1 + s_1 = 1 + f_{0,1}$

This leads us to the fact that spot rates and forward rates are consistent with each other.

Key idea
Spot rates completely determine forward rates, and vice versa

---

Think about it

How can you use spot rates to find the value of $f_{2,3}$? How do you interpret this value?

$$(1+s_3)^3 = 1.022^3 = 1.06743 = (1.01)(1.030206)\left(1 + f_{2,3}\right)$$

Thus, $f_{2,3} = 0.025905$. This means that the market is currently anticipating that money invested at the beginning of year 3 will earn 2.5905% for that year. This is lower than the market anticipated yield in year 2 (3.0206%) but better than year 1 (1%).

Important notes

1. If you look at bond pricing through the lens of spot rates, you can no longer "quickly" compute bond prices using annuity formulas; you have to compute the price of each payment (coupon or redemption) separately.

2. Underlying the principles relating spot rates, yield rates, and forward rates is the principle of no arbitrage. Arbitrage would mean that there was a risk free way for an investor to make money. "No arbitrage" says that's impossible. Further exploration of arbitrage is relegated to future courses.

3. Forward rates offer an opportunity for an investor to consider different investment strategies. For example, if the implied forward rate for a certain class of bonds is 2% for year 2, but you think that by then interest rates will increase, you may choose not to buy bonds now but instead wait a year to buy.

EXPLORATION 9.3. UNDERSTANDING BOND PRICING AS AN INVESTOR

As an investor, you are looking at the bond market and notice that the yield rates for two different bonds have different yield rates (see Table 9.12).

Table 9.12 Yield rates for two grade a, $1,000 bonds with annual 3% coupons

Bond	Term (year)	Yield (effective annual) (%)	Selling price
A	1	3	
B	2	5	

1. Find the selling price for each bond and fill the values into Table 9.12.

2. What are some reasons why the yield rates may be different between the two bonds? Hint: Who determines the yield rate?

Since the bonds have similar grades (this means that the perceived risk of default by the company is the same) this doesn't explain why the yield rates are different. Instead, the more likely driver of the different yield rates is that the market perceives that interest rates will change over time.

Up until now, we've computed bond yield rates as an internal rate of return (dollar-weighted yield rate), which ignores the fact that the marketplace (which is driving yield rates) is typically anticipating changes in interest rates over time.

Key idea

Bond yield rates are dollar-weighted rates of return and, thus, are "average" market yield rates over the term of the bond, averaged over the various coupon payments and the redemption payment.

Spot rates

To help get a somewhat more realistic sense of how the marketplace is arriving at a given yield rate, it is helpful to define a *spot rate*.

Definition

A **spot rate**, s_t, is the annual effective rate of interest earned by money invested now for a period of t years.

---

3. Based on Bond A, what is the value of s_1, the 1-year spot rate? Why?

This brings us to an important key idea involving bonds with a single cash flow.

Key idea

Spot rates equal yield rates for zero-coupon bonds because there is only a single cash flow.

---

4. Finding the 2-year spot rate takes a bit more work, but before we do, make a prediction: Do you think the 2-year spot rate (s_2) will be larger or smaller than the 1-year spot rate, s_1? Why?

   If we think of each of the cash flows for Bond B separately, we can write the present value of Bond B as a function of each cash flow and the spot rates, s_1 and s_2.

$$\text{Present value} = \frac{C_1}{1 + s_1} + \frac{C_2}{(1 + s_2)^2}$$

5. Use the present value of the bond, the cash flow amounts, and the value of s_1 to find the 2-year spot rate, s_2.

Using spot rates to compute zero-coupon bond prices

6. What is the present value of a similarly graded, 2-year zero-coupon bond with face value $1,000?

7. Why is the present value of the 2-year zero-coupon bond less than the present value of the 2-year coupon bond?

Using spot rates to compute yield rates

We've used yield rates to compute spot rates, but how about the other way around?

8. If the 3-year spot rate, s_3, is 6.5%, find the selling price of a 3-year, $1,000 bond with 3% annual coupons.

9. What is the yield rate on the bond? Use the IRR function Excel, your calculator's bond worksheet, or guess-and-check.

10. Why do you think that the yield rate is so close to the 3-year spot rate?

Forward rate

Spot rates give you some information about the anticipated future market performance, but a 3-year spot rate (e.g., $s_3 = 0.065$ above) is still "averaged" over the entire 3-year period. A spot rate doesn't tell you what the market anticipates happening just in year three.

Definition

A forward rate, f_{t_1,t_2}, is the anticipated market interest rate on money invested at time t_1 and held until time t_2.

Spot rates can be thought of as a function of forward rates. For example,

$$(1+s_2)^2 = (1+f_{0,1})(1+f_{1,2})$$
$$1 + s_1 = 1 + f_{0,1}$$

In other words, the rate of return on money invested for 2 years can be thought of as the product of the growth factor for the first year times the growth factor in the second year.

11. What is $f_{0,1}$, the rate the market anticipates earning on money invested now (time 0) until time 1? What other symbol/term did we just use for this?

12. What is $f_{1,2}$? Interpret this value.

These relationships hold in general as shown in the following equation:

$$(1+s_n)^n = (1+f_{0,1})(1+f_{1,2})\ldots(1+f_{n-1,n})$$

This leads us to the fact that spot rates and forward rates are consistent with each other.

Key idea

Spot rates completely determine forward rates, and vice versa

13. What is $f_{2,3}$? Interpret this value.

14. How would you describe consumer sentiments about the next 3 years?

See the end of Example 9.3 for some additional important comments.

HOMEWORK QUESTIONS: SECTION 9.3

Conceptual questions

1. Why do spot rates equal yield rates for zero-coupon bonds?

2. If spot rates are going to be different on a single investment, are they different for each year (or compounding period) or different for each cash flow?

3. Is a spot rate often an average rate over multiple time periods? Is a forward rate often an average rate over multiple time periods?

4. What is the meaning of $f_{3,4}$?

5. Suppose a 2-year \$500 bond with \$10 annual coupons has spot rates of s_1 and s_2 where $s_1 \neq s_2$. Will the yield rate be closer to s_1 or s_2? Explain why.

6. If $f_{0,1} = f_{1,2} = f_{2,3} = 0.02$ for a 3-year bond, what are the values of s_1, s_2, and s_3? What is the value of the yield rate?

7. Which of the following is the correct way to calculate s_2?
   a. $s_2 = \left(1 + f_{0,1}\right)\left(1 + f_{1,2}\right)$
   b. $s_2 = \left(1 + f_{0,1}\right)\left(1 + f_{1,2}\right) - 1$
   c. $s_2 = \sqrt{\left(1 + f_{0,1}\right)\left(1 + f_{1,2}\right)} - 1$
   d. $s_2 = \sqrt{\left(1 + f_{0,1}\right)\left(1 + f_{1,2}\right) - 1}$

Practice questions

8. Suppose a 3-year \$500 bond with \$10 coupons has spot rates of $s_1 = 0.01$, $s_2 = 0.015$, and $s_3 = 0.02$. What is the selling price of the bond?

9. The present value of a 2-year $1,000 bond with $30 annual coupons is $986.01. The spot rate for the first year is $s_1 = 0.03$. What is the value of s_2?

10. The forward rate for a bond for year 1 is 0.01, year 2 is 0.01 and year 3 is 0.03. What is the three-year spot rate, s_3?

11. Suppose the spot rate over a 3-year period is 2.658%, the forward rate for the first year is $f_{0,1} = 4.5\%$, and the forward rate for the second year is $f_{1,2} = 1.5\%$. What is the forward rate for the third year?

12. A 2-year $1,000 bond with annual coupons has a 1-year spot rate of $s_1 = 2\%$ and a 2-year spot rate of $s_2 = 3\%$ If the selling price of the bond is $971.44, what is the value of the coupons?

Application questions

13. A 2-year $1,000 bond with $20 annual coupons has a 1-year spot rate of $s_1 = 2\%$ and a 2-year spot rate of $s_2 = 3.25\%$.
    a. What is the selling price of the bond?
    b. What is the yield rate for the bond?
    c. What is $f_{0,1}$?
    d. What is $f_{1,2}$?

14. A 3-year $1,000 bond with $20 annual coupons has a 1-year spot rate of $s_1 = 2\%$, a 2-year spot rate of $s_2 = 3.25\%$, and an annual yield rate of 3%.
    a. What is the selling price of the bond?
    b. What is the 3-year spot rate, s_3, for the bond?
    c. What is $f_{0,1}$?
    d. What is $f_{1,2}$?
    e. What is $f_{2,3}$?

15. A 3-year $1,000 bond with $20 annual coupons has the following forward rates: $f_{0,1} = 0.02$, $f_{1,2} = 0.025$, $f_{2,3} = 0.03$.
    a. What are the values of s_1, s_2, and s_3?
    b. What is the selling price of the bond?
    c. What is the yield rate for the bond?

16. A 2-year $500 bond with $10 annual coupons sells for $495. If the 1-year spot rate is 2%, find the values of the following.
  a. s_2
  b. $f_{0,1}$
  c. $f_{1,2}$
  d. Yield rate

17. A 3-year $1,000 bond with 3% annual coupons has a 1-year spot rate of $s_1 = 2\%$, a 2-year spot rate of $s_2 = 2.5\%$, and a 3-year spot rate of $s_2 = 3.5\%$.
  a. What is the selling price of the bond?
  b. What is the yield rate for the bond?
  c. What is $f_{0,1}$?
  d. What is $f_{1,2}$?
  e. What is $f_{2,3}$?

END OF CHAPTER SUMMARY

In this chapter, we dug deeper into bonds. In particular, we explored how to compute the amortization schedule for bonds, allowing a company to compute a "book value" (or current valuation of bond debt) for their company's balance sheet. We then saw how a company can make decisions about whether or not to call a bond early based on the market yield rates, call premiums, and the calling rules for the bond they have issued. Finally, we took a look into a bit more about how market yield rates for bonds are really dollar-weighted yield rates (IRR), but these average yield rates can be thought of as a function of spot rates and forward rates.

END OF CHAPTER EXERCISES

(SOA EXAM FM SAMPLE QUESTIONS May 2000, Question 43)

1. A 1,000 par value 5-year bond with 8.0% semi-annual coupons was bought to yield 7.5% convertible semi-annually.

Determine the amount of premium amortized in the 6th coupon payment.

A. 2.00

B. 2.08

C. 2.15

D. 2.25

E. 2.34

(SOA EXAM FM SAMPLE QUESTIONS May 2003, Question 42)

2. A 10,000 par value 10-year bond with 8% annual coupons is bought at a premium to yield an annual effective rate of 6%.

Calculate the interest portion of the 7th coupon.

A. 632

B. 642

C. 651

D. 660

E. 667

(SOA EXAM FM SAMPLE QUESTIONS May 2005, Question 11)

3. A 1,000 par value bond pays annual coupons of 80. The bond is redeemable at par in 30 years, but is callable any time from the end of the 10th year at 1050.

Based on her desired yield rate, an investor calculates the following potential purchase prices, P:

- Assuming the bond is called at the end of the 10th year, $P = 957$
- Assuming the bond is held until maturity, $P = 897$
- The investor buys the bond at the highest price that guarantees she will receive at least her desired yield rate regardless of when the bond is called.
- The investor holds the bond for 20 years, after which time the bond is called.

  Calculate the annual yield rate the investor earns.

  A. 8.56%

  B. 9.00%

  C. 9.24%

D. 9.53%
E. 9.99%

(SOA EXAM FM SAMPLE QUESTIONS November 2005, Question 22)

4. A 1,000 par value bond with coupons at 9% payable semi-annually was called for 1,100 prior to maturity.

   The bond was bought for 918 immediately after a coupon payment and was held to call. The nominal yield rate convertible semi-annually was 10%.
   Calculate the number of years the bond was held.
   A. 10
   B. 25
   C. 39
   D. 49
   E. 54

(SOA EXAM FM SAMPLE QUESTIONS Interest Theory, Question 54)

5. Matt purchased a 20-year par value bond with an annual nominal coupon rate of 8% payable semi-annually at a price of 1,722.25. The bond can be called at par value X on any coupon date starting at the end of year 15 after the coupon is paid. The lowest yield rate that Matt can possibly receive is a nominal annual interest rate of 6% convertible semi-annually.

   Calculate X.
   A. 1,400
   B. 1,420
   C. 1,440
   D. 1,460
   E. 1,480

(SOA EXAM FM SAMPLE QUESTIONS Interest Theory, Question 55)

6. Toby purchased a 20-year par value bond with semi-annual coupons of 40 and a redemption value of 1,100. The bond can be called at 1,200 on any coupon date prior to maturity, starting at the end of year 15.

   Calculate the maximum price of the bond to guarantee that Toby will earn an annual nominal interest rate of at least 6% convertible semi-annually.
   A. 1,251
   B. 1,262
   C. 1,278
   D. 1,286
   E. 1,295

   (SOA EXAM FM SAMPLE QUESTIONS Interest Theory, Question 56)

7. Sue purchased a 10-year par value bond with an annual nominal coupon rate of 4% payable semi-annually at a price of 1,021.50. The bond can be called at par value X on any coupon date starting at the end of year 5. The lowest yield rate that Sue can possibly receive is an annual nominal rate of 6% convertible semi-annually.

   Calculate X.
   A. 1,120
   B. 1,140
   C. 1,160
   D. 1,180
   E. 1,200

   (SOA EXAM FM SAMPLE QUESTIONS Interest Theory, Question 57)

8. Mary purchased a 10-year par value bond with an annual nominal coupon rate of 4% payable semi-annually at a price of 1,021.50. The bond can be called at 100 over the par value of 1,100 on any coupon date starting at the end of year 5 and ending six months prior to maturity.

Calculate the minimum yield that Mary could receive, expressed as an annual nominal rate of interest convertible semi-annually.

A. 4.7%

B. 4.9%

C. 5.1%

D. 5.3%

E. 5.5%

(SOA EXAM FM SAMPLE QUESTIONS Interest Theory, Question 91)

9. An investor purchases a 10-year callable bond with face amount of 1,000 for price P. The bond has an annual nominal coupon rate of 10% paid semi-annually.

   The bond may be called at par by the issuer on every other coupon payment date, beginning with the second coupon payment date.
   The investor earns at least an annual nominal yield of 12% compounded semi-annually regardless of when the bond is redeemed.
   Calculate the largest possible value of P.

   A. 885

   B. 892

   C. 926

   D. 965

   E. 982

   (SOA EXAM FM SAMPLE QUESTIONS Interest Theory, Question 100)

10. An investor owns a bond that is redeemable for 300 in seven years. The investor has just received a coupon of 22.50 and each subsequent semi-annual coupon will be X more than the preceding coupon. The present value of this bond immediately after the payment of the coupon is 1,050.50 assuming an annual nominal yield rate of 6% convertible semi-annually.

    Calculate X.

    A. 7.54

B. 10.04

C. 22.37

D. 34.49

E. 43.98

(SOA EXAM FM SAMPLE QUESTIONS Interest Theory, Question 116)

11. An investor owns a bond that is redeemable for 250 in 6 years from now. The investor has just received a coupon of c and each subsequent semi-annual coupon will be 2% larger than the preceding coupon. The present value of this bond immediately after the payment of the coupon is 582.53 assuming an annual effective yield rate of 4%.

Calculate c.

A. 32.04

B. 32.68

C. 40.22

D. 48.48

E. 49.45

(SOA EXAM FM SAMPLE QUESTIONS Interest Theory, Question 117)

12. An n-year bond with annual coupons has the following characteristics:
    i. The redemption value at maturity is 1,890;
    ii. The annual effective yield rate is 6%;
    iii. The book value immediately after the third coupon is 1,254.87; and
    iv. The book value immediately after the fourth coupon is 1,277.38.
    Calculate n.
    A. 16
    B. 17
    C. 18
    D. 19
    E. 20

(SOA EXAM FM SAMPLE QUESTIONS Interest Theory, Question 118)

13. An n-year bond with semi-annual coupons has the following characteristics:
    i. The par value and redemption value are 2,500;
    ii. The annual coupon rate is 7% payable semi-annually;
    iii. The annual nominal yield to maturity is 8% convertible semi-annually; and
    iv. The book value immediately after the fourth coupon is 8.44 greater than the book value immediately after the third coupon.
    Calculate n.
    A. 6.5
    B. 7.0
    C. 9.5
    D. 12.0
    E. 14.0

(SOA EXAM FM SAMPLE QUESTIONS Interest Theory, Question 62)

14. A 40-year bond is purchased at a discount. The bond pays annual coupons. The amount for accumulation of discount in the 15th coupon is 194.82. The amount for accumulation of discount in the 20th coupon is 306.69.

    Calculate the amount of discount in the purchase price of this bond.
    A. 13,635
    B. 13,834
    C. 16,098
    D. 19,301
    E. 21,135

(SOA EXAM FM SAMPLE QUESTIONS May 2005, Question 10)

15. Yield rates to maturity for zero coupon bonds are currently quoted at 8.5% for one-year maturity, 9.5% for two-year maturity, and 10.5%

for three-year maturity. Let i be the one-year forward rate for year two implied by current yields of these bonds.

Calculate i.
A. 8.5%
B. 9.5%
C. 10.5%
D. 11.5%
E. 12.5%

(SOA EXAM FM SAMPLE QUESTIONS November 2005, Question 15)

16. You are given the following term structure of spot interest rates:

Term (in years)	Spot interest rate
1	5.00%
2	5.75%
3	6.25%
4	6.50%

A three-year annuity-immediate will be issued a year from now with annual payments of 5,000. Using the forward rates, calculate the present value of this annuity a year from now.
A. 13,094
B. 13,153
C. 13,296
D. 13,321
E. 13,401

(SOA EXAM FM SAMPLE QUESTIONS Interest Theory, Question 67)

17. The prices of zero-coupon bonds are:

Maturity	Price
1	0.95420
2	0.90703
3	0.85892

Calculate the third year, one-year forward rate.

A. 0.048
B. 0.050
C. 0.052
D. 0.054
E. 0.056

(SOA EXAM FM SAMPLE QUESTIONS Interest Theory, Question 92)

18. You are given the following term structure of interest rates:

Length of investment in years	Spot rate
1	7.50%
2	8.00%
3	8.50%
4	9.00%
5	9.50%
6	10.00%

Calculate the one-year forward rate for the fifth year implied by this term structure.

A. 9.5%
B. 10.0%
C. 11.5%
D. 12.0%
E. 12.5%

(SOA EXAM FM SAMPLE QUESTIONS Interest Theory, Question 119)

19. For the next four years, the one-year forward rates of interest are estimated to be:

Year	0	1	2	3	4
Forward Rate	4%	6%	8%	10%	12%

Calculate the spot rate for a zero-coupon bond maturing three years from now.
A. 4%
B. 5%
C. 6%
D. 7%
E. 8%

(SOA EXAM FM SAMPLE QUESTIONS Interest Theory, Question 33)

20. You are given the following information with respect to a bond:
   i. par value: 1,000
   ii. term to maturity: 3 years
   iii. annual coupon rate: 6% payable annually
   You are also given that the one, two, and three-year annual spot interest rates are 7%, 8%, and 9% respectively.
   Calculate the value of the bond.
   A. 906
   B. 926
   C. 930
   D. 950
   E. 1,000

(SOA EXAM FM SAMPLE QUESTIONS Interest Theory, Question 34)

21. You are given the following information with respect to a bond:

    i. Par value: 1,000

    ii. Term to maturity: 3 years

    iii. Annual coupon rate: 6% payable annually

You are also given that the one, two, and three-year annual spot interest rates are 7%, 8%, and 9% respectively.

The bond is sold at a price equal to its value.

Calculate the annual effective yield rate for the bond i.

    A. 8.1%

    B. 8.3%

    C. 8.5%

    D. 8.7%

    E. 8.9%

(SOA EXAM FM SAMPLE QUESTIONS November 2001, Question 31)

22. You have decided to invest in two bonds. Bond X is an n-year bond with semiannual coupons, while bond Y is an accumulation bond redeemable in $\frac{n}{2}$ years. The desired yield rate is the same for both bonds. You also have the following information.

Bond X

- Par value is 1,000
- The ratio of the semi-annual bond rate to the desired semi-yield annual yield rate, $\frac{r}{i}$, is 1.03125.
- The present value of the redemption value is 381.50.

Bond Y

- Redemption value is the same as the redemption value of bond X.
- Price to yield is 647.80.

What is the price of bond X?

    A. 1,019

    B. 1,029

    C. 1,050

    D. 1,055

    E. 1,072

CHAPTER TEN

Portfolios Revisited

Abstract

In this chapter, we will revisit portfolios, with a particular eye towards mitigating interest rate risk. When we first visited this topic in Chapter 5, we laid out some basic ideas; now we will dig deeper so that by the end of the chapter you will be able to construct a fully immunized portfolio—that is, a portfolio that is completely protected against changes in the interest rate.

We will start by reviewing Macaulay duration—a measure of the average time of cash flows which is a proxy measurement of interest rate risk since cash flows further into the future will be impacted more greatly by changes in the interest rate. We will see, however, that the modified duration was helpful because it provided a direct estimate of the actual amount of change in the current price of the future cash flows as a function of changes to the yield rate. One downside of measures of duration was that they assumed a linear price—yield relationship. Convexity helps improve these estimates by taking into account the curvature of the price—yield relationship. Furthermore, convexity is one of the three conditions for a portfolio to be immunized, with the convexity of assets needing to be larger than the convexity of liabilities (along with equal durations and present values) in order for a portfolio to be protected against interest rate changes.

Keywords: Macaulay duration; Macaulay convexity; Modified duration; Modified convexity; Redington immunization; Full immunization

SECTION 10.1. COMPARING MEASURES OF INTEREST RATE RISK

Earlier in the course, we looked at Macaulay duration as a measure of interest rate risk. The Macaulay duration gives the weighted average time of future cash flows with larger values of the Macaulay duration indicating more interest rate risk. In this section, we will see how the modified duration (ModD), which can be computed using the Macaulay duration, can be used to directly quantify interest rate risk.

A Spiral Approach to Financial Mathematics.
DOI: https://doi.org/10.1016/B978-0-12-801580-3.00010-1

© 2018 Elsevier Inc.
All rights reserved.

Learning objectives

By the end of this section, you will be able to:

- Use basis points to summarize interest rate changes.
- Compute the ModD given a series of cash flows and estimating the slope of the price—yield curve or by using the Macaulay duration.
- Use the ModD to estimate changes in the price of a portfolio.

EXAMPLE 10.1 HOW RISKY IS MY PORTFOLIO?

Let's again suppose you are starting to develop a portfolio of investments to save for the future. To spread out your investment risk you decide to buy three separate bonds:

Bond 1. A $1,000, 3-year bond with semiannual coupons at 4% nominal annually

Bond 2. A $1,000, 5-year bond with semiannual coupons at 4% nominal annually

Bond 3. A $1,000, 10-year bond with semiannual coupons at 4% nominal annually

You pay par value for each of the bonds. Because the bonds sold for par, the yield rate for each bond is currently at the nominal coupon rate (4% for all 3 bonds).

While the bonds are currently selling at par, you are wondering what will happen if market yield rates change.

Think about it

What will happen to the prices of these bonds if yield rates increase? Decreases? If all bonds experience a 0.1% change in yield rate, which bond(s) will be affected the most?

As we have seen before, the price and yield rate have an inverse relationship because the bond pays fixed amounts in the future. Thus, as yield rates decrease the price increases and as yield rates increase the price decreases. Moreover, the further into the future a payment happens, the more the present value is impacted by a change in yield rate. Thus, a small change in the interest rate today will have a larger impact on Bond

3 (the 10-year bond) than on the shorter term bonds, and Bond 2 will be impacted more than Bond 1.

Table 10.1 illustrates the price—yield relationship. The changes in the price of Bond 1 are minimal for these small changes in the yield rate (e.g., approximately a $6 change in price for a 0.2% change in the yield rate). However, the changes for Bond 3 (the 10-year bond) are more substantial (e.g., a $16 price decrease for a 0.2% increase in the yield rate).

Table 10.1 Prices of Bonds 1, 2, and 3 as yield rates change

Yield rate (nominal, semiannual compounding) (%)	Bond 1 (3-year) ($)	Bond 2 (5-year) ($)	Bond 3 (10-year) ($)
3.8	1,005.62	1,009.03	1,016.51
3.9	1,002.81	1,004.50	1,008.22
4 (current)	1,000.00	1,000.00	1,000.00
4.1	997.20	995.52	991.86
4.2	994.42	991.06	983.81

Fig. 10.1 further illustrates this relationship across a wider range of yield rate changes.

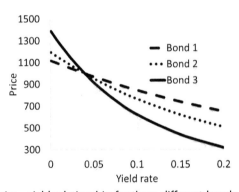

Figure 10.1 The price—yield relationship for three different bonds.

As you can see, especially for Bond 3, the price—yield relationship is a curve, not a straight line. You can also see this in Table 10.1, by recognizing that the increase in price is not the same as the decrease in price for the same-sized change in yield rate. However, the relationship is fairly linear, especially over short distances.

Key idea

The price—yield relationship is a curve but can be approximated by a straight line over short distances.

Think about it

As the term of the bond keeps getting shorter and shorter, what will the price—yield curve look like? What about as the term gets longer and longer?

The slope of the price—yield curve keeps getting closer and closer to zero as the term of the bond shortens. Conceptually, this simply means that as the bond gets closer and closer to its maturity (time when it will pay the face value; in this example, $1,000), changes in the yield rate have less and less impact on its value. In the extreme case, if the bond will redeem tomorrow, changes in the yield rate will not affect the price much at all since there is a guaranteed payment of $1,000 so soon. At the other extreme, as the bond's redemption date is further and further into the future, the slope of the line will get more and more vertical, indicating that even small changes in the yield rate may have dramatic impact on the price. These relationships correlate directly to the relationship between time and value for a savings account with compound interest.

Review: Macaulay duration

Earlier in the text, we used the Macaulay duration as a method to quantify price sensitivity. Recall that the Macaulay duration is the weighted average time of the cash flows and is given by the following equation, where $PV(C_t)$ is the present value of the cash flow, C_t, at time t.

$$\text{MacD} = \sum t \frac{PV(C_t)}{PV(\text{All})}$$

For Bond 1 at a 4% nominal yield, we can compute the Macaulay duration as

$$\text{MacD} = \sum t \frac{PV(C_t)}{PV(\text{All})} = 0.5 \left(\frac{19.6078}{1,000} \right) + 1 \left(\frac{19.22}{1,000} \right) + 1.5 \left(\frac{18.85}{1,000} \right)$$
$$+ 2 \left(\frac{18.48}{1,000} \right) + 2.5 \left(\frac{18.11}{1,000} \right) + 3 \left(\frac{905.73}{1,000} \right)$$
$$= 0.5(0.0196078) + 1(0.01922) + 1.5(0.01885) + 2(0.01848)$$
$$+ 2.5(0.01811) + 3(0.90573) = 2.86 \text{ years}$$

Since the Macaulay duration is 2.86 for Bond 1 and is smaller than that of Bonds 2 and 3 (4.58 and 8.33, respectively), the average cash flow for Bond 1 is sooner and less sensitive to yield rate changes.

We have visually represented the Macaulay duration in Fig. 10.2.

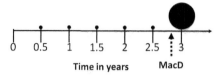

Figure 10.2 Visual representation of Macaulay duration as the weighted average time of the cash flows.

Modified duration

While the Macaulay duration can be useful, especially for portfolios (sets of cash flows), and is useful when working to immunize portfolios (recall Section 5.3, with more coming later in this chapter), one drawback is that the units are years.

The ModD seeks to address this weakness as a direct measure of how much the price of an asset (e.g., a bond or a portfolio) changes when the yield rate changes. Before we formally define ModD, we introduce the helpful concept of *basis points* when talking about yield rate changes.

Definition

Basis points are the most commonly used units when talking about yield rate changes. One basis point is 0.01% and, thus, 100 basis points is equivalent to 1%.

Thus, if a bond yield changes from 4% to 4.2%, it is a 20 basis point change. Describing yield rate changes in terms of basis points makes it clearer than using more vague terminology like "The yield rate increased 1%"—which could mean a 1-percentage point (100-basis point) increase, or a proportional increase of 0.01.

With this in mind, we now define ModD.

Definition

The ModD measures the change in price as a function of the yield rate. In particular, it is the percent rate of change in price for a 100-basis point (1 percentage point) change in yield rate.

Thus, if the ModD is 1.2% then the price of the bond will change 1.2% for a 100-basis point change in yield. Notice that the ModD is a measure of the change in the value of a bond (1.2%) in response to a change in the yield rate (100 basis points). The ModD can be interpreted in terms of the slope of the price—yield curve evaluated at the current yield rate.

Key idea

The ModD is the slope of the price—yield curve at the current yield rate divided by the present value of the bond in order to report price changes as a percentage; in calculus terms, the ModD is the derivative of the price—yield curve evaluated at the current yield rate dived by the present value of the bond.

Here is an equation for ModD

$$\text{ModD} = \frac{-\left(\text{Change in price}/\text{Change in yield}\right)}{\text{Current price}}$$

$$= \frac{-\text{Slope of price} - \text{yield curve}}{\text{Current price}} = \frac{-\text{PV}'(i)}{\text{PV}(i)}$$

where $\text{PV}(i)$ is the present value of a bond at a current yield rate of i and $\text{PV}'(i)$ is its derivative. The negative sign is included since an increase in the yield rate causes a decrease in the bond price.

While this equation helps understand what ModD is measuring, it may not be immediately obvious how to compute it for a particular bond.

Calculating the modified duration

There are two ways to calculate the ModD.

Method 1—estimating the modified duration

Method 1 of calculating the ModD estimates the slope of the price—yield curve by looking at the change in price over a small interval. Table 10.2 illustrates these calculations for a handful of different yield rates. Notice that the estimated slopes are fairly similar. This is because, as we noted in Fig. 10.1, the price—yield curve is fairly linear.

Thus, Table 10.2 tells us that if the yield rate changes by one basis point (0.01%), the price of bond will change by approximately $0.28. It is more typical to report the slope of the price–yield curve in terms of 100 bp changes, so we scale the slope so that the units are 100 bp [1 percentage point (see final column of table)]. Thus, we estimate that the price of the bond will change by approximately $28.00 for every 100 bp (1 percentage point) change in the yield. Here is the equation for what we have just done.

$$100 \times \text{Estimated slope of price} - \text{yield curve}$$
$$= 100 \text{ bp} \times \frac{\text{Total change in price}}{\text{Total change in interest rate(bp)}}$$

While the estimated slopes (and ModDs) are similar in Table 10.2, they do differ a bit. A robust way to estimate the slope is to go up 100 bp and down 100 bp from the current yield rate to generate the estimate.

$$100 \times \text{Robust estimate of slope}$$
$$= 100 \text{ bp} \times \frac{\text{Price(100 bp higher)} - \text{Price(100 bp lower)}}{200 \text{ bp}}$$

Applied to Bond 1, this gives us

$$100 \times \text{Robust estimate of slope}$$
$$= 100 \text{ bp} \times \frac{\text{Price(100 bp lower)} - \text{Price(100 bp higher)}}{200 \text{ bp}}$$
$$= 100 \text{ bp} \times \frac{\$972.46 - \$1,028.49}{200 \text{ bp}} = -\$28.02$$

Thus, we estimate that the bond price will decrease by approximately $28.02 for every 100 bp increase in yield rate.

In order to get the ModD, we scale the slope estimate by the current price of the bond (in this case, $1,000).

$$\text{ModD} = \frac{-\text{Slope of price} - \text{yield curve}}{\text{Current price}} = \frac{\$28.02}{\$1,000} = 2.802\%$$

Thus, we say that the ModD of this bond is 2.802%. This means that the bond price will change by 2.802% for every 100 bp (1 percentage point) change in the yield rate.

Table 10.2 Estimating slope of the price–yield curve for Bond 1

Yield rate (nominal, semiannual compounding) (%)	Bond 1 (3-year) ($)	Change in price from current price ($1,000) ($)	Change in yield rate from current yield (4%). reported in basis points (and percentage)	Estimated slope for 1 bp change (change in price divided by change in yield) ($)	Scaled estimates of slope (100 bp × slope) ($)
3.0	1,028.49	28.49	100 bp (1%)	0.2849	28.49
3.8	1,005.62	5.62	20 bp (0.2%)	0.2810	28.10
3.9	1,002.81	2.81	10 bp (0.1%)	0.2805	28.05
4.0	1,000.00	0.00	0 bp (0.0%)	—	—
4.1	997.20	2.80	10 bp (0.1%)	0.2796	27.96
4.2	994.42	5.56	20 bp (0.2%)	0.2791	27.91
5.0	972.46	27.54	100 bp (1%)	0.2754	27.54

bp, basis point.

Method 2—computing modified duration as a function of the Macaulay duration

A second approach to computing the ModD utilizes the following equation, which relates the two different types of duration

$$\mathrm{ModD} = \frac{\mathrm{MacD}}{1+i},$$

where i is the current effective yield rate. Thus, the ModD is simply a scaled version of the Macaulay duration.

Key idea

The term ModD comes from the fact that the value for the Macaulay duration is modified slightly to get the ModD. Importantly, the ModD is more widely used in practice.

In the case of our bond, $\mathrm{MacD} = 2.86$ years and the effective yield rate is 4.04% (nominal is 4% with semiannual compounding). Thus, the ModD is $2.86\%/1.0404 = 2.75\%$.

Slightly different answers?

Because Method 1 is estimating the slope, you may get a slightly different answer than you get using Method 2 (e.g., 2.8% vs 2.75%). The Method 2 approach is more accurate and should be used in practice. We wanted to show you Method 1, however, because it directly illustrates what ModD is measuring.

It is worth noting that the ModD, as a function of the slope, can be used to quickly predict the change in price of bonds. An equation for estimating the present value at yield rate j is

Estimate of present value at yield rate $j = \mathrm{PV}(i) \times (1 - (j - i)\mathrm{ModD})$

where j is the new yield rate, i is the current yield rate, $\mathrm{PV}(i)$ is the present value at yield rate i, and ModD is entered in percentage points. For example, $\mathrm{ModD} = 2.75\%$ for Bond 1.

Thus, an estimated price for Bond 1 for a yield rate of 5% is

$$\$1000(1 - (0.05 - 0.04)2.75) = \$972.50.$$

The actual price (see Table 10.2 above) is $972.46.

Finding the modified duration for each bond

In order to find the ModD for each bond, we start by finding the Macaulay duration and then simply dividing by 1 plus the annual yield rate (4.04% effective), or 1.0404. (See results in Table 10.3.)

Table 10.3 Modified duration for each bond

	Macaulay duration (years)	Modified duration (%)
Bond 1 (3-year)	2.86	2.75
Bond 2 (5-year)	4.58	4.40
Bond 3 (10-year)	8.34	8.02

Thus, Bond 2 will change by approximately 4.40% in value for a 1% change in yield rate, while Bond 3 will change by approximately 8.02%.

Finding the modified duration for the portfolio

Now, since you own one of each bond, how can you find the impact on your entire portfolio if interest rates change?

Think about it

If all of the bonds in your portfolio experience a similar change in yield rate, predict how much your portfolio will change in value?

Since you own one of each bond, the change in the percent value of your portfolio should be some kind of "average" of the percent change in value of each of the individual bonds. Let's compute this more exactly using both Methods 1 and 2.

Method 1

First, we will compute the value of the portfolio if interest rates drop to 3.9% and then again if interest rates increase to 4.1% by summing the price of each of the three bonds for these two different interest rates. Then, we will estimate the slope, and finally divide by the present value of the portfolio to obtain the ModD. (Note: The values below come from those in Table 10.1.)

Portfolio value if interest rates drop to 3.9%: $1,002.81 + $1,004.50 + $1,008.22 = $3,015.53

Portfolio value if interest rates increase to 4.1%: $997.20 + $995.52 + $991.86 = $2,984.58

Estimated slope per 100 basis points: $100 \times (\$3,015.53 - \$2,984.58)/20 = \$154.75$

Estimated ModD: $\$154.75/\$3,000 = 0.0516 = 5.16\%$

The estimated ModD of the portfolio is 5.16%. In other words, a 100-basis point (1 percentage point) change in the yield rate will change the portfolio value by approximately 5.16%.

Method 2

Find the Macaulay duration of the portfolio by finding the weighted-average time of the cash flows.

$$\text{MacD} = 0.5\left(\frac{19.61}{3,000}\right) + 0.5\left(\frac{19.61}{3,000}\right) + 0.5\left(\frac{19.61}{3,000}\right) + \cdots$$
$$= 0.003268 + 0.003268 + 0.003268 = 5.23 \text{ years}$$

Thus, $\text{ModD} = 5.23/1.0404 = 5.03\%$

Notice that the present value of the portfolio is $3,000. As you might have guessed, this is simply the average of the individual ModDs for the bonds in this portfolio. That is, if you average the ModDs of the three bonds in this portfolio you get $(2.75\% + 4.40\% + 8.02\%)/3 = 5.06\%$. The only difference from what we obtained above is due to rounding. In this case, since all three bonds have present value of $1,000, they each make up 1/3 of the portfolio's present value.

This leads us to the following key idea.

Key idea

The ModD of a portfolio is the weighted average of the ModDs of the assets in the portfolio, where weights are based on the percentage of the present value of the portfolio attributable to that asset.

EXPLORATION 10.1 EVALUATING PORTFOLIO RISK

As we have considered before, suppose you are starting to develop a portfolio of investments to save for the future. To spread out your invest-ment risk, you decide to buy two separate bonds:

Bond 1. A $1,000, 3-year bond with semiannual coupons at 3% nominal annually

Bond 2. A $1,000, 1-year bond with semiannual coupons at 3% nominal annually

1. What is present value of each bond and the total present value of your portfolio if the bonds are both selling at par?

2. Predict what will happen to your portfolio if the yield rate increases. What if it decreases? Which bond will be affected the most? Why?

3. Confirm your predictions by computing the present value of both bonds at all the yield rates listed in Table 10.4.

Table 10.4 Price-yield relationships for two bonds

Yield rate (for both bonds, nominal with semiannual converting) (%)	Bond 1 ($)	Bond 2 ($)
2.0		
2.5	1,014.37	1,004.91
3.0	1,000.00	1,000.00
3.5	985.88	995.13
4.0		

4. For Bond 1, is the change in price linear as the yield rate changes? Hint: Compute the change in price for a yield rate change from 2% to 3% and then from 3% to 4% and compare.

While the change in price as the yield rate changes is fairly linear, it is, in fact a curve.

Key idea

The price—yield relationship is a curve but can be approximated by a straight line over short distances.

Review: Macaulay duration

Earlier in the course, we used the Macaulay duration as a way to quantify price sensitivity. Recall that the Macaulay duration is the weighted average time of the cash flows and is given by the following equation, where $PV(C_t)$ is the present value of the cash flow, C_t, at time t.

$$\text{MacD} = \sum t \frac{PV(C_t)}{PV(\text{All})}$$

5. Assuming a current market yield rate of 3%, predict which Bond will have the larger Macaulay duration. Why?

6. Assuming a current market yield rate of 3%, compute the Macaulay duration of Bond 1. Use t measured in years.

7. Assuming a current market yield rate of 3%, compute the Macaulay duration of Bond 2. Use t measured in years.

Modified duration

While the Macaulay duration can be useful, especially for portfolios (sets of cash flows), and is useful when working to immunize portfolios (recall Section 5.3, with more coming later in this chapter). One drawback is that the units are years.

The ModD seeks to address this weakness as a direct measure of how much the price of an asset (e.g., bond, portfolio) changes when the yield rate changes. Before we formally define ModD, we introduce the helpful concept of **basis points** when talking about yield rate changes.

Definition
Basis points (bps) are the most commonly used units when talking about yield rate changes. One basis point is 0.01% and, thus, 100-basis points is equivalent to 1%.

---

8. If the yield rate increases 20 basis points, by what percentage does it change?

Definition

The ModD measures the change in price as a function of the yield rate. In particular, it is the percent rate of change in price for a 100-basis point (1 percentage point) change in yield rate.

Method 1

There are two ways to compute the ModD. The first is as a function of the observed change in price for changes in yield.

9. How much does the price change as the yield rate increases from 2.5% to 3.5% for Bond 1 (refer to Table 10.4 you filled in earlier)?

10. What is the increase in basis points as the yield rate increases from 2.5% to 3.5%?

11. Use the previous two answers to report an estimate of the slope of the price—yield curve in terms of basis points. Hint: Slope is change in price divided by change in yield. Hint 2: Be careful with the sign of the numerator!

12. What is the slope in terms of a 1-percentage point (100 basis point) change?

From your answer to the previous question, we can say that we estimate that the price of the bond to decrease by $28.49 for every one-percentage point increase. For those of you familiar with calculus, recall that the slope of a line at a particular point is the derivative.

Key idea

The ModD is the slope of the price—yield curve at the current yield rate divided by the present value of the bond in order to report price changes as a percentage; in calculus terms, the ModD is the derivative of the price—yield curve evaluated at the current yield rate dived by the present value of the bond.

Here is an equation for ModD

$$ModD = \frac{-\left(\text{Change in price}/\text{Change in yield}\right)}{\text{Current price}}$$

$$= \frac{-\text{Slope of price} - \text{yield curve}}{\text{Current price}} = \frac{-PV'(i)}{PV(i)}$$

where $PV(i)$ is the present value of a bond at a current yield rate of i and $PV'(i)$ is its derivative. The negative sign is included since an increase in the yield rate causes a decrease in the bond price.

13. Now, let us compute the ModD by dividing our estimate of the slope (100 basis point change version) by the current price of Bond 1. What is the ModD of Bond 1?

The ModD is interpreted as a prediction of the percentage change in price for a one-percentage point (100 basis point) change in the yield. Thus, for Bond 1, we estimate that the price of the bond will change by 2.849% for every one unit (100 bps) change in the price.

It is worth noting that the ModD, as a function of the slope, can be used to quickly predict the change in price of bonds. An equation for estimating the present value at yield rate j is

Estimate of present value at yield rate $j = PV(i) \times (1 - (j - i)ModD)$

14. Use the ModD to find the predicted price of Bond 1 if the yield rate changes from 3% to 2%. How close is this to the true price when the yield rate is 2%?

15. Use the ModD to find the predicted price of Bond 1 if the yield rate changes from 3% to 4%. How close is this to the true price when the yield rate is 2%?

Method 2

Another way to compute the ModD is to use the Macaulay duration. In particular, the following relationship is true.

$$ModD = \frac{MacD}{1 + i}$$

In the equation above, use the effective yield rate, though use of the nominal yield rate typically will have very little impact on your results.

16. Use the Macaulay duration (measured in years) to find the value of the ModD.

17. Compare your answer to the one you received previously. Are they exactly the same? Are they close?

Because Method 1 is estimating the slope, you may get a slightly different answer than you get using Method 2 (e.g., 2.8% vs 2.7%). The Method 2 approach is more accurate and should be used in practice. We wanted to show you Method 1, however, because it directly illustrates what ModD is measuring.

Key idea

The term ModD comes from the fact that the value for the Macaulay duration is modified slightly to get the ModD. Importantly, the ModD is more widely used in practice.

Finding the modified duration for Bond 2

18. Find the ModD for Bond 2.

19. Use the ModD for Bond 2 to predict the price of the bond if the yield drops to 2%.

20. Use the ModD for Bond 2 to predict the price of the bond if the yield increases to 4%.

Finding the modified duration for the portfolio

To find the ModD for the portfolio, we make use of the fact that the ModD of the portfolio is equal to the weighted average of the ModDs of the assets in the portfolio.

Key idea

The ModD of a portfolio is the weighted average of the ModDs of the assets in the portfolio, where weights are based on the percentage of the present value of the portfolio attributable to that asset.

---

21. Find the ModD of the portfolio.

22. Use the ModD of the portfolio to estimate the price of the portfolio if interest rates increase 100 basis points to 4%. Compare your answer to the true portfolio value and confirm that your estimate is reasonable.

SUMMARY

In this section, we revisited the concept of duration as a measure of interest rate risk. The ModD is more applicable than the Macaulay duration if the goal is to directly quantify (estimate) changes in portfolio value as a function of changes in the interest rate. We introduced the concept of basis points as a convenient way to measure interest rate changes $(100 \text{ bp} = 0.001 = 0.1\%)$.

Notation and equation summary

$$\text{ModD} = \frac{\text{MacD}}{1+i} = \frac{-\left(\text{Change in price}/\text{Change in yield}\right)}{\text{Current price}}$$

$$= \frac{-\text{Slope of price} - \text{yield curve}}{\text{Current price}} = \frac{-PV'(i)}{PV(i)}$$

Equation to estimate bond price using ModD

Estimate of present value at yield rate $j = PV(i) \times (1 - (j - i)\text{ModD})$

HOMEWORK QUESTIONS: SECTION 10.1

Conceptual questions

1. As the yield rate decreases on a bond, what happens to the price of the bond?

2. Is the change in the price of a bond, because of a yield-rate change, more pronounced on a short-term or a long-term bond?

3. Macaulay duration is essentially a measure of what?

4. What does a modified duration of 2.5% mean?

5. How are modified duration and Macaulay duration related?

Practice questions

6. If the Macaulay duration on a portfolio is 2.75 years and the yield rate is 3.4%, what is the modified duration?

7. A 3-year $1,000 bond has a yield rate of 3% nominal with semiannual compounding and $20 semiannual coupons. What is the Macaulay duration for this bond?

8. Thirty basis points is equivalent to what percentage? How many basis points 0.3%?

9. If the yield rate went down to 3.9% nominal with semiannual compounding, the price of a 3-year bond would increase to $5,014.03, and if the rate increased to 4.1%, it would drop to $4,986.02. The bond currently sells for $5,000. Using these numbers, what is the negative of the approximate slope of the current price curve divided by the current price?

10. A portfolio has a value of $5,000 and a modified duration of 2.1%. What is the predicted value of the portfolio if the yield rate decreases 100 basis points?

11. Deb's portfolio consists of two bonds; a $500 bond with a modified duration of 1.2% and $1,000 bond with a modified duration of 2%. What is the modified duration of the portfolio?

Application questions

12. A 5-year $1,000 bond is being sold with 4% annual coupons and an annual yield rate of 2%.
    a. What is the value of the coupons?
    b. What is the selling price of the bond?

   c. What is the bond price if the yield changes to 1.9%, but the coupon values do not change?

   d. What is the bond price if the yield changes to 2.1%, but the coupon values do not change?

   e. Using method 1 from the section, calculate the modified duration.

13. A 3-year $1,000 bond is being sold at par with semiannual coupons at a yield rate of 5% compounded semiannually.

   a. What is the value of the coupons?

   b. What is the selling price of the bond?

   c. What is the bond price if the yield changes to 4.9% compounded semiannually, but the coupon values do not change?

   d. What is the bond price if the yield changes to 5.1% compounded semiannually, but the coupon values do not change?

   e. Using method 1 from the section, calculate the modified duration.

   f. What is the Macaulay duration for the bond?

   g. Using method 2 from the section, calculate the modified duration.

14. A 2-year $500 bond is being sold at par with semiannual coupons at a yield rate of 3% compounded semiannually.

   a. What is the value of the coupons?

   b. What is the selling price of the bond?

   c. What is the bond price if the yield changes to 2.9%, but the coupon values do not change?

   d. What is the bond price if the yield changes to 3.1%, but the coupon values do not change?

   e. Using method 1 from the section, calculate the modified duration.

   f. What is the Macaulay duration for the bond?

   g. Using method 2 from the section, calculate the modified duration.

15. Emma has two bonds: a 3-year $1,000 bond that is being sold at par with semiannual coupons at a yield rate of 6% compounded

semiannually and a 5-year $5,000 bond that is being sold at par with semiannual coupons at a yield rate of 6% compounded semiannually.

  a. What is the Macaulay duration for each of the bonds?

  b. Using method 2 from the section, calculate the modified duration for each of the bonds.

  c. What is the modified duration for Emma's portfolio that consists of the two bonds?

16. Tyler has two bonds: a 5-year $1,000 bond that has 4% annual coupons and an annual yield rate of 1.5% and a 10-year $500 bond that has a 6% annual coupons and an annual yield rate of 2%.

  a. What is the Macaulay duration for each of the bonds?

  b. Using method 2 from the section, calculate the modified duration for each of the bonds.

  c. What is the modified duration for Tyler's portfolio that consists of the two bonds?

SECTION 10.2. CONVEXITY

In the previous section, we estimated the change in price of a bond by using a linear approximation of the price–yield curve. In particular, we saw that the ModD estimated the percent change in the price of a bond for a change of 100 basis points in the yield rate. However, this calculation is not as accurate as it could be because it assumes that the yield curves are linear, when in fact they are curved. Learning about how to quantify the convexity (curvature) of the price–yield curve will prove very helpful in Section 10.3 where we will again explore the concept of portfolio immunization.

Learning objectives

By this end of this section, you should be able to:
- Compute and interpret the Macaulay convexity (MacC)
- Compute and interpret the Modified convexity

EXAMPLE 10.2. HOW RISKY IS MY PORTFOLIO? (REVISITED)

Let us again suppose you are starting to develop a portfolio of investments to save for the future. To spread out your investment risk you decide to buy three separate bonds:

Bond 1. A $1,000, 3-year bond with semiannual coupons at 4% nominal annually

Bond 2. A $1,000, 5-year bond with semiannual coupons at 4% nominal annually

Bond 3. A $1,000, 10-year bond with semiannual coupons at 4% nominal annually

You pay par value for each of the bonds. Because the bonds sold for par, the yield rate for each bond is currently at the nominal coupon rate (4% for all 3 bonds). While the bonds are currently selling at par, you are wondering what will happen if market yield rates change.

In the previous section, we used ModD to predict the change in price of bonds. An equation for estimating the present value at yield rate j is

$$\text{Estimate of present value at yield rate } j = PV(i) \times (1 - (j - i)\text{ModD})$$

where j is the new yield rate, i is the current yield rate, $PV(i)$ is the present value at yield rate i, and ModD is entered in percentage points. For example, ModD $= 2.75\%$ for Bond 1.

Thus, an estimated price for Bond 1 for a yield rate of 5% is

$$\$1,000(1 - (0.05 - 0.04)2.75) = \$972.50.$$

However, the actual price is $972.46. While this is close, if you owned thousands of bonds, this small difference could amount to substantial amounts of money. Table 10.5 shows the estimates for all bonds across a variety of interest rates.

As seen in Table 10.5, Bond 3, the longest term bond has the most deviation from predicted to actual values of the bonds. One way to address this difference and improve our estimate is to take the curvature of the price−yield curve into consideration, rather than assuming it is linear (an assumption of the ModD).

Table 10.5 Prices of Bonds 1, 2 and 3 as yield rates change

	Bond 1 (3-Year)		Bond 2 (5-Year)		Bond 3 (10-Year)	
Yield rate (nominal, semiannual compounding) (%)	Actual value ($)	Prediction using modified duration (2.75%) ($)	Actual value ($)	Prediction using modified duration (4.40%) ($)	Actual value ($)	Prediction using modified duration (8.02%) ($)
2	1,057.96	1,055.00	1,094.71	1,088.00	1,180.46	1,180.46
3	1,028.49	1,027.50	1,046.11	1,044.00	1,085.84	1,085.84
4	1,000.00	1,000.00	1,000.00	1,000.00	1,000.00	1,000.00
5	972.46	972.50	956.24	956.00	922.05	922.05
6	945.83	945.00	914.70	912.00	851.23	851.23

Convexity

Convexity is a mathematical term describing a graph's curvature. In Fig. 10.3, we see that the price–yield curves are convex. In particular, they are curved upward (concave up)—this is particularly observable to the naked eye for Bond 3 but is also the case for Bonds 1 and 2 as well.

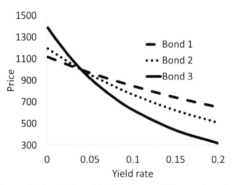

Figure 10.3 The price–yield relationship for three different bonds.

Key idea

Assets with longer durations have the most curvature and, thus, have the poorest estimates of price changes when using ModD.

Macaulay convexity

The MacC is one way to begin to quantify the curvature of a price—yield relationship. It is defined very similarly to the Macaulay duration.

$$\text{MacC} = \sum t^2 \frac{\text{PV}(C_t)}{\text{PV}(\text{All})}$$

Notice that the only difference in the definition of the MacC is that the time, t, is squared first. Thus, you can think of MacC as a weighted average of the square of the times of the cash flow.

Think about it

How will MacC relate to MacD (Macaulay Duration)? How will cash flows further into the future impact the value?

MacC will be larger than MacD because $t^2 > t$ when $t > 1$. Furthermore, because you are squaring the times, MacC will get large quickly when cash flows are far into the future. Thus, MacC is a measure of convexity because the further into the future the cash flows are, the more curvature there is (see key idea above).

Table 10.6 shows the computation for the MacC. Notice that the weighting factors for the cash flows (fourth column) are the same whether you are computing Macaulay duration (fifth column) or MacC (sixth column), the only difference is whether you are multiplying the weights by the time t, or time-squared, t^2.

In Table 10.7, we have computed the MacC for each bond. You can see that the convexity is largest for the longest term bond, meaning that the graph has the most curvature. This should not be at all surprising based on our earlier observations.

Note that we report the MacC in both half years and in years. Because time is squared and $(1/2)^2 = 1/4$, to convert MacC from half years to years we have to multiply by $1/4$ or divide by 4.

Modified convexity

The value of the MacC can be used to compute a value called the modified convexity (ModC). The ModC can be computed as a function of the MacC and the yield rate as shown in the equation below. The ModC

Table 10.6 Macaulay Convexity for Bond 1

Payment date (from now; t) (year)	Payment size (C_t)	Present value at a 4% nominal yield rate; $PV(C_t)$ ($)	Percentage of total cash flow (weighting factor; $PV(C_t)/PV(All)$)	Product of time and weighting factor; $tPV(C_t)/PV(All)$	Product of time-squared and weighting factor; $t^2PV(C_t)/PV(All)$
0.5	20	19.61	$19.61/$1,000 = 0.01961	0.5 × 0.1961 = 0.0098	$(0.5)^2$ × 0.1961 = 0.0049
1.0	20	19.22	0.01922	0.0192	0.0192
1.5	20	18.85	0.01885	0.0283	0.0424
2.0	20	18.48	0.01848	0.0370	0.0739
2.5	20	18.11	0.01811	0.0453	0.1132
3.0	20	17.76	0.01776	0.0533	0.1598
3.0	1,000	887.97	0.8880	2.6639	7.992
Total		PV(All) = $1,000	100%	MacD = 2.86	MacC = 8.41

Table 10.7 Convexity calculations for each of the three bonds

	Macaulay duration (Year)	Modified duration (%)	Macaulay convexity (years)	Macaulay convexity (half-years)
Bond 1 (3-year)	2.86	2.75	8.41	33.64
Bond 2 (5-year)	4.58	4.40	22.01	88.04
Bond 3 (10-year)	8.34	8.02	75.82	303.28

measures the curvature of the price—yield curve and, thus, is based on the second derivative.

$$\text{ModC} = \frac{\text{MacC} + \text{MacD}}{(1+i)^2} = \frac{\text{PV}''(\text{All})}{\text{PV}(\text{All})}$$

As with ModD, i typically represents the effective interest rate in the equation above. Thus, we use the equation above in Table 10.8 to get values for the ModC.

Table 10.8 Convexity calculations for each of the three bonds

	Macaulay duration (years)	Modified duration (%)	Macaulay convexity (years)	Modified convexity (%-squared)
Bond 1 (3-year)	2.86	2.75	2.1025	4.588
Bond 2 (5-year)	4.58	4.40	5.5025	9.32
Bond 3 (10-year)	8.34	8.02	18.955	25.236

Definition

The **convexity** measures the nonlinear relationship between interest rates and price using the second derivative.

Final comments

1. You could use the ModC to improve price changes as a function of changes to the yield rate from those that you made in the previous section using the ModD. However, in modern financial realms this is typically unnecessary because we can let computers do the calculations for us.

2. The real benefit of computing convexity is about immunizing your portfolio (protecting your portfolio against interest rate changes). This is the focus of the next section.

EXPLORATION 10.2 EVALUATING PORTFOLIO RISK (CONTINUED)

Let us once again assume that you are starting to develop a portfolio of investments to save for the future. To spread out your investment risk, you decide to buy two separate bonds:

Bond 1. A $1,000, 3-year bond with semiannual coupons at 3% nominal annually

Bond 2. A $1.000, 1-year bond with semiannual coupons at 3% nominal annually

In the previous section, we used ModD to predict the change in price of bonds. An equation for estimating the present value at yield rate j is

Estimate of present value at yield rate $j = PV(i) \times (1 - (j - i)\text{ModD})$

where j is the new yield rate, i is the current yield rate, $PV(i)$ is the present value at yield rate i, and ModD is entered in percentage points. For example, ModD $= 2.806\%$ for Bond 1.

1. Use the ModD for Bond 1 to estimate the present value of the bond for yield rates of 0.02 and 0.04. Enter the values into Table 10.9.

Table 10.9 Price-yield relationships for two bonds

Yield rate (for both bonds, nominal with semiannual converting) (%)	Bond 1		Bond 2	
	Actual price ($)	Predicted price using ModD ($)	Actual price ($)	Predicted price using ModD ($)
2	1,028.98		1,009.85	
3	1,000.00	1,000.00	1,000.00	1,000.00
4	971.99		990.29	

2. Calculate the ModD for Bond 2 and use it to estimate the present value of the bond for yield rates of 0.02 and 0.04. Enter the values into Table 10.9.

3. Which prediction is the furthest away from the actual price? Why might this be the case?

Convexity

Convexity is a mathematical term describing a graphs curvature.

Key idea

Assets with longer durations have the most curvature and, thus, have the poorest estimates of price changes when using ModD.

One way to address this difference and improve our estimate is to take the curvature of the price–yield curve into consideration, rather than assuming it is linear (an assumption of the ModD).

Macaulay convexity

The MacC is one way to begin to quantify the curvature of a price–yield relationship. It is defined very similarly to the Macaulay duration.

$$\text{MacC} = \sum t^2 \frac{\text{PV}(C_t)}{\text{PV(All)}}$$

Notice that the only difference in the definition of the MacC is that the time, t, is squared first. Thus, you can think of MacC as a weighted average of the square of the times of the cash flow.

4. Find the MacC of Bond 1. Make sure to include the units and do your computation in terms of half-years (6-month period; e.g., $t = 1$ at 6 months, $t = 2$ at 1 year, etc.).

5. Find the MacC of Bond 2. Make sure to include the units and do your computation in terms of half-years (6-month period).

   In order to convert from half years to years, because time is squared in the MacC equation and $(1/2)^2 = 1/4$, take the MacC values you found above and divide by 4.

6. Find the MacC for both bonds using *years*. What are the units of these values?

Modified convexity

The value of the MacC is not very helpful by itself, but it is very helpful when computing a value called the ModC. The ModC can be computed as a function of the MacC and the yield rate. The ModC measures the curvature of the price–yield curve and, thus, is based on the second derivative.

$$\text{ModC} = \frac{\text{MacC} + \text{MacD}}{(1+i)^2} = \frac{PV''(\text{All})}{PV(\text{All})}$$

The unit on ModC is percent-squared. Typically, the effective interest rate is used for i in the equation above.

7. Find the ModC for Bond 1 using years.

8. Find the ModC for Bond 2 using years.

Definition

The **convexity** measures the nonlinear relationship between interest rates and price using the second derivative.

See the end of Example 10.2 for some important final comments.

SUMMARY

In this section, we saw how to compute the MacC and ModC, which help to capture the curvature of the price–yield curve for cash flows. While this curvature can help us better anticipate the true changes in price as a function of changes in yield, the real power to computing convexity comes when we try to immunize a portfolio—that is, make it "immune" to changes in the interest rate. This is the theme and focus of the next section.

Notation and equation summary

$$\text{MacC} = \sum t^2 \frac{PV(C_t)}{PV(\text{All})}$$

$$\text{ModC} = \frac{\text{MacC} + \text{MacD}}{(1+i)^2} = \frac{PV''(\text{All})}{PV(\text{All})}$$

HOMEWORK QUESTIONS: SECTION 10.2

Conceptual questions

1. As the term of a bond increases, does the price–yield curve become more curved or less curved?

2. What is the difference between Macaulay duration and Macaulay convexity?

3. Which is larger in value, Macaulay duration or Macaulay convexity?

4. Modified convexity is a measure of what?

5. What are the units for Macaulay duration? Macaulay convexity? modified duration? modified convexity?

Practice questions

6. What is the estimated present value of a bond if the yield rate changes from 2% to 2.5% for a $1,000 bond that has a modified duration of 2.45?

7. A bond with a present value of $1,000 has a modified duration of 2.7, a modified convexity of 8.5, and a yield rate of 3%. If the yield rate changes to 3.2%, what is the estimated present value of the bond?

8. If a bond has a Macaulay convexity of 26.79 years, a Macaulay duration of 4.59 years, and a yield rate of 3%, what is its modified convexity?

9. A $1,000 1-year bond is being sold at par with coupons every 6 months and 2% annual yield compounded semiannually. What is its Macaulay convexity in terms of half years?

10. A $1,000 1-year bond is being sold at par with coupons every 6 months and 2% annual yield compounded semiannually. What is its Macaulay convexity in terms of years?

Application questions

11. A 5-year $1,000 bond with annual coupons of 3% is sold at par.
    a. Compute the Macaulay duration for the bond.
    b. Using the Macaulay duration, calculate the modified duration for the bond?
    c. Compute the Macaulay convexity for the bond.
    d. Compute the modified convexity for the bond.

12. A 5-year $1,000 bond has annual coupons of 4% and a yield rate of 1.5% annually.
    a. Compute the Macaulay duration for the bond.
    b. Using the Macaulay duration, calculate the modified duration for the bond?
    c. Compute the Macaulay convexity for the bond.
    d. Compute the modified convexity for the bond.

13. A 3-year $1,000 bond with 4% coupons paid semiannually is bought at par.
    a. Compute the Macaulay duration for the bond.
    b. Using the Macaulay duration, calculate the modified duration for the bond?
    c. Compute the Macaulay convexity for the bond.
    d. Compute the modified convexity for the bond.

14. A 4-year $1,000 bond with 4% coupons paid semiannually is bought to yield 1.5% convertible semiannually.
    a. Compute the Macaulay duration for the bond.
    b. Using the Macaulay duration, calculate the modified duration for the bond?
    c. Compute the Macaulay convexity for the bond.
    d. Compute the modified convexity for the bond.

15. You have two bonds in your portfolio: A 3-year $1,000 bond with semiannual coupons of 4% annual that is sold a par and a 2-year $1,000 bond with semiannual coupons of 4% annual that is also sold at par.
    a. Compute the Macaulay duration for the portfolio.
    b. Using the Macaulay duration, calculate the modified duration for the portfolio?
    c. Compute the Macaulay convexity for the portfolio.
    d. Compute the modified convexity for the portfolio.

SECTION 10.3. REDINGTON IMMUNIZATION

In the previous section, we explored convexity as another way, along with duration, to quantify portfolio risk. In particular, convexity measured the curvature of a price–yield curve and, like duration, larger durations and convexities reflect more interest rate sensitivity. While duration and convexity do have some important characteristics in their own light, a key application is through the idea of portfolio immunization.

Earlier in the course, we learned that portfolio immunization is protection against changes in interest rates. That is, for small changes in interest rates, the value of the portfolio increases instead of decreases. Here we will formally revisit the idea of immunizing a portfolio to protect against interest rate changes.

Learning objectives

By the end of the section, you will be able to
- State the three necessary conditions for Redington immunization and the additional condition needed for full immunization.
- Evaluate whether a portfolio is Redington immunized and/or fully immunized.
- Suggest a strategy to make a portfolio Redington immunized and/or fully immunized.

EXAMPLE 10.3. GETTING READY TO PAY BACK A BOND DEBT

Earlier (see Section 5.3) we looked at a case where a company had issued a large zero-coupon bond as an alternative to a loan. At that time, we began to think about ways to prepare to pay off this looming debt. Now we will revisit this scenario knowing more about duration and convexity.

A few years ago, your company issued zero-coupon bonds totaling $100,000. These bonds are now due to be paid off in exactly 3 years. This means that you have to make sure your company has $100,000 on hand in 3 years. Your company has begun selling some products and has a little over $95,000 in the bank. What should you do with this money now?

You look at current selling prices for zero-coupon bonds and see the following yield rates for zero-coupon bonds in Table 10.10. Yield rates are between 2% and 3% (better than leaving the money in the bank), and so you can potentially make the company some extra money by investing in bonds.

Table 10.10 Price of $1,000 zero-coupon bonds

Payoff date (Year)	Present value ($)	Yield rate (%)
2	942.60	3
3	942.32	2
4	888.49	3

Recall that a cash-flow matching strategy would involve buying 3-year, zero-coupon bonds. If you buy 100, 3-year zero-coupon, 2% bonds this will cost you $94,232.00 today. These bonds will pay off $100,000 ($1,000 times 100) in 3 years—exactly what you need. Cash flow matching is a form of immunization—once you buy the bonds, you will be protected against changes in the interest rate.

However, look again at Table 10.10. Notice that the yield rate for 3-year bonds is currently lower than other terms (i.e., the 2-year and 4-year bonds). So, you wonder, can you save your company even more by purchasing bonds with shorter or longer payoff times?

Do you recall the problems with buying just 2-year bonds? The problem is that you will get cash in 2 years and need to find a place to invest it that will earn a high enough interest rate that you will have $100,000 when your lump-sum payment is due. Relatedly, the problem with the 4 year bonds is that you are counting on the market yield rate to be high enough when you go to sell the bonds (before they redeem) to pay off the $100,000 debt. In both cases, you have not fully eliminated interest rate risk.

Key idea

Buying assets with payoffs before the liability is problematic if yield rates go down, and buying assets with payoffs after the liability is problematic if yield rates go up.

Immunizing the liability by buying a mix of bonds

Table 10.11 shows the side-by-side comparison of the different strategies. Since changes in the yield rate for the shorter and longer term bonds have different impacts, this suggests that buying a mix of bonds may be a worthwhile strategy. We began to see this idea earlier in the course.

Table 10.11 Comparison of present and future values of different bond-purchasing strategies

	Buy 100, 3-year bonds ($)	Buy 98, 2-year bonds and reinvest the money for the third year (after bond redemption) ($)	Buy 104, 4-year bonds now and sell at end of third year ($)
Present value (today)	94,232.00	92,374.80	92,402.96
Future value (in 3 years) if rates stay at 3%	100,000.00	100,940.00	100,970.87
Future value (in 3 years) if rates drop to 1%	100,000.00	98,980.00	102,970.30
Future value (in 3 years) if rates rise to 5%	100,000.00	102,900.00	99,047.62

Key idea

Buying bonds with payoff times that fall on either side of a future liability can maximize investment return and mitigate interest-rate risk.

Redington immunization

A portfolio of assets and liabilities meets the criteria for **Redington immunization** if the following conditions are met:

1. The present value of assets is equal to (or greater than) that of liabilities

2. The Macaulay durations of assets and liabilities are equal

3. The MacC of assets is larger than the MacC of liabilities

A portfolio meeting the criteria for Redington immunization will be protected against small changes in the interest rate. In particular, the value of assets will be larger than the value of liabilities if interest rates change (go up or go down).

Definition

A portfolio meets the criteria for **Redington immunization** and is protected against small changes (increases or decreases) in the interest rate if the present value of assets and liabilities are equal, the Macaulay duration of assets and liabilities are equal, and the MacC of assets is larger than the MacC of liabilities.

Now let us check the conditions for Redington immunization. The present value of your company's debt is $94,232, and you have a little over $95,000 in the bank; thus, you have met the first criteria for Redington immunization. Now, how can you make the Macaulay durations of your assets and liabilities equal?

First, recognize that the Macaulay duration of your liability is 3 years—that is, when the entire lump-sum payment of $100,000 is due. Therefore, now, the question is how to structure a portfolio of assets with the same Macaulay duration.

Recall that the equation for Macaulay duration is

$$\text{MacD} = \sum t \frac{\text{PV}(C_t)}{\text{PV(All)}}$$

Therefore, this means that you need

$$3 = \sum t \frac{\text{PV}(C_t)}{94,232}$$

If you remember that Macaulay duration acts like a weighted average, and that you can buy 2- and 4-year bonds, if we can generate a 50–50 mix of 2- and 4-year bonds, the weighted average should be 3. Note, however, that this does not mean buying the same number of 2- and 4-year bonds. Instead, we want the present values of the 2- and 4-year bonds we buy to be the same.

More formally, we can think of the problem this way. We want both of the following equations to be true:

$$3 = 2\frac{\text{PV(2-year bonds)}}{94,232} + 4\frac{\text{PV(4-year bonds)}}{94,232}$$

$$\text{PV(2-year bonds)} + \text{PV(4-year bonds)} = 94,232$$

Solving this system of equations gives

$$PV(2\text{-year bonds}) = PV(4\text{-year bonds}) = 47,116$$

Key idea

The key to finding the appropriate mix of shorter term and longer term bonds needed to "Redington immunize" your portfolio is to set up two linear equations with two unknowns and then solve

---

For \$47,116 you can buy 50, 2-year bonds at \$942.32 each and for another \$47,116 you can buy 53.03 (we will round up to 54) 4-year bonds at \$888.49 each.

Key idea

In practice, values for X and Y may not lead to whole numbers of bonds. Generally, if you round both values up to the nearest whole numbers, you will spend a bit more up front but maintain immunization. If you round down, it is possible you will be slightly underfunded in certain scenarios.

Are we duration matched? Since we have put half of the portfolio in 2-year bonds and half in 4-year bonds, we are duration matched since

$$MacD = 2\left(\frac{PV(2 - \text{year bonds})}{94,232}\right) + 4\left(\frac{PV(4 - \text{year bonds})}{94,232}\right)$$

$$= 2\left(\frac{47,116}{94,232}\right) + 4\left(\frac{47,116}{94,232}\right) = 2\left(\frac{1}{2}\right) + 4\left(\frac{1}{2}\right) = 3$$

Is the MacC of the assets larger than the liabilities?
For assets, we have

$$MacC = 2^2\left(\frac{PV(2 - \text{year bonds})}{94,232}\right) + 4^2\left(\frac{PV(4 - \text{year bonds})}{94,232}\right)$$

$$= 4\left(\frac{47,116}{94,232}\right) + 16\left(\frac{47,116}{94,232}\right) = 4\left(\frac{1}{2}\right) + 16\left(\frac{1}{2}\right) = 2 + 8 = 10$$

For liabilities we have

$$MacC = 3^2\left(\frac{PV(3 - \text{year bonds})}{94,232}\right) = 3^2(1) = 9$$

Yes, the MacC of the assets (10) is larger than the liabilities (9). Thus, we have met the criteria for Redington immunization.

CONFIRMING REDINGTON IMMUNIZATION WORKS

Let us see why a portfolio with an equal mix (present values, not number) of 1-year and 3-year bonds is Redington immunized in this case.

Table 10.12 below adds another column for the mixed portfolio we proposed purchasing above. As you can see, the value of the portfolio is above the target value whether interest rates increase or decrease.

Table 10.12 Comparison of present value and future value of different bond-purchasing strategies

	Buy 100, 3-year bonds ($)	**Buy 98, 2-year bonds and reinvest the money for the third year (after bond redemption) ($)**	**Buy 104, 4-year bonds now and sell at end of third year ($)**	**Buy 50 2-year bonds and 54 4-year bonds ($)**
Present value (today)	94,232.00	92,374.80	92,402.96	95,094.46
Future value (in 3 years) if rates stay at 3%	100,000.00	100,940.00	100,970.87	103,927.20
Future value (in 3 years) if rates drop to 1%	100,000.00	98,980.00	102,970.30	103,965.30
Future value (in 3 years) if rates rise to 5%	100,000.00	102,900.00	99,047.62	103,928.60

You may notice that this portfolio cost us a bit more up front than the others did. This is because we rounded up the number of bonds suggested to be "on the safe side." However, in this case, even if you only bought 53 of the 4-year bonds, your portfolio would cost only $94,205.97 now and yield at least $102,956.30 (details not shown).

Full immunization

Redington immunization only guarantees that assets will be larger than liabilities for small changes in interest rates. A fully immunized portfolio guarantees that assets will be larger than liabilities for any change in interest rates.

Definition

Full immunization is when a portfolios value increases for any change in interest rates. The criteria for full immunization are the same as for Redington immunization but require that there is an asset cash flow before the liability and another one after the liability.

This portfolio is fully immunized since we used a mix of 2- and 4-year bonds (asset cash flows) which fall before and after the liability (3-year payment).

CONCLUDING REMARKS

1. In the exploration above, you actually had $950,000 to invest but only needed to invest $946,267. If you invest all of the $950,000 in approximately a 50−50 mix, you will be Redington (and fully) immunized. Having a larger present value of assets vs liabilities is not a problem!

2. There are some hefty assumptions to Redington and full immunization including yield rates being the same. Of course, this is not going to be actually true in practice but can give insight into strategies you can take to mitigate risk. Computers can be used to quickly evaluate a strategy across a wide-variety of more realistic scenarios (e.g., dissimilar changes in yield rate for different assets, etc.)

EXPLORATION 10.3. REVISITING ANTICIPATING PAYING BACK BONDS

Let us again assume that you are at a company that has issued some large zero-coupon bonds that are coming due in 2 years. In particular, you will owe $1,000,000 in 2 years. Your company currently has $950,000 on hand.

1. What characteristic must the bonds have so the $950,000 you have on hand now can be used to pay back the $1,000,000 bond issue today? What is a potential downside of using this approach?

Recall that cash flow matching is a strategy where future liabilities are matched exactly by future assets.

2. Explain how you could use zero-coupon bonds *to cash flow match* your $1 million liability.

Recall that a portfolio is immunized if it is protected against interest rate risk—that is, if it is not negatively impacted by changes to the interest rate.

3. Explain how buying zero-coupon bonds could immunize your portfolio.

Cash-flowing matching may be a good strategy to mitigate interest-rate risk.

4. If 2-year, zero-coupon bonds are currently yielding 1.5% effective annually (the 2-year spot rate, s_2, is 1.5%), what is the selling price for the bonds if their face value is $1,000? How many bonds will you need to buy today to cash-flow match your liability? What is the problem?

It is possible that other investments may pay better yield rates or have other advantages.

Buying bonds with different payoff times

Let us imagine that 1-year zero-coupon bonds are paying 2.8% effective annually, and 3-year zero-coupon bonds are also currently yielding 2.8% effective annually. Earlier in the course, we began to explore a strategy, which could take advantage of these higher yielding bonds.

Buying a 1-year coupon bond

5. What is the selling price for the 1-year bond? How many can you buy today?

6. What is one practical problem with buying the 1-year bond as a way to invest money to pay off the liability?

7. If you go ahead and buy as many 1-year zero-coupon bonds now as you can, then, after 1 year, you buy more 1-year zero-coupon bonds, what are you hoping is true about the 1-year spot rate at that time? What is the risk?

Buying a 3-year coupon bond

8. What is the selling price for a 3-year zero-coupon bond yielding 2.8% annually? How many can you buy today?

9. If you go ahead and buy as many 3-year zero-coupon bonds now as you can, then, after 2 years, you go to the market to sell the bonds in order to get the cash needed to pay off your liability, what are you hoping is true about the 1-year spot rate at that time? What is the risk?

If you buy the shorter term (1-year) bond, it is problematic if yield rates (in particular, the 1-year spot rate 1 year from now) go down. If you buy the longer term (3-year) bond, it is problematic if yield rates (in particular, the 1-year spot rate 2 years from now) go up. Thus, there is still interest rate risk with either strategy.

Key idea

Buying assets with payoffs before the liability is problematic if yield rates go down, and buying assets with payoffs after the liability is problematic if yield rates go up.

Immunizing the liability by buying a mix of bonds

Since changes in the yield rate for the shorter and longer term bonds have different impacts, this suggests that buying a mix of bonds may be a worthwhile strategy. We began to see this idea earlier in the course.

Key idea

Buying bonds with payoff times that fall on either side of a future liability can maximize investment return and mitigate interest-rate risk

Let us assume that you invest half of your current savings of $950,000 in 1-year bonds and the other half in 3-year bonds.

10. How many 1-year bonds and how many 3-year bonds will you have in your portfolio?

11. Find the Macaulay duration of your portfolio of assets. That is, what is the Macaulay duration of your portfolio of 1- and 3-year bonds?

12. What is the Macaulay duration of your portfolio of liabilities? That is, what is the Macaulay duration of the bonds you are due to pay off in 2 years?

13. How do the Macaulay durations of your assets and liabilities compare?

14. Find the MacC of your portfolio of assets.

15. Find the MacC of your portfolio of liabilities.

16. How do the MacCs of your assets and liabilities compare?

Redington immunization

A portfolio of assets and liabilities meets the criteria for **Redington Immunization** if the following conditions are met:

1. The present value of assets is equal to (or greater than) that of liabilities

2. The Macaulay durations of assets and liabilities are equal

3. The MacC of assets is larger than the MacC of liabilities

A portfolio meeting the criteria for Redington immunization will be protected against small changes in the interest rate. In particular, the value of assets will be larger than the value of liabilities if interest rates change (go up or go down).

Definition

A portfolio meets the criteria for **Redington immunization** and is protected against small changes (increases or decreases) in the interest rate if the present value of assets and liabilities are equal, the Macaulay duration of assets and liabilities are equal, and the MacC of assets is larger than the MacC of liabilities.

Let us see why a portfolio with an equal mix (present values, not number) of 1- and 3-year bonds is Redington immunized in this case.

When examining Redington immunization, you need to pick a market yield rate that applies to all assets and liabilities. In this case, we will use 2.8%.

17. First, find the present value of your 2-year bond liability at a market yield rate of 2.8%. Is this more or less than $950,000 you have on hand?

The fact that you have more than the present value of your liability at a market yield rate of 2.8% is why investing at 2.8% is a doable strategy to meet your liability.

Key idea

The key to finding the appropriate mix of shorter term and longer term bonds needed to "Redington Immunize" your portfolio is to set up two linear equations with two unknowns and then solve.

Let X be the amount you will invest in 1-year bonds and Y be the amount that you will invest in 3-year bonds. Thus, you want to have $X + Y = \$946,267$.

18. Now, write an equation for the Macaulay duration for your asset portfolio in terms of the unknowns X and Y. Hint: You need the

Macaulay duration for the assets to equal the Macaulay duration of the liabilities. What is the Macaulay duration of the liabilities?

19. Use your answer to the previous question and the fact that $X + Y = \$946,267$ to find the values of X and Y. Interpret these values.

Notice that earlier, we looked at a portfolio that did invest half the assets in 1-year bonds and the other half in 3-year bonds and the MacC was five, and this is larger than the MacC for the liability (2-year bond). Thus, we have met the criteria for Redington immunization.

20. Starting with \$946,267, how many 1-year bonds should you buy and how many 3-year bonds should you buy? Your answers should be in fractions.

Note that in this case, the values of X and Y we calculated do not lead to whole numbers of bonds. In practice, buying fractions of bonds may not be possible.

Key idea

In practice, values for X and Y may not lead to whole numbers of bonds. Generally, if you round both values up to the nearest whole numbers, you will spend a bit more up front but maintain immunization. If you round down, it is possible you will be slightly underfunded in certain scenarios.

Confirming redington immunization works

Since the portfolio is Redington immunized by investing half of your money in 1-year bonds and half in 3-year bonds, we should be in good shape to pay back the liability if interest rates change.

21. Assume that you invest \$946,267 today with half in 1-year bonds and half in 3-year bonds. Confirm that you have enough to pay back your liability if effective annual interest rates increase to 2.9% after you buy the bonds. Round up the number of bonds purchased.

22. Assume that you invest \$946,267 today with half in 1-year bonds and half in 3-year bonds. Confirm that you have enough to pay back your liability if effective annual interest rates decrease to 2.7% after you buy the bonds. Round up the number of bonds purchased.

Fig. 10.4 illustrates the fact that this portfolio is Redington immunized since the assets curve is strictly above the liabilities curve for small changes in the yield rate.

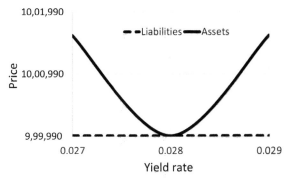

Figure 10.4 A visual look at Redington immunization.

Full immunization

Redington immunization only guarantees that assets will be larger than liabilities for small changes in interest rates. A fully immunized portfolio guarantees that assets will be larger than liabilities for any change in interest rates.

Definition

Full immunization is when a portfolios value increases for any change in interest rates. The criteria for full immunization are the same as for Redington immunization but require that there is an asset cash flow before the liability and another one after the liability.

---

23. Does the strategy proposed above yield a fully immunized portfolio?

See the end of Example 10.3 for a few concluding remarks.

▷ SUMMARY

In this section, we have seen how Redington immunizing a portfolio helps protect against interest rate risk by ensuring that assets will be greater than liabilities regardless of changes in the interest rate. When cash flow matching is not possible, Redington immunization provides a reasonable way to protect your current assets from leading to a situation where you cannot afford to cover your future liabilities.

HOMEWORK QUESTIONS: SECTION 10.3

Conceptual questions

1. If you have a liability that is due in 3 years, and you want to cover it with a bond purchase now, why might it be to your advantage to do something other than just buy 3-year bonds?

2. What does it mean for a portfolio to be immunized?

3. Buying assets with payoffs before a liability is due to be paid could be a problem if yield rates go _____(up/down) while buying assets with payoffs after a liability is due to be paid could be a problem if yield rates go _____(up/down).

4. What things need to be equal for a portfolio to meet the conditions of Redington immunization? What else has to occur for a portfolio to meet the conditions of Redington immunization?

5. What additional condition is needed for full immunization that is not needed for a Redington immunization?

Practice questions

6. The yield rate on zero-coupon bonds is 1.5% and you have $400,000 to invest, $250,000 in 2-year bonds and $150,000 in 5-year bonds. If both types of bonds have a face value of $1,000, how many bonds of each type can you buy?

7. If your portfolio is set up, so you will be receiving $250,000 in 2 years and $150,000 in 5 years, what is the Macaulay duration for these assets?

8. If your portfolio is set up so you will be receiving $250,000 in 2 years and $150,000 in 5 years, what is the Macaulay convexity for these assets?

9. If you have plan to invest $400,000 in 2-year and 5-year zero-coupon bonds, how much should you invest in each if you want the Macaulay duration of this investment to be three?

10. You invest $130,000 in 5-year zero-coupon bonds with a yield rate of 1.5% and a face value of $1,000.
   a. How many bonds can you buy?
   b. After 3 years, you decide to sell, and the yield rate increases to 1.6%. What is the value of your bonds?

Application questions

11. You have a payment of $500,000 that is due in 5 years. You will be using 3-year and 10-year zero-coupon bonds to immunize your liability. The annual effective yield rate is 2% on both the assets and liability.
   a. What is the present value of the liability?
   b. What is the Macaulay duration of the liability?
   c. If you have the same present value on your assets, how much should you invest in each type of bond so your assets have the same Macaulay duration as your liability?
   d. What is the Macaulay convexity of the liability?
   e. What is the Macaulay convexity of your bonds investment from part (c)?
   f. Does this portfolio meet the conditions to be Redington immunized? Full immunization?

12. Your company has a liability that is composed of $10,000 due in 1 year and $20,000 due in 2 years. This liability has spot rates of $s_1 = 0.01$ and $s_2 = 0.02$. You will be using 1- and 4-year zero-coupon bonds to immunize this liability. The yield rates of the assets are the same as the liability.
   a. What is the present value of the liability?
   b. What is the Macaulay duration of the liability?

    c. If your assets have the same present value on your liability, how much should you invest in each type of bond so your assets have the same Macaulay duration as your liability?

    d. What is the Macaulay convexity of the liability?

    e. What is the Macaulay convexity of your bonds investment from part (c)?

    f. Does this portfolio meet the conditions to be Redington immunized? Full immunization?

13. Your company has a liability that is composed of $20,000 due in 1 year and $50,000 due in 2 years. This liability has forward rates of $f_{0,1} = 0.02$ and $f_{1,2} = 0.025$. You will be using 1- and 3-year zero-coupon bonds to immunize this liability. The yield rate on the assets is the same as the liability.

    a. What is the present value of the liability?

    b. What is the Macaulay duration of the liability?

    c. If your assets have the same present value on your liability, how much should you invest in each type of bond so your assets have the same Macaulay duration as your liability?

    d. What is the Macaulay convexity of the liability?

    e. What is the Macaulay convexity of your bonds investment from part (c)?

    f. Does this portfolio meet the conditions to be Redington immunized? Full immunization?

END OF CHAPTER SUMMARY

In this chapter, we have revisited portfolios, with a particular focus on evaluating and mitigating interest rate risk. We started by reviewing Macaulay duration—a measure of the average time of cash flows which is a proxy measurement of interest rate risk since cash flows further into the future will be impacted more greatly by changes in the interest rate. We saw, however, that the ModD was helpful because it provided a direct estimate of the actual amount of change in the current price of the future cash flows as a function of changes to the yield rate. One downside of measures of duration was that they assumed a linear price-yield relationship. Convexity helped improved these estimates by taking into account the curvature of the price-yield relationship. Furthermore, convexity was one of the three conditions for a portfolio to be immunized, with the convexity of assets needing to be larger than the convexity of liabilities (along with equal durations and present values) in order for a portfolio to be protected against interest rate changes.

END OF CHAPTER EXERCISES

(SOA EXAM FM SAMPLE QUESTIONS November 2005, Question 21)

1. Which of the following statements about immunization strategies are true?
   I. To achieve immunization, the convexity of the assets must equal the convexity of the liabilities.
   II. The full immunization technique is designed to work for any change in the interest rate.
   III. The theory of immunization was developed to protect against adverse effects created by changes in interest rates
   A. None
   B. I and II only
   C. I and III only
   D. II and III only
   E. The correct answer is not given by (A), (B), (C), and (D).

(SOA EXAM FM SAMPLE QUESTIONS Interest Theory, Question 36)

2. A common stock pays a constant dividend at the end of each year into perpetuity.

   Using an annual effective interest rate of 10%, calculate the Macaulay duration of the stock.
   A. 7 years
   B. 9 years
   C. 11 years
   D. 19 years
   E. 27 years

(SOA EXAM FM SAMPLE QUESTIONS Interest Theory, Question 37)

3. A common stock pays dividends at the end of each year into perpetuity. Assume that the dividend increases by 2% each year.

Using an annual effective interest rate of 5%, calculate the Macaulay duration of the stock in years.

A. 27
B. 35
C. 44
D. 52
E. 58

(SOA EXAM FM SAMPLE QUESTIONS Interest Theory, Question 51)

4. Joe must pay liabilities of 1,000 due 6 months from now and another 1,000 due one-year from now. There are two available investments:

Bond I: A 6-month bond with face amount of 1,000, an 8% nominal annual coupon rate convertible semi-annually, and a 6% nominal annual yield rate convertible semi-annually;

Bond II: A one-year bond with face amount of 1,000, a 5% nominal annual coupon rate convertible semi-annually, and a 7% nominal annual yield rate convertible semi-annually.

Calculate the amount of each bond that Joe should purchase to exactly match the liabilities.

A. Bond I—1, Bond II—0.97561
B. Bond I—0.93809, Bond II—1
C. Bond I—0.97561, Bond II—0.94293
D. Bond I—0.93809, Bond II—0.97561
E. Bond I—0.98345, Bond II—0.97561

(SOA EXAM FM SAMPLE QUESTIONS Interest Theory, Question 52)

5. Joe must pay liabilities of 2,000 due one year from now and another 1,000 due two years from now. He exactly matches his liabilities with the following two investments:

Mortgage I: A one-year mortgage in which X is lent. It is repaid with a single payment at time one. The annual effective interest rate is 6%.

Mortgage II: A two-year mortgage in which Y is lent. It is repaid with two equal annual payments. The annual effective interest rate is 7%.

Calculate $X + Y$.

A. 2,600
B. 2,682
C. 2,751
D. 2,825
E. 3,000

(SOA EXAM FM SAMPLE QUESTIONS Interest Theory, Question 53)

6. Joe must pay liabilities of 1,000 due one year from now and another 2,000 due three years from now. There are two available investments:

Bond I: A one-year zero-coupon bond that matures for 1,000. The yield rate is 6% per year

Bond II: A two-year zero-coupon bond with face amount of 1,000. The yield rate is 7% per year.

At the present time, the one-year forward rate for an investment made two years from now is 6.5%

Joe plans to buy amounts of each bond. He plans to reinvest the proceeds from Bond II in a one-year zero-coupon bond. Assuming the reinvestment earns the forward rate; calculate the total purchase price of Bond I and Bond II where the amounts are selected to exactly match the liabilities.

A. 2,584
B. 2,697

    C. 2,801

    D. 2,907

    E. 3,000

(SOA EXAM FM SAMPLE QUESTIONS Interest Theory, Question 68)

7. Sam buys an eight-year, 5,000 par bond with an annual coupon rate of 5%, paid annually. The bond sells for 5,000. Let d_1 be the Macaulay duration just before the first coupon is paid. Let d_2 be the Macaulay duration just after the first coupon is paid.

    Calculate $\frac{d_1}{d_2}$.

    A. 0.91

    B. 0.93

    C. 0.95

    D. 0.97

    E. 1.00

(SOA EXAM FM SAMPLE QUESTIONS Interest Theory, Question 70)

8. Determine which of the following statements is false with respect to Redington immunization.
    A. Modified duration may change at different rates for each of the assets and liabilities as time goes by.
    B. Redington immunization requires infrequent rebalancing to keep modified duration of assets equal to modified duration of liabilities.
    C. This technique is designed to work only for small changes in the interest rate.
    D. The yield curve is assumed to be flat.
    E. The yield curve shifts in parallel when the interest rate changes.

(SOA EXAM FM SAMPLE QUESTIONS Interest Theory, Question 71)

9. Aakash has a liability of 6,000 due in four years. This liability will be met with payments of A in two years and B in six years. Aakash is

employing a full immunization strategy using an annual effective interest rate of 5%.

Calculate $|A - B|$.

A. 0
B. 146
C. 293
D. 586
E. 881

(SOA EXAM FM SAMPLE QUESTIONS Interest Theory, Question 72)

10. Jia Wen has a liability of 12,000 due in eight years. This liability will be met with payments of 5,000 in five years and B in $8 + b$ years. Jia Wen is employing a full immunization strategy using an annual effective interest rate of 3%.

Calculate $\dfrac{B}{b}$.

A. 2,807
B. 2,873
C. 2,902
D. 2,976
E. 3,019

(SOA EXAM FM SAMPLE QUESTIONS Interest Theory, Question 73)

11. Trevor has assets at time 2 of A and at time 9 of B. He has a liability of 95,000 at time 5. Trevor has achieved Redington immunization in his portfolio using an annual effective interest rate of 4%.

Calculate $\dfrac{A}{B}$.

A. 0.7307
B. 0.9670
C. 1.0000
D. 1.0132
E. 1.3686

(SOA EXAM FM SAMPLE QUESTIONS Interest Theory, Question 121)

12. Annuity A pays 1 at the beginning of each year for three years. Annuity B pays 1 at the beginning of each year for four years.

The Macaulay duration of Annuity A at the time of purchase is 0.93. Both annuities offer the same yield rate.
Calculate the Macaulay duration of Annuity B at the time of purchase.
  A. 1.240
  B. 1.369
  C. 1.500
  D. 1.930
  E. 1.965

(SOA EXAM FM SAMPLE QUESTIONS Interest Theory, Question 124)

13. Rhonda purchases a perpetuity providing a payment of 1 at the beginning of each year. The perpetuity's Macaulay duration is 30 years.

Calculate the modified duration of this perpetuity.
  A. 28.97
  B. 29.00
  C. 29.03
  D. 29.07
  E. 29.10

(SOA EXAM FM SAMPLE QUESTIONS Interest Theory, Question 126)

14. Which of the following statements regarding immunization are true?
  I. If long-term interest rates are lower than short-term rates, the need for immunization is reduced.
  II. Either Macaulay or modified duration can be used to develop an immunization strategy.

III. Both processes of matching the present values of the flows or the flows themselves will produce exact matching.

A. I only

B. II only

C. III only

D. I, II, and III

E. The correct answer is not given by (A), (B), (C), or (D).

(SOA EXAM FM SAMPLE QUESTIONS Interest Theory, Question 127)

15. A company owes 500 and 1,000 to be paid at the end of year one and year four, respectively. The company will set up an investment program to match the duration and the present value of the above obligation using an annual effective interest rate of 10%.

The investment program produces asset cash flows of X today and Y in three years.

Calculate X and determine whether the investment program satisfies the conditions for Redington immunization.

A. $X = 75$ and the Redington immunization conditions are not satisfied.

B. $X = 75$ and the Redington immunization conditions are satisfied.

C. $X = 1,138$ and the Redington immunization conditions are not satisfied.

D. $X = 1,138$ and the Redington immunization conditions are satisfied.

E. $X = 1,414$ and the Redington immunization conditions are satisfied

(SOA EXAM FM SAMPLE QUESTIONS Interest Theory, Question 128)

16. An insurance company has a known liability of 1,000,000 that is due 8 years from now. The technique of full immunization is to be employed. Asset I will provide a cash flow of 300,000 exactly 6 years

from now. Asset II will provide a cash flow of X, exactly y years from now, where $y > 8$.

The annual effective interest rate is 4%.
Calculate X.

A. 697,100
B. 698,600
C. 700,000
D. 701,500
E. 702,900

(SOA EXAM FM SAMPLE QUESTIONS Interest Theory, Question 129)

17. A company has liabilities of 573 due at the end of year 2 and 701 due at the end of year 5.

    A portfolio comprises two zero-coupon bonds, Bond A and Bond B. Determine which portfolio produces a Redington immunization of the liabilities using an annual effective interest rate of 7.0%.
    A. Bond A: 1-year, current price 500; Bond B: 6-years, current price 500
    B. Bond A: 1-year, current price 572; Bond B: 6-years, current price 428
    C. Bond A: 3-years, current price 182; Bond B: 4-years, current price 1,092
    D. Bond A: 3-years, current price 637; Bond B: 4-years, current price 637
    E. Bond A: 3.5 years, current price 1,000; Bond B: Not used

(SOA EXAM FM SAMPLE QUESTIONS Interest Theory, Question 130)

18. A company has liabilities of 402.11 due at the end of each of the next three years. The company will invest 1,000 today to fund these payouts. The only investments available are one-year and three-year zero-coupon bonds, and the yield curve is flat at a 10% annual effective rate. The company wishes to match the duration of its assets to the duration of its liabilities.

Determine how much the company should invest in each bond.

A. 366 in the one-year bond and 634 in the three-year bond.

B. 484 in the one-year bond and 516 in the three-year bond.

C. 500 in the one-year bond and 500 in the three-year bond.

D. 532 in the one-year bond and 468 in the three-year bond.

E. 634 in the one-year bond and 366 in the three-year bond.

(SOA EXAM FM SAMPLE QUESTIONS Interest Theory, Question 131)

19. You are given the following information about a company's liabilities:

  - Present value: 9,697
  - Macaulay duration: 15.24
  - Macaulay convexity: 242.47

The company decides to create an investment portfolio by making investments into two of the following three zero-coupon bonds: 5-year, 15-year, and 20-year. The company would like its position to be Redington immunized against small changes in yield rate.

The annual effective yield rate for each of the bonds is 7.5%.

Determine which of the following portfolios the company should create.

  A. Invest 3,077 for the 5-year bond and 6,620 for the 20-year bond.

  B. Invest 6,620 for the 5-year bond and 3,077 for the 20-year bond.

  C. Invest 465 for the 15-year bond and 9,232 for the 20-year bond.

  D. Invest 4,156 for the 15-year bond and 5,541 for the 20-year bond.

  E. Invest 9,232 for the 15-year bond and 465 for the 20-year bond.

(SOA EXAM FM SAMPLE QUESTIONS Interest Theory, Question 132)

20. A bank accepts a 20,000 deposit from a customer on which it guarantees to pay an annual effective interest rate of 10% for two years. The customer needs to withdraw half of the accumulated value at the end of the first year. The customer will withdraw the remaining value at the end of the second year.

The bank has the following investment options available, which may be purchased in any quantity:

Bond H: A one-year zero-coupon bond yielding 10% annually

Bond I: A two-year zero-coupon bond yielding 11% annually

Bond J: A two-year bond that sells at par with 12% annual coupons

Any portion of the 20,000 deposit that is not needed to be invested in bonds is retained by the bank as profit.

Determine which of the following investment strategies produces the highest profit for the bank and is guaranteed to meet the customer's withdrawal needs.

A. 9,091 in Bond H, 8,264 in Bond I, 2,145 in Bond J

B. 10,000 in Bond H, 10,000 in Bond I

C. 10,000 in Bond H, 9,821 in Bond I

D. 8,910 in Bond H, 731 in Bond I, 10,000 in Bond J

E. 8,821 in Bond H, 10,804 in Bond J

(SOA EXAM FM SAMPLE QUESTIONS Interest Theory, Question 69)

21. An insurance company must pay liabilities of 99 at the end of one year, 102 at the end of two years and 100 at the end of three years. The only investments available to the company are the following three bonds. Bond A and Bond C are annual coupon bonds. Bond B is a zero-coupon bond.

Bond	Maturity (in years)	Yield-to-Maturity (Annualized)	Coupon Rate
A	1	6%	7%
B	2	7%	0%
C	3	9%	5%

All three bonds have a par value of 100 and will be redeemed at par. Calculate the number of units of Bond A that must be purchased to match the liabilities exactly.

A. 0.8807

B. 0.8901

C. 0.8975

D. 0.9524

E. 0.9724

GLOSSARY

Annual percentage yield (APY) *annual percentage yield (APY)* is the annual effective rate of interest.

Account chart when solving problems with multiple deposits and withdrawals and/or changes in effective interest rate, an *account chart* is a useful way to summarize information. An account chart summarizes account balances, interest, deposits, and withdrawals over time, usually with one row for each compounding period.

Accumulated value the *accumulated value* of a series of payments of $1 at effective interest rate i, over n payment periods, each payment happening at the end of the period, is equal to $s_{\overline{n}|i}$, pronounced "s-angle-n."

Amortization *amortization* is a term used to describe how a debt is paid off with a fixed repayment schedule of equally sized payments.

Amortization table an *amortization table* is a table that shows the principal balance, interest accrued, and amount of money paid toward principal each period when payments are equally sized.

Amount of premium (or discount) the *amount of premium (or discount)* is the absolute value of the difference between the selling price of the bond and the face value of the bond.

Annual effective discount rate the *annual effective discount rate (d)* is an alternative way to communicate how much interest is earned on an investment. In particular, it is computed as interest earned divided by the future value of the account. It is commonly used in financial situations where the future value of the account is predetermined.

Annuity an *annuity* is a series of often equally sized (level) payments which continue for a finite amount of time. Unless otherwise specified, you can assume that the payments are equally sized and spaced equally apart.

Annuity-due an *annuity-due* is an annuity where the payments occur at the beginning of the period.

Annuity-immediate an *annuity-immediate* is an annuity where the payments occur at the end of the period.

Arithmetically increasing (decreasing) annuity an *arithmetically increasing (or decreasing) annuity*, increases (decreases) by a fixed amount each period.

Basis points *basis points* are the most commonly used units when talking about yield rate changes. One basis point is 0.01% and, thus, 100 basis points is equivalent to 1%.

Bond a *bond* is a formal agreement between the borrower (the bond issuer—often a company or government) and the lender (the bond purchaser—often an individual or another company) for the borrower to pay the lender certain amounts at future dates.

Book value the *book value* of a bond is the present value of the future coupon payments plus the present value of the redemption price calculated at the original yield rate at the time the bond was sold. It is the amount shown on the issuing companies balance sheet or "books" (hence the name "book" value).

Callable bond a *callable bond* is a bond with rules that allow for the issuer (e.g., company) to pay the bond off early.

Callable bonds typically come with one of three options: **European** *(one call date),* **Bermuda** *(multiple call dates), or* **American** *(range of call dates after an initial lockdown period where the bond cannot be called). The bond is called when it is redeemed early, and is typically redeemed for a higher price — the redemption value plus the call premium.*

Capitalizing *capitalizing* interest on a loan occurs when no interest payment is made and so the interest on the loan gets added to the loan balance.

Cash-flow matching *cash-flow matching* is a strategy where future liabilities are matched exactly by future assets. This means that, regardless of whether or not yield rates change, the liability can be paid off.

Cash flow problem a *cash flow problem* is a financial problem where there are multiple deposits and/or withdrawals to an account with a constant or variable rate of interest. Goals of such problems are usually to calculate the total fund balance, find the value of particular deposits or withdrawals given the final fund balance or to find the interest rate needed or total amount of time of the investment to achieve some final fund balance.

Certificate of deposit a *certificate of deposit* is type of savings account that prespecifies the length of time that the deposit will be held by the bank with a prespecified, usually unchanging, interest rate. Penalties are often incurred if money is withdrawn (taken out) sooner.

Compound interest *compound interest* is when the amount of interest that is paid grows over time reflecting the fact that interest paid at the end of each period is reinvested in the account. In essence, compound interest means that you are earning "interest on the interest."

Compounding period the *compounding period* is the period over which the savings institution pays interest.

Convexity the *convexity* measures the nonlinear relationship between interest rates and price using the second derivative.

Coupon rate *coupon rate* is the value that is multiplied by the face value of the bond to find the coupon size. Most coupon rates are stated as a nominal coupon rate with semiannual compounding.

Coupons *coupons* are periodic payments made from the bond issuer to the investor throughout the loan term, and are usually paid out in addition to a lump-sum at the end of the term (the redemption value).

Defaulting if a borrower cannot pay back their loan it is called *defaulting* on the loan and the lender may be able to take things the borrower owns (repossession) or garnish wages (take a portion of the borrower's income).

Discount (bond) a bond is selling at a *discount* if its selling price is less than the face value.

Discount factor the *discount factor*, represented by the Greek letter nu (v), but sometimes called "v" in practice, is the present value of $1 paid in 1 year at an effective annual rate of interest, i. Thus, $v = 1/(1 + i)$ since $v(1 + i) = 1$

Dollar-weighted rate of return the *dollar-weighted rate of return* (or internal rate of return; IRR) is the rate so that if all deposits and withdrawals were subject to the same interest rate over the entire investment time period, the individual transactions would accumulate to the investments ending balance.

Drop payment a *drop payment* is the final payment on a loan and is typically of a slightly different size than the rest of the payments in order to make the balance on the loan exactly zero. It is standard practice to set the regular payments through the life of the loan slightly larger, so that the drop payment will be slightly lower than the rest.

Duration matching *duration matching* involves creating a portfolio with a duration equal to the time of the future liability and can create an immunized portfolio.

Dynamic account chart a *dynamic account chart* uses technology to instantly update all balances in an account chart to alleviate tedious by hand calculations. Microsoft Excel is a popular business tool to create dynamic account charts.

Effective rate of interest the *effective rate of interest*, often denoted by the letter i, is the number which, when multiplied by the beginning deposit balance, K, yields the dollar amount of the interest earned at the end of the first period. i is typically reported as a decimal, not as a percentage.

Face value the *face value* (par value) of the bond is the value multiplied by the coupon rate of the bond to find the coupon size. Typically, the face value is equal to the redemption value.

Force of interest the *force of interest* (∂) is the nominal annual interest rate if there is continuous compounding (infinitely many compounding periods in the year).

Forward rate a *forward rate* (f_{t_1,t_2}) is the anticipated market interest rate on money invested at time t_1 and held until time t_2.

Geometrically increasing (decreasing) annuity a *geometrically increasing* (or decreasing) annuity (or perpetuity) grows (declines) by a percentage each period.

Grade the *grade* of a bond is measure of its investment risk. Market yield rates are generally higher for more risky bonds.

Immunized a portfolio is *immunized* if it is protected against interest rate risk (changing interest rates).

Inflation *inflation* is the increase in prices and decrease in the purchasing power of money over time.

Interest *interest* is the amount of money the bank or other depositing institution pays you for the privilege of storing (and using!) your money. Usually, interest is paid as a percentage of the amount deposited and is paid at regular, predetermined intervals.

Liability a *liability* is a future debt that is owed. For example, a company issuing a bond views the coupon payments and future redemption as liabilities to be paid in the future.

Limit the *limit* of a sequence of numbers is the value that the sequence approaches (or converges to) as the sequence continues indefinitely.

Loan a *loan* is when one entity (e.g., a bank) lends money to another entity (e.g., an individual). Typically, the borrower pays back the original amount of the loan plus interest.

Maccaulay duration the *Macaulay duration* is the weighted average time that future investment payments will occur.

Modified duration the *modified duration* (*ModD*) measures the change in price as a function of the yield rate. In particular, it is the percent rate of change in price for a 100 basis point (1 percentage point) change in yield rate.

Nominal rate of discount a *nominal rate of discount* ($d^{(p)}$) is like a nominal rate of interest in that it gives the (typically) annual rate found by multiplying p (the number of compounding periods in a year) by the effective discount rate, d, per period. Note: We use p here for discount rate, but the idea is the same as the variable m, which we use for nominal interest rates.

Nominal rate of interest with monthly compounding the *nominal rate of interest with monthly compounding (or APR)*, denoted $i^{(12)}$, and pronounced "i upper 12," is the interest rate such that the effective interest rate for each month is $i^{(12)}/12$. The compounding period for APR will be monthly unless otherwise stated since in practice APR can sometimes to refer to other (nonmonthly) compounding periods.

Par (bond) a bond is selling a *par* if the selling price equals its face value.

Perpetuity a *perpetuity* is a series of payments that continues forever. When organizations or individuals "live off the interest"—never spending any of the balance—this amounts to a perpetuity.

Perpetuity-due a *perpetuity-due* is a perpetuity where the payments occur on the first day of the period.

Perpetuity-immediate a *perpetuity-immediate* is a perpetuity where the payments occur on the last day of the period.

Portfolio a *portfolio* is a collection of investments (e.g., stocks, bonds, etc.) held by a person or organization. While not necessary, portfolios often span multiple market sectors to spread out investment risk.

Preferred stock *preferred stock* is part ownership in a company, but comes with the right to regular (usually quarterly) dividend payments. Payments of dividends on preferred stock are guaranteed as long as the company has paid its creditors.

Present value the *present value* of a series of payments of $1 at an effective interest rate of i, over n payment periods, with each payment happening at the end of the period, is equal to $a_{\overline{n}|i}$, pronounced "a-angle-n." If $n = \infty$ then this is a perpetuity.

Premium (bond) if a bond's selling price is more than the face value, the bond is said to be selling at a *premium*.

Principal the *principal* of a loan is the amount that the borrower owes the lender at any particular time; it is the loan balance.

Recursive approach a *recursive approach* to solving cash flow problems computes account balances by moving forward in time with each transaction. For accounts with many transactions this can be tedious to do by hand, but technology can often speed the process, especially when there are patterns in the transactions (e.g., same deposit amount each period).

Redemption value the *redemption value* of the bond is the amount that is paid from the bond issuer to the bond holder at the end of the bond term.

Redington immunication a portfolio meets the criteria for *Redington immunization* and is protected against small changes (increases or decreases) in the interest rate if the present value of assets and liabilities are equal, the Macaulay duration of assets and liabilities are equal and the Macaulay convexity of assets is larger than the Macaulay convexity of liabilities.

Refinancing *refinancing* involves ending the terms of the original loan and taking the principal balance on the original loan and making that the starting balance on a new loan, with new terms.

Retrospective method the *retrospective method* for finding payment sizes and loan balances views loans as a form of a sinking fund where the loan balance accumulates.

Simple interest *simple interest* is when the amount of interest that is paid stays the same over time reflecting the fact that interest paid at the end of each period is not reinvested in the account. In essence, simple interest means that you are not earning "interest on the interest" as you are in the case of compound interest.

Sinking fund a *sinking fund* is a fund that receives regular payments from the borrower to accumulate value so it can be used later for some other purpose—for example, against the principal on an interest-only loan. Sometimes the entire approach of an interest-only loan combined with a sinking fund is called the sinking fund approach to paying back a loan. Typically, sinking funds receive regular payments, at a fixed rate of interest with a goal of accumulating the principal balance at the end of the loan term.

Spot rate a *spot rate* $(s_t,)$ is the annual effective rate of interest earned by money invested now for a period of t years.

Term the *term* of a bond is the length of time from the time the bond is issued until the final payment is made.

Time weighted yield rate the *time-weighted yield rate* is an overall measure of an investment's performance which ignores timing and size of transactions. It is computed as the product of all individual period yield rates.

Treasury bill (T-bill) a *Treasury bill (T-bill)* is a government financial security which acts like a short-term loan to the government and like a short-term investment for the lender. An investor buys treasury bills today (gives money to the government) for the promise of a payment of a fixed amount sometime in the future. T-bills are typically issued over short terms (e.g., 4, 13, 26, and 52 weeks).

Writing down a bond *writing down a bond* is when a bond sold at a premium has its book value decrease over time until it reaches par value when the bond is redeemed. Conversely, when a bond is sold at a discount, the coupon payments do not cover interest and so the bond is written up until it reaches par value when the bond is redeemed.

Yield rate the *yield rate* (or yield to maturity) of a bond is the interest rate earned by the investor.

FORMULAS

CHAPTER ONE SAVING: FUNDAMENTALS OF INTEREST

- The balance in an account, $A(t)$, with compound interest at annual effective interest rate i after t years, when starting value of with K, is given as $A(t) = K(1+i)^t$.
- The balance in an account, $a(t)$, with compound interest at annual effective interest rate i after t years, when starting with \$1, is given as $a(t) = (1+i)^t$.
- If the monthly effective rate of interest is j, then the equivalent annual effective rate of interest, i, can be found by solving this equation for i: $1 + i = (1+j)^{12}$.
- The general formula for the ending account balance, $A(t)$, for an account with a starting value of K, a nominal rate of interest of $i^{(m)}$, for m compounding periods per year for t years is given as $A(t) = K(1 + (i^{(m)}/m))^{tm}$.

CHAPTER TWO LOANS: FUNDAMENTALS OF BORROWING AND LENDING

- To determine the Sinking Fund Goal where you have payments of P dollars at an effective interest rate of i for n total compounding periods is given by

$$\text{Sinking fund goal} = (P)\left(\frac{(1+i)^n - 1}{i}\right) = (P)s_{\overline{n}|i}.$$

- To formula to determine the amortized payment, P, where you are given the present value (the value of the loan), PV, the effective interest rate per compounding period, i, and the total number of compounding periods n is determine by

$$P = (\text{PV})\left(\frac{i}{1-(1+i)^{-n}}\right).$$

CHAPTER THREE ANNUITIES: FUNDAMENTALS OF REGULAR PAYMENTS

- Perpetuity payment (P) = account balance (B) × interest rate (i).
- The discount factor, v, is given by $v = 1/(1+i)$, where i is the annual effective rate of interest.
- The present value of a future payment of size P, with n periods in the future, in an account earning an effective interest rate i and corresponding discount factor $v = 1/(1+i)$ is present value $= P/(1+i)^n = Pv^n$.
- The amount of money needed today in an annuity where P is the payment received, i is the effective interest per compounding period, n is the total number of compounding periods, and v is the discount factor is given by

$$\text{Amount needed today} = Pa_{\overline{n}|i} = P\left(\frac{1-\left(1/(1+i)\right)^n}{i}\right) = P\left(\frac{1-v^n}{i}\right)$$

CHAPTER FOUR STOCKS AND BONDS: FUNDAMENTALS OF INVESTMENT STRATEGIES

- The present value (or selling price) of a bond with a face value of F, effective yield rate per period of j, coupon rate of r (per period), and n compounding periods and coupons earned is

$$\text{PV} = \frac{F}{(1+j)^n} + Fra_{\overline{n}|j} = \frac{F}{(1+i)^n} + Fr\left(\frac{1-\left(1/(1+i)\right)^n}{i}\right)$$

- The above can also be written as
$\text{PV} = Fv^n + Fra_{\overline{n}|j} = Fv^n + Fr\left((1-v^n)/j\right)$.

- The predicted price of a preferred stock, P, using the dividend discount model is $P = D/i$ where D is the value of the dividend payment and i is the effective interest rate per dividend period.

CHAPTER FIVE PORTFOLIOS: FUNDAMENTALS OF COLLECTIONS OF ASSETS AND LIABILITIES

- To find the dollar-weighted rate of return, solve the following equation for i, the unknown rate of return. In this equation, m represents the different deposits and withdrawals from the account, C_m is the mth deposit amount (using a minus sign for a withdrawal), and t_m is the length of time from the deposit (or withdrawal) until the account end date.

$$\text{Account ending value} = \sum_{\text{all values of } m} C_m(1+i)^{t_m}$$

- To determine the time-weighted yield rate over the entire investment period, use the following:

$$1 + (\text{Time-weighted yield rate over entire investment time})$$
$$= (1 + \text{yield rate period 1})(1 + \text{yield rate period 2})$$
$$\cdots(1 + \text{yield rate period } k)$$
$$= \left(\frac{\text{End balance for period 1}}{\text{Start balance for period 1}}\right)\left(\frac{\text{end balance for period 2}}{\text{start balance for period 2}}\right)\cdots$$
$$\left(\frac{\text{end balance for period } k}{\text{start balance for period } k}\right)$$
$$= (1 + \text{Annual time-weighted yield rate})^m$$

- The equation for MacCaulay duration is

$$\text{MacD} = \sum t\frac{\text{PV}(C_t)}{\text{PV(All)}}$$

where C_t is the cash flow at time t, PV indicates present value, and All is all future cash flows.

CHAPTER SIX SAVINGS REVISITED

- The effective annual interest rate, given the force of interest, ∂, is given by effective annual rate $= e^{\partial} - 1$.
- The force of interest at time t, $\partial(t)$, has the following relationship with $a(t)$, the accumulated amount in the account at time t, if you deposited \$1 today, and $a'(t)$, the derivative of $a(t)$ in terms of t:

$$\partial(t) = \frac{a'(t)}{a(t)}$$

- For compound interest, $\partial(t) = \ln(1 + i)$.
- To find balances in accounts with continuous compounding, use $A(t) = Pe^{rt}$ where $A(t)$ is the future balance of an account in t years, P is the present value of the account, e is 2.178..., and r is the force of interest.
- The discount rate, d, is found by the following:

$$d = \frac{\text{Interest earned}}{\text{Future account value}}$$

- The discount rate, d, and interest, i, have the following relationships:

$$d = \frac{i}{1 + i} \qquad i = \frac{d}{1 - d} \qquad (1 + i)^t = (1 - d)^{-t}$$

- The relationship between discount factor, v, and discount rate, d, is given as $d = 1 - v$.
- The relationship between present value and future value for the discount rate, d, is

$$\text{Present value} = \text{future value} - \text{future value} \times d = \text{future value}(1 - d)$$

- The account balance after t years, where d is the annual effective discount rate, is $a(t) = (1 - d)^{-t}$.
- The conversion equation between annual effective rate of discount, d, and the nominal rate of discount, $d^{(p)}$, where p is the number of compounding periods per year, is

$$1 - d = \left(1 - \frac{d^{(p)}}{p}\right)^{p}$$

- To convert nominal discount rate, $d^{(p)}$, to the force of interest, δ, use $1 - e^{d^{(p)}} = 1 - \delta$.

CHAPTER SEVEN LOANS REVISITED

- A loan can be thought of as an annuity with the following equation:

$$\text{Initial loan balance} = Pa_{\overline{n}|i} = P\frac{1 - v^{n}}{i}$$

- The general formula for a loan balance after k payments, where D is the drop payment, P is the payment amount, and n is the original number of payments, is

$$\text{Loan balance after } k \text{ payments} = Pa_{\overline{n-k-1}|i} + Dv^{n-k}$$

- The amount of interest in the

$$k\text{th payment} = (\text{loan balance after } k-1 \text{ payments})$$
$$i = P\left(1 - v^{n-k}\right) + iDv^{n-k+1}.$$

- The retrospective method for finding a loan payment says that $B(1+i)^{n} = Ps_{\overline{n}|i}$, where B is the initial loan balance and P is the equal size payments.
- The outstanding loan balance after the kth payment is $B(1+i)^{k} - Ps_{\overline{k}|i}$.
- The amount of interest in the $(k + 1)$th payment is $(1+i)^{k}(iB - P) + P$.
- The loan balance before the final payment (which can be used to find the drop payment) is $B(1+i)^{n-1} - Ps_{\overline{n-1}|i}$.
- An important relationship between $s_{\overline{n}|i}$ (the accumulated value of \$1 paid for n periods) and $a_{\overline{n}|i}$ (the present value of \$1 paid for n periods) is $a_{\overline{n}|i}(1+i)^{n} = s_{\overline{n}|i}$.

CHAPTER EIGHT ANNUITIES REVISITED

- The initial balance of an annuity where the first payment is P and the payments increase at a rate of k for n periods is

$$\text{Initial balance} = P\frac{1-(v(1+k))^n}{i-k}$$

- The initial balance of a perpetuity where the first payment is P and the payments increase at a rate of k is

$$\text{Initial balance} = \frac{P}{i-k}$$

- The accumulated value of a geometrically increasing annuity is given by

$$\text{Accumulated value} = P\left(\frac{(1+i)^n - (1+k)^n}{i-k}\right)$$

- The initial balance of an annuity where the first payment is P and the payments increase by Q for n periods is

$$\text{Initial balance} = Pa_{\overline{n}|i} + \frac{Q}{i}\left(a_{\overline{n}|i} - nv^n\right)$$

- The initial balance of a perpetuity where the first payment is P and the payments increase by Q each period is

$$\text{Initial balance} = \frac{P}{i} + \frac{Q}{i^2}$$

- The accumulated value of an arithmetically increasing annuity is given by

$$\text{Accumulated value} = Ps_{\overline{n}|i} + \frac{Q}{i}\left(s_{\overline{n}|i} - nv^n\right)$$

- The present value of \$1 in a perpetuity-due is

$$\ddot{a}_{\overline{\infty}|i} = (1+i)a_{\overline{\infty}|i} = \frac{1+i}{i} = \frac{1}{d}$$

- The present value of a perpetuity due is

$$\text{Present value} = P\ddot{a}_{\overline{\infty}|i} = P\left(\frac{1+i}{i}\right) = \frac{P}{d}$$

- The relationship between an annuity due and an annuity immediate is

$$P\ddot{a}_{\overline{n}|i} = P + Pa_{\overline{n-1}|i} = (1+i)Pa_{\overline{n}|i} = P\left(\frac{1-v^n}{d}\right)$$

- The accumulated value for an annuity-due is

$$\ddot{s}_{\overline{n}|i} = (1+i)s_{\overline{n}|i} = \frac{(1+i)^n - 1}{d}$$

- The accumulated value for an annuity-immediate is

$$s_{\overline{n}|i} = \frac{(1+i)^n - 1}{i}$$

- A convenient way to think about inflation-adjusted annuities is as a variation on an annuity-due. First, you define a new rate of interest, i^*, as $1 + i^* = (1+i)/(1+k)$, or $i^* = (1+i)/(1+k)$. (You can think of i^* as an inflation-adjusted interest rate.) With this formula, you can find the present value of the inflation-adjusted annuity as

$$\left(\frac{1}{1+i}\right)\ddot{a}_{\overline{n}|i^*} = \left(\frac{1+i^*}{1+i}\right)a_{\overline{n}|i^*}$$

CHAPTER NINE BONDS REVISITED

- The book value, B_k, at period k with a face value of F, effective yield rate per period of j, coupon rate of r (per period), and n compounding periods and coupons earned is

$$B_k = F(v)^{n-(k+1)} + Fra_{\overline{n-(k+1)}|j}$$

- The amortization of premium is the difference between the coupon payment and the accrued interest or

$$Fr - jB_{k-1}$$

- The present value of a bond can be determined using its spot rates, s, and cash flows, C:

$$\text{Present value} = \frac{C_1}{1+s_1} + \frac{C_2}{(1+s_2)^2} + \cdots + \frac{C_n}{(1+s_n)^n}$$

- The following relationship holds between spot rates and forward rates

$$(1+s_n)^n = (1+f_{0,1})(1+f_{1,2})\cdots(1+f_{n-1,n})$$

CHAPTER TEN PORTFOLIOS REVISITED

- Modified duration (ModD) can be determined by the following:

  - $\text{ModD} = \frac{-\text{PV}'(i)}{\text{PV}(i)}$

  - $\text{ModD} = \frac{\text{MacD}}{1+i}$

  where $\text{PV}(i)$ is the present value of a bond at a current yield rate of i, $\text{PV}'(i)$ is its derivative, MacD is the Macaulay duration.

- An equation for estimating the present value at yield rate j is

  Estimate of present value at yield rate $j = \text{PV}(i) \times (1 - (j-i)\text{ModD})$,

where j is the new yield rate, i is the current yield rate, $\text{PV}(i)$ is the present value at yield rate i, and ModD is entered in percentage points.

- The equation for Macaulay convexity (MacC) is

$$\text{MacC} = \sum t^2 \frac{\text{PV}(C_t)}{\text{PV(All)}}$$

where t is a time index variable, C_t is the cash flow at time t, PV indicates present value, and All is all future cash flows.

- Modified convexity (ModC) can be computed as a function of the Macaulay convexity, Macaulay duration, and yield rate.

$$\text{ModC} = \frac{\text{MacC} + \text{MacD}}{(1+i)^2} = \frac{\text{PV}''(\text{All})}{\text{PV(All)}}$$

APPENDIX

CHAPTER 1

Section 1.1

1. Because the interest earned in one period is reinvested for subsequent periods, leading you to be able to earn "interest on the interest." Over long enough of periods of time and/or at high enough interest, the interest earned on an account will eventually be more than initial deposits.

3. Simple interest does not reinvest the interest, whereas compound interest does.

5. More.

7. $A(t)$ is the amount of money in account at time t when the account starts with any amount K. $a(t)$ is the amount of money in the account at time t, when the account starts with $K = 1$.

9. $150 interest. Ending balance = $5,150.

11. $3,535 after 1 year; $3,570.35 after 2 years.

13. 3.2% interest rate.

15. $19,920.20 if $i = 0.001$; $19,219.61 if $i = 0.01$; $13,660.27 if $i = 0.1$.

17. $10,285.72.

19. Approximately $4,780.54 for each of the four summers.

21. $55.12.

Section 1.2

1. Effective rates are the actual interest rates earned per period. Nominal rates are a shorthand used by banks to report interest rates and are reported as the effective rate per period times the number of periods in a year. APR is the most popular "nominal" rate which is computed as 12 times the effective monthly interest rate.

3.   A nominal rate of interest of 6% compounded quarterly yields a 6.1364% effective annual rate (more than 6%) because interest is compounded four times during the year instead of only once.

5.   Increases because interest is being compounded more frequently.

7.   12%; 6%.

9.   0.005; 0.061678; Monthly compounding.

11. $2,040.37.

13.   (a) $102,857.18.   (b) $106,408.91.   (c) $109,574.54.   (d) $110,210.02.

15. $8,870.53.

17.   (a) (i) 10.4713067%, (ii) 10.5155782%, (iii) 10.5170365%, (iv) 10.5170913%, (v) 10.5170927%. (b) 10.5170918%.

Section 1.3

1.   Sooner because the deposit has more time to earn interest.

3.   You will earn more interest if you deposit money into a savings account monthly rather than annually.

5.   (Day 1 of month balance) $\times$ (1 + effective interest rate/ month) = end of month balance

7.   11.90 years.

9. $607.20, $1,221.69, $1,843.55. Interest earned = $43.55.

11. $5,120.80.

13. $20,616.07.

15.   (a) $702,856.24. (b) $930,597.05.

Section 1.4

1.   Recursive.

3.   Withdrawals are treated like a deposit, but their value (including interest) is subtracted to find the final amount left in the account.

5.   Time.

7. $1,805.67.

9. $23,493.19.

11.   (a) $25,116.87. (b) $3,868.33.

13.   (a) $12,689.79. (b) $1,103.25.

15.   (a) $4,120.80. (b) $i = 3.30$.

17.   (a) 87 months. (b) $276.25.

END OF CHAPTER 1

1. B.
3. A.
5. E.
7. D.
9. E.

CHAPTER 2

Section 2.1

1. Sooner.
3. Increase; decrease; decrease.
5. If the payment amount is first applied to principal before the interest is computed, the amount of interest accumulated each period will be lower. With the same size payment made monthly, the payoff period and total interest paid will be lower.
7. $6,600.
9. $6,992.65.
11. $343.75.
13. (a) $350.03. (b) $325.75. (c) $10.11. (d) $12,000. (e) $601.20. (f) The total principal paid stays the same; total interest paid is $483.52 ($117.68 less); the loan term becomes 30 months.
15. (a) (Below). (b) $6,282.53. (c) $4,634.34.

Year	Principal balance (Jan 1) ($)	Interest accrued (Jan 1–Dec 31) ($)	Payment (Dec 31) ($)	New loan balance (Dec 31) ($)
1	20,000	1,023.24	3,500	17,523.24
2	17,523.24	896.52	3,500	14,919.76
3	14,919.76	763.32	3,500	12,183.08
4	12,183.08	623.31	3,500	9,306.39
5	9,306.39	476.13	3,500	6,282.53

17. (a) $20,000(1.04) - P$. (b) $0 = 20,000(1.04)^2 - P(1.04) - P$. (c) $P = \$10,603.93$. (d) $P = \$7,206.97$.

Section 2.2

1. Increases; decreases.
3. More.
5. To make more money on the interest.
7. (a) Interest = $484.38; principal = $414.74. (b) 0.54.
9. 20-year loan: $65,789.03; 30-year loan: $103,928.03. The 30-year loan pays more interest (a difference of $38,139).
11.

Date	Payment ($)	Amount of payment going to interest ($)	Amount of payment going to principal ($)
2018	2,754.90	400	2,354.90
2019	2,754.90	305.80	2,449.10
2020	2,754.90	207.84	2,547.06
2021	2,754.90	105.96	2,648.94

13. (a) $119,158.40. (b) $134,053.20. (c) $14,894.80. (d) You can increase your monthly payment so that the term becomes shorter than 30 years.
15. (b) $2,645.52. (c) (i) $8,603.16, (ii) $161.86, (iii) $3,298.72, (iv) No.
17. (a) $P(1.03)$; $P(1.03) - 10{,}000$. (b) $P(1.03)^2 - 10{,}000(1.03)$; $P(1.03)^2 - 10{,}000(1.03) - 10{,}000$. (c) $P(1.03)^3 - 10{,}000(1.03)^2 - 10{,}000(1.03) - 10{,}000$; 0. (d) $28,286.11.

Section 2.3

1. True.
3. Alli, because her monthly payments will have more time spent in the bank account to accumulate interest.
5. Divide the sinking fund goal by $s_{\overline{n}|i}$.
7. $1,559.73.
9. 64.65.
11. (a) $167.59. (b) $P = \$138.83$; $1.2P = \$166.60$; $1.5P = \$208.25$.
13. 39 months.
15. (a) $66,810 (Original mortgage) vs $69,360 (refinanced offer). (b) $42,607.76. (c) − $26,752.24. (d) $31,789.60. (e) − $35,020.40. (f) Yes.
17. (a) $P = \frac{PV(1+i)^n \times i}{(1+i)^n - 1}$. (c) $983.88.

END OF CHAPTER 2

1. C.
3. C.
5. C.
7. C.
9. E.
11. B.

CHAPTER 3

Section 3.1

1. (a) End. (b) Stay the same. (c) Increase.
3. (a) They decrease. (b) They increase.
5. No, 1/12 is too much money for the account to remain a perpetuity. The interest accrued in 1 month is less than 1/12 of the set amount of money.
7. 4.4%.
9. 14.
11. (a) $800. (b) $1,500.
13. (a) $1,689,867.85. (b) $856,215.04. (c) $1,667,068. (d) $833,534.
15. (a) $1,000,000. (b) $1,250,000. (c) $1,153,478.31.

Section 3.2

1. Larger.
3. Decreases.
5. Decreases.
7. $1 will be paid out infinitely; perpetuity.
9. $62,311.05.
11. $83,395.81.
13. 0.969273.
15. (a) 25.9. (b) 32.1. (c) 46.6. (d) An infinite amount.
17. (a) Forever. (b) 495 months. (c) Forever.

19. (a) $3,438.65. (b) $3,933.61. (c) $3,762.06. (d) $3,762.06. (e) Answers are the same. This is because both accounts are earning the same nominal interest rate. (f) $P\left(\frac{1-v^n}{i}\right) \times (1+i)^n = P\left(\frac{(1+i)^n - 1}{i}\right)$.

21. (a) $A =$ "amount needed today"; $P =$ payment per period; $n =$ number of total periods.

(b) (i) $A(1+i) = P + \frac{P}{(1+i)} + \frac{P}{(1+i)^2} + \ldots + \frac{P}{(1+i)^{n-1}}$

(ii) $A(1+i) - A = P + \frac{P}{(1+i)^n}$

(iii) $Ai = P + \frac{P}{(1+i)^n}$

(iv) $A = P\left(\frac{1 - (1/(1+i))^n}{i}\right)$

> **END OF CHAPTER 3**

1. D.
3. B.
5. A.
7. A.
9. B.
11. A.
13. E.
15. D.
17. D.

> **CHAPTER 4**

Section 4.1

1. Will get paid out at the end of the term.
3. Increases.
5. Present value of the coupon payments and present value of the redemption value.
7. (a) $50. (b) $33.33.
9. (a) $10. (b) $6.67.
11. 5.92%.
13. (a) $1,019.27. (b) $1,046.11.

15. $1,000.
17. $739,550.05.
19. (a) $PV = Fra_{\overline{n}|i} + \frac{F}{(1+i)^n}$ (b) $PV = Fra_{\overline{n}|r} + \frac{F}{(1+r)^n}$ (c) $PV = Fr \times \frac{1-v^n}{r} + Fv^n$, $PV = F(1 - v^n) + Fv^n$, $PV = F - Fv^n + Fv^n$, $PV = F$

Section 4.2

1. Yield rate is the interest rate earned by the investor.
3. They will be the same.
5. The yield rate is higher than the coupon rate.
7. 4%.
9. 11.69; $1,402.91.
11. (a) $4,179.65. (b) Premium. (c) $5,000.
13. (a) $5,000. (b) $100. (c) (i) $1,046.22, (ii) 3.87%.
15. (a) 8 years. (b) 7 years. (c) 6 years.

Section 4.3

1. Decrease.
3. Common stock represents a share of ownership in the company, while preferred stock is a type of stock that also comes with the right to future dividend payments.
5. Dividends are payouts of a company's profits.
7. $28.08.
9. $12.40.
11. (a) $154.43. (b) $137.75. (c) $124.41. (d) Decreases.
13. (a). $7.99. (b) $37.50. (c) $25.52. (d) $33.51.
15. (a) $17.16. (b) $22.84. (c) $47.07. (d) $3.53. (e) $4.48.

END OF CHAPTER 4

1. E.
3. B.
5. B.
7. C.
9. D.
11. A.
13. B.

CHAPTER 5

Section 5.1

1. Dollar-weighted yield rate will be larger.
3. Since you are attempting to maximize your rate of return, you should compare each other's dollar-weighted rate of return because it shows whether or not the investor timed his/her deposits well.
5. It will be the same.
7. 4.49%.
9. $4,100 = 3,000(1 + i) + 1,000(1 + i)^{0.25}$.
11. (a) \$3,151.20. (b) $3,151.2 = 1,000(1 + i)^2 + 2,000(1 + i)$. (c) 3.745%.
13. (a) 2.77%. (b) 5.62%. (c) No. (d) Yes, $i = 2.43\%$.
15. (a) 12.5%. (b) 4%. (c) 17%. (d) $5,460 = 2000(1 + i) + 3,000(1 + i)^{0.5}$. (e) 13.32%. (f) (i) Yes, the dollar-weighted rate considers deposits/withdrawals. In this case, the larger deposit was made at the correct time when the rate of return was high. (ii) No, the time-based rate of return does not account for the mount of deposits/withdrawals.

Section 5.2

1. More sensitive.
3. Weighted average; future investment payments.
5. Decrease to \$484.51 (a decrease of \$15.49).
7.

Payment Date (years from now)	Payment size	Present value ($)	% of Total cash flow (weighting factor)	Product of time and weighting factor
0.5	12	11.65	0.02913	0.01456
1	12	11.31	0.02828	0.02828
1.5	12	10.98	0.02745	0.04118
2	12	10.66	0.02665	0.05331
2	400	355.39	0.8885	1.7770
	Total	400	100	1.9143

9. 1.86 years.
11. 2.70 years.

13. The price changes $37.19 for a 4 percentage point change in yield rate, or $9.30/point. For a bond that is $500 currently, this amounts to a $9.30/$500 = 0.0186 or 1.86% change in price per 1-percentage point change in yield.

Section 5.3

1. Assets and liabilities,

3. Buy some short-term bonds—bonds that expire before the due date of the liability—and some long-term bonds—bonds that expire after the due date of the liability.

5. The due date of the liability.

7. (a) $970.87. (b) $980.39.

9. $942.60.

11. (a) $450.77. (b) 166.

13. (a) $40,007.84. (b) $40,030.77.

15. (a) $48,669.67. (b) $46,388.58.

17. (a) Bond A: $613.91; Bond B: $783.53. (b) Bond A: $666.34; Bond B: $934.58. (c) Bond A: 2.07%; Bond B: 4.51%.

END OF CHAPTER 5

1. B.
3. D.
5. C.
7. C.
9. A.
11. C.
13. D.
15. E.
17. C.
19. B.
21. D.

CHAPTER 6

Section 6.1

1. Increases; by approaching a limit.
3. 4% force of interest.
5. No, a quick calculation, $i = e^{0.05} - 1 = 0.0513$, shows that the largest effective interest rate a 5% nominal rate of interest could be is 5.13%, which would be the case under continuous compounding.
7. $975.31.
9. 3.0%.
11. $2,003.66.
13. $16,550.63.
15. (a) 4.1%. (b) 12.7%. (c) 3,678.3%. (d) No, in continues indefinitely. (e) Effective annual rate $= \lim_{m \to \infty} ((1+i)^m - 1) = \infty$.
17. (a) $2P = Pe^{ti}$. (b) $ti = 0.69315$. (c) 69.315. (d) Increased, because there are less compounding periods, so a slightly longer time is needed to double the investment.
19. The effective annual rate is equal to this equation, but you must subtract 1 from each side.

Section 6.2

1. Future value.
3. Effective discount rate.
5. Yes.
7. 2.56%.
9. 4%.
11. 0.98.
13. Highest rate of return: option 2; lowest rate of return: option 1.
15. (a) $542.53. (b) $542.08. (c) $541.72.
17. 2.07%.

Section 6.3

1. Decrease.
3. Better.
5. False.
7. 5%.

9. 5.84%.
11. (a) $516.59. (b) 3.21%. (c) 3.32%. (d) No.
13. $2,846.63.
15. (a) 10%. (b) 10.8%.

END OF CHAPTER 6

1. E.
3. B.
5. C.
7. A.
9. A.
11. A.
13. C.

CHAPTER 7

Section 7.1

1. Level payments are fixed payment amounts for each period.
3. The last payment will be slightly larger.
5. $\frac{1-v^n}{i}$, where $v = \frac{1}{1+i}$.
7. $632.65.
9. $8,171.25.
11. (a)$158,342.24—this is the present value of the remaining future payments, excluding the drop payment. (b) $617.91—this is the present value of the drop payment, after k (180) payments have been made.
13. (a) $1,157.79. (b) $145,601.88. (c) $455.01 in interest; $702.78 in principal.
15. (a) $1,013.38. (b) (i) $160,177.45, (ii) $949.68, (iii) $15,280.88.
17. 2.625% APR.

Section 7.2

1. $a_{\overline{n}|i}$ finds the present value of all n, future payments of $1 at an interest rate of i. $s_{\overline{n}|i}$ finds the accumulated value of all payments of $1 after n periods at and interest rate of i.

3. You are finding the difference in the initial loan amount accumulated with no payments, and the value in the sinking fund.

5. You multiply that balance by (1 + the periodic interest rate), because a whole period will pass before you make the drop payment.

7. $9,684.75.

9. $191.84

11. (a) $238.12. (b) $237.34. (c) $18.82 in interest; $219.30 in principal.

13. (a) 20 years: $1,333.16; 30 years: $1,050.32. (b) 20 years: $1,331.96; 30 years: $1,045.92 (c) 20 years: $101,290.36; 30 years: $158,110.80.

15. (a) (i) 0.3675%, (ii) $1,253.35, (iii) $201,206. (b) (i) 0.1836%, (ii) $626.10, (iii) $200,792. (c) Beth. Her payments are made more regularly, which leaves less time for interest to accrue on the balance.

END OF CHAPTER 7

1. B.
3. D.
5. A.
7. C.
9. A.
11. D.
13. D.
15. C.
17. D.

CHAPTER 8

Section 8.1

1.   The payouts are increasing each payment in an inflation-adjusted annuity, whereas a regular annuity has equal payouts throughout the life of the annuity.

3.   Lower.

5.   If the initial balance of an inflation-adjusted perpetuity is calculated as $Pv + P(1 + k)v^2 + P(1+k)^2v^3 + \dots$,   and $i = k$,   then   the initial balance $= Pv + Pv + Pv + \dots$, which doesn't sum to a finite number.

7.   \$631,343.02.

9.   \$2,108.21.

11. \$4,183.69.

13. (a) \$172,122.55. (b) \$344,245.11. (c) \$516,367.66. (d) Yes.

15. (a) Since $v = \frac{1}{1+i}$, $Pv + P(1+k)v^2 + \dots$ can be rewritten as $\frac{P}{1+i} + \frac{P(1+k)}{(1+i)^2} + \frac{P(1+k)^2}{(1+i)^3} + \dots$.(b) (i) \$97.08, (ii) \$36.97, (iii) \$0.01, (iv) 0. (c) (i) \$99.01, (ii) \$99.01, (iii) \$99.01, (iv)\$99.01, (v) the initial balance must be $\left(P/(1 + i)\right) \times n$, where n is the number of payments. If the series goes on indefinitely, there isn't a finite initial balance possible.

17. (a) $S(1 + k)v = v^2(1 + k) + (1+k)^2v^3 + (1+k)^3v^4 + (1+k)^4v^5 + \dots + (1+k)^nv^{n+1}$.

   (b) $S(1 - v(1 + k)) = v - (1 + k)^nv^{n+1}$ $S = \frac{v - (1+k)^nv^{n+1}}{1 - v(1 + k)}$.

   (c) $S = \frac{1 - (1+k)^nv^n}{\frac{1}{v} - (1 + k)}$.

   (d) $S = \frac{1 - (1+k)^nv^n}{(1 + i) - (1 + k)} \rightarrow S = \frac{1 - \left((1+k)/(1+i)\right)^n}{i - k}$.

   (e) $\left(\frac{1+k}{1+i}\right)^n = (v(1+k))^n$.

Section 8.2

1.   (a) Neither. (b) Arithmetically. (c) Geometrically.

3.   Annuity A; annuity B.

5.   Q.

7.   \$1,080; \$1,100; \$3,100.

9.   \$21,666.66.

11. \$182,469.13.

13. \$211,831.38.

15. \$77,689.60.

Section 8.3

1. An annuity-due has payments occurring at the beginning of the period, whereas an annuity-immediate has payments occurring at the end of the period.
3. Sooner.
5. The discount rate (d).
7. $997.51.
9. $86,076.87.
11. (a) $55,186.31. (b) $53,063.76. (c) (i) $4516.64; total sum of payments is $1,083,993.76 monthly and $1,103,726.25 annually, so monthly is less. This makes sense because the money has less time to accumulate interest (e.g., first payment is in 30 days vs 1 year). (ii) $4,501.90; total sum of payments is $1,080,456.60 monthly and $1,061,275.25 annually, so monthly is more. This makes sense because the money has more time to accumulate interest with the monthly payments since your initial payment (today) is much smaller with the monthly payouts.
13. (a) $57,830.10. (b) $55,605.86. (c) $40,000. (d) $38,461.54.
15. $31,133.47.
17. (a) $41,883.29. (b) $56,287.64.

Section 8.4

1. An annuity with arithmetically increasing payments has payments that increase by a fixed amount. A geometrically increasing annuity has payments that increase as a percentage from the previous payment.
3. You can use the perpetuity-due formula and "roll forward" year 7 using the interest rate. First payment = (Initial investment) $\times d \times (1+i)^7$.
5. No, any perpetuity where the rate of increase is larger than the interest rate earned will deplete at some point in time, regardless of how long the first payment is deferred.
7. $161.81.
9. $18,258.50.
11. (a) $5,825.24. (b) $4,000. (c) $2,491.90.
13. (a) $123,000. (b) $307,500. (c) $287,000. (d) $253,666.18.
15. (a) $15,000. (b) (i) 0.01735, 0.00995, (ii) $7,399.00, (iii) $7,472.63, (iv) Less. Because deposits are made quicker, there is less time for interest to build up on each other. (c) (i) $7,527.37, (ii)

$7602.27, (iii) More. Because more time is left for to investment to accumulate interest, the payments are slightly larger.

17.

$$s_{\overline{n}|} = (1+i)^n a_{\overline{n}|} = (1+i)^n * \left(\frac{1 - v^n}{i} \right)$$

$$= (1+i)^n \times \frac{1 - \left(1/(1+i)^n \right)}{i}$$

$$= \frac{(1+i)^n - 1}{i} = s_{\overline{n}|}$$

END OF CHAPTER 8

1. C.
3. B.
5. E.
7. C.
9. D.
11. E.
13. A.
15. C.
17. D.
19. B.
21. E.
23. B.
25. B.
27. C.
29. A.
31. C.
33. E.
35. B.
37. C.
39. A.
41. D.
43. D.
45. E.
47. C.

CHAPTER 9

Section 9.1

1. Same as; more than; less than.
3. The present value of both the future coupon payments and the redemption price.
5. 0.
7. $990.36.
9. $50.
11. (a) $986.23. (b) $990.60. (c) $22.50. (d) Accrued interest = $24.76; accumulation of discount = $2.26.
13. (a) $1,000. (b) $1,000. (c) $25. (d) accrued interest = $25; accumulation of discount/premium = $0.
15.

Half-year	Coupon payment ($)	Interest accrued ($)	Amortization of premium ($)	Book value ($)
0				1,019.04
1	25	20.38	4.62	1,014.42
2	25	20.29	4.71	1,009.71
3	25	20.19	4.81	1,004.90
4	25	20.10	4.90	1,000

Section 9.2

1. The bond issuer can pay the bond off early, before the redemption date.
3. Down.
5. No.
7. $1,009.78; 758.
9. $10,000; $510,000.
11. (a) $510; $510,000. (b) $507.36. (c) 1,005. (d) (See below). (e) The total loss would be $2,600.

Time	Keep original bond (1,000 bonds sold) ($)	Refinance (1,005 bonds sold) ($)	Savings (loss) ($)
3rd half year	10,000	10,050	(50)
4th half year	510,000	512,550	(2,550)
Total	520,000	522,600	(2,600)

13. (a) $1,020; $10,200,000. (b) $1,022.04. (c) 9,978. (d) (See below). (e) The total loss would be $76,900. (f) Refinancing was not advantageous in this case because the coupon rate increased. If the number of bonds sold is less than the number currently issued, in order for refinancing to be advantageous, the terms must be the same as the original bond.

Time	Keep original bond (1,000 bonds sold) ($)	Refinance (9,978 bonds sold) ($)	Savings (loss) ($)
3rd half year	200,000	249,450	(49,450)
4th half year	10,200,000	10,227,450	(27,450)
Total	10,400,000	10,476,900	(76,900)

15. The total loss for the company would be $28,080.

Section 9.3

1. Because there is only one single cash flow.

3. A spot rate is often an average rate over multiple periods; forward rate is not.

5. s_2—the larger proportion of the payout of the bond occurs at the end of the second period, and so, the yield rate will be pulled toward the 2-year spot rate.

7. D. $s_2 = \sqrt{(1+f_{0,1})(1+f_{1,2})} - 1$

9. $s_2 = 0.0375$.

11. $f_{2,3} = 2.00\%$.

13. (a) $976.41. (b) 3.237%. (c) $f_{0,1} = 2.0\%$. (d) $f_{1,2} = 4.515\%$.

15. $s_1 = 2\%$; $s_2 = 2.25\%$; $s_3 = 2.5\%$. (b) $985.91. (c) 2.493%.

17. (a) $986.97. (b) 3.465%. (c) $f_{0,1} = 2\%$. (d) $f_{1,2} = 3.00\%$. (e) $f_{2,3} = 5.529\%$.

END OF CHAPTER 9

1. B.
3. C.
5. C.
7. E.
9. A.
11. A.
13. A.
15. C.
17. E.
19. C.
21. E.

CHAPTER 10

Section 10.1

1. Increases.
3. Macaulay duration is the weighted average time of future cash flows.
5. MacD and ModD are related through the equation $ModD = MacD/(1 + i)$, where modified duration takes into account price sensitivity when there is a change in the yield to maturity.
7. 2.86.
9. 2.80%.
11. 1.6%.
13. (a) $25. (b) $1,000. (c) $1,002.76. (d) $997.25. (e) 2.76%. (f) 2.82. (g) 2.69%.
15. (a) 3-year bond: 2.79; 5-year bond: 4.39. (b) 3-year bond: 4.14%; 5-year bond: 2.63%. (c) 3.39%.

Section 10.2

1. More curved.
3. Macaulay convexity.
5. Years; squared years; percent-squared.

7. $994.62.

9. 3.97 squared half-years.

11. (a) 4.72 years. (b) 4.58%. (c) 23.03 squared years. (d) 26.15 percent-squared.

13. (a) 2.86 years. (b) 2.75%. (c) 8.41 squared years. (d) 10.40 percent-squared.

15. (a) 2.40 years. (b) 2.31%. (c) 6.12 squared years. (d) 7.87 percent-squared.

Section 10.3

1. If there are interest rate changes in longer or shorter term bonds, you could maximize your investment and make money after the liability has been paid.

3. Down; up.

5. There needs to be a cash flow before and after the liability.

7. 3.125 years.

9. $266,666.67 in the 2-year bonds; $133,333.33 in the 5-year bonds.

11. (a) $452,865.40. (b) 5 years. (c) $323,475.29 in the 3-year bond; $129,390.11 in the 10-year bond. (d) 25. (e) 35. (f) Yes; yes.

13. (a) $67,413.85. (b) 1.71 years. (c) $43,519.84 in 1-year bonds; $23,912.01 in 3-year bonds. (d) 3.13 squared years. (e) 3.84 squared years. (f) Yes; yes.

END OF CHAPTER 10

1. D.

3. B.

5. C.

7. C.

9. D.

11. D.

13. C.

15. A.

17. A.

19. A.

21. A.

INDEX

Note: Page numbers followed by "*f*" and "*t*" refer to figures and tables, respectively.